ORBIT 8

is the latest in this unique series of anthologies of the best new SF: fourteen stories written especially for this collection by some of the top names in the field.

—Harlan Ellison in "One Life, Furnished in Early Poverty" tells a moving story of a man who goes back in time to help his youthful self.

—Avram Davidson finds a new and sinister significance in the first robin of Spring.

—R. A. Lafferty reveals a monstrous microfilm record of the past.

—Kate Wilhelm finds real horror in a story of boy-meets-girl.

—and ten other tales by some of the most original minds now writing in this most exciting area of today's fiction are calculated to blow the mind.

OTHER ORBIT ANTHOLOGIES

AVAILABLE AS BERKLEY MEDALLION

PAPERBACKS

ORBIT 8

EDITED BY
DAMON KNIGHT

An Anthology
of New Science Fiction Stories

A BERKLEY MEDALLION BOOK
PUBLISHED BY
BERKLEY PUBLISHING CORPORATION

Copyright © 1970 by Damon Knight

Published by arrangement with the editor

Originally published by G. P. Putnam's Sons

BERKLEY MEDALLION EDITION,
MARCH, 1971

SBN-01970-5

*BERKLEY MEDALLION BOOKS are published by
Berkley Publishing Corporation
200 Madison Avenue
New York, N. Y. 10016*

BERKLEY MEDALLION BOOKS ® TM 757,375

Printed in the United States of America

CONTENTS

ORBIT 8

GARDNER R. DOZOIS

HORSE OF AIR

Sometimes when the weather is good I sit and look out over the city, fingers hooked through the mesh.

—The mesh is weather-stained, beginning to rust. As his fingers scrabble at it, chips of rust flake off, staining his hands the color of crusted blood. The heavy wire is hot and smooth under his fingers, turning rougher and drier at a rust spot. If he presses his tongue against the wire, it tastes slightly of lemons. He doesn't do that very often—

The city is quieter now. You seldom see motion, mostly birds if you do. As I watch, two pigeons strut along the roof ledge of the low building several stories below my balcony, stopping every now and then to pick at each other's feathers. They look fatter than ever. I wonder what they eat these days? Probably it is better not to know. They have learned to keep away from me anyway, although the mesh that encloses my small balcony floor to ceiling makes it difficult to get at them if they do land nearby. I'm not really hungry, of course, but they are noisy and leave droppings. I don't really bear any malice

9

toward them. It's not a personal thing; I do it for the upkeep of the place.

(I hate birds. I will kill any of them I can reach. I do it with my belt buckle, snapping it between the hoops of wire.)

—He hates birds because they have freedom of movement, because they can fly, because they can shift their viewpoint from spot to spot in linear space, while he can do so only in time and memory, and that imperfectly. They can fly here and look at him and then fly away, while he has no volition: if he wants to look at them, he must wait until they decide to come to him. He flicks a piece of plaster at them, between the hoops—

Startled by something, the pigeons explode upward with a whir of feathers. I watch them fly away: skimming along the side of a building, dipping with an air current. They are soon lost in the maze of low roofs that thrust up below at all angles and heights, staggering toward the Apartment Towers in the middle distance. The Towers stand untouched by the sea of brownstones that break around their flanks, like aloof monoliths wading in a surf of scummy brown brick. Other Towers march off in curving lines toward the horizon, becoming progressively smaller until they vanish at the place where a misty sky merges with a line of low hills. If I press myself against the mesh at the far right side of the balcony, I can see the nearest Tower to my own, perhaps six hundred yards away, all of steel and concrete with a vertical line of windows running down the middle and rows of identical balconies on either side. Nearest to me on the left is a building that rises about a quarter of the way up my Tower's flank: patterns of dark brown and light red bricks, interlaced with fingers of mortar; weathered grey roof shingles, a few missing here and there in a manner reminiscent of broken teeth; a web of black chimney and sewage pipes crawling up and across the walls like metallic creepers. All covered with the pale splotches of bird droppings. The Towers are much cleaner; not so many horizontal surfaces. Windows are broken in the disintegrating buildings down there; the dying sunlight glints from fangs of shattered glass. Curtains hang in limp shreds that snap and drum when a wind comes up. If you squint, you can see that the wind has scattered broken twigs and rubbish all over the floors inside. No, I am much happier in one of the Towers.

(I hate the Towers. I would rather live anywhere than here.)

——He hates the Towers. As the sun starts to dip below the horizon, settling down into the concrete labyrinth like a hog into a wallow, he shakes his head blindly and makes a low noise at the back of his throat. The shadows of buildings are longer now, stretching in toward him from the horizon like accusing fingers. A deep grey gloom is gathering in the corners and angles of walls, shot with crimson sparks from the foundering sun, now dragged under and wrapped in chill masonry. His hands go up and out, curling again around the hoops of the mesh. He shakes the mesh violently, throwing his weight against it. The mesh groans in metallic agony but remains solid. A few chips of concrete puff from the places where the ends of the mesh are anchored to the walls. He continues to tear at the mesh until his hands bleed, half-healed scabs torn open again. Tiny blood droplets spatter the heavy wire. The blood holds the deeper color of rust——

If you have enough maturity to keep emotionalism out of it, the view from here can even be fascinating. The sky is clear now, an electric, saturated blue, and the air is as sharp as a jeweler's glass. Not like the old days. Without factories and cars to keep it fed, even the eternal smog has dissipated. The sky reminds me now of an expensive aquarium filled with crystal tropical water, me at the bottom: I almost expect to see huge eyes peering in from the horizon, maybe a monstrous nose pressed against the glass. On a sunny day you can see for miles.

But it is even more beautiful when it rains. The rain invests the still landscape with an element of motion: long fingers of it brushing across the rooftops or marching down in zigzag sheets, the droplets stirring and rippling the puddles that form in depressions, drumming against the flat concrete surfaces, running down along the edges of the shingles, foaming and sputtering from downspouts. The Towers stand like lords, swirling rain mists around them as a fine gentleman swirls his jeweled cloak. Pregnant grey clouds scurry by behind the Towers, lashed by wind. The constant stream of horizontals past the fixed vertical fingers of the Towers creates contrast, gives the eye something to follow, increases the relief of motion. Motion is heresy when the world has become a still-life. But it soothes, the old-time religion. There are no atheists in foxholes, nor abstainers when the world begins to flow. But does that prove the desirability of God or the weakness of men? I drink when the world flows, but unwillingly, because I know the price. I have to drink, but I also have to pay. I will pay later when the motion stops and the world returns to lethargy, the doldrums made more unbearable by the contrast known a moment before. That is another cross that I am forced to bear.

But it is beautiful, and fresh-washed after. And sometimes there is a rainbow. Rain is the only esthetic pleasure I have left, and I savor it with the unhurried leisure of the aristocracy.

—When the rain comes, he flattens himself against the mesh, arms spread wide as if crucified there, letting the rain hammer against his face. The rain rolls in runnels down his skin, mixing with sweat, counterfeiting tears. Eyes closed, he bruises his open mouth against the mesh, trying to drink the rain. His tongue dabs at the drops that trickle by his mouth, licks out for the moisture oozing down along the links of wire. After the storm, he sometimes drinks the small puddles that gather on the balcony ledge, lapping them noisily and greedily, although the tap in the kitchen works, and he is never thirsty—

Always something to look at from here. Directly below are a number of weed-overgrown yards, chopped up unequally by low brick walls, nestled in a hollow square formed by the surrounding brownstones. There is even a tree in one corner, though it is dead and its limbs are gnarled and splintered. The yards were never neatly kept by the rabble that lived there, even in the old days: they are scattered with trash and rubbish, middens of worn-out household items and broken plastic toys, though the weeds have covered much. There was a neat, bright flower bed in one of the further yards, tended by a bent and leather-skinned foreign crone of impossible age, but the weeds have overgrown that as well, drowning the rarer blossoms. This season there were more weeds, fewer flowers—they seem to survive better, though God knows they have little else to recommend them, being coarse and ill-smelling.

In the closest yard an old and ornate wicker-back chair is still standing upright; if I remember correctly, a pensioner bought it at a rummage sale and used it to take the sun, being a parasite good for nothing else. Weeds are twining up around the chair; it is half-hidden already. Beyond is a small concrete court where hordes of ragged children used to play ball. Its geometrical white lines are nearly obliterated now by rain and wind-drifted gravel. If you look sharp at this clearing, sometimes you can see the sudden flurry of a small darting body through the weeds: a rat or a cat, hard to tell at this distance.

Once, months ago, I saw a man and a woman there, my first clear indication that there are still people alive and about. They entered the court like thieves, crawling through a low window, the man lowering the girl and then jumping down after. They were dressed in rags, and the man carried a rifle and a bandolier. After reconnoitering, the man forced one of the rickety doors into a brownstone, disappearing inside. After a while he came out dragging a mattress—filthy, springs jutting through fabric—and carried it into the ball court. They had intercourse there for the better part of the afternoon, stopping occasionally while the man prowled about with the rifle. I remember thinking that it was too bad the gift of motion had been wasted on such as these. They left at dusk. I had not tried to signal them, leaving them undisturbed to their rut, although I was somewhat sickened by the coarse brutality of the act. There *is* such a thing as *noblesse oblige*.

(I hate them. If I had a gun I would kill them. At first I watch greedily as they make love, excited, afraid of scaring them away if they should become aware of me watching. But as the afternoon wears on, I grow drained, and then angry, and begin to shout at them, telling them to get out, get the hell out. They ignore me. Their tanned skin is vivid against asphalt as they strain together. Sweat makes their locked limbs glisten in the thick sunlight. The

rhythmic rise and fall of their bodies describes parabolic
lines through the crusted air. I scream at them and tear at
the mesh, voice thin and impotent. Later they make love
again, rolling from the mattress in their urgency, sprawling
among the lush weeds, coupling like leopards. I try to
throw plaster at them, but the angle is wrong. As they
leave the square, the man gives me the finger.)

Thinking of those two makes me think of the other
animals that howl through the world, masquerading as
men. On the far left, hidden by the nearest brownstones
but winding into sight further on, is a highway. Once it
was a major artery of the city, choked with a chrome flood
of traffic. Now it is empty. Once or twice at the beginning
I would see an ambulance or a fire engine, once a tank. A
few weeks ago I saw a jeep go by, driving square in the
middle of the highway, ridden by armed men. Occasionally I have seen men and women trudge past, dragging
their possessions behind them on a sledge. Perhaps the
wheel is on the way out.

Against one curb is the overturned, burned-out hulk of
a bus: small animals use it for a cave now, and weeds are
beginning to lace through it. I saw it burning, a week after
the Building Committee came. I sat on the balcony and
watched its flames eat up at the sky, although it was too
dark to make out what was happening around it; the street
lights had been the first things to go. There were other
blazes in the distance, glowing like campfires, like blurred
stars. I remember wondering that night what was happening, what the devil was going on. But I've figured it out
now.

It was the niggers. I hate to say it. I've been a liberal
man all my life. But you can't deny the truth. They are
responsible for the destruction, for the present degeneration of the world. It makes me sad to have to say this. I
had always been on their side in spirit, I was more than
willing to stretch out a helping hand to those less fortunate
than myself. I always said so; I always said that. I had
high hopes for them all. But they got greedy, and brought
us to this. We should have known better, we should have
listened to the so-called racists, we should have realized
that idealism is a wasting disease, a cancer. We should

have remembered that blood will tell. A hard truth: it was the niggers. I have no prejudice; I speak of cold facts. I had always wished them well.

(I hate niggers. They are animals. Touching one would make me vomit.)

—He hates niggers. He has seen them on the street corners with their women, he has seen them in their juke-boxed caves with their feet in sawdust, he has heard them speaking in a private language half devised of finger snaps and motions of liquid hips, he has felt the inquiry of their eyes, he has seen them dance. He envies them for having a culture separate from the bland familiarity of his own, he envies their tang of the exotic. He envies their easy sexuality. He fears their potency. He fears that in climbing up they will shake him down. He fears generations of stored-up hate. He hates them because their very existence makes him uncomfortable. He hates them because sometimes they have seemed to be happy on their tenement street corners, while he rides by in an air-conditioned car and is not. He hates them because they are not part of the mechanism and yet still have the audacity to exist. He hates them because they have escaped—

Dusk has come, hiding a world returned to shame and barbarism. It occurs to me that I may be one of the few members of the upper class left. The rabble were always quick to blame their betters for their own inherent inferiority and quick to vent their resentment in violence when the opportunity arose. The other Apartment Towers are still occupied, I think; I can see the lights at night, as they can see mine, if there is anyone left there to see. So perhaps there are still a few of us left. Perhaps there is still some hope for the world after all.

Although what avail to society is their survival if they are as helpless as I? We may be the last hope of restoring order to a land raped by Chaos, and we are being wasted. We are born to govern, to regulate, prepared for it by station, tradition and long experience: leadership comes as naturally to us as drinking and fornication come to the masses of the Great Unwashed. We are being wasted, our experience and foresight pissed away by fools who will not listen.

And we dwindle. I speak of us as a class, as a corporate "we." But there are fewer lights in the other Towers every month. Last night I counted less than half the number I could see a year ago. On evenings when the wind grows bitter with autumn cold, I fear that I will soon be the only one left with the courage to hold out. It would be so easy to give in to despair; the quietus of hopelessness is tempting. But it is a siren goddess, made of tin. Can't the others see that? To give up is to betray their blood. But still the lights dwindle. At times I have the dreadful fancy that I will sit here one night and watch the last light flicker out in the last Tower, leaving me alone in darkness, the only survivor of a noble breed. Will some improbable alien archaeologist come and hang a sign on my cage: the last of the aristocracy?

Deep darkness now. The lights begin to come on across the gulfs of shadow, but I am afraid to count them. Thinking of these things has chilled me, and I shudder. The wind is cold, filled with dampness. There will be a storm later. Distant lightning flickers behind the Towers, each flash sending jagged shadows leaping toward me, striking blue highlights from every reflecting surface. Each lightning stroke seems to momentarily reverse the order of things, etching the Towers in black relief against the blue-white dazzle of the sky, then the brilliance draining, leaving the Towers as before: islands of light against an inky background of black. The cycle is repeated, shadows lunging in at me, in at me, thrusting swords of nigger-blackness. It was on a hellish night like this that the Building Committee came.

It was a mistake to give them so much power. I admit it. I'm not too proud to own up to my own mistakes. But we were tired of struggling with an uncooperative and unappreciative society. We were beaten into weariness by a horde of supercilious bastards, petty and envious little men hanging on our coattails and trying to chivy us down. We were sick of people with no respect, no traditions, no heritage, no proper ambitions. We were disgusted by a world degenerating at every seam, in every aspect. We had finally realized the futility of issuing warnings no one would listen to. Even then the brakes could have been applied to our skidding society if someone had bothered to listen, if anyone had had the guts and foresight to take the necessary measures. But we were tired, and we were no longer young.

So we traded our power for security. We built the Towers; we formed a company, turned our affairs over to them, and retired from the world into our own tight-knit society. Let the company have the responsibility and the problems, let them deal with the pressures and the decisions, let them handle whatever comes; we will be safe and comfortable regardless. They are the bright, ambitious technicians; let them cope. They are the expendable soldiers; let them fight and be expended as they are paid for doing; we shall be safe behind the lines. Let them have the mime show of power; we are civilized enough to enjoy the best things of life without it. We renounce the painted dreams; they are hollow.

It was a mistake.

It was a mistake to give them the voting proxies; Anderson was a fool, senile before his time. It was all a horrible mistake. I admit it. But we were no longer young.

And the world worsened, and one day the Building Committee came.

It was crisis, they said, and Fear was walking in the land. And the Charter specified that we were to be protected, that we must not be disturbed. So they came with the work crews and meshed over my balcony. And welded a slab of steel over my door as they left. They would not listen to my protest, wrapped in legalities, unvulnerable in armor of technical gobbledygook. Protection was a specific of the Charter, they said, and with the crisis this was the only way they could ensure our protection should the outer defenses go down; it was a temporary measure.

And the work crews went about their business with slap-dash efficiency, and the balding, spectacled foreman told me he only worked here. So I stood quietly and watched them seal me in, although I was trembling with rage. I am no longer young. And I would not lose control before these vermin. Every one of them was waiting for it, hoping for it in their petty, resentful souls, and I would let myself be flayed alive before I would give them the

satisfaction. It is a small comfort to me that I showed them
the style with which a gentleman can take misfortune.

(When I finally realize what they are doing, I rage and
bluster. The foreman pushes me away. "It's for your own
good," he says, mouthing the cliché halfheartedly, not
really interested. I beat at him with ineffectual fists. Annoyed, he shrugs me off and ducks through the door. I try
to run after him. One of the guards hits me in the face
with his rifle butt. Pain and shock and a brief darkness.
And then I realize that I am lying on the floor. There is
blood on my forehead and on my mouth. They have almost finished maneuvering the steel slab into place, only a
man-sized crack left open. The guard is the only one left
in the room, a goggled technician just squeezing out
through the crack. The guard turns toward the door. I
hump myself across the room on my knees, crawling after
him, crying and begging. He plants his boot on my shoulder and pushes me disgustedly away. The room tumbles, I
roll over twice, stop, come up on my elbows and start to
crawl after him again. He says, "Fuck off, Dad," and
slaps his rifle, jangling the magazine cartridge in the
breech. I stop moving. He glares at me, then leaves the
room. They push the slab all the way closed. It makes a
grinding, rumbling sound, like a subway train. Still on my
knees, I throw myself against it, but it is solid. Outside
there are welding noises. I scream.)

There is a distant rumbling now. Thunder: the storm is
getting nearer. The lightning flashes are more intense, and
closer together. They are too bright, too fast, blending into
one another, changing the dimensions of the world too
rapidly. With the alternating of glare and thrusting shadow
there is too much motion, nothing ever still for a second,
nothing you can let your eye rest on. Watching it strains
your vision. My eyes ache with the motion.

I close them, but there are squiggly white afterimages
imprinted on the insides of my eyelids. A man of breeding
should know how to control his emotions. I do; in the old
circles, the ones that mattered, I was known for my self-
discipline and refinement. But this is an unseasonable
night, and I am suddenly afraid. It feels like the bones are

being rattled in the body of the earth, it feels like maybe It will come now.

But that is an illusion. It is not the Time; It will not come yet. Only I know when the Time is, only I can say when It will come. And It will not come until I call for It, that is part of the bargain. I studied military science at Annapolis. I shall recognize the most strategic moment, I shall know when the Time is at hand for vengeance and retribution. I shall know. And the Time is not now. It will not come tonight. This is only an autumn storm.

I open my eyes. And find my stare returned. Windows ring me on all sides like walls of accusing, lidless eyes. Lightning oozes across the horizon: miniature reflections of the electric arc etched in cold echoes across a thousand panes of glass, a thousand matches struck simultaneously in a thousand dusty rooms.

A sequence of flares. The sky alternates too quickly to follow. Blue-white, black. Blue-white. Black again. The roofs flicker with invested motion, brick dancing in a jerky, silent-movie fashion.

Oh God, the chimneys, humped against dazzle, looming in shadow. Marching rows of smoky brick gargoyles, ash-cold now with not an ember left alive. The rows sway closer with every flash. I can hear the rutch of mortar-footed brick against tile, see the waddling, relentless rolling of their gait. They are people actually, the poor bastard refugees of the rabble frozen into brick, struck dumb with mortar. I saw it happen on the night of the Building Committee, thousands of people swarming like rats over the roofs to escape the burning world, caught by a clear voice of crystal that metamorphosed them with a single word, fixing them solid to the roofs, their hands growing into their knees, their heels into their buttocks, their heads thrown back with mouths gaped in a scream, flesh swapped for brick, blood for mortar. They hump toward me on their blunt knees in ponderously bobbing lines. With a sound like fusing steel, nigger-black shadows humping *in* at me. Christ hands sealing my eyes with clay stuffing down my mouth my throat filling Oh God oh christ christ *christ*

It is raining now. I will surely catch a chill standing here; there are vapors in the night air. Perhaps it would be advisable to go inside. Yes, I do think that would be best. Sometimes it is better to forget external things.

—He crawls away from the mesh on his hands and knees, although he is healthy and perfectly able to stand. He often crawls from place to place in the apartment; he thinks it gives him a better perspective. Rain patters on the balcony behind, drums against the glass of the French windows that open into the apartment. He claws at the framework of the windows, drags himself to his feet. He stands there for a moment, face pressed flat against the glass, trembling violently. His cheeks are wet. Perhaps he has been crying. Or perhaps it was the rain—

I turn on the light and go inside, closing the French windows firmly behind me. It is the very devil of a night outside. In here it is safe, even comfortable. This place is only a quarter of my actual apartment of course. The Building Committee sealed me in here, cut me off from the rest of my old place, which occupied most of this floor. Easier to defend me this way, the bastards said. So this apartment is smaller than what I'm used to living in, God knows. But in a strange way the smallness makes the place more cozy somehow, especially on a piggish night like this when fiends claw the windowpane.

I cross to the kitchen cubicle, rummage through the jars and cans; there's some coffee left from this week's shipment, I think. Yes, a little coffee left in one of the jars: instant; coarse, murky stuff. I had been used to better; once we drank nothing but fine-ground Colombian, and I would have spat in the face of any waiter who dared to serve me unpercolated coffee. This is one of the innumerable little ways in which we pay for our folly. A thousand little things, but together they add up into an almost unbearable burden, a leering Old Man of the Sea wrapped leech-fashion around my shoulders and growing heavier by the day. But this is defeatist talk. I am more tired than I would allow myself to admit. Here the coffee will help; even this bitter liquid retains that basic virtue in kind with the more palatable stuff. I heat some water, slosh it over the obscene granules into a cup. The cup is cracked, no replacement for it: another little thing. A gust of wind rattles the glass in the French windows. I will not listen to it.

Weary, I carry the steaming cup into the living room, sit down in the easy chair with my back to the balcony. I try to balance the cup on my knee, but the damn thing is too hot; I finally rest it on the chair arm, leaving a moist ring on the fabric, but that hardly matters now. Can my will be weakening? Once I would have considered it sacrilege to sully fine furniture and would have gone to any length to avoid doing so. Now I am too wrapped in lassitude to get up and go into the kitchen for a coaster. Coffee seeps slowly into fabric, a widening brownish stain, like blood. I am almost too tired to lift the cup to my lips.

Degeneration starts very slowly, so deviously, so patiently that it almost seems to be a living thing; embodied it would be a weasellike animal armed with sly cunning and gnawing needle teeth. It never goes for your throat like a decent monster, so that you might have a chance of beating it down: it lurks in darkness, it gnaws furtively at the base of your spine, it burrows into your liver while you sleep. Like the succubi I try to guard against at night, it saps your strength, it sucks your breath in slumber, it etches away the marrow of your bones.

There is enough water in the tank for one more bath this week; I should wash, but I fear I'm too tired to manage it. Another example? It takes such a lot of *effort* to remain civilized. How tempting to say, "It no longer matters." It does matter. I say it does. I will make it matter. I cannot afford the seductive surrender of my unfortunate brethren; I have a responsibility they don't have. Perhaps I am luckier to have it in a way. It is an awesome responsibility, but carrying it summons up a corresponding strength, it gives me a reason for living, a goal outside myself. Perhaps my responsibility is what enables me to hang on, the knowledge of what is to come just enough to balance out the other pressures. The game has not yet been played to an end. Not while I still hold my special card.

Thinking of the secret, I look at the television set, but the atmospherics are wrong tonight for messages, and it's probably too late for the haphazard programming they put out now. Some nights I leave the test pattern on, enjoying the flickering highlights it sends across the walls and ceilings, but tonight I think it will be more comfortable with just the pool of yellow glow cast by the lamp next to my chair, a barrier against the tangible darkness.

Looking at the television always reawakens my curiosity about the outside world. What is the state of society? The city I can see from my balcony seems to have degenerated into savagery, civilization seems to have been destroyed, but there are contradictions, there are ambiguities. Obviously the Building Committee must still be in existence somewhere. The electric lights and the plumbing still work in the Towers, a shipment of food supplies rattles up the pneumatic dumbwaiter into the kitchen cubicle twice a week, there are old movies and cartoons on television, running continuously with no commercials or live programming, never a hint of news. Who else could it be for but us? Who else could be responsible for it but the Building Committee? I've seen the city; it is dark, broken, inhabited by no one but a few human jackals who eke out a brute existence and hunt each other through the ruins. These facilities are certainly not operated for them—the other Towers are the only lighted buildings visible in the entire wide section of city visible from here.

No, it is the Building Committee. It must be. They are the only ones with the proper resources to hold a circle of order against a widening chaos. Those resources were vast. I know: we built them, we worked to make them flexible, we sweated to make them inexhaustible. We let their control pass out of our hands. One never finishes paying for past sins.

What a tremendous amount of trouble they've gone to, continuing to operate the Towers, even running a small television station somewhere to force-feed us the "entertainment" specified in the Charter. And never a word, never a glimpse of them, even for a second. Why? Why do they bother to keep up the pretense, the mocking hypocrisy of obeying the Charter? The real power is theirs now, why do they bother to continue the sham and lip service? Why don't they just shut down the Towers and leave us to starve in our plush cells? Is it the product of some monstrous, sadistic sense of humor? Or is it the result of a methodical, fussily prim sense of order that refuses to deny a legal technicality even when the laws themselves have died? Do they laugh their young men's laughter when they think of the once-formidable old beasts they have caged?

I feel a surge of anger. I put the half-emptied cup carefully down on the rug. My hand is trembling. The Time is coming. It will be soon now. Soon they will heap some further indignity on me and force my hand. I will not have them laughing at me, those little men with maggots for eyes. Not when I still have it in my power to change it all. Not while I still am who I am. But not just yet. Let them have their victory, their smug laughter. An old tiger's fangs may be blunt and yellowing, but they can still bite. And even an old beast can still rise for one more kill.

I force myself to my feet. I have the inner strength, the discipline. They have nothing, they are the rabble, they are children trying out as men and parading in adult clothing. It was we who taught them the game, and we still know how to play it best. I force myself to wash, to fold the bed out from the wall, to lie still, fighting for calm. I run my eyes around the familiar dimensions of the apartment, cataloguing: pale blue walls, red draw curtains for the French windows, bookshelves next to the curtains, a black cushioned stool, the rug in patterns of orange and green against brown, a red shaggy chair and matching couch, the archways to the kitchen and bath cubicles. Nothing alien. Nothing hostile. I begin to relax. Thank God for familiarity. There is a certain pleasure in looking at well-known, well-loved things, a certain unshakable sense of reality. I often fall asleep counting my things.

(I hate this apartment. I hate everything in this apartment. I cannot stand to live here any longer. Someday I will chop everything to unrecognizable fragments and pile it in the middle of the floor and burn it, and I will laugh while it burns.)

—He is wakened by a shaft of sunlight that falls through the uncurtained French windows. He groans,

stirs, draws one foot up, heel against buttock, knee toward
the ceiling. His hand clenches in the bedclothes. The
sound of birds reaches him through the insulating glass.
For a moment, waking, he thinks that he is elsewhere,
another place, another time. He mutters a woman's name
and his hand goes out to grope across the untouched,
empty space beside him in the double bed. His hand encounters only the cool of sheets, no answering warmth of
flesh. He grimaces, his bent leg snaps out to full length
again, his suddenly desperate hand rips the sheet free of
the mattress, finding nothing. He wrenches to his feet,
neck corded, staggering. By the time his eyes slide open he
has begun to scream—

I will not allow it. Do you hear me, bastards? *I will not
allow it.* I will not stand for it. You've gone too far, I warn
you, too far, I'll kill you. D'you hear? Niggers and thieves.
The past is all I have. I will not have you touching it, I
will not have you sliming and defiling it with your shitty
hands. You leave her out of it, you leave her alone. What
kind of men are you using her against me? *What kind of
men are you?* Rabble not worth breath. Defiling everything you touch, everything better than you finer than you.
I will not allow it.

It is time. It is *Time.*

The decision brings a measure of calm. I am committed now. They have finally driven me too far. It is time for
me to play the final card. I will not let them remain un-
punished for this another second, another breath. I will call
for It, and It will come. I must keep control, there must be
no mistakes. This is retribution. This is the moment I have
waited for all these agonizing months. I must keep control,
there must be no mistakes. It must be executed with
dispatch, with precision. I breathe deeply to calm myself.
There will be no mistakes, no hesitations.

Three steps take me to the television. I flick it on, waiting for it to warm. Impatience drums within me, tightly
reined as a rearing Arabian stallion. So long, so long.

A picture appears on the screen: another imbecilic movie. I think of the Building Committee, unaware, living in
the illusion of victory. Expertly, I remove the back of the
television, my skilled fingers probing deep into the maze

of wires and tubes. I work with the familiarity of long practice. How many hours did I crouch like this, experimenting, before I found the proper frequency of the Others by trial and error? Patience was never a trait of the rabble; it is a talent reserved for the aristocracy. They didn't count on my patience. Mayflies themselves, they cannot understand dedication of purpose. They didn't count on my scientific knowledge, on my technical training at Annapolis. They didn't count on the resources and ingenuity of a superior man.

I tap two wires together, creating sparks, sending messages into ether. I am sending on the frequency of the Others, a prearranged signal in code: the Time is now. Let It come. Sweat in my eyes, fingers cramping, but I continue to broadcast. The Time is now. Let It come. At last a response, the Others acknowledging that they've received my order.

It is over.

Now It will come.

Now they will pay for their sins.

I sit back on my heels, drained. I have done my part. I have launched It on Its way, given birth to retribution, sowed the world with dragon's teeth. And they laughed. Now It is irreversible. Nothing can stop It. An end to all thieves and niggers, to all little men, to all the rabble that grow over the framework like weeds and ruin the order of the world. I stagger to the French windows, throw them open. Glass shatters in one frame, bright fragments against the weave of the rug. Onto the balcony where buildings press in at me unaware of Ragnarok. I collapse against the mesh, fingers spread, letting it take my weight. No motion in the world, but soon there will be enough. Far north, away from the sight of the city, the spaceships of the Others are busy according to plan, planting the thermal charges that will melt the icecap, shattering the earth-old ice, liberating the ancient waters, forming a Wave to thunder south and drown the world. I think of the Building Committee, of the vermin in the ruins of the city, even of my fellows in the other Towers. I am not sorry for them. I am no longer young, but I will take them with me into darkness. There will be no other eyes to watch a sun I can no longer see. I have no regrets. I've always hated them. I hate them all.

(I hate them all.)

—He hates them all—

A moaning in the earth, a trembling, a drumming as of a billion billion hooves. The Tower sways queasily. A swelling, ragged shriek of sound.

The Wave comes.

Over the horizon, climbing, growing larger, stretching higher, filling up the sky, cutting off the sunlight, water in a green wall like glass hundreds of feet high, topped with fangs of foam, the Wave beginning to topple in like the closing fist of God. Its shadow over everything, night at noon as it sweeps in, closes down. The Towers etched like thin lines against its bulk. It is curling overhead is the sky now there is no sky now but the underbelly of the Wave coming down. I have time to see the Towers snapped like matchsticks broken stumps of fangs before it hits with the scream of grating steel and blackness clogs my throat to

(I have destroyed the world.)

—The shadow of the mesh on his face—

Sometimes you can see other people in the other Tower apartments, looking out from their own balconies. I wonder how they destroy the world?

—He turns away, dimly remembering a business appointment. Outside the lazy hooting of rush-hour traffic. There is a cartoon carnival on Channel Five—

HARLAN ELLISON

ONE LIFE, FURNISHED IN EARLY POVERTY

And so it was—strangely, strangely—that I found myself standing in the backyard of the house I had lived in when I was seven years old. At thirteen minutes till midnight on no special magical winter's night, in a town that had held me only till I was physically able to run away. In Ohio, in winter, near midnight—certain I could go back.

Not truly knowing *why* I even wanted to go back. But certain that I could. Without magic, without science, without alchemy, without supernatural assistance; just *go back*. Because I had to, I needed to . . . go back.

Back; thirty-five years and more. To find myself at the age of seven, before any of it had begun; before any of the directions had been taken; to find out what turning point in my life it had been that had wrenched me from the course all little boys took to adulthood and set me on the road of loneliness and success that ended here, back where I'd begun, in a backyard at now-twelve minutes to midnight.

At forty-two I had come to the point in my life I had

27

struggled toward since I was a child: a place of security, importance, recognition. The only one from this town who had made it. The ones who had had the most promise in school were now milkmen, used-car salesmen, married to fat, stupid *dead* women who had themselves been girls of exceeding promise in high school. *They* had been trapped in this little Ohio town, never to break free. To die there, unknown. I had broken free, had done all the wonderful things I'd said I would do.

Why should it all depress me now?

Perhaps it was because Christmas was nearing and I was alone, with bad marriages and lost friendships behind me.

I walked out of the studio, away from the wet-ink-new fifty-thousand-dollar contract, got in my car and drove to International Airport. It was a straight line made up of inflight meals and jet airliners and rental cars and hastily purchased winter clothing. A straight line to a backyard I had not seen in over thirty years.

I had to find the dragoon to go back.

Crossing the rime-frosted grass that crackled like cellophane, I walked under the shadow of the lightning-blasted pear tree. I had climbed in that tree endlessly when I was seven years old. In summer, its branches hung far over and scraped the roof of the garage. I could shinny out across the limb and drop onto the garage roof. I had once pushed Johnny Mummy off that garage roof . . . not out of meanness, but simply because I had jumped from it many times and I could not understand anyone's not finding it a wonderful thing to do. He had sprained his ankle, and his father, a fireman, had come looking for me. I'd hidden on the garage roof.

I walked around the side of the garage, and there was the barely visible path. To one side of the path I had always buried my toy soldiers. For no other reason than to bury them, know I had a secret place, and later dig them up again, as if finding treasure.

(It came to me that even now, as an adult, I did the same thing. Dining in a Japanese restaurant, I would hide small pieces of *pakkai* or pineapple or *terriyaki* in my rice bowl and pretend to be delighted when, later in the meal, my chopsticks encountered the tiny treasures down in among the rice grains.)

I knew the spot, of course. I got down on my hands and knees and began digging with the silver penknife on my watch chain. It had been my father's penknife—almost the only thing he had left when he died.

The ground was hard, but I dug with enthusiasm, and the moon gave me more than enough light. Down and down I dug, knowing eventually I would come to the dragoon.

He was there. The bright paint rusted off his body, the saber corroded and reduced to a stub. Lying there in the grave I had dug for him thirty-five years before. I scooped the little metal soldier out of the ground and cleaned him off as best I could with my paisley dress handkerchief. He was faceless now, and as sad as I felt.

I hunkered there, under the moon, and waited for midnight, only a minute away, knowing it was all going to come right for me. After so terribly long.

The house behind me was silent and dark. I had no idea who lived there now. It would have been unpleasant if the strangers who now lived here had been unable to sleep and, rising to get a glass of water, had idly looked into the backyard. *Their* backyard. I had played here and built a world for myself here, from dreams and loneliness. Using talismans of comic books and radio programs and matinee movies and potent charms like the sad little dragoon in my hand.

My wristwatch said midnight, one hand laid straight on the other.

The moon faded. Slowly, it went gray and shadowy, till the glow was gone, and then even the gray afterimage was gone.

The wind rose. Slowly, it came from somewhere far away, and built around me. I stood up, pulling the collar of my topcoat around my neck. The wind was neither warm nor cold, yet it rushed, without even ruffling my hair. I was not afraid.

The ground was settling. Slowly, it lowered me the tiniest fractions of inches. But steadily, as though the layers of tomorrows that had been built up were vanishing.

My thoughts were of myself: *I'm coming to save you. I'm coming, Gus. You won't hurt anymore . . . you'll never have hurt.*

The moon came back. It had been full; now it was new. The wind died. It had carried me where I'd needed to go. The ground settled. The years had been peeled off.

I was alone in the backyard of the house at 89 Harmon Drive. The snow was deeper. It was a different house, though it was the same. It was not recently painted. The Depression had not been long ago; money was still tight. It wasn't weather-beaten, but in a year or two my father would have it painted. Light yellow.

There was a sumac tree growing below the window of the dinette. It was nourished by lima beans and soup and cabbage.

"You'll just sit there until you finish every drop of your dinner. We're not wasting food. There are children starving in Russia."

I put the dragoon in my topcoat pocket. He had worked more than hard enough. I walked around the side of the house. I smiled as I saw again the wooden milk box by the side door. In the morning, very early, the milkman would put three quarts of milk there, but before anyone could bring them in, this very cold winter morning in December, the cream would push its way up and the little cardboard caps would be an inch above the mouths of the bottles.

The gravel talked beneath my feet. The street was quiet and cold. I stood in the front yard, beside the big oak tree, and looked up and down.

It was the same. It was as though I'd never been away. I started to cry. Hello.

Gus was on one of the swings in the playground. I stood outside the fence of Lathrop Grade School, and watched him standing on the seat, gripping the ropes, pumping his little legs. He was smaller than I'd remembered him. He wasn't smiling as he tried to swing higher. It was serious to him.

Standing outside the hurricane fence, watching Gus, I was happy. I scratched at a rash on my right wrist, and smoked a cigarette, and was happy.

I didn't see them until they were out of the shadows of the bushes, almost on him.

One of them rushed up and grabbed Gus's leg, and tried to pull him off the seat, just as he reached the bottom of his swing. Gus managed to hold on, but the chain ropes twisted crazily and when the seat went back up, it hit the metal leg of the framework.

Gus fell, rolled face down in the dust of the playground, and tried to sit up. The boys pushed through between the swings, avoiding the berserk one that clanged back and forth.

Gus managed to get up, and the boys formed a circle around him. Then Jack Wheeldon stepped out and faced him. I remembered Jack Wheeldon.

He was taller than Gus. They were *all* taller than Gus, but Wheeldon was beefier. I could see shadows surrounding him. Shadows of a boy who would grow into a man with a beer stomach and thick arms. But the eyes would always remain the same.

He shoved Gus in the face. Gus went back, dug in and charged him. Gus came at him low, head tucked under, fists tight, arms braced close to the body. He hit him in the stomach and wrestled him around. They struggled together like inept club fighters, raising dust.

One of the boys in the circle took a step forward and hit Gus hard in the back of the head. Gus turned his face out of Wheeldon's stomach, and Wheeldon punched him in the mouth. Gus started to cry.

I'd been frozen, watching it happen, but he was crying—

I looked both ways down the fence and found the break far to my right. I threw the cigarette away as I dashed down the fence, trying to look behind me. Then through the break and I was running toward them the long distance from far right field of the baseball diamond, toward the swings and seesaws. They had Gus down now, and they were kicking him.

When they saw me coming, they started to run away. Jack Wheeldon paused to kick Gus once more in the side; then he, too, ran.

Gus was lying there, on his back, the dust smeared into

mud on his face. I bent down and picked him up. He
wasn't moving, but he wasn't really hurt. I held him very
close and carried him toward the bushes that rose on a
small incline at the side of the playground. The bushes
were cool overhead and they canopied us, hid us; I laid
him down and used my handkerchief to clean away the
dirt. His eyes were very blue. I smoothed the straight
brown hair off his forehead. He wore braces; one of the
rubber bands hooked onto the pins of the braces, used to
keep them tension-tight, had broken. I pulled it free.

He opened his eyes and started crying again.

Something hurt in my chest.

He started snuffling, unable to catch his breath. He
tried to speak, but the words were only mangled sounds,
huffed out with too much air and pain.

Then he forced himself to sit up and rubbed the back of
his hand across his runny nose.

He stared at me. It was panic and fear and confusion
and shame at being seen this way. "Th-they hit me from in
back," he said, snuffling.

"I know. I saw."

"D'jou scare'm off?"

"Yes."

He didn't say thank you. It wasn't necessary. The backs
of my thighs hurt from squatting. I sat down.

"My name is Gus," he said, trying to be polite.

I didn't know what name to give him. I was going to tell
him the first name to come into my head, but heard myself
say, "My name is Mr. Rosenthal."

He looked startled. "That's *my* name, too. Gus Rosenthal!"

"Isn't that peculiar," I said. We grinned at each other,
and he wiped his nose again.

I didn't want to see my mother or father. I had those
memories. They were sufficient. It was little Gus I wanted
to be with. But one night I crossed into the backyard at 89
Harmon Drive from the empty lots that would later be a
housing development.

And I stood in the dark, watching them eat dinner.

There was my father. I hadn't remembered him being so handsome. My mother was saying something to him, and he nodded as he ate. They were in the dinette. Gus was playing with his food. *Don't mush your food around like that, Gus. Eat, or you can't stay up to hear* Lux Presents Hollywood.

But they're doing "Dawn Patrol."

Then don't mush your food.

"Momma," I murmured, standing in the cold, "Momma, there are children starving in Russia." And I added, thirty-five years late, "Name two, Momma."

I met Gus downtown at the newsstand.

"Hi."

"Oh. Hullo."

"Buying some comics?"

"Uh-huh."

"You ever read *Doll Man* and *Kid Eternity*?"

"Yeah, they're great. But I got them."

"Not the new issues."

"Sure do."

"Bet you've got *last* months. He's just checking in the new comics right now."

So we waited while the newsstand owner used the heavy wire snips on the bundles, and checked off the magazines against the distributor's long white mimeographed sheet. And I bought Gus *Airboy* and *Jingle Jangle Comics* and *Blue Beetle* and *Whiz Comics* and *Doll Man* and *Kid Eternity*.

Then I took him to Isaly's for a hot fudge sundae. They served it in a tall tulip glass with the hot fudge in a little pitcher. When the waitress had gone to get the sundaes, little Gus looked at me. "Hey, how'd you know I only liked crushed nuts, an' not whipped cream or a cherry?"

I leaned back in the high-walled booth and smiled at him.

"What do you want to be when you grow up, Gus?"

He shrugged. "I don't know."

Somebody put a nickel in the Wurlitzer in his booth, and Glenn Miller swung into "String of Pearls."

"Well, did you ever think about it?"

"No, huh-uh. I like cartooning, maybe I could draw comic books."

"That's pretty smart thinking, Gus. There's a lot of money to be made in art." I stared around the dairy store, at the Coca-Cola posters of pretty girls with pageboy hairdos, drawn by an artist named Harold W. McCauley whose style would be known throughout the world, whose name would never be known.

He stared at me. "It's fun, too, isn't it?"

I was embarrassed. I'd thought first of money, he'd thought first of happiness. I'd reached him before he'd chosen his path. There was still time to make him a man who would think first of joy, all through his life.

"Mr. Rosenthal?"

I looked down and across, just as the waitress brought the sundaes. She set them down and I paid her. When she'd gone, Gus asked me, "Why did they call me a dirty Jewish elephant?"

"Who called you that, Gus?"

"The guys."

"The ones you were fighting that day?"

He nodded. "Why'd they say elephant?"

I spooned up some vanilla ice cream, thinking. My back ached, and the rash had spread up my right wrist onto my forearm. "Well, Jewish people are supposed to have big noses, Gus." I poured the hot fudge out of the little pitcher. It bulged with surface tension for a second, then spilled through its own dark-brown film, covering the three scoops of ice cream. "I mean, that's what some people *believe*. So I suppose they thought it was smart to call you an elephant, because an elephant has a big nose . . . a trunk. Do you understand?"

"That's dumb. I don't have a big nose . . . do I?"

"I wouldn't say so, Gus. They most likely said it just to make you mad. Sometimes people do that."

"That's dumb."

We sat there for a while and talked. I went far down inside the tulip glass with the long-handled spoon, and finished the deep dark, almost black bittersweet hot fudge. They hadn't made hot fudge like that in many years. Gus got ice cream up the spoon handle, on his fingers, on his chin, and on his T-shirt. We talked about a great many things.

We talked about how difficult arithmetic was. (How I would still have to use my fingers sometimes even as an adult.) How the guys never gave a short kid his "raps" when the sandlot ball games were in progress. (How I overcompensated with women from doubts about stature.) How different kinds of food were pretty bad-tasting. (How I still used ketchup on well-done steak.) How it was pretty lonely in the neighborhood with nobody for friends. (How I had erected a façade of charisma and glamor so no one could reach me deeply enough to hurt me.) How Leon always invited all the kids over to his house, but when Gus got there, they slammed the door and stood behind the screen laughing and jeering. (How even now a slammed door raised the hair on my neck and a phone receiver slammed down, cutting me off, sent me into a senseless rage.) How comic books were great. (How my scripts sold so easily because I had never learned how to rein in my imagination.)

We talked about a great many things.

"I'd better get you home now," I said.

"Okay." We got up. "Hey, Mr. Rosenthal?"

"You'd better wipe the chocolate off your face."

He wiped. "Mr. Rosenthal . . . how'd you know I like crushed nuts, an' not whipped cream or a cherry?"

We spent a great deal of time together. I bought him a copy of a pulp magazine called *Startling Stories* and read him a story about a space pirate who captures a man and his wife and offers the man the choice of opening one of two large boxes—in one is the man's wife, with twelve hours of air to breathe, in the other is a terrible alien fungus that will eat him alive. Little Gus sat on the edge of the big hole he'd dug, out in the empty lots, dangling his feet, and listening. His forehead was furrowed as he listened to the marvels of Jack Williamson's "Twelve Hours to Live," there on the edge of the fort he'd built.

We discussed the radio programs Gus heard every day: *Tennessee Jed, Captain Midnight, Jack Armstrong, Super-*

man, *Don Winslow of the Navy*. And the nighttime programs: *I Love a Mystery, Suspense, The Adventures of Sam Spade*. And the Sunday programs: *The Shadow, Quiet, Please, The Mollé Mystery Theater*.

We became good friends. He had told his mother and father about "Mr. Rosenthal," who was his friend, but they'd spanked him for the *Startling Stories,* because they thought he'd stolen it. So he stopped telling them about me. That was all right; it made the bond between us stronger.

One afternoon we went down behind the Colony Lumber Company, through the woods and the weeds to the old condemned pond. Gus told me he used to go swimming there, and fishing sometimes, for a black oily fish with whiskers. I told him it was a catfish. He liked that. Liked to know the names of things. I told him *that* was called nomenclature, and he laughed to know there was a name for knowing names.

We sat on the piled logs rotting beside the black mirror water, and Gus asked me to tell him what it was like where I lived, and where I'd been, and what I'd done, and everything.

"I ran away from home when I was thirteen, Gus."

"Wasn't you happy there?"

"Well, yes and no. They loved me, my mother and father. They really did. They just didn't understand what I was all about."

There was a pain on my neck. I touched a fingertip to the place. It was a boil beginning to grow. I hadn't had a boil in years, many years, not since I was a . . .

"What's the matter, Mr. Rosenthal?"

"Nothing, Gus. Well, anyhow, I ran away, and joined the carny."

"Huh?"

"A carnival. The Tri-State Shows. We moved through Illinois, Ohio, Pennsylvania, Missouri, even Kansas . . ."

"Boy! A carnival! Just like in *Toby Tyler or Ten Weeks with the Circus?* I really cried when Toby Tyler's monkey got killed, that was the worst part of it, did you do stuff like that when you were with the circus?"

"Carnival."

"Yeah. Uh-huh. Didja?"

"Something like that. I carried water for the animals sometimes, although we only had a few of those, and mostly in the freak show. But usually what I did was clean up and carry food to the performers in their tops—"

"What's that?"

"That's where they sleep, in rigged tarpaulins. You know, tarps."

"Oh. Yeah, I know. Go on, huh."

The rash was all the way up to my shoulder now. It itched like hell, and when I'd gone to the drugstore to get an aerosol spray to relieve it, so it wouldn't spread, I had only to see those round wooden display tables with their glass centers, under which were bottles of Teel tooth liquid, Tangee Red-Red lipstick and nylons with a seam down the back, to know the druggist wouldn't even know what I meant by Bactine or Liquid Band-Aid.

"Well, along about K.C. the carny got busted because there were too many moll dips and cannons and paperhangers in the tip . . ." I waited, his eyes growing huge.

"What's all *thaaat* mean, Mr. Rosenthal?"

"Ah-ha! Fine carny stiff *you'd* make. You don't even know the lingo."

"Please, Mr. Rosenthal, please tell me!"

"Well, K.C. is Kansas City, Missouri . . . whèn it isn't Kansas City, Kansas. Except, really, on the other side of the river is Weston. And busted means thrown in jail, and . . ."

"You were in *jail*?"

"Sure was, little Gus. But let me tell you now. Cannons are pickpockets and moll dips are lady pickpockets, and paperhangers are fellows who write bad checks. And a tip is a group."

"So what happened, what happened?"

"One of these bad guys, one of these cannons, you see, picked the pocket of an assistant district attorney, and we all got thrown in jail. And after a while everyone was released on bail, except me and the Geek. Me, because I

wouldn't tell them who I was, because I didn't want to go
home, and the Geek, because a carny can find a wetbrain
in *any* town to play Geek."

"What's a Geek, huh?"

The Geek was a sixty-year-old alcoholic. So sunk in his
own endless drunkenness that he was almost a zombie . . .
a wetbrain. He was billed as The Thing, and he lived in a
portable pit they carried around, and he bit the heads off
snakes and ate live chickens and slept in his own dung.
And all for a bottle of gin every day. They locked me in
the drunk tank with him. The smell. The smell of sour liquor, oozing with sweat out of his pores, it made me sick,
it was a smell I could never forget. And the third day, he
went crazy. They wouldn't fix him with gin, and he went
crazy. He climbed the bars of the big freestanding drunk
tank in the middle of the lockup, and he banged his head
against the bars and ceiling where they met, till he fell
back and lay there, breathing raggedly, stinking of that
terrible smell, his face like a pound of raw meat.

The pain in my stomach was worse now. I took Gus
back to Harmon Drive and let him go home.

My weight had dropped to just over a hundred and ten.
My clothes didn't fit. The acne and boils were worse. I
smelled of witch hazel. Gus was getting more antisocial.

I realized what was happening.

I was alien to my own past. If I stayed much longer,
God only knew what would happen to little Gus . . . but
certainly I would waste away. Perhaps just vanish. Then
. . . would Gus's future cease to exist, too? I had no way of
knowing; but my choice was obvious. I had to return.

And couldn't! I was happier here than I'd ever been
before. The bigotry and violence Gus had known before I
came to him had ceased. They knew he was being watched
over. But Gus was becoming more erratic. He was
shoplifting toy soldiers and comic books from the Kresge's
and constantly defying his parents. It was turning bad. I
had to go back.

I told him on a Saturday. We had gone to see a Lash La
Rue Western and Val Lewton's *The Cat People* at the

Lake Theater. When we came back I parked the car on Mentor Avenue, and we went walking in the big, cool, dark woods that fronted Mentor where it met Harmon Drive.

"Mr. Rosenthal," Gus said. He looked upset.

"Yes, Gus?"

"I gotta problem, sir."

"What's that, Gus?" My head ached. It was a steady needle of pressure above the right eye.

"My mother's gonna send me to a military school."

I remembered. *Oh, God,* I thought. It had been terrible. Precisely the thing *not* to do to a child like Gus.

"They said it was 'cause I was rambunctious. They said they were gonna send me there for a *year* or two. Mr. Rosenthal . . . don't let'm send me there. I didn't mean to be bad. I just wanted to be around you."

My heart slammed inside me. Again. Then again. "Gus, I have to go away."

He stared at me. I heard a soft whimper.

"Take me with you, Mr. Rosenthal. Please. I want to see Galveston. We can drive a dynamite truck in North Carolina. We can go to Matawatchan, Ontario, Canada, and work topping trees, we can sail on boats, Mr. Rosenthal!"

"Gus . . ."

"We can work the carny, Mr. Rosenthal. We can pick peanuts and oranges all across the country. We can hitchhike to San Francisco and ride the cable cars. We can ride the boxcars, Mr. Rosenthal . . . I promise I'll keep my legs inside an' not dangle 'em. I remember what you said about the doors slamming when they hook'm up. I'll keep my legs inside, honest I will. . . ."

He was crying. My head ached hideously. But he was *crying!*

"I'll *have* to go, Gus!"

"You don't care!" He was shouting. "You don't care about me, you don't care what happens to me! You don't care if I die . . . you don't—"

He didn't have to say it: *you don't love me.*

"I do, Gus. I swear to God, I do!"

I looked up at him; he was supposed to be my friend. But he wasn't. He was going to let them send me off to that military school.

"I hope you die!"

Oh, dear God, Gus, I am! I turned and ran out of the woods as I watched him run out of the woods.

I drove away. The green Plymouth with the running boards and the heavy body; it was hard steering. The world swam around me. My eyesight blurred. I could feel myself withering away.

I thought I'd left myself behind, but little Gus had followed me out of the woods. Having done it, I now remembered: why had I remembered none of it before? As I drove off down Mentor Avenue, I came out of the woods and saw the big green car starting up, and I ran wildly forward, crouching low, wanting only to go with him, my friend, me. I threw in the clutch and dropped the stick into first and pulled away from the curb as I reached the car and climbed onto the rear fender, pulling my legs up, hanging onto the trunk latch. I drove weaving, my eyes watering and things going first blue then green, hanging on for dear life to the cold latch handle. Cars whipped around, honking madly, trying to tell me that I was on the rear of the car, but I didn't know what they were honking about, and scared their honking would tell me I was back there, hiding.

After I'd gone almost a mile, a car pulled up alongside, and a woman sitting next to the driver looked down at me crouching there, and I made a *please don't tell* sign with my finger to my freezing lips, but the car pulled ahead and the woman rolled down her window and motioned to me. I rolled down my window and the woman yelled across through the rushing wind that I was back there on the rear fender. I pulled over and fear gripped me as the car stopped and I saw me getting out of the door, and I crawled off the car and started running away. But my legs were cramped and cold from having hung on back there, and I ran awkwardly; then coming out of the dark was a road sign, and I hit it, and it hit me in the side of the face, and I fell down, and I ran toward myself, lying there, crying, and I got to him just as I got up and ran off into the gravel yard surrounding the Colony Lumber Company.

Little Gus was bleeding from the forehead where he'd struck the metal sign. He ran into the darkness, and I knew where he was running . . . I had to catch him, to tell him, to make him understand why I had to go away.

I came to the hurricane fence and ran and ran till I found the place where I'd dug out under it, and I slipped down and pulled myself under and got my clothes all dirty, but I got up and ran back behind the Colony Lumber Company, into the sumac and the weeds, till I came to the condemned pond back there. Then I sat down and looked out over the black water. I was crying.

I followed the trail down to the pond. It took me longer to climb over the fence than it had taken him to crawl under it. When I came down to the pond, he was sitting there with a long blade of saw grass in his mouth, crying softly.

I heard him coming, but I didn't turn around.

I came down to him, and crouched behind him. "Hey," I said quietly. "Hey, little Gus."

I wouldn't turn around. I wouldn't.

I spoke his name again, and touched him on the shoulder, and in an instant he was turned to me, hugging me around the chest, crying into my jacket, mumbling over and over, "Don't go, please don't go, please take me with you, please don't leave me here alone . . ."

And I was crying, too. I hugged little Gus, and touched his hair, and felt him holding onto me with all his might, stronger than a seven-year-old should be able to hold on, and I tried to tell him how it was, how it would be: "Gus . . . hey, hey, little Gus, listen to me . . . I *want* to stay, you *know* I want to stay . . . but I can't."

I looked up at him; he was crying, too. It seemed so strange for a grown-up to be crying like that, and I said, "If you leave me *I'll* die. I will!"

I knew it wouldn't do any good to try explaining. He was too young. He wouldn't be able to understand.

He pulled my arms from around him, and he folded my hands in my lap, and he stood up, and I looked at him. He was gonna leave me. I knew he was. I stopped crying. I wouldn't let him see me cry.

I looked down at him. The moonlight held his face in a

pale photograph. I wasn't fooling myself. He'd understand. He'd know. I turned and started back up the path. Little Gus didn't follow. He sat there looking back at me. I only turned once to look at him. He was still sitting there like that.

He was watching me. Staring up at me from the pond side. And I knew what instant it had been that had formed me. It wasn't all the people who'd called me a wild kid, or a strange kid, or any of it. It wasn't being poor or being lonely.

I watched him go away. He was my friend. But he didn't have no guts. He didn't. But I'd show him! I'd really show him! I was gonna get out of here, go away, be a big person and do a lot of things, and some day I'd run into him someplace and see him and he'd come up and shake my hand and I'd spit on him. Then I'd beat him up.

He walked up the path and went away. I sat there for a long time, by the pond. Till it got real cold.

I got back in the car, and went to find the way back to the future, where I belonged. It wasn't much, but it was all I had. I would find it . . . I still had the dragoon . . . and there were many stops I'd made on the way to becoming me. Perhaps Kansas City; perhaps Matawatchan, Ontario, Canada; perhaps Galveston; perhaps Shelby, North Carolina.

And crying, I drove. Not for myself, but for myself, for little Gus, for what I'd done to him, forced him to become. Gus . . . Gus!

But . . . oh, God . . . what if I came back again . . . and again? Suddenly, the road did not look familiar.

AVRAM DAVIDSON

RITE OF SPRING

"The winter meat is about all *gone*," said Mrs. Robinson.

"So's the winter, for that matter," her husband said. "Al*most* . . ."

". . . *and* the potatoes . . ."

Mr. Robinson got up rather quickly and looked in the bin. "Guess there's enough, though. I can do without greens with my meat. If I have to. But I sure hate to do without potatoes."

"Yes," she said, drily. "I've noticed."

He looked at her, as though for a moment mildly surprised or puzzled. Then, with a faint smile, he put his arm around her. For a moment she stood there, her head bent and touching his. With a little sound of content, next, she moved away. She gestured toward one of the cabinets. "There'll be all *that* to do."

He nodded. "Not time *yet*, though . . . Alice . . ."

"Yes?"

Mr. Robinson coughed. "Boy was trying to get in the girl's room again last night."

She whirled around, quicker than you might have

thought. A look of alarm or concern faded from her face. "He didn't, though . . ."

Mr. Robinson shook his head. "Scuttled off quick enough, he heard me coming." And did quick brief mimicry of himself, bleary-eyed, clutching an imaginary bathrobe, coughing a rheumy, old-man's-nighttime cough, and shuffling along noisily. Abruptly he stopped and straightened up, ceased to be an ill and probably querulous old man, was once again stalwart, thickset, and vigorous, for all his grey hairs. He and his wife chuckled.

"Well," he said, "it's natural enough. Healthy young boy. Pretty young girl."

"*That*," she said, "is beside the point— You speak to him, now, Henry. I'll speak to her."

"Done and done and Bradstreet," said Mr. Robinson. He looked out the tightly closed windows. "Getting to be about that time of the season. Fact, it *is* that time of the season. Oh, I shouldn't be surprised . . . any day now . . . Boy out to the shed?"

His wife nodded. As he started getting into his sweater and jacket, she said, "Button up warm now."

Mr. Robinson stepped out the back door and started across the yard. The remnants of last year's vegetable garden lay stark and dead beneath his feet. Looking down, he said, "Well, old friend, we'll put new life into you very soon now." He pushed open the door of a weathered and sturdy old outbuilding. Its smell was cold and faint. Hanging from a beam was a block and tackle and rope and chain. Mr. Robinson pulled, tested, made adjustments, grunted his approval, and went out.

The sound of sawing and chopping ceased as he appeared in the door of the shed. "You doing pretty good, Roger," he said. "Yes, sir, you doing pretty good, Mr. Ames."

Roger picked up an armful of wood and carried it over and stacked it. He wiped his face. He had on it a few freckles and a few pimples and a few hairs. Mr. Robinson put a hand on the boy's biceps and doubled up the boy's arm. "That's good, too," he said. "Better than lifting dumbbells."

A sudden look of cunning came over Roger's stolid face. He swiftly seized the older man in a wrestling hold, heaved. They swayed together for a moment. Then, suddenly, Roger lay on the sawdusty floor and Mr. Robinson was pinning his shoulders to it. "Can't do it yet, can you?" he asked.

"Hey," said Roger. The grip relaxed, the boy started to get up, Mr. Robinson flopped him down again. "Pretty good for an old man with one foot in the grave and another on a banana peel . . . *Now* . . . I got something to tell you, young Roger Ames, and you are going to listen to it, too. You were trying to sneak into Betty's room last night. Weren't you. Yes you were." Roger's face, only faintly flushed, still, from the wrestling, now flooded as red as his shirt. "Now you listen. I am not some old prune who doesn't know that females are built different from men. I know all about that. You ever learn as much about that as me, you be doing pretty well. *I* know what's fun and natural between the sects. *But.* And here's the point, you see, boy. There is a *time.* You been *told* that. And when that time comes, why fine. That's what makes the world go round. That's what makes the grasses grow. The flowers bloom. But that time has not yet come for you. You just *wait,* now, till it does. *I* waited. It won't kill you." He got up.

Roger scrambled up as well. He looked embarrassed and, at the same time, respectful. And, for the present moment, just a bit uncertain. Mr. Robinson said, "Well, now. You've cut wood. You've wrestled. So now let's see you practice catching for a while." And for a while there, in the winter-stale garden between the old house and the outbuildings, he watched and instructed Roger as Roger practiced catching. Somewhere in the house a little bell rang.

Mrs. Robinson was putting things on a tray with attention and dispatch at the same time as she was speaking with Betty. "Toast, butter, jam, honey, cocoa," she counted. "Bless me, *how* that woman does eat. It's a pleasure to behold . . . cookies . . . is there any piece of crisp bacon, cold, from breakfast? She is *very* fond of that . . . What was I saying . . . Oh, there's always so much to think about and to *do* at this time of the year . . ."

"About Roger and, *you* know," Betty said: a slim young girl, rather blossomy about the bosom, with a pale-and-pink and shiny face. "Well, I never encouraged him. I don't even . . . well . . . oh . . . I guess I do *like* him okay, but, oh, sort of like a brother, if you know what I mean, Grandma Robinson." The little bell rang and rang.

Grandma Robinson said that she did know what Betty meant. A little smile crinkled the corners of her mouth and eyes. "As for 'a brother,' well, my, many a girl says that, until a certain time comes, and *then* her mind gets changed quick enough." She deftly laid a neatly ironed napkin over the tray and picked it up. Betty went ahead and opened doors. "Oh, I've no reason to complain of you, dear," said the older woman. "You've been as nice as any girl who's ever lived with us. And I'm sure your mother will be pleased, too. Because it's just as she *said,* child, it's just as she *said.* It's hard raising children right, in the city, teaching them the right ways, the old ways, the things to *know* . . . to *do* . . . and, for *that* matter, *not* to do . . ."

Betty said, "And all those things, you know, in the woods, too . . ."

Mrs. Robinson turned her face, slightly creased with the effort of carrying the tray, and nodded over her shoulder. Betty knocked on the last door. There was a noise from inside, and she opened the door, standing aside for the other to go in.

"Well, Mrs. Machick," said Grandma Robinson, cheerfully, "and here we are, with your half-past ten snack." The room was clean, but it did not smell so.

"Half-past *ten*? You mean more like half-past *twelve,*" the woman sitting on the bed said. She was fat. She was very, very fat. Betty deftly pulled up a little table. Mrs. Robinson set the tray down. "No, dear, it's only half-past ten," she said.

"*Sure* it is," said Mrs. Machick, in a low, tight voice. "Oh, sure." She had a small, tight, tiny-tiny mouth, set into the middle of a vast, loose face. Her eyes darted quickly between the lady of the house and the girl, but she didn't meet their own eyes, and then she had eyes only for the tray and what was on it.

"Now. Is that all right?" Mrs. Robinson cocked her head.

"Could you spare it?" the woman on the bed asked. Her brows made quirky little motions. She sighed. She shrugged. All down the front of her nightgown were food stains.

"Now, if there's anything else you'd like, just ring your little bell for it," Mrs. Robinson said, without the slightest trace of annoyance. "If we have it, we'll be glad to bring it to you."

"*Sure* you would," Mrs. Machick said. "*Oh,* yeah." She fluttered her nostrils with the breath of the long-suffering, gave her frowzy head a little shake, and began to feed.

Betty and Grandma closed the door and exchanged faint sighs. They were halfway across the front room when a low whistle was heard from outside. They looked at each other, wide-eyed and open-mouthed, then turned and tiptoed swiftly to the windows, not touching the lace curtains. A bird was on the ground in front of the house, investigating the sere remains of last year's grass. Out from behind an evergreen came Roger. It was a marvel how, body crouched, on the tips of his toes, hands out just so, how swiftly and how silently he sped; for all his size and all.

It was over in a matter of seconds.

Everybody cried out, but not very loudly. Roger, followed by Mr. Robinson, turned toward the house. Grandma and Betty bustled about, taking things from drawers and closets. The men came in, Roger with a wide and surprised-silly grin on his face. "Welcome, welcome, first harbinger of spring," said Mrs. Robinson; and, "Sir, we bid you welcome," her husband said, with a slight bow. She poured wine into a silver goblet. The bird's head peeped out between the boy's fingers. He held them over the goblet, as though he were offering the bird a drink. Mr. Robinson took its head between the thumb and forefinger of his left hand and with his right hand he took the shears Betty gave him and cut off its head. The bright blood made little swirls in the pale wine, till Mrs. Robin-son, with a silver spoon on the handle of which were quaint and curious engravings much more than half-obscured, stirred the goblet. Then the liquid turned pink. She gave everybody a spoonful of it.

For a moment the house was utterly still.

Then Betty gave her lips an absentminded smack. Then she went absolutely pale. Her eyes flew to Roger. From her now white lips came a sound like the rim of a glass being squeaked. His mouth fell open. His eyes bulged. She fled the room in an instant. The door to the hall slammed behind her. Then another door slammed—the back one. But in between the two times, Roger, uttering a noise be-tween a growl and a howl, had begun his pursuit. There was a crash. ("Didn't even *try* to open *that* one," Mr. Robinson said.) There was a cry, first shrill, then full-throated. There were two noises, quick together, as it might be thud-*thump* or thump-*thud*.

"Well, now," said Mr. Robinson, gently. "He did wait. And it didn't kill him." There were some more noises. A lot more. "Isn't killing *her,* either, presumably," he added.

"It always pays to do things right," his wife said. "You'll get some good greens and potatoes and garden truck *this* year, I shouldn't wonder."

He gave a slow, reflective nod. "You decided what kind of annuals you want out front?" he asked. She started to reply; then, with a tongue click of self-reproof, flung open the front door and emptied the goblet in a wide-scattered toss. Her lips moved. "*There,*" she said, after a moment, closing up. The two older people looked at each other in quiet contentment. They sighed. Nodded briskly.

"Plenty to do," he said. "Even before *those* two are ready to help us. Got to get all those knives and cleavers out of the cabinet and sharpen— Oh. *Oh,* yes. Before I forget." He fetched a pad and an envelope, ink bottle and pen, sat. "To the Editor, Dear Sir," he wrote, in his neat, slow hand. "This morning at"—he pursed his lips, con-sulted his pocket watch, considered—"at about a quarter-to eleven we sighted the first robin of spring in our front yard. Wonder if this is any kind of a record for recent years? Would be glad to hear from any devoted 'robin-watchers' and followers of other good old ways and customs, who may write me directly if they care to."

In her room across the other side of the house, fat Mrs. Machick rang her little bell.

THOM LEE WHARTON

THE BYSTANDER

Harry Van Outten was sitting on the tall stool behind the bar at Decline And Fall when the chunky man with the straw snap-brim and the attaché case came in. He stood blinking as his eyes got used to the dark, and Harry got a good long look at him and decided who he was. The man ambled over to the bar and Harry took the usual deep breath and waited. The case was put down gently between the man and Harry, and of course the man did not sit down.

"If it's about the fire policy, you'll have to go see Pardie in the Maritime and Commercial Building. Suite H, tell him I sent you."

"Mr. Van Outten?"

"Doctor. DDS. No matter. Listen, I'd like to help you, but the lawyer said I wasn't to mess around with this insurance mess."

"Dr. Harry Van Outten, Orthodontic Surgeon, NLP, 22053 Oceanic Avenue, Bournemouth, N.J." (He said it "EnJay.") "This address."

"NLP?"

"No Longer Practicing."

"How'd you know that? Would you like a drink?"

"My name is Roseboom," said the chunky man, and pulled out a little vinyl card case with his picture and thumbprint set into it. The card had "Federal Bureau of Investigation" printed across the top.

"*Oh,* yeah," said Harry, leaning forward on the stool. "What can I do for you, Mr. Rosenbloom?"

"That's Rose-boom." The man looked at Harry's hand and took it and shook it.

"Sorry," said Harry. "Drink?" He clinked the rocks in his gin-gin.

"Maybe later." He looked closely at Harry for a moment. "You know, Doctor . . . Mister. . . ."

"Call me Harry," said Harry.

"You know, Doctor, you don't look very much like your description."

"I've been sick. What description?"

"Bureau files description."

"Why would the FBI have a description of me?"

"Oh, you'd be surprised," said Roseboom vaguely. "Could I talk to you? For a while?"

"How long? What about?"

"A while. Some of your . . . associates."

"Which?"

"Your business associates."

"You mean Joe the Nuts?"

"I hoped you'd come to the point."

"We'll come to the point of an icepick in here," said Harry in a raspy whisper, "this place is bugged to the ears. We'll go for a ride."

Roseboom led the way out the door by several yards, and Harry gimped across the parking lot after him. "Slow down," he called, "this hot blacktop is murder."

"You could've gotten your shoes. I'd wait."

"Never wear 'em. Here." Harry jumped up on the running board of an absolutely mint 1934 Packard Twin Six Phaeton, in buff aluminum with red piping and gray watered-silk upholstery. He twitched his scorched toes for a few seconds and scraped his feet on the running board,

then deftly swung the door open and fell behind the tower-
ing wheel. "Come on."

Roseboom walked cautiously around the beast and
climbed up and in the passenger's side. Harry piloted the
big silver car out of the parking lot and turned north on
Oceanic Avenue. Roseboom craned his neck to look
behind, then slowly turned again to the front.

"That second windshield keeps the wind off your neck
if you're riding in front and is vital if you're in the back."
Roseboom looked over the dash, which was real ebony,
taking in the expanse of dials and instruments. "This
hickey here is a stopwatch for testing your speedometer,
this is a brake fluid gauge, this is a . . . now what the hell
is this? Might be a manifold pressure gauge, but then
again. . . ."

"What would a car like this cost?"

"Invaluable. Priceless. There *aren't* any more, you see."

Roseboom looked straight ahead through the tall
windshield. "You are a successful orthodontist," he said.
"Yet most of your income comes from that gin mill we
just left. You command a very great deal of money. But I
think a toy like this might be beyond even you." He
looked over at Harry.

"The car was a gift," said Harry.

"From whom, may I ask?"

"Why?"

"I'm wondering—this is for the record—if any taxes
were paid on this gift."

"I honestly wouldn't know," said Harry, glancing back
at Roseboom for an instant. The agent narrowed his eyes
but saw no guile in Harry's face. "My lawyer takes care of
the money."

"Which brings us back to the source of the gift."

"Oh, Joe saw the thing at the opera one night—parked
outside the opera house, that is—in Hollywood, I think it
was. Said it reminded him of *The Untouchables*." Harry
gave one soundless snicker.

"And he bought it then."

"I've got a bill of sale, title, everything's in order."

"I know," said Roseboom after a time. He sat quietly,

watching the honky-tonks on Oceanic Avenue fly past. Shortly, Harry noticed that the agent was inspecting him again.

"Something the matter?"

"This nags at me. There are only two elements of the description we have of you that jibe with your actual appearance. The height. The glasses. Now, it says here"—and he was not looking at any paper—"six feet, two thirty-five, brown hair, gray eyes—"

"Gray is right," said Harry.

"If you like. And you are about six feet. The stoop fools you. *White* hair now, and you weigh"—a pause and a sidewise glance—"about one sixty, one fifty-five."

"I told you I was sick."

"Also, the beard. And mustache."

"I quit shaving when I sold my practice. Only psychiatrists get away with beards. Who brings their kids to a dentist with a beard? You know, that poopsheet you have on me sounds like about four, five years ago."

"At date of compilation, subject forty-two years of age."

"I'm forty-six. This birthday." He thumped the wheel with the heel of his hand. "You must've gotten that stuff from my driver's license or something."

"Mmmm," said Roseboom, nodding vaguely, "I concede that you were sick."

"*Oh,* yeah," said Harry.

"What with?"

"Gastroenteritis," said Harry, after a pause. "Recurrent. Gets worse as you get older, I guess."

"I knew dysentery was recurrent. I never heard that about gastro-whoozis. When contracted?"

"You sound like a doctor."

"Small talk. I don't care—professionally—what you've got. What *illness.*"

"I picked it up in the Caribbean about four years ago," said Harry, softly. "Somebody forgot to wash their hands Before Leaving This Rest Room and went and put together our hors d'oeuvres."

" 'Our'?"

"My wife and boy. They died of it. The boy on the island, my wife in Miami. After she heard. Never eat raw fish."

"I'm sorry."

"Thanks. I mean it," he added quickly.

"To get back to Joe the Nuts," said Roseboom.

"Just a minute," said Harry. There was a pause of ten or fifteen seconds, then Harry braked the car to a near stop and turned sharply to the right, up a dirt road that was really only two ruts through a vacant lot overgrown with brown marsh grass. They breasted a low hill—really a sand dune, Roseboom realized—and saw the ocean. Harry let the car roll ahead a little into softening sand and then stopped it and turned off the motor. "Come on," said Harry. They got out of the car. Roseboom sank to his ankles in soft, hot sand. "Leave your shoes and socks." Roseboom sat on the wide running board and pulled them off. He knocked the shoes together, sending a cloud of sand downwind. "Don't get it on the car," called Harry.

Roseboom caught up with him, and they trudged together through the sand and grass tufts toward a tall oblong structure half on the beach and half in the low surf. There was a rusty metal ladder set in its landward side. Harry shouldered ahead, heaved himself up, and continued to climb without a word. Roseboom saw him disappear into a low doorway about twenty feet from the ground and then followed him. Roseboom heaved himself into a low-celinged room about thirty feet square and saw Harry on the seaward side, looking out a narrow horizontal window. The walls, Roseboom saw, must have been a foot thick. There were pocks and cracks in them, and bits of rusty reinforcing skeleton were visible here and there. He guessed that the thing must have been fifty feet high altogether. "What's upstairs?"

"Another room like this. Roof. We could go up there now, but it's like a frying pan this time of day." He intercepted Roseboom's look. "Watchtower left from War Two. There were a lot of tankers getting sunk off this coast. There'd be six or eight guys in here, Coast Guard, all weathers, looking for submarines, smoke, like that."

Roseboom looked at him with a grin. "Not bugged?"

"Someday the thing'll fall into the water. Anyway, I don't think anybody knows the way I come here. At least nobody ever followed me or was here, except some kids who come to roast marshmallows and screw and like that."

"You come here often."

"*Oh*, yeah. I like to watch the sea," he said simply, looking out the view slit again.

"How did you know your own place was bugged?"

"Well, I did it myself. Early in the game, that was. Then somebody, I don' know, maybe Christmas Angel, some of the boys, added some little hickeys of their own. You can hear 'em on the phones. Lights dim out every once in a while. You'd be surprised—no, I guess you wouldn't—at what goes on in those back rooms some nights." Roseboom nodded and continued to look straight at Harry, who wiped his rust-stained palms on his spotless white bell-bottomed slacks, looked once around the room, then back out at the ocean.

"You bought into Decline And Fall in nineteen sixty-six," prompted Roseboom.

"*Oh,* yeah. I came back here, tried to pick up my practice. You know. I had this big-ass house down the coast, in Lochmere, on the Bay. Hundred'n a quarter thousand. Pool. Heated pool. Vacuum cleaners in the baseboards. Boat dock. Big playroom. You know how I felt when I saw that playroom. Jesus Christ.

"Well, I tried to stick it out there. The place wasn't quite paid off, I had a good practice, lots of consulting work, my own lab, four bright young kid associates, going to all be partners someday. Whole floor in a new building. Eight chairs, little operating theater, even. Mostly just for show.

"And. I never had much time to indulge myself, really, just in that upper-middle suburbs kind of way. The lawn. The parties. The concerts. Running the pie throw at the church fair. You know. I really didn't know how to go about it any other way.

"I tried. I had the people from Dunhill's come down and survey the place, turn the next-to-biggest bathroom into a room-size humidor. Bought three thousand Royal

Jamaica Churchills. Ever smoke a Churchill?" Roseboom
shook his head. "Here. Buck twenty-five a crack."

Roseboom did not smoke. He took the big cigar
anyway.

"Then I called Frederick Wildman. I don't mean
Frederick Wildman's goddamn secretary, I mean Frederick. Wildman. He came down. Him. We put together a
wine and cordial cellar. He also sold me a couple of barrels
of scotch. Glenlivet Waters, it's called. Apparently they
don't bottle it at all. That's how Decline And Fall got such
a reputation for wines and brandies, by the way. That's *my*
cellar down in the cellar. If you follow me.

"I *drank* the scotch," he added after a pause.

"Then I had a few more alterations made. A sauna. A
seven-foot-deep bathtub. That just about killed my wife's
insurance. Turned the Buick in on a Cad with a few
refinements. Mostly a bar.

"I got myself a maid after the first couple of big dinner
parties I gave to dispel the . . . what? It wasn't *gloom,* exactly. . . . A maid, after a decent period of mourning.
Lives-in-gives-out, as the saying goes. *That* was a little
girl. Between her and that fountain of booze, I wouldn't
have lasted long. It was that empty, empty house. And I
hadn't even gotten *started* on drugs yet." He was talking
quietly, conversationally, but Roseboom saw that he was
wringing his hands very slowly and very hard.

"Then one night. I think it was New Year's, sixty-six, I
was driving along Oceanic Avenue, blitzed out of my
mind, as usual, when all of a sudden, this fire engine
comes blasting by me on the *right.* Of course I was probably driving on the left anyway. Well, this aroused some
atavistic drunk-ass response in me, so I took off chasing
it. Now that was a wild ride. I should mention that there
were a bunch of others behind me. I kept those red lights
in sight up ahead and drove. Spray was coming over the
seawall and freezing in the air, and that road was just like
glass. Anyway, I stayed alive until I came up on the place
that was burning. I spun out turning into the lot—hit the
big marble seal by the exit sign—and crumpled the Cad
up a little.

"Anyway, I was out there looking over the damage,

freezing to death and staggering and falling on my face, half from ice and half from booze, up comes this little guy with tears running down his face, yelling, 'No insurance! No insurance! No insurance even for fires! You might's well go away, no money for you here!'

"Well, I told him I wasn't going to sue, it was my fault, I was drunk, and so on for about a minute. After the third time I said 'drunk,' his face lit up, and he grabbed me and hugged me and said 'Me, too!' And be damned if he didn't have half a Pinch bottle under his apron.

"So then, we got in the Cad and watched the fire and butchered the Pinch. What he'd left. The place didn't burn badly, just a lot of decor and the kitchen wiped out. And there were some fur coats and so on that they were going to be liable for. Just for the record, his name was Tibor Telredy, and the place was called Ungaria, Goulash Our Specialty. Telredy was a Hungarian Freedom Fighter who'd gone into his family pretty deep to set up the place; his mother did the cooking, his father played violin and so on, besides their life savings on the line. He just hadn't had anything left over for insurance.

"I don't know if it was booze, boredom, or genius, but I started to talk the deal right then and there. Him being drunk didn't hurt any. Anyhow, we worked it out, sitting there in that bunged-up Cadillac with the heater running fit to roast your ass off, guzzling raw booze right from that bulky bottle. My collar was wilted next morning from what ran down my chin that night. Anyhow, we worked it out. I'd cover all his liabilities, pay for incidentals like legal fees and so on, and buy him out for . . ." Harry looked appraisingly at the FBI man for a second. "If you want to know, I guess you could find out. Ninety thou. Go on, you say it if you want. Others have accused me of setting bombs in orphanages.

"I had to sell the house to cover it all, which wasn't a bad idea. Didn't take much of a loss. It cost me about forty to cover liabilities—there were a few cars on fire behind the place that he neglected to point out at the time—and about another sixty to get the place fixed up the way I wanted. The way it is now. With my penthouse on the third floor, the pool tables, the stage and all. You know, I looked up the original title on that land and house. Decline And Fall is a restaurant, bar, cocktail lounge, grill, and cabaret with occasional dinner-theater, which can seat four hundred people on two floors and in the Wine Cellar Room. It was built in nineteen ten as a *summer* house for *one* family! We've lost something somewhere."

"What happened to the former owner?"

"I got a postcard from him about a year ago. He's teaching Slavic history at Southern California. Asked if I wanted to join the Minutemen."

"Did you?"

"Why should I? When I've got the Mafia?"

They looked each other in the eye for a little while, and then Harry looked back out to sea.

"Well, Decline And Fall opened, all right. I handed over the practice to the boys—taught them how to incorporate, first—and arranged for them to pay me a percentage for ninety-nine years or until my death, whichever happens first. Then I moved in on the third floor and tended bar and washed glasses. Didn't even get help, at first. But this resort-area trade just keeps coming and coming. I got tired out at last. But it took time to build up a clientele, especially without a working kitchen—I didn't know much about the business then—and I had some problems."

"Such as what?"

"I'll skip over the little ones, because you want to hear about Joe and the Family. Anyway, that summer, there was a motorcyle gang hit town. Remember?"

"No."

"Well, they hit it. First it was just messing around a lot in the streets. Then the cops got on 'em and they had to go to ground someplace." Harry looked over his shoulder at the FBI man. "Usually it's a bar they pick."

"And it was yours."

"You bet it was. My regular customers—gone! The furniture was crumbling. The bastards never drank anything but draft beer and they'd get on a jag where they'd break glasses after each round. Then they dragged some woman in off the street and just about gangbanged her on the pool table before I got back from upstairs with the shotgun. I kept it under the bar after that."

"Got a permit?"

"You be damned. Anyhow, that cooled them down a little. Things were halfway back to normal. Things looked good, I was meeting expenses and beating trade out of the other locals. Then. Then one night the Big Sprocket or whatever they call him got paroled and crushed into town from California. The whole bunch came in and set up a long course of getting pie-eyed for themselves. They chased off the other customers in about five minutes.

"Except for a bunch of guys sitting in the back. In the big booth. These were guys I'd never seen before, off a charter boat. They were the usual fishing types—baseball caps, polo shirts, three-day beards—you know. They weren't paying any attention to what was going on up front, and the Big Sprocket saw that they weren't. He hitched up his jeans and walked back there and told them to buy a round for the house or get the hell out. One says, 'Can we drink up before we leave?' but Big Sprocket had wandered away.

"I guess somebody must've gone to the phone. I don't know who or when. Anyway, a half hour later, Big Sprock remembered them, and he went back with a mug of beer in each hand and said, 'Are you mutherfuckers still here?' And the first guy he'd talked to stood up, very soft-spoken and almost fatherly, and said, 'We better take this discussion outside,' and Big Sprocket says, 'You bet your ass we better,' and he led the way out, with his whole mob following him. And those fishing types.

"By that time, *I* was on the phone, but somebody'd popped the wires out. So I had a gin-gin and I got the shotgun and filled my pockets with shells and started for the porch. By then, there were sounds of a real, earnest difference of opinion to be heard issuing from the front parking lot." Harry grinned and smacked his lips at the memory.

"I opened those swinging doors and walked out like Long John Silver onto that quarterdeck," said Harry, "and there was quite a rumble out there. But it was just about over. Down at the end of each driveway, somebody had parked a dump truck. In the middle of the lot there was a big pile of motorcycle parts. There were four or five guys down there, taking their time about tossing these little bits of motorcycles onto the one truck, the one parked in the 'enter' driveway. Then there were four or five guys with sledgehammers and spud bars tearing what must've been the last few motorcycles apart and throwing the bits and pieces onto the pile. And right in front of the big front steps were forty or fifty guys with baseball bats, brass knucks, sandbags, blackjacks, loaded canes, and what-all, just beating the living hell out of Big Sprocket and his mob.

"I just sort of stood there. Frozen, you know, at the sight. I thought I was really going to have to shoot somebody, and I was so relieved that I didn't have to, at least right away, that I just fell into one of those big rattan chairs. You saw 'em, the ones on the front porch for the neckers and honeymooners, moon over the vasty sea, and all that. Then, somebody put a hand on my shoulder. I practically had a stroke. Then I looked over beside me. There were those fishermen, sitting in these chairs, taking their lordly ease, sipping fresh boozes—and I don't know where they came from, I didn't serve 'em—watching the show just like they'd watch the Wednesday night fights.

" 'Here, old buddy,' says one of them, the one closest to me, who'd put his hand on my shoulder. 'Have a drink. These are almost as good as yours.' And I took it. What it was, I couldn't tell you. I made it go in three seconds, and he grinned at me, and squeezed my shoulder really buddy-buddy and handed me another one.

"Well, to keep from boring you, those guys in the lot and in the driveway finished beating those motorbikers to a bloody pulp and disposing of their mounts at the same time. Some of them took a whack or two at some of the bodies, then started to throw the remains onto the other truck, the one parked in the exit.

" 'Hey, Frank!' the guy beside me calls out. One of the batmen turned and came a few paces toward us. 'Dump 'em in the quarry. My quarry, not yours. Show 'em the Hand.' And the guy nodded and laughed and went about his business. Then the guy next to me turned and said, 'And now a gentleman can drink in peace,' and he drained his drink. Then he said, 'You've got one of the best places I ever saw. Come on back in and build us some more.' Then he said, 'You like Italian food?' "

Harry looked at Roseboom. "I guess that was the first hint I ever had." Roseboom nodded.

"We got back into the bar," said Harry, "and I was setting them up for the house—the fishermen and about five others—when he introduced himself. 'I'm Joe Nucci,' he said, and I told him who I was. He nodded and said, 'Uh-huh. Glad to meet you.' Then he told me who the other guys were." Harry looked at Roseboom again. "All out-of-towners, except Christmas Angel."

"Yeah," said Roseboom.

"Well, we all socked 'em down with both hands for about two hours, and a couple of guys all covered with dust, T-shirts, work pants, you know, came in, and they looked at Joe and he lifted his eyebrows and they just nodded and sat down at the other end of the bar. I just served them two triples and they said 'Thank you,' and 'Thank you.'

"I guess it was that 'Italian food' business that got Joe and I talking about . . . business. 'Goddamn it, Harry old buddy,' he kept saying, 'a guy who runs such a hell of a bar has got to have a kitchen, too! And what could it be with a name like that but a *guinea* kitchen?' And I explained how I was going to get the kitchen running early next year, with help and all, and hire a pianist, and have a free lunch in the bar, and he kept pounding on the bar and hissing, 'Yeah! Right! Great!' Hell, I told it to him just like it is now—you saw it. And he nodded, and grinned, and kept punching me in the shoulder, and I never had a chance to think about closing time, so they stayed till four thirty. But somebody thought to shut off the sign." Harry stared off at the sea, remembering. "We were telling each other our life stories all night. Then he waved from the front porch, wiggled his fingers, he still had a drink in each hand, and he yelled, 'Don't forget what I said, Harry, boy!' and he said, 'Don't worry any more about that dentist shit! You're a *community service* now!' " Harry turned around. "And you know, I'm as good a restaurateur as I ever was an orthodontist?"

"What then?" asked Roseboom.

"Well, I started to get phone calls. This designer. That manufacturer. Beautiful terms. If I sounded reluctant, why, they'd come down a few thousand! I couldn't afford *not* to get that goddamn kitchen all outfitted and working! Then, when the stuff was all installed, and painted, and the drawers full of knives and like that, and we had lots of flour and all around, this fat guy comes walking in one day. 'I am Ercole Barone,' he says. 'Where is my kitchen?' " Harry paused. "You don't know who Ercole Barone is."

"No," said Roseboom. "Should I?"

Harry sighed. "Vulgarian," he said. "I shouldn't say that, because I didn't know myself. All I knew was that this huge guy who looked like Oliver Hardy, if Oliver Hardy had been born in Rome, had come in and started to turn out these unbelievable meals. There was one sent to me on the third floor, every day, nine a.m., three thirty, and nine p.m., unless I sent word to hold it. My God," said Harry, remembering.

He recovered himself. "Ercole Barone is the master chef of a well-known restaurant in New York whose name I dare not divulge. He plans the menus for a shipping line and four airlines on the side. He works in town nine months out of the year." Harry looked at Roseboom, saw he was not impressed, and scowled. "The other three, he works for me. The Italian legation and the Italian Mission to the UN drives here once a week, summers, in DPL-licensed cars, to eat Barone's cooking. I have seen a silver-haired diplomat weeping into a plate of *scampi Fra Diavolo,* and there is hardly a man among them who is not in tears when he has to leave.

"Then there is the little old lady who comes in every day to make the pasta dough and pizza crusts. She does not speak a word of English. She arrives in a rented limousine. She turns out more starch than the farms of Idaho, finishes at four p.m., walks to the back door, and Barone gives her two twenty-dollar bills I have given him for this purpose. I ask why only forty bucks? Why two twenties? And I always get the same reply: 'Twenty for pay, twenty for carfare.' She comes in by private plane from *somewhere,* is met by a limousine, driven to my doorstep, and then every day at four, driven back to meet her plane at the local airport.

"Then there's the clientele. And the entertainment. The old days of serving gin and tonics to the beach bums are long gone. Sure, we let the suntanned, windblown crowd in afternoons, but at night, it's different. If we ever had a fire like poor Telredy's, the bill for the furs in the checkroom would be bigger than the cost of the whole building, burned flat. We don't just get the gold-plate trade from the trotting track, and the wanderers from the city! There were plates from nineteen states in that parking lot one night!"

Harry caught himself and lowered his voice. "The entertainment. Yeah. We don't *have* any. It's taxed. But what do we do when a truck rolls up one afternoon, delivers us a very special concert piano, and at nine that night, a certain blind jazz pianist shows up for dinner and then kids on the keys for a few hours afterward? Or when a British rock group comes for *fettucine Alredo* and gigs until five the next morning? Now, this is not every day. The everyday stuff is Joe the Nuts singing Verdi, or his buddies singing . . . what they sing. What *he* sings."

Roseboom started to speak, and Harry put up his hand wearily. "I'm not naming any names." He scratched his chest reflectively. "One night he even had his *daughter* with him. Nobody even thought to turn out the sign that night.

"And then there's Joe. He's really pretty good. And he puts his heart into it, it's as much fun to watch as to listen. You know how he worked as a singing waiter when he was a kid. Do you know one thing that preys on Joe's mind? That he's never been able to get Franco Corelli to come in for a few days. Corelli is his idol."

"A *capo don* of the Mafia," said Roseboom, "working as a singing waiter. Dear God, no!"

"We don't say 'Mafia,' " said Harry. " 'Mafia' is a bad word. Old hat. It's usually 'the Family,' or 'the Honored Society,' or—this is Joe talking—'We the People.' "

Roseboom gave him a hard look. "When were the firm financial arrangements made?"

"Weren't," said Harry.

"You keep no records? I think, just speaking off the top of my head, that you people are all in trouble."

"Records? My taxes are in order. I'm not a vital industry, subject to audits by state or federal governments. As somebody or other once said, as long as the law can't require me to be a literate, it can't make me keep records. They tell me I've got a pretty good tax lawyer."

"Don't you know for sure?"

"I'm in pretty good shape," said Harry, quietly. "I'm rich, and I'm not in jail. I'm enjoying life for the first time . . . in a long time."

Roseboom was silent for a while. Then he said, "I was going to ask you—I *do* ask you to testify at some future date, to a grand jury soon to be constituted, against your Mafia connections."

"Why?" said Harry.

"Why?" yelled Roseboom. "They've taken over your business, they've put you under their thumb—"

"How's that? *I* run my business. And I do a good job. What they're doing is throwing business my way and helping me keep on top. And, mister, it's pure cream." He paused reflectively. "Now, it is true that Joe put a safe in my office that only he and Christmas Angel know the combination to, and that the Angel handles the receipts. But the Angel is Joe's employee, and Joe is my friend. My own take has gone up every year, and I can't see anything significant being drained off."

" 'Thou shalt not muzzle the ox, when that he treadeth out the grain,' " said Roseboom, through his teeth. "What do you mean by 'significant'?"

"I mean that two places have changed hands on that strip this year. Nothing to do with the Family. They just couldn't hack it. If I was being milked the way you seem to think I am, I'd be in the street myself. As it is, I was asked to bid on one of them. By the owner's lawyer, not by the Family. And as far as being under any thumbs," Harry continued, "I went to Martinique last spring to visit my son's grave. To Miami to visit my wife's. I visited my

uncle in Chicago, he's a surgeon. I went to St. Petersburg to look into some real estate stuff I got into in the fifties. I could've run out any time, if I wanted to. Your point eludes me."

"Listen to me," said Roseboom. "Joe the Nuts, born Giuseppe Nucci, known as Joseph Nucci, is a *capo don.* He is a big, big gangster, if I may use an old-hat word." He sneered just the slightest bit. "He has operated all over the country as a special representative of the Mafia, gouging small businessmen into signing over their livelihoods to his . . . organization."

"Did you ever hear of the Supreme Protective Agency in New York?" asked Harry. "They go around hitting shopkeepers for ten bucks a month, for 'protection.' Now, that is *really* old hat. And all they do for that ten is to string tape around the edges of the shopwindows, you know, like a burglar alarm, but without alarm wires in it."

"Well?" said Roseboom.

"But it *works,*" said Harry. "That green tape is like a danger signal. Joe described it to me once in very memorable terms. He said, 'Those storefronts are *Territory.*' " He paused. "Maybe what you're saying is that I'm Territory, too."

"Yes," said Roseboom, between his teeth, "I guess you are."

"And there's another thing," said Harry. "Joe Nucci is my friend. Now, I've had friends who were drunks. Queers. *Cruel* people, both men and women, and that's the worst of all. Joe is just a nice little guy who loves singing and booze and screwing and who takes pleasure keeping his house in order. That could be *me,* except I can't sing. When I compare him to some of the other friends I've had, he comes out pretty good.

"And now you come in here and tell me that I've got to chuck away my livelihood, my friend, and put myself in criminal suspicion, just because somebody sent you a report or a memo or what the hell to that effect. 'Casino owner'—these places like mine are always 'casinos' in your language—'with Mafia connections,' that's what I'll be for the rest of my life."

"Wait a minute," said Roseboom.

"No. Let me finish with the most cogent argument I've got, again, so as not to stretch this interview out unduly. Now, suppose I *am* a Mafia patsy. What happens? I'm caught between them and you, remember. They come to me and they threaten to cut off my balls, pull out my tongue, kill me, sink me in a block of cement into the bottom of New York Harbor. Kill a few of my friends, burn my house—and my business, they're in the same building—poison my cats, sink my boat . . . and so on.

"Now, what do you threaten? You threaten to put me in *jail*." Harry looked at Roseboom for a long time. Roseboom was looking at the floor. "I'm afraid, Mr. Roseboom, that the Mafia is leading in the bidding for my ass."

"Don't you know we can protect you?" asked Roseboom, but Harry could see that he was tired, and he himself knew that he spoke without conviction.

"Thirty years?" asked Harry. "I might live thirty years. But the chances are against it if I listen to you."

Roseboom stood up and automatically brushed a cloud of cement dust off the seat of his pants. He moved toward the doorway, turned and faced Harry, then stepped gingerly down onto the ladder.

Harry took one last look at the sea, sighed deeply, and followed him down.

* * *

Sleet and snow were racketing at the front windows of Decline And Fall, and Harry looked up, and then curled closer to the blaze in the new fireplace in the empty cocktail lounge. He guessed that he had another hour before the first of the wintertime regulars pulled in—if they came out at all on a night like this. The floodlit pillar Joe the Nuts had sent from Leptis Magna was sheathed in ice. Harry looked out at it and grinned to himself. "Good for the image," Joe had said. God knew it was phallic and classic and Roman enough for anybody. Harry had his sixth gin-gin of the evening at hand and was feeling no pain, literally. The small of his back had begun to bother him late in the fall. He pulled out the letter that had arrived with the pillar and read it again.

Dear Harry:

Thanks for the news about Uncle Freddie once again. Everybody needs a vacation. But you know them bastards wouldnt even let me in to SICILY? Then when I left Palermo I couldnt get into Rome. Anyway I got the pillar for you then, dont ask me how, you keep your nose clean like always. Beirut was nice but I like Spain much better. This is just a little fishing village Harry the name of which I will divulge when you call at Wagon-Lits Internationales, Barcelona. There are lots of Swede college girls here, made me think of my man the DUTCHMAN. Im making out OK with the wife of the local boss of guardia civil, thats state cops. Harry the wine here is as good as real Vino Rosso and is thirtyfive cents a quart. Oops thats a leter here in the old country. I never was as happy traveling for the family as I am here. To tell you the truth Harry I think them bastards are just as happy if I stay over here indefinitely. I didnt mention I get to sing in the local bar, what they call a bodega! And for money! Its the greatest moment of my life, more fun than when I was a kid. You know I love to sing. All I really need to die happy is to get paid to sing in your place Harry with Corelli beside me. But its real good here too. When are you coming over Harry? It isnt going to be too cool for you now that theres been all that noise around there. Frankie Buttons was pulled in to a special grand jury they convened just for him. You remember Frank. Come over here Harry, well have a ball. Between the two of us theres nothing we cant do.

                           Joe (The Nuts)

Harry refolded the letter and put it back in his breast pocket. He was glad Joe had gotten out. Of course, he thought, it would be easy anywhere for Joe. He was like a cat, always landed on his feet. Now, he, Harry . . . But that was water under the bridge. Harry drained the gin. He got up—it took him a distressingly long time—and walked to the bar. The barman came to him, but he continued around behind it. "Never mind," he said. "I'll build my own."

He sat on the high stool—his high stool—as he worked. He could not feel the rung of the stool under his feet, and knew that his ankles and feet must be swelling again. Sitting there reminded him of the previous summer, when Inspector Roseboom had finally appeared, as Harry had known he, or some other, would.

Roseboom had been blown to tatters by the bomb under the floorboards of his car two days after the interview with Harry. Then an anonymous call had sent FBI men from the local office after one Angelo Christofori, known as Christmas Angel, who was suspected of killing an agent. The Angel might have gotten clear if he hadn't locked his car. As he stood there, panting, trying to work the lock on his Lincoln Continental, two agents had come up on him and shot him eleven times, as he attempted to escape and/or resist arrest. The coroner noted that no single one of these bullets lodged in a vital spot.

After that, it had gone back and forth, for five months or more. An agent here, two or three torpedoes there, killed, bombed, wounded, taken into custody. A file of documents confiscated. An informer made to disappear. A little war, up and down the Jersey coast from the storm center at Decline And Fall. Harry thought that what he had done was better than what Roseboom had wanted him to do. First Harry had warned the Family, through Joe, that the FBI was interested in Decline And Fall. Joe had escaped, Roseboom was murdered, and Harry had blown the whistle on Christmas Angel. By then both sides were at each other, and Harry saw in each day's papers how the battle raged around him. Each morning's edition was delivered by special courier to Decline And Fall at eleven fifteen the previous night. Harry liked a head start on the news.

He had known for fourteen months that he was dying. The back pains had been cancer of both kidneys. It was a while before he could handle his gin-gins altogether comfortably. But Harry persevered. He had been a dentist, and a good one, all his life, except for a few timid and colorless childhood years. His student days were a blank to him once they had passed. He had never been able to get close to any woman but his dead wife. The passing of the boy who had been partly his wife and partly himself had burned something out of him. He reflected that he had not lied completely to Roseboom when he laid his sickness to a plate of pickled fish on a hot night in Martinique. Then he had bought Decline And Fall; he had discovered that his only pleasure was in making, rather than merely doing. He had made Decline And Fall well, and it would be his monument. With Joe's help, he had made it good beyond his dreams. Then came the thing that would unmake him and his creation, and he had done a bit of unmaking himself. Except for Joe, they were all expendable; and he would live—he would—to see the outcome of the battle that he had posed between his enemies as it raged around his house.

He finished the mixing and laid the long spoon down carefully, took up the fresh gin-gin and walked slowly back to his chair by the fire. The paper boy was on his way out but came back for his tip. Harry sat down gently and opened the paper, flipping it so that the pages stood by themselves, the headline boldly exposed. He could hardly wait to see what he had done tonight.

R. A. LAFFERTY

ALL PIECES OF A
RIVER SHORE

It had been a very long and ragged and incredibly in-
terlocked and detailed river shore. Then a funny thing had
happened to it. It had been broken up, sliced up into
pieces. Some of the pieces had been folded and com-
pressed into bales. Some of them had been rolled up on
rollers. Some of them had been cut into still smaller pieces
and used for ornaments and as Indian medicine. Rolled
and baled pieces of the shore came to rest in barns and old
warehouses, in attics, in caves. Some were buried in the
ground.

And yet the river itself still exists physically, as do its
shores, and you may go and examine them. But the shore
you will see along the river now is not quite the same as
that old shore that was broken up and baled into bales and
rolled onto rollers, not quite the same as the pieces you
will find in attics and caves.

His name was Leo Nation and he was known as a rich
Indian. But such wealth as he had now was in his collec-

tions, for he was an examining and acquiring man. He had cattle, he had wheat, he had a little oil, and he spent everything that came in. Had he had more income he would have collected even more.

He collected old pistols, old ball shot, grindstones, early windmills, walking-horse threshing machines, flax combs, Conestoga wagons, brass-bound barrels, buffalo robes, Mexican saddles, slick horn saddles, anvils, Argand lamps, rush holders, hay-burning stoves, hackamores, branding irons, chuck wagons, longhorn horns, beaded serapes, Mexican and Indian leatherwork, buckskins, beads, feathers, squirrel-tail anklets, arrowheads, deerskin shirts, locomotives, streetcars, mill wheels, keelboats, buggies, ox yokes, old parlor organs, blood-and-thunder novels, old circus posters, harness bells, Mexican oxcarts, wooden cigar-store Indians, cable-twist tobacco a hundred years old and mighty strong, cuspidors (four hundred of them), Ferris wheels, carnival wagons, carnival props of various sorts, carnival proclamations painted big on canvas. Now he was going to collect something else. He was talking about it to one of his friends, Charles Longbank who knew everything.

"Charley," he said, "do you know anything about 'The Longest Pictures in the World' which used to be shown by carnivals and in hippodromes?"

"Yes, I know a little about them, Leo. They are an interesting bit of Americana: a bit of nineteenth-century back country mania. They were supposed to be pictures of the Mississippi River shore. They were advertised as one mile long, five miles long, nine miles long. One of them, I believe, was actually over a hundred yards long. They were badly painted on bad canvas, crude trees and mudbank and water ripples, simplistic figures and all as repetitious as wallpaper. A strong-armed man with a big brush and plenty of barn paint of three colors could have painted quite a few yards of such in one day. Yet they are truly Americana. Are you going to collect them, Leo?"

"Yes. But the real ones aren't like you say."

"Leo, I saw one. There is nothing to them but very large crude painting."

"I have twenty that are like you say, Charley. I have

three that are very different. Here's an old carnival poster
that mentions one."

Leo Nation talked eloquently with his hands while he
also talked with his mouth, and now he spread out an old
browned poster with loving hands:

"*The Arkansas Traveler,* World's Finest Carnival,
Eight Wagons, Wheel, Beasts, Dancing Girls, Baffling
Acts, Monsters, Games of Chance. And Featuring the
World's Longest Picture, Four Miles of Exquisite Paint-
ing. This is from the Original Panorama; it is Not a
Cheap-Jack Imitation."

"So you see, Charley, there was a distinction: there
were the original pieces, and there were the crude imitations."

"Possibly some were done a little better than others,
Leo; they could hardly have been done worse. Certainly,
collect them if you want to. You've collected lots of less
interesting things."

"Charley, I have a section of that panoramic picture
that once belonged to the Arkansas Traveler Carnival. I'll
show it to you. Here's another poster:

"King Carnival, The King of them All. Fourteen
Wagons. Ten Thousand Wonders. See the Rubber Man.
See the Fire Divers. See the Longest Picture in the World,
see Elephants on the Mississippi River. This is a Genuine
Shore Depictment, not the Botches that Others show."

"You say that you have twenty of the ordinary pictures,
Leo, and three that are different?"

"Yes I have, Charley. I hope to get more of the genuine. I hope to get the whole river."

"Let's go look at one, Leo, and see what the difference
is."

They went out to one of the hay barns. Leo Nation kept
his collections in a row of hay barns. "What would I do?"
he had asked once, "call in a carpenter and tell him to
build me a museum? He'd say, 'Leo, I can't build a museum without plans and stuff. Get me some plans.' And
where would I get plans? So I always tell him to build me
another hay barn one hundred feet by sixty feet and fifty
feet high. Then I always put in four or five decks myself
and floor them, and leave open vaults for the tall stuff.

Besides, I believe a hay barn won't cost as much as a museum."

"This will be a big field, Charley," Leo Nation said now as they came to one of the hay-barn museums. "It will take all your science in every field to figure it out. Of the three genuine ones I have, each is about a hundred and eighty yards long. I believe this is about the standard length, though some may be multiples of these. They passed for paintings in the years of their display, Charley, *but they are not paintings.*"

"What are they then, Leo?"

"I hire you to figure this out. You are the man who knows everything."

Well, there were two barrel reels there, each the height of a man, and several more were set further back.

"The old turning mechanism is likely worth a lot more than the picture," Charles Longbank told Leo Nation. "This was turned by a mule on a treadmill, or by a mule taking a mill pole round and round. It might even be eighteenth century."

"Yeah, but I use an electric motor on it," Leo said. "The only mule I have left is a personal friend of mine. I'd no more make him turn that than he'd make me if I was the mule. I line it up like I think it was, Charley, the full reel north and the empty one south. Then we run it. So we travel, we scan, from south to north, going upstream as we face west."

"It's funny canvas and funny paint, much better than the one I saw," said Charles Longbank, "and it doesn't seem worn at all by the years."

"It isn't either one, canvas or paint," said Ginger Nation, Leo's wife, as she appeared from somewhere. "It is picture."

Leo Nation started the reeling and ran it. It was the wooded bank of a river. It was a gravel and limestone bank with mud overlay and the mud undercut a little. And it was thick timber to the very edge of the shore.

"It is certainly well done," Charles Longbank admitted. "From the one I saw and from what I had read about these, I wasn't prepared for this." The rolling picture was certainly not repetitious, but one had the feeling that the

riverbank itself might have been a little so, to lesser eyes
than those of the picture.

"It is a virgin forest, mostly deciduous," said Charles
Longbank, "and I do not believe that there is any such
temperate forest on any large river in the world today. It
would have been logged out. I do not believe that there
were many such stretches even in the nineteenth century.
Yet I have the feeling that it is a faithful copy of something, and not imaginary."

The rolling shores: cottonwood trees, slash pine,
sycamore, slippery elm, hackberry, pine again.

"When I get very many of the pictures, Charley, you
will put them on film and analyze them or have some kind
of computer do it. You will be able to tell from the sun's
angle what order the pictures should have been in, and
how big are the gaps between."

"No, Leo, they would all have to reflect the same hour
of the same day to do that."

"But it *was* all the same hour of the same day," Ginger
Nation cut in. "How would you take one picture at two
hours of two days?"

"She's right, Charley," Leo Nation said. "All the pictures of the genuine sort are pieces of one original authentic picture. I've known that all along."

Rolling shore of pine, laurel oak, butternut, persimmon,
pine again.

"It is a striking reproduction, whatever it is," Charles
Longbank said, "but I'm afraid that after a while even this
would become as monotonous as repeating wallpaper."

"Hah," said Leo. "For a smart man you have dumb
eyes, Charley. Every tree is different, every leaf is different. All the trees are in young leaf too. It's about a last-
week-of-March picture. What it hangs on, though, is what
part of the river it is. It might be a third-week-in-March
picture, or a first-week-in-April. The birds, old Charley
who know everything, why don't we pick up more birds in
this section? And what birds are those there?"

"Passenger pigeons, Leo, and they've been gone for
quite a few decades. Why don't we see more birds there?
I've a humorous answer to that, but it implies that this
thing is early and authentic. We don't see more birds be-

cause they are too well camouflaged. North America is to-day a bird watchers' paradise because very many of its bright birds are later European intrusions that have replaced native varieties. They have not yet adjusted to the native backgrounds, so they stand out against them visually. Really, Leo, that is a fact. A bird can't adapt in a short four or five hundred years. And there are birds, birds, birds in that, Leo, if you look sharp enough."

"I look sharp to begin with, Charley; I just wanted you to look sharp."

"This rolling ribbon of canvas or whatever is about six feet high, Leo, and I believe the scale is about one to ten, going by the height of mature trees and other things."

"Yeah, I think so, Charley. I believe there's about a mile of river shore in each of my good pictures. There's things about these pictures though, Charley, that I'm almost afraid to tell you. I've never been quite sure of your nerves. But you'll see them for yourself when you come to examine the pictures closely."

"Tell me the things now, Leo, so I'll know what to look for."

"It's all there, Charley, every leaf, every knob of bark, every spread of moss. I've put parts of it under a microscope, ten power, fifty power, four hundred power. There's detail there that you couldn't see with your bare eyes if you had your nose right in the middle of it. You can even see cells of leaf and moss. You put a regular painting under that magnification and all you see is details of pigment, and canyons and mountains of brush strokes. Charley, you can't find a brush stroke in that whole picture! Not in any of the real ones."

It was rather pleasant to travel up that river at the leisurely equivalent rate of maybe four miles an hour, figuring a one to ten ratio. Actually the picture rolled past them at about half a mile an hour. Rolling bank and rolling trees, pin oak, American elm, pine, black willow, shining willow.

"How come there is shining willow, Charley, and no white willow, you tell me that?" Leo asked.

"If this is the Mississippi, Leo, and if it is authentic,

then this must be a far northern sector of it."

"Naw. It's Arkansas, Charley. I can tell Arkansas anywhere. How come there was shining willow in Arkansas?"

"If that is Arkansas, and if the picture is authentic, it was colder then."

"Why aren't there any white willow?"

"The white willow is a European introduction, though a very early one, and it spread rapidly. There are things in this picture that check *too* well. The three good pictures that you have, are they pretty much alike?"

"Yeah, but not quite the same stretch of the river. The sun's angle is a little different in each of them, and the sod and the low plants are a little different."

"You think you will be able to get more of the pictures?"

"Yeah. I think more than a thousand miles of river was in the picture. I think I get more than a thousand sections if I know where to look."

"Probably most have been destroyed long ago, Leo, if there ever were more than the dozen or so that were advertised by the carnivals. And probably there were duplications in that dozen or so. Carnivals changed their features often, and your three pictures may be all that there ever were. Each could have been exhibited by several carnivals and in several hippodromes at different times."

"Nah, there were more, Charley. I don't have the one with the elephants in it yet. I think there are more than a thousand of them somewhere. I advertise for them (for originals, not the cheap-jack imitations), and I will begin to get answers."

"How many there were, there still are," said Ginger Nation. "They will not destroy. One of ours has the reel burned by fire, but the picture did not burn. And they won't burn."

"You might spend a lot of money on a lot of old canvas, Leo," said Charles Longbank. "But I will analyze them for you: now, or when you think you have enough of them for it."

"Wait till I get more, Charley," said Leo Nation. "I will

make a clever advertisement. 'I take those things off your hands,' I will say, and I believe that people will be glad to get rid of the old things that won't burn and won't destroy, and weigh a ton each with reels. It's the real ones that won't destroy. Look at that big catfish just under the surface there, Charley! Look at the mean eyes of that catfish! The river wasn't as muddy then as it is now, even if it was springtime and the water was high."

Rolling shore and trees: pine, dogwood, red cedar, bur oak, pecan, pine again, shagbark hickory. Then the rolling picture came to an end.

"A little over twenty minutes I timed it," said Charles Longbank. "Yes, a yokel of the past century might have believed that the picture was a mile long, or even five or nine miles long."

"Nah," said Leo. "They were smarter then, Charley; they were smarter then. Most likely that yokel would have believed that it was a little less than a furlong long, as it is. He'd have liked it, though. And there may be pieces that are five miles long or nine miles long. Why else would they have advertised them? I think I can hit the road and smell out where a lot of those pictures are. And I will call in sometimes and Ginger can tell me who have answered the advertisements. Come here again in six months, Charley, and I will have enough sections of the river for you to analyze. You won't get lonesome in six months, will you, Ginger?"

"No. There will be the hay cutters, and the men from the cattle auctions, and the oil gaugers, and Charley Longbank here when he comes out, and the men in town and the men in the Hill-Top Tavern. I won't get lonesome."

"She jokes, Charley," said Leo. "She doesn't really fool around with the fellows."

"I do not joke," said Ginger. "Stay gone seven months, I don't care."

Leo Nation did a lot of traveling for about five months. He acquired more than fifty genuine sections of the river and he spent quite a few thousands of dollars on them. He went a couple of years into hock for them. It would have been much worse had not many people given him the things and many others sold them to him for very small amounts. But there were certain stubborn men and women who insisted on a good price. This is always the hazard of collecting, the thing that takes most of the fun out of it. All these expensively acquired sections were really prime pieces and Leo could not let himself pass them by.

How he located so many pieces is his own mystery, but Leo Nation did really have a nose for these things. He smelt them out; and all collectors of all things must have such long noses.

There was a professor man in Rolla, Missouri, who had rugged his whole house with pieces of a genuine section.

"That sure is tough stuff, Nation," the man said. "I've been using it for rugs for forty years and it isn't worn at all. See how fresh the trees still are! I had to cut it up with a chain saw, and I tell you that it's tougher than any wood in the world for all that it's nice and flexible."

"How much for all the rugs, for all the pieces of pieces that you have?" Leo asked uneasily. There seemed something wrong in using the pieces for rugs, and yet this didn't seem like a wrong man.

"Oh, I won't sell you any of my rugs, but I will give you pieces of it, since you're interested, and I'll give you the big piece I have left. I never could get anyone much interested in it. We analyzed the material out at the college. It is very sophisticated plastic material. We could reproduce it, or something very like it, but it would be impossibly expensive, and plastics two-thirds as tough are quite cheap. The funny thing, though, I can trace the history of the thing back to quite a few decades before any plastic was first manufactured in the world. There is a big puzzle there, for some man with enough curiosity to latch onto it."

"I have enough curiosity; I have already latched onto it," Leo Nation said. "That piece you have on the wall—it looks like—if I could only see it under magnification—"

"Certainly, certainly, Nation. It looks like a swarm of bees there, and it is. I've a slide prepared from a fringe of it. Come and study it. I've shown it to lots of intelligent people and they all say 'So what?' It's an attitude that I can't understand."

Leo Nation studied the magnification with delight. "Yeah," he said. "I can even see the hairs on the bees' legs. In one flaking-off piece there I can even make out the cells of a hair." He fiddled with low and high magnification for a long while. "But the bees sure are funny ones," he said. "My father told me about bees like that once and I thought he lied."

"Our present honeybees are of late European origin, Nation," the man said. "The native American bees *were* funny and inefficient from a human viewpoint. They are not quite extinct even yet, though. There are older-seeming creatures in some of the scenes."

"What are the clown animals in the piece on your kitchen floor?" Leo asked. "Say, those clowns are big!"

"Ground sloths, Nation. They set things as pretty old. If they are a hoax, they are the grandest hoax I ever ran into. A man would have to have a pretty good imagination to give a peculiar hair form to an extinct animal—a hair form that living sloths in the tropics do not have . . . a hair form that sloths of a colder climate just possibly might have. But how many lifetimes would it have taken to paint even a square foot of this in such microscopic detail? There is no letdown anywhere, Nation; there is prodigious detail in every square centimeter of it."

"Why are the horses so small and the buffaloes so big?"

"I don't know, Nation. It would take a man with a hundred sciences to figure it out, unless a man with a hundred sciences had hoaxed it. And where was such a man two hundred and fifty years ago?"

"You trace your piece that far back?"

"Yes. And the scene itself might well be fifteen thousand years old. I tell you that this is a mystery. Yes, you can carry those scraps with you if you wish, and I'll have the bale that's the remaining big piece freighted up to your place."

There was a man in Arkansas who had a section of the picture stored in a cave. It was a tourist-attraction cave, but the river-shore picture had proved a sour attraction.

"The people all think it is some sort of movie projection I have set up in my cave here," he said. " 'Who wants to come down in a cave to see movies,' they say. 'If we want to see a river shore we will go see a river shore,' they say, 'we won't come down in a cave to see it.' Well, I thought it would be a good attraction, but it wasn't."

"How did you ever get it in here, man?" Leo Nation asked him. "That passage just isn't big enough to bring it in."

"Oh, it was already here, rock rollers and all, fifteen years ago when I broke out that little section to crawl through."

"Then it had to be here a very long time. That wall has formed since."

"Nah, not very long," the man said. "These limestone curtains form fast, what with all the moisture trickling down here. The thing could have been brought in here as recent as five hundred years ago. Sure, I'll sell it. I'll even break out a section so we can get it out. I have to make the passage big enough for people to walk in anyhow. Tourists don't like to have to crawl on their bellies in caves. I don't know why. I always liked to crawl on my belly in caves."

This was one of the most expensive sections of the picture that Nation bought. It would have been even more expensive if he had shown any interest in certain things seen through trees in one sequence of the picture. Leo's heart had come up into his mouth when he had noticed those things, and he'd had to swallow it again and maintain his wooden look. This was a section that had elephants on the Mississippi River.

The elephant (*Mammut americanum*) was really a mastoden, Leo had learned that much from Charles Longbank. Ah, but now he owned elephants; now he had one of the key pieces of the puzzle.

You find a lot of them in Mexico. Everything drifts down to Mexico when it gets a little age on it. Leo Nation was talking with a rich Mexican man who was as Indian as himself.

"No, I don't know where the Long Picture first came from," the man said, "but it did come from the North, somewhere in the region of the River itself. In the time of De Soto (a little less than five hundred years ago) there was still Indian legend of the Long Picture, which he didn't understand. Yourselves of the North, of course, are like children. Even the remembering tribes of you like the Caddos have memories no longer than five hundred years.

"We ourselves remember longer. But as to this, all that we remember is that each great family of us took a section of the Long Picture along when we came south to Mexico. That was, perhaps, eight hundred years ago that we came south as conquerors. These pictures are now like treasures to the old great Indian families, like hidden treasures, memories of one of our former homes. Others of the old families will not talk to you about them. They will even deny that they have them. I talk to you about it, I show it to you, I even give it to you because I am a dissident, a sour man, not like the others."

"The early Indian legends, Don Caetano, did they say where the Long Picture first came from or who painted it?"

"Sure. They say it was painted by a very peculiar great being, and his name (hold onto your *capelo*) was Great River Shore Picture Painter. I'm sure that will help you. About the false or cheap-jack imitations for which you seem to have contempt, don't. They are not what they seem to you, and they were not done for money. These cheap-jack imitations are of Mexican origin, just as the shining originals were born in the States. They were done for the new great families in their aping the old great families, in the hope of also sharing in ancient treasure and ancient luck. Having myself just left off aping great families of another sort, I have a bitter understanding of these imitations. Unfortunately they were done in a late age that lacked art, but the contrast would have been as great in any case: all art would seem insufficient beside that of the Great River Shore Picture Painter himself.

"The cheap-jack imitation pictures were looted by gringo soldiers of the U.S. Army during the Mexican War, as they seemed to be valued by certain Mexican families.

From the looters they found their way to mid-century carnivals in the States."

"Don Caetano, do you know that the picture segments
stand up under great magnification, that there are details
in them far too fine to be seen by the unaided eye?"

"I am glad you say so. I have always had this on faith
but I've never had enough faith to put it to the test. Yes,
we have always believed that the pictures contained
depths within depths."

"Why are there Mexican wild pigs in this view, Don
Caetano? It's as though this one had a peculiar Mexican
slant to it."

"No. The peccary was an all-American pig, Leo. It
went all the way north to the ice. But it's been replaced by
the European pig everywhere but in our own wilds. You
want the picture? I will have my man load it and ship it to
your place."

"Ah, I would give you something for it surely—"

"No, Leo, I give it freely. You are a man that I like.
Receive it, and God be with you! Ah, Leo, in parting, and
since you collect strange things, I have here a box of
bright things that I think you might like. I believe they are
no more than worthless garnets, but are they not pretty?"

Garnets? They were not garnets. Worthless? Then why
did Leo Nation's eyes dazzle and his heart come up in his
throat? With trembling hands he turned the stones over
and worshiped. And when Don Caetano gave them to him
for the token price of one thousand dollars, his heart rejoiced.

You know what? They really were worthless garnets.
But what had Leo Nation thought that they were in that
fateful moment? What spell had Don Caetano put on him
to make him think that they were something else?

Oh well, you win here and you lose there. And Don
Caetano really did ship the treasured picture to him free.

Leo Nation came home after five months of wandering
and collecting.

"I stand it without you for five months," Ginger said.
"I could not have stood it for six months, I sure could not
have stood it for seven. I kidded. I didn't really fool

around with the fellows. I had the carpenter build another hay barn to hold all the pieces of picture you sent in. There were more than fifty of them."

Leo Nation had his friend Charles Longbank come out.

"Fifty-seven new ones, Charley," Leo said. "That makes sixty with what I had before. Sixty miles of river shore I have now, I think. Analyze them, Charley. Get the data out of them somehow and feed it to your computers. First I want to know what order they go in, south to north, and how big the gaps between them are."

"Leo, I tried to explain before, that would require (besides the presumption of authenticity) that they were all done at the same hour of the same day."

"Presume it all, Charley. They *were* all done at the same time, or we will assume that they were. We will work on that presumption."

"Leo, ah—I had hoped that you would fail in your collecting. I still believe we should drop it all."

"Me, I hoped I would succeed, Charley, and I hoped harder. Why are you afraid of spooks? Me, I meet them every hour of my life. They're what keeps the air fresh."

"I'm afraid of it, Leo. All right, I'll get some equipment out here tomorrow, but I'm afraid of it. Damn it, Leo, *who was here?*"

"Wasn't anybody here," Ginger said. "I tell you like I tell Charley, I was only kidding, I don't really fool around with the fellows."

Charles Longbank got some equipment out there the next day. Charles himself was looking bad, maybe whiskeyed up a little bit, jerky, and looking over his shoulder all the time as though he had an owl perched on the back of his neck. But he did work several days running the picture segments and got them all down on scan film. Then he would program his computer and feed the data from the scan films to it.

"There's like a shadow, like a thin cloud on several of the pictures," Leo Nation said. "You any idea what it is, Charley?"

"Leo, I got out of bed late last night and ran two miles up and down that rocky back road of yours to shake myself up. I was afraid I was *getting* an idea of what those thin clouds were. Lord, Leo, who was here?"

Charles Longbank took the data in to town and fed it to his computers.

He was back in several days with the answers.

"Leo, this spooks me more than ever," he said, and he looked as if the spooks had chewed him from end to end. "Let's drop the whole thing. I'll even give you back your retainer fee."

"No, man, no. You took the retainer fee and you are retained. Have you the order they go in, Charley, south to north?"

"Yes, here it is. But don't do it, Leo, don't do it."

"Charley, I only shuffle them around with my lift fork and put them in order. I'll have it done in an hour."

And in an hour he had it done.

"Now, let's look at the south one first, and then the north one, Charley."

"No, Leo, no, no! Don't do it."

"Why not?"

"Because it scares me. They really *do* fall into an order. They really could have been done all at the same hour of the same day. Who was here, Leo? Who is the giant looking over my shoulder?"

"Yeah, he's a big one, isn't he, Charley? But he was a good artist and artists have the right to be a little peculiar. He looks over my shoulder a lot too."

Leo Nation ran the southernmost segment of the Long Picture. It was mixed land and water, island, bayou and swamp, estuary and ocean mixed with muddy river.

"It's pretty, but it isn't the Mississippi," said Leo as it ran. "It's that other river down there. I'd know it after all these years too."

"Yes," Charles Longbank gulped. "It's the Atchafalaya River. By the comparative sun angle of the pieces that had been closely identified, the computer was able to give close bearings on all the segments. This is the mouth of the Atchafalaya River which has several times in the geological past been the main mouth of the Mississippi. But how did he know it if he wasn't here? Gah, the ogre is looking over my shoulder again. It scares me, Leo."

"Yeah, Charley, I say a man ought to be really scared

at least once a day so he can sleep that night. Me, I'm
scared for at least a week now, and I like the big guy.
Well, that's one end of it, or mighty close to it. Now we
take the north end.

"Yes, Charley, yes. The only thing that scares you is
that they're real. I don't know why he has to look over our
shoulders when we run them, though. If he's who I think
he is he's already seen it all."

Leo Nation began to run the northernmost segment of
the river that he had.

"How far north are we in this, Charley?" he asked.

"Along about where the Cedar River and the Iowa
River later came in."

"That all the farther north? Then I don't have any segments of the north third of the river?"

"Yes, this is the farthest north it went, Leo. Oh God,
this is the last one."

"A cloud on this segment too, Charley? What are they
anyhow? Say, this is a pretty crisp scene for springtime on
the Mississippi."

"You look sick, Long-Charley-Bank," Ginger Nation
said. "You think a little whiskey with possum's blood
would help you?"

"Could I have the one without the other? Oh, yes, both
together, that may be what I need. Hurry, Ginger."

"It bedevils me still how any painting could be so wonderful," Leo wondered.

"Haven't you caught on yet, Leo?" Charles shivered.
"It isn't a painting."

"I tell you that at the beginning if you only listen to
me," Ginger Nation said. "I tell you it isn't either one,
canvas or paint, it is only picture. And Leo said the same
thing once, but then he forgets. Drink this, old Charley."

Charles Longbank drank the healing mixture of good
whiskey and possum's blood, and the northernmost segment of the river rolled on.

"Another cloud on the picture, Charley," Leo said. "It's
like a big smudge in the air between us and the shore."

"Yes, and there will be another," Charles moaned. "It
means we're getting near the end. Who were they, Leo?
How long ago was it? Ah—I'm afraid I know that part

pretty close—but they couldn't have been human then, could they? Leo, if this was just an inferior throwaway, why are they still hanging in the air?"

"Easy, old Charley, easy. Man, that river gets chalky and foamy! Charley, couldn't you transfer all this to microfilm and feed it into your computers for all sorts of answers?"

"Oh, God, Leo, it already is!"

"Already is what? Hey, what's the fog, what's the mist? What is it that bulks up behind the mist? Man, what kind of blue fog-mountain—?"

"The glacier, you dummy, the glacier," Charles Longbank groaned. And the northernmost segment of the river came to an end.

"Mix up a little more of that good whiskey and possum's blood, Ginger," Leo Nation said. "I think we're all going to need it."

"That old, is it?" Leo asked a little later as they were all strangling on the very strong stuff.

"Yes, that old," Charles Longbank jittered. "Oh, who was here, Leo?"

"And, Charley, it already is *what*?"

"It already *is* microfilm, Leo, to them. A rejected strip, I believe."

"Ah, I can understand why whiskey and possum's blood never caught on as a drink," Leo said. "Was old possum here then?"

"Old possum was, we weren't." Charles Longbank shivered. "But it seems to me that something older than possum is snuffing around again, and with a bigger snufter."

Charles Longbank was shaking badly. One more thing and he would crack.

"The clouds on the—ah—film, Charley, what are they?" Leo Nation asked.

And Charles Longbank cracked.

"God over my head," he moaned out of a shivering face, "I wish they *were* clouds on the film. Ah, Leo, Leo, who were they here, who were they?"

"I'm cold, Charley," said Leo Nation. "There's bone-chill draft from somewhere."

The marks . . . too exactly like something, and too big to be: the loops and whorls that were eighteen feet long.
. . .

GENE WOLFE

SONYA, CRANE WESSLEMAN, AND KITTEE

The relation between Sonya and Crane Wessleman was an odd one, and might perhaps have been best described as a sort of suspended courtship, the courtship of a poor girl by a wealthy boy, if they had not both been quite old. I do not mean to say that they are old *now*. Now Sonya is about your age and Crane Wessleman is only a few years older, but they do not know one another. If they had, or so Sonya often thought, things might have been much different.

At the time I am speaking of every citizen of the United States received a certain guaranteed income, supplemented if there were children, and augmented somewhat if he or she worked in certain underpaid but necessary professions. It was a very large income indeed in the mouths of conservative politicians and insufficient to maintain life according to liberal politicians, but Sonya gave them both the lie. Sonya without children or augmentation lived upon this income, cleanly but not well. She was able to do this because she did not smoke, or attend any public entertainment that was not free, or use drugs, or drink except when Crane Wessleman poured her a small glass of one of his liqueurs. Then she would hold it up to the light to see if it were yellow or red or brown, and sniff it in a delicate and ladylike way, and roll a half teaspoon on her tongue until it was well mixed with her saliva, and then swallow it. She would go on exactly like this, over and over, until she had finished the glass, and when she had swallowed it all it would make her feel somewhat younger; not a great deal younger, say about two years, but somewhat younger; she enjoyed that. She had been a very attractive girl, and a very attractive woman. If you can imagine how Debbie Reynolds will look when she attends the inauguration of John-John Kennedy, you will about have her. With her income she rented two rooms in a converted garage and kept them very clean.

Crane Wessleman met Sonya during that time when he still used, occasionally, to leave his house. His former partner had asked him to play bridge, and when he accepted had called a friend, or (to be truthful) had his wife call the friend's wife, to beg the name of an unattached woman of the correct age who might make a fourth. A name had been given, a mistake made, Sonya had been called instead, and by the time the partner's wife realized what had occurred Sonya had been nibbling her petits fours and asking for sherry instead of tea. The partner did not learn of his wife's error until both Crane Wessleman and Sonya were gone, and Crane Wessleman never learned of it. If he had, he would not have believed it. The next time the former partner called, Crane Wessleman asked rather pointedly if Sonya would be present.

She played well with him, perhaps because she was what Harlan Ellison would call an empath—Harlan meaning she gut-dug whether or not Crane Wessleman was going to make the trick—or perhaps only because she had what is known as card sense and the ability to make entertaining inconsequential talk. The partner's wife said she was cute, and she was quite skillful at flattery.

Then the partner's wife died of a brain malignancy; and the partner, who had only remained where he was because of her, retired to Bermuda; and Crane Wessleman stopped

going out at all and after a very short time seldom
changed from his pajamas and dressing gown. Sonya
thought that she had lost him altogether.

Sonya had never formed the habit of protesting the
decisions of fate, although once when she was much,
much younger she had assisted a male friend to distribute
mimeographed handbills complaining of the indignity of
death and the excretory functions—a short girl with blond
braids and chino pants, you saw her—but that had been
only a favor. Whatever the handbills said, she accepted
those things. She accepted losing Crane Wessleman too,
but at night when she was trying to go to sleep, she would
sometimes think of Crane Wessleman among The Things
That Might Have Been. She did not know that the
partner's wife was dead or that the partner had moved to
Bermuda. Nor did she know how they had first gotten her
name. She thought that she was not called again because
of something—a perfectly innocent thing which everyone
had forgotten in five minutes—she had said to the
partner's wife. She regretted it, and tried to devise ways, in
the event that she was ever asked again, of making up for
it.

It was not merely that Crane Wessleman was rich and
widowed, although it was a great deal that. She liked him,
knowing happily and secretly as she did that he was hard
to like; and, deeper, there was the thought of something
else: of opening a new chapter, a wedding, flowers, a new
last name, a not dying as she was. And then four months
after the last game Crane Wessleman himself called her.

He asked her to have dinner with him, at his home; but
he asked in a way that made it clear he assumed she
possessed means of transportation of her own. It was to be
in a week.

She borrowed, reluctantly and with difficulty, certain
small items of wearing apparel from distant friends, and
when the evening came she took a bus. You and I would
have called it a helicopter, you understand, but Sonya
called it a bus, and the company that operated it called it a
bus, and most important, the driver called it a bus and had
the bus driver mentality, which is not a helicopter pilot
mentality at all. It was the ascendant heir of those cheap

wagons Boswell patronized in Germany. Sonya rode for half because she had a Golden Age card, and the driver resented that.

When she got off the bus she walked a considerable distance to get to the house. She had never been there before, having always met Crane Wessleman at the former partner's, and so she did not know exactly where it was although she had looked it up on a map. She checked the map from time to time as she went along, stopping under the infrequent streetlights and waving to the television cameras mounted on them so that if the policeman happened to be looking at the time and saw her he would know that she was all right.

Crane Wessleman's house was large, on a lot big enough to be called an estate without anyone's smiling; the house set a hundred yards back from the street. A Tudor house, as Sonya remarked with some pleasure—but there was too much shrubbery, and it had been allowed to grow too large. Sonya thought roses would be nicer, and as she came up the long front walk she put pillar roses on the gas lantern posts Crane Wessleman's dead wife had caused to be set along it. A brass plate on the front door said:

C. WESSLEMAN
AND
KITTEE

and when Sonya saw that she *knew.*

If it had not been for the long walk she would have turned around right there and gone back down the path past the gas lamps; but she was tired and her legs hurt, and perhaps she would not really have gone back anyway. People like Sonya are often quite tough underneath.

She rang the bell and Kittee opened the door. Sonya knew, of course, that it was Kittee, but perhaps you or I might not. We would have said that the door was opened by a tall, naked girl who looked a good deal like Julie Newmar; a deep-chested, broad-shouldered girl with high cheekbones and an unexpressive face. Sonya had forgotten about Julie Newmar; she knew that this was Kittee, and

she disliked the thing, and the name Crane Wessleman
had given it with the whining double *e* at the end. She said
in a level, friendly voice, "Good evening, Kittee. My name
is Sonya. Would you like to smell my fingers?" After a
moment Kittee did smell her fingers, and when Sonya
stepped through the door Kittee moved out of the way to
let her in. Sonya closed the door herself and said, "Take
me to Master, Kittee," loudly enough, she hoped, for
Crane Wessleman to hear. Kittee walked away and Sonya
followed her, noticing that Kittee was not really completely naked. She wore a garment like a short apron put
on backward.

The house was large and dirty, although the air fil-
tration units would not allow it to be dusty. There was an
odor Sonya attributed to Kittee, and the remains of some
of Crane Wessleman's meals, plates with dried smears still
on them, put aside and forgotten.

Crane Wessleman had not dressed, but he had shaved
and wore a clean new robe and stockings as well as slippers. He and Sonya chatted, and Sonya helped him un-
pack the meal he had ordered for her and put it in the
microwave oven. Kittee helped her set the table, and Crane
Wessleman said proudly, "She's wonderful, isn't she."
And Sonya answered, "Oh yes, and very beautiful. May I
stroke her?" and ran her fingers through Kittee's soft
yellow hair.

Then Crane Wessleman got out a copy of a monthly
magazine called *Friends*, put out for people who owned
them or were interested in buying, and sat beside Sonya as
they ate and turned the pages for her, pointing out the ads
of the best producers and reading some of the poetry put
at the ends of the columns. "You don't know, really, what
they were anymore," Crane Wessleman said. "Even the
originators hardly know." Sonya looked at the naked girl
and Crane Wessleman said, "I call her Kittee, but the germ
plasm may have come from a gibbon or a dog. Look
here."

Sonya looked, and he showed her a picture of what
seemed to be a very handsome young man with high
cheekbones and an unexpressive face. "Look at that
smile," Crane Wessleman said, and Sonya did and noticed

that the young man's lips were indeed drawn back slightly. "Kittee does that sometimes too," Crane Wessleman said. Sonya was looking at him instead of at Kittee, noticing how the fine lines had spread across his face and the way his hands shook.

After that Sonya came about once a week for a year. She learned the way perfectly, and the bus driver grew accustomed to her, and she invented a pet of her own, an ordinary imaginary chow dog, so that she could take a certain amount of leftover meat home.

The next to last time, Crane Wessleman pointed out another very handsome young man in *Friends,* a young man who cost a great deal more than Sonya's income for a year, and said, "After I die I am going to see to it that my executor buys one like this for Kittee. I want her to be happy." Then, Sonya felt, he looked at her in a most significant way; but the last time she went he seemed to have forgotten all about it and only showed Sonya a photograph he had taken of himself with Kittee sitting beside him very primly, and the remote control camera he had used, and told her how he had ordered it by mail.

The next week Crane Wessleman did not call at all, and when it was two days past the usual time Sonya tried to call him, but no one answered. Sonya got her purse, and boarded the bus, and searched the area around Crane Wessleman's front door until she found a key hidden under a stone beneath some of the shrubbery.

Crane Wessleman was dead, sitting in his favorite chair. He had been dead, Sonya decided, for several days, and Kittee had eaten a portion of his left leg. Sonya said aloud, "You must have been very hungry, weren't you, Kittee, locked in here with no one to feed you."

In the kitchen she found a package of frozen *mouton Sainte-Menebould,* and when it was warm she unwrapped it and set it on the dining-room table, calling, "Kittee! Kittee! Kittee!" and wondering all the time whether Crane Wessleman might not have left her a small legacy after all.

LIZ HUFFORD

TABLETS OF STONE

After months in flight, the crew of the merchant ship was happy to land *almost* anywhere: Galen was an exception. When they learned that a repair stop on the planet was unavoidable, morale dropped. "Solitary confinement" was the captain's wry comment to Lorn Newent, the other unmarried crewman. Lorn, the ship's communications man, contacted the stationmaster just as he had three years before. He focused the image on the screen.

"Hello . . ."

This time the station operator was female. She looked very young, and pretty enough for Lorn to term fragile. He usually described her race as scrawny nondescripts.

"Communicator Newent. Have received your request: permission granted. We sympathize with your mechanical difficulties. Three weeks is an extended tour; however, regulations must be maintained. Please order the crew to remain within the restricted area. We apologize for the limited facilities, but unfortunately no more space is available. Any requests may be registered with me. We will, of course, expect reimbursement for the extra two-week occupancy."

"Yes," he said, struggling with the language, "we are prepared to unload three times the usual amount of nutrient."

The tip of her small tongue appeared for a moment at corner of her mouth. She wouldn't be half bad if you fattened her up a little.

"I have a request," Lorn said as he leaned across the desk.

The girl's shoulders tightened as she refused to acknowledge him.

"I said I have a request."

She turned, unsure in her response and angry because of it.

"Mr. Newent, you *always* have a request. My position requires that I serve the crew. I am not personally responsible for your individual happiness."

"Would you like to be?" he asked with his most earnest expression.

"Would I like to be what?" she replied. "Mr. Newent, for a communications expert you are quite inept. I have no idea what the literal content of this conversation is!"

"That's all right," he muttered apologetically, "I don't think it has any. It's all subjective: I like to talk to you."

She blushed. "It's just that I have other work to do. I'm planning the use of this field until it is again needed for a landing."

"That pushed for room?" he asked. "I thought the population was being controlled."

"For the moment," she said, "but only for the moment."

"About my request," he continued, "would you like to use the recreational facilities with me?"

She frowned.

"Okay, okay, you're very busy. I just thought sometime . . ." He paused, stuffed his hands in his pockets, and looked toward the climbing white housing modules and narrow, teeming streets of Galen. "I don't suppose you could give me an ashore?"

"Sorry," she said.

"Well, maybe sometime we could walk down to the fence and talk to the guards or do sit-ups together in the exercise room." He turned to leave. She watched him, glanced at the papers on her desk, and rose.

"Mr. Newent . . ."

Lorn reached for her hand and again she was angry.

"That's immoral, Lorn," she said.

"Immoral," he chuckled. He was beginning to develop his own theory of relativity.

"Yes," she replied firmly, "it would be the beginning of evil. If you touch my hand, you will want to touch more of me. If you touch more of me, I would probably want you to touch *more* of me. Do not think that I am foolishly ignorant of these things, but it would be evil. I would deserve death."

"Death!" Lorn was suddenly alert.

"How do you stop evil on your planet?" she asked.

Lorn watched as the planet Galen dotted, specked, and finally winked its way into oblivion. He wondered how much hell he'd catch. At least there would be no fine. He had told Tessca he would not see her until she had been discovered. He would deny knowledge of her act: she would claim it was her own idea. No one could prove him accomplice. The crew was composed of three couples, the captain, and himself. Surely sympathy would lie with the "star-crossed lovers."

"Lorn!"

He whirled around. "Captain?"

"Tessca's on board."

Lorn screwed up his face and tilted it quizzically. "Sir?"

"Come off it, Lorn," the captain said, "you know damn well she's here."

"Sir, you know I wasn't anxious to leave, but surely you don't think . . ."

"Like hell I don't. You know we carry extra supplies, although not many, I assure you. *Authorized Personnel Only.*" The captain drummed his fingers on the regulations book. "I have a professional crew and you bring in a pretty little bitch from a crowded, worthless planet we know next to nothing about. Now I could understand if it were one of those broads from . . ."

He paused to reflect on some enjoyable leave spent on a still-unnamed planet. "Still, she was a charming little thing. I should have said something, but no, I thought, the kid needs a bit of fun. Didn't think you'd do a fool thing like this. I can't throw her off. We're not turning back. By God . . ."

The captain bit the side of his mouth. A moment passed before he spoke.

"I suppose you'll want me to do the honors."

Lorn looked at the darkness where Galen had been.

"Well, if you would, sir."

"Your ways are very strange, Lorn," she said. "He says those words and it's all right. I will not be evil."

"That's right," Lorn smiled.

"We never tried that," she said.

"You would have been a frustrated old maid if it weren't for me."

Lorn placed his hands on her shoulders and steered her to the bunk.

Tessca was pregnant. The captain shuddered at the thought of explaining two stowaways, but the imminence of life renewed everyone's spirits. Everyone but Tessca. Pregnancy did not agree with her. Her face was haggard. She moved slowly and complained of being tired.

"I am going to be evil, aren't I, Lorn?" she whimpered.

"Evil," he said, "no, you're just the most wretched moralist I've ever seen. I've explained to you our custom. We are married. That means it won't be evil. You should be happy to have a child."

"A child," she said, thoughtfully pulling her hair. "But I still look and feel to myself very evil."

He pulled her on his lap.

"I love you, Tessca."

When Tessca gave birth, two of the wives assisted. When she saw it *was* evil, Tessca let herself die. The women shrieked their way from the birthplace.

LOGBOOK ENTRY: "There were about fifty of the tiny infants. From what we deduced about Tessca's aging process, their approximate growth rate was calculated. The oxygen will not hold out. By the time we realized what must be done some of them could crawl. The women could not bring themselves to help us. We have not finished the task. Some of them have found their way into the nutrient chambers.

"Lorn has hung himself."

ROBERT F. YOUNG

STARSCAPE WITH FRIEZE
OF DREAMS

The orbital shipyards of Altair IV are both a source of
beauty and a source of prosperity to the planet's inhabitants. The beauty derives from the reflective quality of the
orbiting spacewhales that are being converted into
spaceships; the prosperity, from the employment afforded
by the conversion process and from its perennial need of
supplies.

Although the number of these huge, asteroidlike
creatures varies, there are seldom fewer than twelve of
them in orbit at any given time, for generally as soon as
one of them becomes a full-fledged ship and is deorbited,
another arrives to take its place. The night skies of Altair
IV are the richer for their presence. Like bright Venuses
they rise at uneven intervals in the east, climb rapidly to
zenith, then slide down the dark slope of the heavens and
set in the west. The interested observer can watch the
passage of these lovely moonstars the whole night
through, and speculate, if he is so inclined, on how far

back into the past they have traveled; for the present, as every schoolboy knows, is only the surface of the space-time sea, and a living spacewhale can dive beneath this surface and sojourn in times past, can return, if it so desires, to the primordial moment when the cosmos was born.

The shipyards are sometimes referred to as the Spacewhale Graveyard, but in the connotative sense of the term this is a misnomer. Spacewhales do not come here of their own free will or because they wish to die. They are brought here by the whalers who have pursued them and by the Jonahs who have deganglioned them. They are dead upon arrival—

Or at least they are presumed to be.

The curtain rises upon a man who once upon a time was a Jonah himself. *Name:* John Starfinder. *Race*: Naturalized Terraltairan. *Occupation*: Drive Tissueman.

The scene is the belly of one of the orbiting whales. It is a pleasant scene, because this particular whale is nearing apotheosis, which is to say that most of its honeycombed interior has been converted into compartments, holds, corridors, and companionways, that its fissured and meteor-cratered skin has been inlaid with numerous portscopes and burnished to the smoothness of a woman's thigh, that its asymmetrical lines have been made symmetrical, that locks have been installed in its transsteel flanks, and that artificial gravity and a thermostatically controlled atmosphere now supplant near weightlessness and an absolute-zero vacuum.

An alien image has come unbidden into Starfinder's mind and has caused him to pause in the phosphorescent corridor along which he has been walking. The corridor runs the length of the lowest deck and gives access to the two major holds, the machine shop, a dozen compartments, and three storage areas. In addition, it gives access to the drive-tissue chamber where Starfinder has been working all day adapting the whale's natural propulsion unit to an outside power source. He has been working on the drive tissue ever since conversion began, and it will take him at least another week to finish the job.

The image that has appeared in his mind can be indicated thus:

$$((*))$$

Starfinder is nonplussed. He has been thinking of the angel Gloria Wish, and he can see no connection between $((*))$ and his thoughts.

Presently $((*))$ fades away, and he resumes walking down the corridor toward the companionway which leads up to the main deck and the boarding locks. The twelve-hour workday is done, and like Jonah he is eager to be regurgitated from the belly of the whale; eager to see the angel and ride down with her on a starbeam to the city he has come to call Home.

Perhaps this is why the image has appeared in his mind. Because he is tired from too much work and too much Gloria Wish. Perhaps this is why it appears again, this time in duplicate:

$$((*)) \qquad ((*))$$

Again Starfinder comes to a halt. He is abreast of the machine-shop door; the base of the companionway is just around a bend in the corridor. He knows fear now, as well as mystification. He has had good reason once before to doubt his sanity; now he doubts it again.

The double $((*))$ does not remain long, but no sooner does it fade than it is replaced by another. This one is slightly different:

$$•((*))• \qquad ((*))$$

Moreover, words accompany it; but the words come from within Starfinder's mind:

Morning a thousand Roses brings, you say; Yes, but where leaves the Rose of Yesterday? And this first Summer month that brings the Rose Shall take Jamshyd and Kaikobád away.

The first image, then, denotes a rose; the second, two roses; and the third, a dead rose and a living one. Starfinder's subconscious knows what the hieroglyphs stand for, if Starfinder does not.

His subconscious supplys yet another clue:

Roses are blue.

Starfinder is staring at the machine-shop door now. The machine shop formerly constituted the whale's ganglion chamber. Here in its ganglion the whale kept its memories; here the whale thought its thoughts; here the whale made its decisions; here the whale dreamed its dreams. And the ganglion, like all such ganglions, was shaped like an enormous rose—

An enormous *blue* rose.

It makes sense now. Roses *are* blue.

Breaking free from his inertia, Starfinder rounds the bend in the corridor and starts up the companionway steps. By the time he arrives on the main deck the heiroglyphs have faded completely from his mind. None come to take their place; nevertheless, he is still shaken when he joins the other converters, all clad in gray coveralls like his own. One of them is the shift leader. He stands nearest the locks, awaiting like the others the arrival of the angel Gloria Wish. Starfinder does not like him. The shift leader is aggressive, domineering, and insensitive. No doubt this is why he is a shift leader.

The arrival of Gloria Wish is greeted with cheers, although she appears every evening at this time to post the watchguard and to take the converters home. Starfinder has slept with her; so have most of the other converters whom she ferries to and from their whales. But with Starfinder it is different, because it is he whom she has chosen to be made 1 with. Her silvery skin-tight coveralls enhance the fullness of her breasts, the paps of which protrude through little peepholes made especially for the purpose. She has wide but wiry hips and long slim legs. Her ageless face is of classic cut; beauty radiates from its smooth clear skin, iridesces in her eyes. Her hair is coiffed to form a sunbright halo round her head.

Not only does she own her own shuttle service, but she is a major stockholder in the company that owns the shipyards. This is not unusual on Altair IV. Terraltairan women have climbed the evolutionary ladder faster than Terraltairan men and during the ascent have acquired not only surpassing beauty but surpassing business acumen as well. Unfortunately, the faster they climbed the more of them fell off, and on Altair IV the males now outnumber the females four to one, which makes premarital promiscuity a must. Few men on Altair IV have the good fortune to be able to call a woman exclusively their own, as Starfinder shortly will be able to do. In less than a week now one of his ribs will be removed and fashioned into a circlet for Gloria Wish's neck as a symbol of their 1-ness.

The converters file through the boarding tube into the shuttleship, and the watchguard takes over the whale. The angel sends the little ship dropping dizzily toward the blue-greenness of Altair IV; on all sides pulse the stars, and up above the whale turns into an ovoid moon; down, down, down falls the ship out of heaven, and the cities of the plain can be seen sparkling beyond Altair IV's twilight belt, and now the belt advances to meet the plummeting ship, and there, advancing also, is Starfinder's city; but he has no eyes for it, he is looking up through the overhead spacescope at the dead whales in the sky and at the stars beyond them blooming in the space-time night. In the vast distances forget-me-nots grow, and parsecs to their right glow daffodils; over there are bluebells, lilies of the valley . . . *Someday I will go a-Maying in the heavens—touch a bluebell, breathe the fragrance of a lily, pluck a ((*))* . . .

The angel Gloria Wish sees him home in her late-model flyabout as she does every night. She has offered to buy him a flyabout of his own, but he has refused. This is because he is new to Terraltairan culture and has not wholly accepted its ways. But sooner or later he will accept them.

At the base of the tall bright building where he lives she bids him good-night and tells him she will see him later on after she has totaled the day's receipts. He waves goodbye to her as she flits away.

His apartment comprises three rooms, but they share a
single ceiling, as the partitions are only waist-high. The
ceiling is the sky. Like all the other ceilings in the building
it is televised from the building's roof, but the picture is
flawless and indistinguishable from the reality. Centered
in it at the moment is the faint yellow pinpoint of the
Earth Mother. Earth herself of course is not visible, but
she can be sensed if not seen. Even Starfinder, who has
never laid eyes on her, senses her presence. An umbilical
cord light-years long stretches from his navel to her
storied shores; like all his contemporaries he is as much of
Earth as though he had been born there; they and he are
the children of Earth—the inheritors of her ethos.

He undresses, showers, shaves, dons a lounge-around
ensemble. He sits down and dials his evening meal. The
apartment's 3V screen has come on the minute he walked
in the door; as he dines, he glances at it now and then. In
it, a man and a woman are copulating, but he hardly sees
them. Instead, he sees the rose—

$$((\ast)) \dots$$

"So, whale, you are not dead after all," he says to the
four walls and the three half-walls of the subdivided room.

After his meal, he lies down on the bed and stares up at
the televised heavens. A whale has risen in the east and is
climbing toward zenith. It transits the Earth Mother,
begins its downward journey. However, it is not Starfinder's whale. It is a different leviathan.

He thinks of the final hieroglyphs, pictures them in his
mind—

$$\bullet((\ast))\bullet \qquad ((\ast)) \dots$$

The message is clear enough. The whale, unknown to
the Jonah who deganglioned it, had two ganglions. The
Jonah destroyed only one of them. The other?

Clearly, it was damaged. Else the whale would have
dived long ago and resurfaced elsewhere.

Starfinder has heard of biganglioned whales. They are

extremely rare, but they exist. But the ganglions in the cases he has heard of have been located side by side, and when one was destroyed, the other was destroyed also. Obviously this whale's second ganglion is in a different compartment from the first—a natural chamber that has gone undiscovered by the converters. Probably it is close to the machine shop, though not necessarily. The Jonah's explosives could have damaged the second ganglion by shock waves alone, regardless of its location.

However, Starfinder has never heard of a whale trying to communicate with a human being. It is an established fact that they can and do communicate with each other, sometimes across light-years. But with a human being? It is unthinkable.

Still, this whale has had a long time to mull things over. Maybe it has decided there are worse ignominies in the universe than asking one of its mortal enemies to repair its ganglion. Death, for instance.

Suddenly Starfinder grins. "What will you give me, whale, if I fix it for you?"

Abruptly he realizes what the whale *can* give him, and a tightness afflicts his throat and he lies immobile on the bed, staring starward. But he does not see the stars, they are occulted by a leviathan vessel that is part spacewhale and part spaceship; he sees himself standing on the bridge of the great whale vessel and he hears himself say, "Dive, whale—dive!" . . . and the whale plunges beneath the surface of the space-time sea and plummets into the past; the stars move backward in the spacescopes and the constellations subtly change . . . down, down, down into the mists of mankind's yesterdays the whale travels, and then, as suddenly as it began, the dive ends and the whale surfaces light-years away and eons ago, and nearby in the black vastness the golden Earth Mother glows, her brood not far away; he sees the blue Earth wearing her filmy nightgown of clouds, he glimpses the naked moon, he says, "Go in closer, whale—I want to see the clods who called themselves kings, the ancient empires; I want to see the armored elephants of Carthage, Hadrian at work on his wall, I want to see Attila riding over a hill, his hideous horde behind him . . . I want to see all the things I read about when I was blind—when *you* blinded me, whale —no, not you, your brother."

Sweat shines on Starfinder's forehead; there is a terrible ache in his chest. "If you would give me *that*, whale—"

A chime sounds, and a cathode tube comes to life. In it is the radiant face of the angel Gloria Wish. "Let me in, my love. I've brought you a basket of kisses."

She is wearing skin-tight gossamer lace through which her paps peep like a pair of roses. With goddess mien she sweeps into the room, putting the drab appointments to shame. She deactivates her single garment and it slips from her to the floor. She is like a table spread before him, and he is a traveler from a far land, eager to taste the viands upon which he gorged himself the night before.

` She extinguishes the lights and takes him in her arms; the stars look coldly down upon their lovemaking. As coldly when, her lover spent, she takes one of the priapean hypodermics she always carries with her and injects its contents into his bloodstream . . . insatiably she climbs upon him, goddess-beast, angel fallen from heaven, this is the day of Starfinder; thus womankind has become.

This is the way it is with Starfinder: as a cabin boy on an ore freighter that was once a whale he was blinded by 2-omicron-vii radiation seeping from the residue of an incompletely destroyed ganglion, and he stayed blind for two years, during which time he learned Braille and, ironically, read all the books he had ignored when he could see, and he swore that when his sight returned he would kill all spacewhales, and when it did return he became a Jonah and entered into the bellies of many whales and deganglioned them, which is to say blew out their brains, but the killing affected him strangely, afflicting him with a malaise of the mind from which he recuperated only after a certain experience caused him to give up killing spacewhales, but he could not give them up altogether, because they were all he knew, so he came to Altair IV and went to work in the orbital shipyards, and lo!—an angel appeared in the heavens and Starfinder fell in love.

Gorged, yet strangely empty, Starfinder sinks into a fitful sleep. During it, he dreams an atavistic dream that he has dreamed increasingly often of late. In the dream he is a Cro-Magnon savage walking weaponless across a starlit plain. Just ahead of him and to his right is a small shadow-filled copse. He dreads the copse and wishes to give it a wide berth, but he seems to have no control over his legs and continues walking in a straight line. As he comes abreast of the copse a huge saber-toothed tiger leaps out of the shadows and bears him to the ground. It crouches above him, its massive forelegs resting on his chest, shutting off his breath, its horrible tusked face grinning down into his own. Growls emanate from deep in the beast's bowels; its fetid breath overwhelms him. Slowly the jaws part. They part to an incredible width to accommodate the long yellowed tusks. Slowly the face descends—

Starfinder knows that in a moment he will be dead, and yet he cannot move. This, far more than the tiger, constitutes the nightmarish quality of the dream. This numbing paralysis that grips him, that makes it impossible for him even to try to save himself. His arms lie like lead at his sides. He cannot so much as lift a single finger. All he can do is lie there helplessly and wait for those gaping jaws to complete their relentless journey, and close.

He wills his arms to rise; he wills his fingers to sink into the tiger's tawny throat. But his arms do not stir; his fingers do not even tremble. The great face occults the entire heavens. The jaws, which have opened to a 45° angle, begin to close. One of the tusks pricks Starfinder's jugular vein, wrenching him awake—

He wakes sweating. Beside him, Gloria Wish sleeps. Above him pulse the stars.

He lets his gaze roam the body of the woman he loves, and presently the last dregs of the dream dissolve. What masochistic quirk of his subconscious, he wonders, caused it to occur?

Gloria Wish's eyes have opened, and she is smiling at him in the starlight. Suddenly he remembers the whale, and realizes that he must tell her it is not dead. As a major stockholder in the company that owns it she is responsible for the potential danger its second ganglion represents. Besides, there should be no secrets between them, for soon they will be 1.

But he doesn't tell her, lying there beside her in the starlight, nor does he tell her afterward as they loll before the 3V screen and chat. Tomorrow he will tell her, he promises himself—after he makes certain that the whale really does have a second ganglion.

Or better yet, he will tell the shift leader. But first he must make sure that his mind is not playing him false.

Back in the belly of the whale the next morning, Starfinder descends the companionway to the lowest deck, just as he does each working day. He is tired, but no more so than usual. The only aspect of his appearance that betrays both his fatigue and his suppressed excitement is the slightly heightened color of the 2-omicron-vii scar on his right cheek.

He enters the machine shop warily. Little is known about 2-omicron-vii radiation save that it is deadly, as his erstwhile blindness and the scar on his cheek testify. But clearly the second ganglion is safely sealed off from the rest of the whale; if it were not, he and the other converters would have long since been reduced to ashes.

He closes the machine-shop door behind him. He "listens." He "hears" nothing. Then he concentrates on the whale's first message, visualizing it in his mind—

$$((*))$$

At first, he receives no answer. Then:

$$\cdot((*))\bullet \qquad ((\bullet))$$

Starfinder concentrates again: *Where?*

This time there is no response.

Starfinder is not surprised. How can a mere word convey anything to a spacewhale? So for the moment Starfinder forgets words and concentrates successively on the nearest hold, on the nearest compartment, and finally on the drive-tissue chamber, visualizing each with a $((*))$ in it. Then he blanks his mind and waits.

He feels a shadow. It is pale, and cold as death, and vanishes the moment he becomes aware of it. He has no difficulty interpreting it. It is fear. Desperation has driven the whale into revealing the existence of its second ganglion, but desperation is not enough to overcome its distrust of man.

Strategy is called for. Starfinder must somehow trap the whale into revealing the location of the second ((*)). So he visualizes the whale much as he visualized it in his daydream the previous night, fully converted, except for its drive tissue, and with himself in full command. "Now dive," he says in his mind, cementing the words in the whale's awareness. "Damn you, whale—dive!" And in his mind the whale dives, bearing him, its sole passenger, into the past. "Resurface, whale!" he says. "Return to when we were," and the whale does so, reemerging into the present.

Next, Starfinder visualizes the whale as the freighter it is destined to become in the near future. He pictures its holds brimful of raw materials, and he pictures a surly commander standing on its bridge, a beetle-browed mate pacing its main deck, an obese astrogator poring over charts in its chartroom, a sullen chef cooking in its galley, and a slovenly crew scattered throughout its interior. Finally, to make certain the whale gets the message and understands that of the two alternatives the first is far preferable to the second, Starfinder visualizes the drive-tissue chamber as it will look after the outside power source has been installed and is in operation—concrete proof, were any needed, that man will have taken over and that the whale will be dead.

Then he waits.

As he waits, he realizes belatedly that he has made a bargain with the whale. He has implied that if it will reveal the location of the second ((*)), he, Starfinder, will repair whatever damage has been done to it, and that in return the whale must become his personal property and obey his every command. In his eagerness to trap the whale, he has trapped himself.

But this is ridiculous. Men cannot enter into bargains with animated asteroids that however human they may

sometimes seem are nothing of the sort. Besides, how can
a spacewhale—any more than a man—be trusted? And
all of this is futile speculation anyway, because the whale
will not accept such bondage, no matter how desperate it
may be, no matter how reluctant to die—

The hieroglyphic image that abruptly appears in Starfinder's mind can be indicated thus:

Starfinder is stunned.

The whale *will* enter into bondage.

Clearly, death to a spacewhale is as dreadful a prospect
as death is to a man.

The second ganglion is located just beneath the first in
a natural chamber the converters have overlooked, probably because of its proximity to the whale's skin. Now
that he knows its location, Starfinder must tell the shift
leader. Any other course of action would be insane.

Since the machine shop itself is close to the whale's
skin, the deck separating the shop from the chamber
below cannot be more than three or four feet thick.
Transsteel, which constitutes the whale's subtissue, is a
super-hard organic-metallic two-phase material, but it
yields readily to the hyperacetylene flame which the Altair
IV shipyards developed to cope with it. Since the deck is
of a much softer material, burning through it will take but
a few minutes; blasting the rose into extinction will require
but a few more. It is one thing to dream of commanding a
spacewhale and holding the past in the palm of your hand;
it is quite another to make such a dream a reality when to
do so will mean ostracizing yourself forever from your
adopted society and alienating yourself completely from
the woman you adore. Starfinder realizes that up until this
moment he has been quite mad. Now, thankfully, sanity
has returned.

Starfinder quits the machine shop and seals the door
behind him. It is his intention to seek out the shift leader

and reveal that the whale is not dead. Why, then, does he turn right instead of left and continue down the corridor to the drive-tissue chamber? The reason is that the shift leader can just as well be apprised of the second ganglion during the lunch break as now, because in its present condition it does not represent a true hazard.

Starfinder resumes work where he left off yesterday. It is his job to adapt the original structure so that those aspects of it which are incomprehensible to man can be bypassed. This requires a certain amount of hyper-acetylene surgery (none of which he has performed as yet) and it is a terribly complicated operation.

As Starfinder works, he thinks of how the ancient Carthaginians used to convert elephants into war machines. How they attached armor to the beasts' flanks and forelegs; how they built towers atop the beasts' ungainly backs; how they taught the huge animals to charge and trample the enemy.

For some reason he cannot get these Carthaginian elephants out of his mind, and he thinks of them all morning long. When the lunch-break bell sounds over the intercom, he leaves the drive-tissue chamber and walks down the corridor toward the foot of the companionway. He hurries past the machine-shop door, but not quite fast enough to avoid having a pair of roses implanted in his mind—a living and a dead one.

The dining room is on the second deck, directly above the galley. The galley has been stocked for the ship-to-be's trial voyage, but the working crew's fare is meager. However, Starfinder isn't hungry and hardly notices. There are elephants milling about in his mind, trampling his thoughts, and every now and then a rose appears incongruously among the huge ungainly beasts, and he knows he cannot go on like this, that he must either get rid of his burden or shoulder it in earnest, and since that is out of the question, he approaches the shift leader, who has finished eating and is sitting at his personal table, picking his teeth.

Starfinder has every intention of stopping at the table, and he very nearly does so. But at the last moment the shift leader glances up at him, and Starfinder is reminded

by those bleached blue eyes that the shift leader is not
only aggressive, domineering, and insensitive, but is
frustrated as well. There is nothing that would please him
more than to have Starfinder tell him that the whale is still
alive, because then he would be able to relieve that
frustration, temporarily at least, by destroying the second
ganglion.

But Starfinder wants the second ganglion destroyed by
someone other than himself, doesn't he? Apparently not,
for he walks past the shift leader without a word and descends the companionway to the third deck. Here, in the
main supply room, he procures an anti-2-omicron-vii suit.
Both the supply room and the third-deck corridor are
deserted, and in moments he has reached the lowest deck
and is heading for the drive-tissue chamber. He drops off
the suit by the machine-shop door, picks up his
hyperacetylene torch and tanks in the drive-tissue chamber, and returns. Then he is in the machine shop, the door
sealed behind him.

He marks off the center of the shop, dons the anti-2-
omicron-vii suit and begins burning through the deck.

The machine-shop door is constructed of transsteel
filched from the whale's subtissue and is six inches thick.
Even radiation from a healthy ganglion would be unable
to penetrate it; hence Starfinder has no fears on that score.

Hyperacetylene does not melt metal—it vaporizes it. A
depression three feet in diameter begins to take shape.

Starfinder's mind wanders as he burns . . . The towers
the Carthaginians built atop their war beasts housed
bowmen, and when the enemy was within range the
bowmen unleashed their arrows from the safety of their
portable forts, killing many of their foes and wounding
others. Astride each elephant's neck sat a pilot armed with
a sledgehammer, with which to smash the animal's ver-
tebrae should it panic and go berserk. The Carthaginians
were master converters. They thought of everything.

Much later in his history, as he grew more civilized,
man devised subtler means of converting animals. The
dolphins are a classic example. While publicly making
friends with a few of them, man privately trained others to

carry explosives to the hulls of enemy ships and to detonate both the explosives and themselves at exactly the right moment. The Technologists were master converters too.

Thoughts of the dolphin lead ineluctably to thoughts of the whale that once flourished in the seas of Earth. For a time, Starfinder's mind dwells upon *Moby Dick,* which he read while he was blind, and he wonders whether Melville meant evil to be symbolized by the whale, as so many scholars seem to think, or by Captain Ahab?

What does *this* whale symbolize?

Freedom? Death? Both?

What do *I,* Starfinder, symbolize?

Burn, Starfinder—burn! Leave your soul alone. You did not create the elephant. You did not create the dolphin. You did not create the whale. You did not create *this* whale. And above all, *you did not create man.* Burn, burn, burn!—and when you see the rose, burn that too!

But when he sees the rose he does not burn it. Instead, he extinguishes the torch and lowers himself into the second-ganglion chamber. It is surprisingly large, and its walls emit the same pale phosphorescence that illumines the rest of the whale's interior. The rose is huge, but although its radiation is still deadly, its blueness is not the blueness of the other roses he has known—the roses he has killed . . .

Starfinder kneels, and examines the stem. It is cracked—probably from the shock waves of the explosion that destroyed the first ganglion—and the energy stored in the whale's transsteel subtissue cannot reach the rose in sufficient quantities to sustain it.

But the injury is a minor one. Starfinder can repair the damage in a matter of minutes. Both the stem and the rose consist of transsteel: all he needs to set them right are a welder and a packet of transsteel welding rods, both of which items are no farther away than the drive-tissue chamber.

But, damn it!—he didn't come here to fix the rose. He came to destroy it.

Why, then, didn't he bring the special explosives that alone can do the job? Only Jonah's charges can ef-

fectively eradicate a rose, and there is a whole box of
them in the supply room.

Slowly Starfinder straightens. As though to make his
burden heavier yet, the whale transmits a new combination of hieroglyphs:

°((•))•   ☆   ((•))   ((•☆))   ⌐ᴢ

At first Starfinder doesn't understand the meaning of
the message. Then he realizes that the whale is referring to
their bargain. ((*)) represents the rose in its present
damaged condition; the stickman represents Starfinder.
((*)) stands for the rose after Starfinder shall have
repaired it, and   ((•☆))   the resultant oneness of Star-

finder and the whale   ⌐ᴢ   can mean only one
thing; spacetime, the three-sided figure   ⌐⌐   signi-

fying space, and   ᴢ , with its abrupt descent, time.

There is a long silence. Then the whale, as though
afraid it has failed to make itself clear (and perhaps growing desperate because it is so close to death) discards its
pride and spells out its acceptance of the bargain in a
single hieroglyph which Starfinder cannot fail to understand:

And Starfinder? He climbs out of the second-ganglion
chamber, picks up his hyperacetylene torch and tanks,
quits the machine shop and seals the door behind him.
Then he returns to the drive-tissue chamber, removes the
anti-2-omicron-vii suit and goes back to work. Somehow
he manages to get through the rest of the day.

Lying abed, hands clasped behind his head, Starfinder
gazes up at the celestial ceiling of his room. His whale is
the evening star.

It is distinguishable from the others because its surface is burnished, causing it to reflect even more of the rays of Altair than its dead brothers. It is the brightest object in the heavens.

Lying on his bed, waiting for the angel Gloria Wish, he watches it rise and set, and he wonders how he will be able to live with himself after he tells her that the whale is still alive and that he has made a bargain with it.

He does not need to wonder how she will react when he does tell her. He knows. She will say, "Starfinder, are you insane? Get hold of the shift leader and go up there and kill it at once!"

And Starfinder will say, "Very well, Gloria Wish—I will do as you command."

He will say this because Gloria Wish is stronger than he. She is neither god nor goddess, but she comes very close to being both. It has taken only three centuries for modern Terraltairan woman to evolve, but she is the culmination of everything womankind ever wanted to be. She is the glory of womankind incarnate. To look at a Terraltairan woman is to fall in love.

But seldom is that love returned in kind. It cannot be on a planet where there are so many men. Starfinder knows how lucky he is, and he is grateful. It is true that Gloria Wish will outlive him, then she will become 1 with many lovers after he is dead. But right now she is his, and his alone. Only he can have her. The appeasing of her appetite is his responsibility alone.

But *can* he appease that gargantuan appetite? Can he alone—even with the assistance of priapean injections —perform a task that up till now has required the energies of twenty men?

There are two sayings on Altair IV that crop up regularly during barroom conversations and appear periodically on rest-room walls. The first one rises to poetic heights of a sort, and goes like this:

> With this rib I do thee wed;
> In ten more years I shall be dead.

The second is a simple statement of fact, and goes like this:

The only old men on Terraltair are queers.

Lying on his bed waiting for Gloria Wish, Starfinder stares straight up into the black and infinite immensities where yesterday is the sparkle of a distant star and tomorrow the twinkle of another and today a drop of darkness; he sees the climbing into heaven of the dead whales, the sad promenade of the ((*)) less leviathans across the face of ⌐⫟ ; he sees the yellow mote of the Earth Mother and he visualizes the filmy-nightgowned Earth waiting with all her treasures—Earth Past, the great green orb with all her seas and the ships upon them, and the ancient armies marching over her lands; the pith of history, queens and kings, a pageant colorful and cruel—*all this I hold in the palm of my hand; all this is mine for the taking—*

Enter Gloria Wish, bearing a basket of kisses: "Starfinder, my starfinder—why are you so pale?"

She divests herself of gossamer lace, puts out the lights and sits down on the edge of the bed. Her breasts are like twin pale hills looming above him, and beyond them hovers her face. Its beauty intensifies as he looks up at it, outshines the stars themselves. She is like a wind that has come up from the south, and the wind is warm upon him as the pale hills descend toward his face. Famished, he feeds. And now the wind grows warmer, enveloping him and lifting him into the sky, the stars shine brightly as they pinwheel in the night, and the wind lifts him higher yet, and now he is among the pinwheeling stars. One by one, they nova around his head and fall like flowers past his face, down, down, down . . . Dimly he feels the faint prick of the first hypodermic, wakes to the quickening of his blood; the wind, a hot and searing blast now, whips him aloft again, and now there are supernovas in the heavens, he can see them from the Aurignacian plain across which he is walking, weaponless and alone. Once again the great gaunt beast leaps out of the shadows of the copse and bears him to the earth. Once again the Cyclopean jaws spread wide. Foul saliva drips upon his face. His lungs are a holocaust of pain. Growls of anticipation reverberate in the beast's throat as it lowers its face for the feast.

If he could but move. He tries to break the invisible bonds that hold him helpless to the earth. He tries with every shred of himself, with every molecule, with every atom—break! break! break! . . . and suddenly there is a terrible rending within him, a spasm of incomprehensible pain, and then his arms are free and rising, his fingers are sinking into the tawny throat. Deeper still, and deeper, and now the growls have given way to screams; but the screams do not remain long, Starfinder's fingers drive them away. He rises to his feet with a strength that amazes him, and shakes the dying sabertooth as though it were an empty sack. And shakes and chokes and shakes and chokes. Then he realizes that his eyes are tightly closed, and opens them . . . and sees the face of the angel Gloria Wish, and even then his fingers do not fall away, although the blueness of her face testifies that she is dead.

Up the ladder into heaven climbs Starfinder once again. This time he climbs alone.

He docks the shuttleship against the flank of the whale and passes through the boarding tube into the whale's belly. He overpowers the watchguard and carries him back into the shuttleship. He programs the automatic pilot to orbit the ship three times and then go in for a landing. He reenters the belly of the whale and proceeds directly to the lowest deck. He waits till his hands have stopped trembling; then he repairs the rose.

After sealing the machine-shop door from the outside, he makes his way to the bridge. He gives the rose time to absorb the energy it needs, then says, "Deorbit, whale —break free!" And the whale disengages itself from the oribital shipyards of Altair IV, which are both a source of beauty and a source of prosperity to the planet's inhabitants, and parts company forever with its dead brothers.

Ravenous after months of starvation, it feeds upon the dust and debris of space. Its interior phosphorescence takes on a brighter hue; a throbbing comes from below as its drive tissue comes to life. Replenished, the whale floats upon the surface of the sea. "Now," Starfinder says, and the whale gathers itself for the plunge. "Now, whale." The throbbing of the drive tissue becomes a powerful pulse. "Dive!" And the whole dives, deep into ⌐⌐⁊ , and ⅄ and the ▭• go free.

ROBERT E MARGROFF
AND ANDREW J. OFFUTT

THE BOOK

The book lay on a rough stone shelf, its pages and golden
script unfaded by the sun. To the near-man crouched over
the pages he really could not comprehend, the book
seemed the answer to all wants and longings.

He crouched there, drooling slightly from the corners of
his mouth. His skin was goosefleshed from the morning
cold; his joints were swollen. His name was Brandon.

He went back on his heels to cough and choke. From
the cave's entrance, greasy smoke had backed to fill his
lungs and redden his eyes.

Brandon bellowed his anger. "Dammit, Jilly! Put out
that fire!"

Slowly the smoke cleared.

But the only vision it had concealed was that of Jilly's
broad face and pendulous udders. Her mouth opened to
reveal the yellowed stubs of her teeth.

"Can't bake a snake without a fire."

Brandon tried to glare. "*Move* the fire, woman! Over to
the cliff's edge!"

119

"You want someone see? You want them come take me?"

Brandon considered. It wasn't as if a woman were always easy to find, and he would miss Jilly on cold nights. In the old days when the world was not-old, there had been more people than was good for Brandon's ease of mind. He had been very strong in body, so strong that every male he had challenged had given up what he wanted, whether it was a woman, a haunch of deer or a bigger club. He had taken other men's women, and their brains. Remembering, Brandon licked his lips. But as the years passed it had become harder to swing the club; the book was safer. He had retreated to this valley and raised his deadfalls.

Jilly was insisting: "Brandon?"

He straightened, his spine making a snapping sound. He tried to walk to the cave's mouth as a young warrior walks. It was an absurdly short journey.

The tree branch with its knobbed end was leaning against the cave wall at the entrance. He took it up, raised it and feinted at Jilly.

"Move it far enough," he said. "Far enough; not too far. You hear, woman? Must I bash dirt loose from your ears?"

"N-no, Brandon. I move it." She was not really frightened of him any longer. Brandon returned to the book.

He had often thought, *How to build a better deadfall? How to trap more game?* And because he had brooded long over the open pages, answers had come to him. Sometimes they made little sense, those thoughts that tortured his slow mind. Why did it work for him? He did not know. He did not know.

There had been a time:

His young muscles straining against the boulder that had concealed the cave's entrance. It moved, because everything moved to his shoulder, then. Inside was the book, with all its magic. It took him long to learn its use: concentrating, staring, watching the lines crawl and gradually, gradually become a thought for him. For him only.

He wondered, sometimes, why he stared at the book for

so many hours each day. Time not spent picking the fruits and berries that crowded each other in this valley; time not spent in spearing fish in the chuckling stream, or in setting animal traps, or in watching for strangers. It had first occurred to him while staring at the book that he might stay here and protect himself. A new thought: traps for defense. But why should he not eat of certain roots, and why should Jilly eat of them? Why should they make clay vessels to hold their food? Why should they plunge into the stream at least every moon to scrub the dirt from their sides, rubbing a rough, foaming root all over their bodies?

It was unmanly, this slavery to the book. It had kept him from the fresh air, stooped his back, dimmed his eyesight. Because of the book, he had done things that would have provoked the young Brandon to howls of outrage. It had persuaded him to keep but one wife, to send away the children of his own seed and the women he could not protect—send them away from the valley, rather than destroy them. Why save a woman for another man? Why raise young if not to satisfy his own appetites?

That reminded him: Jilly had been acting strangely.

"Jilly," he said. "You carrying again?"

She scowled at him. Her hand went to the bit of sharp flint in her hair. "You will not sacrifice it," she said fiercely. "You will not kill this one on the Sun stone! You will not eat of its brain and make me eat!"

"No," Brandon said, frowning at the book. "No. It is written here, in gold."

"Written?" Her voice was suspicious. "What is 'written'?"

"These . . . marks" he told her. "They are *written*. Made. Someone put them here so they would mean something to someone else." The thoughts and the phrasing of them threatened to split his brain. "They mean what I need them to mean." He touched his chest. "I read them. You can read too."

Shaking her head, she backed to the cave wall. Her hand rose again to the flint. "No!"

Brandon shrugged. He could force her, of course, but there was no desire in him to make her behave as a man.

A woman, after all, was just a woman. If she were to learn to read, let her next mate—

Her next mate! With a growl, he seized his club. Blood pounded behind his eyes and in his wrists. Her eyes went wide, then narrow as she crouched. Her flint was out and ready, her teeth bared. She expected him to kill her, he saw. It would be no more than a natural act, for no man wishes to enter the shadow-world without at least one wife to accompany him and serve him there.

He raised the club. His muscles quivered. He had to! It was the book's fault!

Jilly fell to her knees. "The new one!" she pleaded.

He paused. Had she knowledge of his thought?

"What new one?" he demanded.

"Here," she said in a small voice, touching her belly. "New one kick. Don't hit me now. I learn if you want."

But he knew she would not, and he did not care. Nor did he want to kill her. But if she should live after him, for long. . . . Brandon stopped. Hating her, hating himself, hating the book, he stopped. Hating the book most of all.

He picked up her shard of flint and walked to the book. He raised a sharp edge above the pages. His hand trembled. Before his eyes the symbols seemed to twist and writhe, begging him: *Do not strike me! Do not strike me!* How could he destroy what had been so good to him?

His arm still quivered. He tried. Slowly he brought the flint down until it touched the page. Averting his face, he gripped the flint strongly and pushed it down. The sharp edge gouged, twisted—and slipped from his fingers.

He lifted his hand to stare. Blood. It was his blood, not the book's. The page remained unmarked. Even his blood ran off without leaving a trace. And Brandon knew fear.

He told himself that he would wait until after the child was born, after Jilly had known the happiness of it. He pictured her on the rock ledge outside, singing and crooning to the new one, her breasts big and her belly flat and wrinkled again. He would have to destroy it then, before it demanded the little new one.

But now Jilly was sobbing and moaning, and the book lay before him. He would close it, and he would not look at it again. If he did not read, perhaps he would not be compelled to do the things it made him want to do. The senseless, foolish things so much worse than bathing in the stream or sending away the wives and children.

Yes, that was it. He would close the book.

His hand was slick with blood and sweat as he attempted to grasp the book's edge. No sign of wear marred the covers; none ever would. He was certain of that, if of nothing else.

But what, he wondered, lay beyond? What came next?

Again Brandon wrestled with curiosity, and once again curiosity won. Brandon turned the page.

Jilly changed gradually. Since giving birth to Little New One she had behaved as Brandon had expected. Every day she nursed the infant beneath the living sun, waiting for Brandon to perform the Great Father role. He went daily into the rich valley, returning with her wants. One day it was fish. Another blueberries. Today crayfish, which was indeed strange, because never, never even during pregnancy, had she cared to eat the hard-shelled creatures with their outsize pincers and alarming eyes. He had pursued them all morning amid the stones, and now he returned, laden with them. He peered inside. Jilly! With the infant on her back, fingers twined fast in her stringy hair, Jilly was leaning over the book!

Brandon's mouth worked, but he found no words. He had told her, he remembered, to learn to read. What an idiotic thing to say! A woman had no business with magic, other than the art of birth. What had he been thinking of? Was it only to make her defy him that he had suggested she read?

Or . . . had the book? Was the book suggesting that he was to admit strangers to his valley, and die, without even Jilly to comfort him? Or perhaps it had been the book that had persuaded him to tell Jilly to read . . . where did the book's power leave off and his own thoughts begin? When had the two become indistinguishable?

"You are angry," she said. She was trembling.

"Read!" he commanded angrily, and he stamped out. He had more important matters, though he was uncertain what they were.

In the valley, surrounded again by greenery, and the

blues and scarlets of the berries, the flickering black and gold and brown of birds, surrounded by the strident hum of insects and the muted roar of the brook, Brandon vented his new frustration. He ripped up bushes and hurled them from him with ridiculous force. He discovered a harmless yellowish snake and jumped up and down upon it, breaking and tearing its twisting body until it was a red jelly upon the grass. He pounded his fists on the boles of trees until his hands bled. He jerked his limbs in an arthritic travesty of a hate dance. He brought down oaths of fire and thunder and hailstone and flood upon oblivious nature. Blowing like a winded animal, foaming in his beard, he snarled down at the darting fish in the little stream.

Then he grunted.

The new thing began with a very small pain somewhere in his chest, like the first ray of the morning sun. And like the sun, it rose and grew and widened until he saw the landscape dim and swirl and he fought his breathlessness with sobs. He fell.

He was dying.

Dying! Dying, after having given his days and his eyesight to an illusion, and it hurt him, more than the dying, to know that what he had given had not been given but *spent*, spent in the way that his seed had sometimes been spent as he slept.

"Brandon?" The softer voice was not Jilly's.

"Brandon?" Not Jilly's, but a voice he recognized: Jalene's. She had been his wife once and he had let her leave him rather than kill her. He twisted, strove desperately to look up at her.

They swam in the mist. There were two of them: Jalene and a strange man with a strong, cruel face.

He tried to think. His mind wanted rest, but it came, filtering, creeping: she had returned, disobedient woman, and she had brought with her a stranger. An enemy, and a man should challenge his enemies. But there was so little time—and no strength.

"You are dying, old man," the stranger said. His voice held malicious joy. "Soon you will lie breathless and stiff. I will take your wives and your valley, and when you're eaten, I will make a medicine of your bones. Does that anger you, old man?" He was grinning.

Brandon flickered his eyelids, an effort. The light did not seem right, but it was there, it and the sun and the faces above him. The face of the stranger—big, corded neck with some whiskers and some patches of skin discolored and scarred from having been scraped with flint; bristly cheek, flattened nose, smallish eyes set deep in his powerful skull. A brute. A brute such as Brandon had been. The thought filled him with horror and longing; the book had changed him so much!

"You want something, old man? Cold water? Shade? Roots? Medicine? You want me to break your head?"

The club did not waver. He watched it descend slowly, felt it touch his skull, watched it ascend. The man made a show of bunching his muscles, settling his feet, tightening his hands on his log of a weapon. He was taking his time, delighting in the torment. As Brandon had.

"You are not afraid? You not want say love words to wives? Maybe see something in cave?" The brute face smiled: immense white teeth.

Brandon struggled to lift his head. His jaw muscles worked, seeming somehow detached from him. It was a strange thing he said, even to his own ears. He fought to phrase it:

"I must ask you not—"

"*Not!*" The giant's nostrils flared. Brandon knew how he himself would have reacted.

"You must not take other wife. You must kill her, Jilly, and Little New One. Bring them here. Their spirits must accompany me."

The brute smiled. "Your wives all be mine, old man. All *are* mine. Baby will live, too. You will not want to be bothered with baby, old man; you have no milk." He chuckled. So, obediently, did Jalene. "What else you want?"

Brandon had set the pattern. What he said he wanted would be doubled back on itself. What he asked would be denied. He would have what he wished because he would ask the opposite.

"I want—you must not look at book in cave. *My* book,

not yours. Never go and look at it. It—tears things in you.
Makes you too wise. Makes you change, like me. Never
look at it!"

The strong man hesitated, frowning, but only for a moment. He smiled confidently.

"I will look. Every day. I am strong. I can bear to look
at it!" His muscles bunched. He glanced at the woman to
be certain she had heard his boast and would remember.

"Wait!" Brandon croaked. "One thing more. One thing
you must not do—this above all else. You must not—"

"Tell me, old man. I have no fear of your shadow-
spirit. Tell me what I must *not* do." Grinning, white teeth
flashing, knuckles whitening about the club.

As from a great distance Brandon forced out the words
that expressed the strangest wish. The most important
wish of all.

"You must not eat of my brain."

CAROL CARR

INSIDE

The house was a jigsaw puzzle of many dreams. It could not exist in reality and, dimly, the girl knew this. But she wandered its changing halls and corridors each day with a mild, floating interest. In the six months she had lived here the house had grown rapidly, spinning out attics, basements, and strangely geometric alcoves with translucent white curtains that never moved. Since she believed she had been reborn in this house, she never questioned her presence in it.

Her bedroom came first. When she woke to find herself in it she was not frightened, and she was only vaguely apprehensive when she discovered that the door opened to blackness. She was not curious and she was not hungry. She spent most of the first day in her four-poster bed looking at the heavy, flowered material that framed the bay window. Outside the window was a yellow-gray mist. She was not disturbed; the mist was a comfort. Although she experienced no joy, she knew that she loved this room and the small bathroom that was an extension of it.

On the second day she opened the carved doors of the

mahogany wardrobe and removed a quilted dressing gown. It was a little large and the sleeves partially covered her hands. Her fingers, long and pale, reached out uncertainly from the edge of the material. She didn't want to open the bedroom door again but felt that she should; if there were something outside to discover, it too would belong to her.

She turned the doorknob and stepped out into a narrow hall paneled, like the wardrobe in her room, in carved mahogany. There were no pictures and no carpet. The polished wood of the floor felt cool against her bare feet. When she had walked the full distance to the end and touched a wall, she turned and walked to the other end. The hall was very long and there were no new rooms leading from it.

When she got back to her bedroom she noticed a large desk in the corner near the window. She didn't remember a desk but she accepted it as she accepted the rest. She looked out and saw that the mist was still there. She felt protected.

Later that afternoon she began to be hungry. She opened various drawers of the desk and found them empty except for a dusty tin of chocolates. She ate slowly and filled a glass with water from the bathroom sink and drank it all at once. Her mouth tasted bad; she wished she had a toothbrush.

On the second day she had wandered as far as the house allowed her to. Then she slept, woke in a drowsy, numb state, and slept again.

On the third day she found stairs, three flights. They led her down to a kitchen, breakfast area and pantry. Unlike her room, the kitchen was tiled and modern. She ate a Swiss cheese sandwich and drank a glass of milk. The trip back to her room tired her and she fell asleep at once.

The house continued to grow. Bedrooms appeared, some like her own, some modern, some a confusion of periods and styles. A toothbrush and a small tube of toothpaste appeared in her medicine cabinet. In each of the bedrooms she found new clothes and wore them in the order of their discovery.

She began to awaken in the morning with a feeling of

anticipation. Would she find a chandeliered dining room or perhaps an enclosed porch whose windows looked out on the mist?

At the end of a month the house contained eighteen bedrooms, three parlors, a library, dining room, ballroom, music room, sewing room, a basement and two attics.

Then the people came. One night she awoke to their laughter somewhere beyond her window. She was furious at the invasion but comforted herself with the thought that they were outside. She would bolt the downstairs door, and even if the mist disappeared she would not look. But she couldn't help hearing them talk and laugh. She strained to catch the words and hated herself for trying. This was *her* house. She stuffed cotton into her ears and felt shut out rather than shut in, which angered her even more.

The house stopped growing. The mist cleared and the sun came out. She looked through her window and saw a lake made up of many narrow branches, its surfaces covered with a phosphorescent sparkle like a skin of dirty green sequins. She saw no one—the intruders came late at night, dozens of them, judging from the sound they made.

She lost weight. She looked in the mirror and found her hair dull, her cheeks drawn. She began to wander the house at odd hours. Her dreams were haunted by the voices outside, the splash of water, and, worst of all, the endless laughter. What would these strangers do if she suddenly appeared at the doorway in her quilted robe and demanded that they leave? If she said nothing but hammered a "No Trespass" sign to the oak tree? What if they just stood there, staring at her, laughing?

She continued to wander. There were no new rooms, but she discovered hidden alcoves and passageways that connected bedroom to bedroom, library to kitchen. She used these passageways over and over again, avoiding the main halls.

Now when she woke, it was with a feeling of dread. Had any of them got in during the night, in spite of her precautions? She found carpenters' tools in a closet and nailed the windows shut. It took weeks to finish the job, and then she realized she had forgotten the windows in the basement. That part of the house frightened her and she put off going down. But when the voices at night began to sound more and more distinct, when she imagined that they were voices she recognized, she knew that she had no choice.

The basement was dark and damp. She could find no objects to account for the shadows on the walls. There was not enough light to work by, and when she finished, she knew she had done badly. If they really wanted to come in, these crooked nails would not stop them.

The next morning she found that the house had a new wing of three bedrooms. They were smaller than those in the rest of the house and more cheaply furnished.

She never knew exactly when the servants moved in. She saw the first one, the cook, when she walked into the kitchen one morning. The woman, middle-aged and heavy, wearing a black uniform with white apron, was taking eggs from the refrigerator.

"How would you like them, madam?"

Before she could reply, the doorbell rang. A butler appeared.

"No, don't answer it!" He continued to walk. "Please —"

"I beg your pardon, madam. I am partially deaf. Would you repeat your statement?"

She screamed: "*Do not answer the door.*"

"Scrambled, fried, poached?" said the cook.

"It may be the postman," said the butler.

"Would madam like to see today's menu? Does madam plan to have guests this evening?" The housekeeper was dark and wiry. She hardly moved her lips but her words were clear.

"Some nice cinnamon toast, I think," the cook said, and she placed two slices of bread in the toaster.

"If you're having twelve to dinner, madam, I would suggest the lace cloth," said the housekeeper.

The doorbell was still ringing. It wouldn't stop. She ran to the stairs, toward the safety of her room.

"Madam?" said the cook, the housekeeper, the butler.

That night they came at sunset. She climbed into bed and drew the covers up around her, but still she could hear their laughter, rising and falling. The water made splashing sounds. She pulled the covers over her head and burrowed beneath them.

A new sound reached her and she threw off the covers, straining to hear. They were downstairs, in the dining room. She could make out the clink of silverware against dishes, the kind of laughter and talking that came up at her from the water. The house was alive with a chattering and clattering she could not endure. She would confront them, explain that this was her house; they would have to leave. Then the servants.

She went down the stairs slowly, rehearsing the exact words she would use. When she reached the ballroom floor she stopped for a second, then crossed it to the open doors of the dining room. She flattened herself against the wall and looked inside.

There were twelve of them, as the housekeeper had suggested—and she knew every one.

Her husband, bald, bold, and precise. "I told her, 'Go ahead and jump; you're not scaring me.' And she jumped. The only brave thing she ever did."

Her mother, dry as a twig, with dead eyes: "I told her it was a sin—but she never listened to me, never."

A friend: "She didn't seem to feel anything. When other people laughed she always looked serious, as if she was mulling it over to find the joke."

"She used to laugh when she was very small. Then she stopped."

"She was a bore."

"She was a sparrow."

"She was a failure. Everyone knew. When she found out for herself, she jumped."

"Was it from a bridge? I was always curious about that."

"Yes. They found her floating on the surface, staring into the sun like some would-be Ophelia." Her husband smiled and wiped his lips with a napkin. "I don't think I'll recommend this place. I've got a stomachache."

The others agreed. They all had stomachaches.

The guests returned, night after night, but each night it was a different group. Always she knew them and always she watched as they ate. When the last party left, joking about the food being poisoned, she was alone. She didn't have to dismiss the servants; they were gone the next day. The yellow-gray mist surrounded her windows again, and for the first time she could remember, she laughed.

PIP WINN

RIGHT OFF THE MAP

It was Mayson, my bunkmate at the Ministry, who insisted on the guns. I must make that clear. But I anticipate.

I was dozing on my bunk when he came in, hot, flushed and untidy, and carrying a long, thin cylinder. I recognized the material as paper.

"A close shave," he remarked. "I thought I wasn't going to make it." They had been tightening up the travel regulations, and a confiscated walking permit was a serious matter.

"What is it this time?" I stretched and climbed down to his bunk.

"An old map."

I looked pointedly at the regulation plastic map of the World Union which hogged most of the wall space. Not that I ever complained. We were better off than most of the couples with apartment rooms Outside; the tap and the heating worked, and we were spared the trouble of applying for Workers' Travel Disks.

"This is different. It's an antique," said Mayson, unrolling it. "Mid-twentieth century."

· With the single men's shopping ration recently reduced to one hour weekly, most of us had time only to fight our way to the queue outside the nearest store, if we bothered at all. But Mayson had a theory about "first things first" and usually returned with something useless, offbeat and space-wasting.

I had to admit that the tattered old map was esthetically pleasing. It showed, in various colors, the political divisions which existed in the twentieth century, with mountain ranges in brown and the landmasses offset by pale-blue sea.

"Well, keep it rolled up, or stick it on the ceiling," I said acidly. "You've got half my storage space already." But I couldn't resist a few comparisons with the modern map. The Department of London, then called "England," was still quite sparsely populated in the west and north. The Department of Khartoum was colored yellow and marked "Sahara Desert," showing that in those days there was still some land actually left barren.

"There's something I want to check." Mayson's finger moved from the old to the new and back again. "Yes, by God! I thought so. Tell me what you see here." He pointed to a place which is now part of the border between the departments of Karachi and Delhi.

I looked. "Two lines of hills, parallel, but converging at both ends. An offshoot of the Himalayas, apparently."

"Good. And the space between?"

"A long, narrow valley, green with black spots." I consulted the index at the foot of the map. "Forest land."

"Right. Now find the place on the standard map."

"It isn't— Yes. Here. But there's only one line of hills. Well, I suppose, with their primitive instruments—"

"No!" I had never seen Mayson so excited. "Cartography was dead accurate by the nineteenth century. Don't you see what this means?"

"You're the historian. I'm only a biologist."

"I'm a sociologist. But never mind that. Suppose it's the modern map that's wrong. There may be lebensraum there—the first to be found in over a century. We're going

to see the Boss. If we handle him right, we'll get an
Orange Disk for this."

For an Orange Disk, anything was worth trying. I
followed Mayson along the crowded corridor.

Phillips was a harassed man. His title, Chief Surveyor,
was a concession to tradition, and he was really a glorified
house matron, pessimistically grappling with the problems
of housing five thousand people in a fifty-year-old building designed for two thousand. He was placating the telephone as we entered. "Sorry, Stevens, not a square inch at
the moment. Yes, of course, at once, if anything turns
up."

He compared the map carefully with the one on his
wall.

"Too good to be true," he said. "But I suppose it *is* just
possible that Karachi and Delhi both thought they had
stopped developing on opposite sides of the same range of
hills. The place is well off the air routes, and the valley, if
it's there, is narrow and completely enclosed. Would you
two like to go and find out?"

"Us?" If I hadn't known his thoughts, I'd have sworn
Mayson was genuinely surprised.

"Why not? I could do with your bunks for a while.
Computers are expecting two girls from the Department of
Paris, and we're a bit stuck. Send Stores a list of the things
you'll need, and I'll recommend you for Orange Disks." I
caught Mayson's triumphant glance. "But you won't get
any transport off the regular routes, so travel light."

He waved us away and picked up the phone. "Computers? About those two girls, Stevens—"

A week later, hung over and sore from our injections,
we plunged into the inferno of the morning shopping ration. The long-delayed One-Way (Streets) Bill was expected to be passed at the next reading. And not before
time.

The shoppers who, struggling and cursing, filled the
wide streets were nearly all women, wearing Yellow Disks
marked "Housewife. Wed. Shift 1."

Mayson had done some homework, and we were in

period costume: trousers, shirts, socks and hooded jack-
ets, all of natural cotton, and leather shoes. The trousers
would protect our legs against thorns, insects or snakes, he
said, and the natural materials would be better than syn-
thetics in a hot, humid atmosphere. On our backs were
knapsacks containing water, food and other necessities—these were anybody's guess—and the guns hung
from our shoulders by straps. On our chests were the
Orange Disks, bearing our photographs and the legend
"Urgent Priority at All Times." They were valid for a year
and were literally priceless.

Thanks to the Disks, we made good speed. They took
us through, instead of around, the Parks, and to the front
of every queue at both Airstrips, and enabled us to stand
by the windows for the whole of the two-hour flight. We
saved at least a week by simply ignoring the customs
queue, and nobody dared challenge us.

At the other end the driver of an orange garbage-wagon
spotted our Disks and picked us up. He used his siren to
good advantage and was able to speed up during the comparative lulls between the Workers' and Shoppers' travel
shifts. He dropped us within sight of the hills, having
saved us many days of battle.

Less than a month after leaving the Ministry we flourished our Disks at the gate in the wall behind the last housing block. The guard saluted and let us through.

At last we sat resting on the cold hilltop, exhausted from
the climb and uneasily aware of the unfamiliar space and
quietness. Below us lay the valley, its treetops shimmering
in the sunshine. I realized that we need no longer stay so
close together, and self-consciously moved away, suddenly
irritated by Mayson, who was already busy calculating the
area of the valley.

I think it was here that I lost the camera. I remember
photographing the contrasting views before and behind,
and the next day it was missing. The loss seemed trivial at
the time. We had the packets of old-fashioned paper
notebooks and pencils which Stores had dug out of the
Ministry basement (the fewer gadgets, the fewer technical
hitches), and these would be adequate for collecting the

notes and diagrams which would be of more interest to
Phillips than the scenery, when translated into potential
bunk space.

We followed a spring which cascaded down to a small
lake, emerging as a stream that, ignorant of its destiny
when it should pass beneath the Wall of Civilization into
an underground reservoir, meandered peacefully along
the valley, overhung by trees. We should not be able to
wander far from its banks at first, because the floor of the
forest was covered by dense undergrowth, and we had
brought no hatchets. In time, the bulldozers would make
short work of this problem.

When we came to a break in the trees we cleared a
small area, using knives and branches, and camped for the
night. After supper, Mayson worked by torchlight for an
hour or so and then, with a muttered "Good night,"
turned in.

But I sat with my back to a tree, far into the hot, damp
night, idly waving the insects away, and savoring for the
first time in my life the peace, and the sounds and scents
of the wild: bird calls, the chattering of monkeys, the scuf-
fling of small night creatures, the smell of foliage and
moist earth. No doubt there would be snakes—perhaps
dangerous. I had once been allotted a Zoo Disk, and an
indescribable emotion possessed me as I contrasted this
solitude and freedom with the plight of the animals
crouching mournfully in their three-tiered cages at home. It
occurred to me that the whole world must have been like
this before man had destroyed it with the spread of his
teeming millions. Suddenly lonely, and frightened by the
unquiet forest, I huddled into my blanket and slept.

"What the hell do you think you're doing?" Mayson's
voice shattered the peace of the dawn. He grabbed his
water flask (replenished by courtesy of the Orange Disks
at the last block before we reached the Wall) and cuddled
it as though it were his only child.

I continued to empty mine over a bush and nodded
toward the stream. "That's fresher."

"You're nuts. It hasn't been purified."

"It's never been polluted. And in a few days we shan't

need these anymore." I indicated the plastic containers full of synthetic food concentrate. "We'll make some paths, find edible plants. And we can catch animals for meat."

It's funny, but I never thought of using the guns for hunting. My mind was set on the idea that they were for whatever unimaginable emergencies Mayson had envisaged when he insisted on bringing them.

He stowed his food and water into his knapsack, and closed it elaborately. "Oh well, if you want to poison yourself with natural food, stinking with bacteria—"

I grabbed his arm. "Sh! Look! Over there."

I must have been looking at it through the trees for some time without seeing it, so perfect was its camouflage. Elegantly draped over a low branch thirty yards or so from the stream was the most glorious creature I had ever seen: a huge cat, as big as a lion, but colored in black and gold stripes which blended harmoniously with the shafts of morning sunlight slanting into the forest. Its underparts were a vivid white. It lay relaxed, eyes half-closed, a poem of grace, dignity and serenity.

"A tiger! A living tiger!" I breathed. I would have sent the whole civilized world to perdition for the camera.

It is not generally known that there were at one time many species of cat. The only surviving members of this once numerous family were the so-called domestic cat, formerly a popular pet, now a pest, which had successfully defied all attempts at extermination, and the lion, which, being gregarious, lazy and friendly to man, is easily tamed and thrives in captivity. The others, solitary and independent, failed to adapt to close confinement and ceased to breed. Though the leopard was the fiercest, the most beautiful of the wild cats was the tiger, the last of which died in London Zoo early in the twenty-first century.

Nevertheless, a tiger this undoubtedly was—a "living fossil." You may have seen films, or museum exhibits, of tigers, but these could give you no idea of the shining glory and awe-inspiring presence of the living animal.

Mayson had seen it now. His face wore the bleak, let's-get-it-over-with expression that I had begun to hate. He went over and picked up his gun.

"Put that down," I said. "And for God's sake keep still, or you'll frighten it."

He examined the mechanism of the safety catch. "We'll have to take it back with us. It'll be the scoop of the century."

I planted myself between the gun and the tiger. "Look, Mayson, you can't mean that. You couldn't do it. And anyway, we've no equipment for taking it over the mountain dead or alive."

"Not the carcass. Just the skin. We have knives. Think of the price it will fetch—the sensation!"

I dived for his gun. I was almost crying with rage and horror.

"You're bloody well *not* going to kill it. It may be the last tiger in the world. What would be the use of it dead?"

He caught me in the midriff with the butt of the gun, and I fell heavily, gasping for breath.

"So what?" he said. "Who lost the camera, for that matter? And who do you think would ever believe we'd seen a tiger, without proof?" He began to push his way into the undergrowth, ignoring the thorns that tore his trousers and hands.

As a sociologist, Mayson should have known about the territorial instinct which mankind once shared with the rest of creation. I, as a biologist, certainly did. I had by now noticed that the tiger was a female, and pregnant. I knew that a breeding female was the most dangerous and unpredictable of all wild animals. Alarmed or provoked, that lovely, placid creature could change, in a moment, into a spitting tornado. Also, there was likely to be a male somewhere nearby. Mayson was in deadly danger. I collected my gun and followed him, plucking frantically at his shirt. "Come back, you damned fool! You'll get yourself killed."

The tigress, aroused by our noisy approach, now stood up, glaring at Mayson. Her ears lay flat, her back was arched, and a ferocious snarl distorted her beautiful face. Mayson had never fired a gun. The closeness of the range was no guarantee that he wouldn't miss. It might even cause him to fire too late. I was equally inexperienced, but obviously I was about to learn fast.

Still oblivious to his danger, Mayson took aim. The tigress crouched, gathering herself for the spring. I had about two seconds. Either that glorious creature and her precious progeny were going to be destroyed for the sake of a bedraggled skin, inexpertly hacked from her warm body, or Mayson, my fellow human, was going to die a very sticky death.

There was no time for sentimentality. No civilized man could dare to take the risk. I raised my gun and fired, a split second before the tigress could leap, like a darting golden flame, at Mayson. There was a snarl, a flurry of limbs, and the sound of the gunshot sent every living thing diving for cover. I stood there, in the sinister, unnatural silence, and saw that I had not missed.

I left Mayson in the clearing we had made, with both the guns, the remainder of the food, and most of the kit. I wanted never to see him again.

I'll wrap this report in a plastic bag and leave it somewhere. But no one will come for it. Phillips is in no hurry to have us on his bunk roll again.

My second notebook is nearly full of drawings—of tiger cubs.

TED THOMAS

THE WEATHER ON THE SUN

. . . . the name "Weather Bureau" continued to be used, although the organization itself was somewhat changed in form. Thus the Weather Congress consisted of three arms. First was the political arm, the Weather Council. Second was the scientific arm, the Weather Advisors. Third was the operating arm, the Weather Bureau. . . .

—*The Columbia Encyclopedia*, 32 Edition, Columbia University Press

The mass of colors on the great globe shimmered and twisted in silence. The dials on the instruments along the curved walls dimmed and brightened each time the needles moved. The Weather Room presented an indecipherable complex of color to the untrained eye, but to the eyes of the Advisors who lounged there it presented an instantaneous picture of the world's weather, when they bothered to look at it. The day shift was near its end, and the mathemeteorologists were waiting to go home. Now and then one of them would look at some spot on the great globe to see how the weather pattern reacted—to check on a bit of his own work carried out earlier in the day. But he was not really interested; his mind was on the evening's date, or dinner, or a hockey game. Even Greenberg, head of the Weather Advisors, felt the general lassitude.

Anna Brackney was too bored to sit still. She got up and wandered into the computer room, plopped down again and punched a 2414 computer to check the day's match. It was 90.4 percent. She muttered, "Lousy," and then looked around guiltily. She punched the call-up to see what the match had been last week. Ninety point six. She started to say aloud, "Not bad," but stopped herself in time. James Eden would not approve of her talking to herself. Idly she punched call-up and looked at the results for last month and the month before that. Then she sat bolt upright, and punched for data for the last six months. Very loudly she said, "Well, well, well, well, what do you know about that?" Ignoring the stares of two computer operators, she marched back into the Weather Room, right up to Greenberg.

"Do you realize," she said, "that our fit has been slipping a little each week? We are now operating on a fit of a little better than ninety percent, when as recently as six months ago our fit was better than ninety-three percent? Did you realize that?"

Greenberg sat up and looked alert. "No. Are you sure?"

Anna did not bother to answer. Greenberg leaned aside and spoke into a communicator. "Charlie, get me a summary of the weekly fit for the last six months." He touched a button and said, "Upton, come on out to the Weather Room, will you? We may have a problem."

Greenberg touched several more buttons. In two minutes there was a circle of people around him, and he held a slip of paper in one hand. He said, "Somehow, in the last six months, we've slipped three percentage points in our match. How could that happen?"

The people looked at one another. Upton said, "Everybody thought somebody else was checking the long-term fit. I only compared it with the week before."

There was a chorus of "So did I," and Greenberg slapped his forehead. "How in hell could a thing like that happen?" He was a man who normally did not swear. "We've been drifting away from acceptable performance for six months and nobody even noticed it? What about the complaints? What kind of complaints we been getting?"

The people shrugged, and Upton spoke for them again. "Nothing special. Just the usual gripes. Two weeks ago the Manitoba Council complained the breeze we made to blow away the mosquitoes was too strong, but—"

"Never you mind," said Anna Brackney. "That was my mathematical model on that problem, and the twenty-knot wind they got was just right to eliminate the mosquitoes because the foresters—"

"Knock it off," said Greenberg. "I take it there have been no serious complaints? I'd better check further." He talked into the phone with one of the secretaries, then said to the group, "Well, it seems we've been lucky. Anyhow, we've got to find out what's wrong. And we've got to find it before somebody else notices it, or we'll have the Weather Council on our necks. I wonder if I ought to call President Wilburn."

The people shook their heads, and Upton said, "I don't like to be sneaky or anything like that. But if we've somehow slipped in our procedures and got away with it, let's correct them without stirring up trouble. You know politicians."

Greenberg said, "We'll all have to stay on this until we find it. All of you willing?"

The people gave up their visions of dinner and dates and hockey games and nodded.

"Okay, then. Each of you set up a program designed to make an independent repeat of your models for the last six months. Most of it was routine stuff, so it won't be bad. Call in the computer technicians and utilize all of the university's staff and equipment you need. If you need more, I'll set up a net and we can pull in everything we need from beyond Stockholm. Monitor your steps and when you find an error feed it into the 9680 as a collecting computer. Any other suggestions?"

The people shook their heads.

"All right. Let's get to work and solve this before anybody else even knows there's a problem. Good luck." A red light flashed on the phone at Greenberg's elbow, and the operator's voice said, "Dr. Greenberg, President Wilburn is on the phone. Some kind of emergency."

Greenberg looked startled. He picked up the phone and listened. In a moment he turned up the audio so that the people could hear what Wilburn was saying.

The ox was almost done, and it smelled mighty good to Big John Sommerville. He stood at the edge of the great patio and looked across it through the morning groups of people to where the ox slowly turned on the spit. A cloud of steam rose above it and quickly disappeared in the still, dry air. Beyond the barbecue pit with its automatic basters, auxiliary heaters, powder sprinklers, temperature sensors and color detectors stood one of the cattle barns, and beyond that the roll of the prairie began. It was picture-pretty: a stand of oak and maple on the forward slope, a road winding up, a stream meandering down the dip at the foot of the first hill fed from some hidden subterranean channel that groped its way to the low mountains. Big John Sommerville turned to look at the house.

It rambled and twisted behind him, cloaked in brown-stained shingles and roofed with cedar. It sprawled and sprouted unexpected wings and went on for three hundred feet. There was a story that two years ago there had been eight guests in that house for a week before Big John found out about it. It was a good house, built for comfort, and it had a sense of belonging.

Big John Sommerville hooked his thumbs in his belt and started to stroll over toward the roasting ox. His face was craggy with little sags in the right places, and his body was big with a thin layer of fat over hard muscles, a good Texas face on a good Texas body.

"Hey, John, when do we eat?"

"Half an hour, I reckon." He walked on.

A hand slapped him on the shoulder, jolted him a little off-balance. As he turned he said, "You hungry, too, Brian?"

"Sure am." It was Brian Travers, mayor of Austin, the

third most potent political figure in the area, and he held a large glass of straight bourbon. "I can wait through another pint or so of bourbon, but then I'm going to put me away a hindquarter of that ox. Hope it's as good as the last."

"Ought to be. Why, hello, Henry. Just get here?"

Henry Carpenter shook hands and looked around cautiously. "Everything under control? They all here?"

Travers said, "They're here. Quit worrying, Henry. We'll get it." The three of them had arranged the ox roast for a hundred of the major and minor citizens of the region to win over their support for a proposed monorail shipping line. It never hurt to line up the solid citizenry on your side before you tackled the local, state and national officials. "We'll get them feeling comfortable on John's bourbon and ox, and then we'll tell them what we want to do. They'll go along, all right."

"Got a surprise," said Big John Sommerville. "I got to a few ears and I made out a case for a little water table replenishment around here. In exactly an hour and a half we will have a gentle rainfall on the mountains right behind the house, just over that near ridge. The time and position will be just right for the damnedest rainbow you ever saw in your life—the pot of gold will be right on top of that rise there. I'll announce the rainfall a half hour before it's due, and we'll let these fellows think I got extra-special connections at the Weather Council. When these fellows see what I can do with the Council, they'll split their britches to get behind us on the monoline. Right?"

Travers and Carpenter raised their glasses and took a long pull in honor of Big John Sommerville.

The bourbon was smooth, the ox was tender and tasty, and the announcement came at just the right time. The clouds formed on schedule. And then the rains came. The black heavens opened up and poured out their watery hell all over the spread of Big John Sommerville. Something like twelve inches of rain fell in the first twenty minutes, and the meandering stream turned into a devastating giant that swept away the barn and the stand of trees and the winding road. The water roared down the gentle slope behind the house and burst through the glass doors that opened out on the concealed porches and little hideaway nooks at the back of the house. The basement quickly filled with water, and the water lifted the floor joists from the plates. The little subterranean waterways built up pressure and quickly saturated the soil to a depth of fifteen feet. A mud slide started that transformed the entire house into a kind of roller coaster. Big John Sommerville felt it start and succeeded in getting everybody out of the house, so there were no casualties. In a final cloudburst, the rainstorm passed away.

One hundred and three men stood on a rocky ledge and looked in awe at all that was left of the house, garages, barns, corral, fences, and trees: a sea of soupy mud with occasional pieces of lumber protruding at crazy angles. The bare bones of the hill showed, and the barbecue pit lay somewhere downslope under fifty feet of mud.

"Big John," said Travers, "when you order yourself a rain, you really order yourself a rain."

It took Big John Sommerville three hours to reach a phone, and by that time his plans were made. First he called the Governor, explained what had happened and what he intended to do. It turned out that the Governor also had some information about a weather order or two that had gone wrong. So the Governor made a few calls himself, ending with a call to Wilburn's office to say that an important constituent named Big John Sommerville would soon be calling to talk to Wilburn about an important problem, and please arrange to have President Wilburn take the call. Big John Sommerville placed a few additional calls to other district councilmen, to three other governors, to several mayors and to half a dozen wealthy industrialists. As it happened, many of these people had some small pieces of information of their own about weather mishaps. When these folk called President Wilburn's office to suggest the President listen to what Big John Sommerville had to say, they also tossed into the conversation a few pointed remarks about weather control and sloppy management.

In two hours' time, the communications network surrounding President Wilburn's office in Sicily was in a snarled mess out of which, nevertheless, two pertinent facts stood out: One, many good citizens were acutely unhappy about the weather control, and, two, Big John Sommerville was acoming.

When Big John Sommerville himself got on the line, President Wilburn was sitting there waiting. The five hours of pent-up anger burst into his office while he sat and marveled. The dirty red face that glared at him, the mud-caked hair, the ripped shirt, the glorious, near incoherence of the teeth-clenched stream of words were all fascinating. Never in his political life had President Wilburn received such a dressing down. Partway through it, Wilburn had to remind himself that the situation was not funny. He was, in fact, in the midst of a totally unexpected crisis.

The screen went blank. Big John Sommerville had had his say.

Wilburn sat quietly and reflected. The world government was not so mighty that one influential and irate citizen could not shake it a little. There should be no false moves now. First, he had to find out what had gone wrong. He called Greenberg at the Advisors.

Greenberg had just turned up the audio.

"Let me make certain there is no misunderstanding," said Wilburn. "Every staff member of the Advisors and all associated personnel are hereby placed on an emergency basis, and you have authority to do whatever is necessary—I repeat, whatever is necessary—to get to the bottom of this and correct it. Money, time, people, equipment, anything you need you get. In twelve hours I want a preliminary report from you, and hopefully you will have the complete answers by that time. If not, your entire organization will stay on the problem until it is solved. Routine work will be suspended except for weather control requests you receive personally from me. Do you have any questions?"

"No, Mr. President," and they hung up.

Anna Brackney said, "Why didn't you tell him we had just discovered the problem ourselves?"

Greenberg gave her a look, then said to the group, "All right, let's go the way we planned. I guess we were dreaming a little to think we were going to solve this before anybody else caught on."

As they turned and walked away, Greenberg heard Anna Brackney say to Hiromaka, "But I don't understand why he didn't tell him we had already found out there was a problem."

Hiromaka said, "Aw, shut up."

At breakfast the next morning Harriet Wilburn said to Jonathan, "I guess this will be a bad one. We'd better make it a good breakfast; lunch may be a little tense." She poked the Diner for his coffee and then began making his onion-flavored eggs basted with pork sauce.

"Why is it," he said, "every time something pops I wind up having the breakfast I used to have when I was a boy? You suppose there's an element of regression there?"

"I certainly hope so. I'd hate to think it was some deep, undefined craving. Do you really think you ought to look at that now?" Wilburn had picked up a morning English-language newspaper.

"Oh, don't worry," he said. "I know I'm going to get the most severe castigation of my career. I'm sort of looking forward to how imaginative the press will be." He began to read.

When his eggs were ready he put down the paper and said, "Yes, they're in full cry. The editors, the seers and columnists say they have been fully aware that things haven't been going right with the Weather Congress for several months, but they were just waiting to see if I would get going and do my job."

Harriet said, "Well, you know, and I know, and your friends know the truth. Eat your eggs, dear."

He ate his eggs. He sipped coffee when he was done, read through another paper, then went out into the soft Sicilian air, stepped on a walk and rode awhile. He got off and walked for a mile as was his custom, but a slight numbness crept into his legs, so he finished the trip on the slidewalk. He entered the Great Hall and went straight to his office through the private door.

Before he closed the door, Tongareva was there. Wilburn said, "Just the man I wanted to see. Come in, Gardner."

On his way to a seat, Tongareva started talking. "I have been reflecting on the events. I think we are caught up in some kind of world hysteria. I think the people have resented the Congress and the Council the way a small boy resents his authoritative father, and now they have found an excuse to let off steam. On top of that, elections are coming. I think we must be very careful."

Wilburn sank into his chair, ignoring the flashing lights on his phones and visuals. "Did you hear about that rained-out picnic in Texas?"

Tongareva nodded, a shade of a smile on his face. "That must have been the granddaddy of all rained-out picnics. The Texan knew just what to do to make an international issue out of it."

"The way he told it to me, it *was* an international issue. He led me to believe that everyone of any international importance was at that picnic, except you and me. Well, let me call Greenberg to see if he's found out what's gone haywire here. Please stay with me, Gardner."

Greenberg took the call in his office, with Upton and Hiromaka. "The information I have for you is incomplete, Mr. President. In fact, I hope it is so incomplete as to be incorrect. But you see, twelve hours is not really enough—"

"What are you trying to say, Dr. Greenberg?"

Greenberg glanced at Upton, took a deep breath and said, "A detailed check of all the procedures, all the mathematical models, all the parameters used here, shows that no error has been made and that our mathematical fit matches the prediction. This would indicate that the error was elsewhere. So we got in touch with Base Lieutenant Commander Markov; Hechmer and Eden are on vacation. We told Markov what we were doing and asked him to check out his results, too. We have his results now, and at least preliminarily, neither he nor we can find any fault with his operations. In short, the Weather Bureau on the Sun accomplished each of its missions within tolerance.

There's no error there either." Greenberg stopped and rubbed his face.

Wilburn asked gently, "What is your conclusion?"

Greenberg said, "Well, since the data were used and applied as correctly as we know how, and since the theory checks out as well as ever—"

He fell silent. After a moment Wilburn said, "Well?"

Greenberg looked straight at him and said, "The trouble might be in the Sun itself. The Sun is changing, and our theories are no longer as valid as they used to be."

Wilburn's breath caught, and he felt his body grow cold. He understood what Greenberg had said, but he did not immediately allow the full thought to enter his mind. He held it in front of him where it could not really frighten him, where it hung like a rotted piece of meat that would have to be eaten eventually, but not now. No one spoke or moved in either office. Greenberg and Tongareva did not want to force the swallowing, and so they waited. Finally, Wilburn took it in.

He sat back and groaned, and then stood up and paced out of range of the viewer. Greenberg sat and waited. Then he heard Wilburn's voice asking, "If what you say is true, our whole system of weather control is faulty. Is that right?"

"Yes, if it proves out," said Greenberg.

"Our entire culture, our entire civilization, the world over, is built on weather control. It is the primary fact of life for every living being. If our ability to control weather is destroyed, our world will be destroyed. We go back to sectionalism, predatory individualism. The one factor that ties all men everywhere together would disappear. The only thing left—chaos."

No one answered him, and for another full minute they were all silent.

Wilburn came back and sat down at his desk. He said to Greenberg, "I have to think. How much time will you need to verify your findings so far?"

"Another twelve hours. The European computer net is on it now, and we are in the process of bringing in the United States net and the Asian net simultaneously. Both of them will be on line in an hour. I might say this is the most intensive effort the Advisors have ever made, and it is causing talk already. There will be no secrets about our findings when we finally get them."

"I understand. I have twelve hours to think of something, and I am going to assume you will confirm what you've already found; that's the worst result I can think of, so I'll get ready to face it." The snap was coming back to Wilburn's voice. "If anything comes up along the way that makes you change your mind, let me know immediately. And thanks for the effort, Dr. Greenberg."

Wilburn looked around his office. The men gathered there did not look happy, and several of them, his political enemies, were frowning. Yet Wilburn needed them all. This was the group that served as a kind of unofficial executive for the entire Council. But it was a difficult group to work with, primarily because they represented such diverse interests.

Councilman Maitland said, "I am afraid, President Wilburn, that you have brought the Council to its lowest point of public esteem that I can remember."

Barstow reared up. "Now just a minute here. How do you—"

Wilburn waved a hand. "It's all right, Arthur. We all agree we have an enormous problem. I called this meeting to ask this group to think about what we do now."

Barstow sat back and nodded. The others were quiet, and then Tongareva said, "You give the impression that you have a plan to solve our present crisis, Jonathan. Are you ready to discuss it?"

"Yes. Although it isn't much of a plan, really." He leaned forward. "We have been this route before. We are confronted with a scientific crisis. The Sun is changing. Our weather control is no longer as accurate, and we may have other dangers we don't even know about yet. The Advisors tell me that these unexpected changes in the Sun might be serious, far more so than our failure to control weather accurately. We don't know what's happening. So here we go again, but this time I'm afraid we will have to mount the largest and most expensive research program the world has ever seen. It is already possible to tell that the answers won't be easy to get. The Weather Bureau has not seen any changes at all, so the Advisors think things must be happening deep inside the Sun. We've never been able to go deep, so the first scientific order of business will be to solve that one."

"Costs, Jonathan?" It was Du Bois, always a worrier about other people's money.

"Enormous, Georges. This is why we will have to be so careful. The tax burden will be the largest we've ever asked our people to bear. But unless someone can think of another program, I think we'll have to sell it."

Barstow said, "Do you mind if I talk to Greenberg? I want to be able to assure my constituents that I've looked into this personally."

"I hope everyone here will do that, and more. Please talk to any person you want, scientific or not, on any possible solutions he may have. Let's adjourn now and meet here in twenty-four hours to thrash it out."

Tongareva stayed, as Wilburn knew he would. He said, "Who's going to head up the program?"

Wilburn looked at him and smiled. "Need you ask? Aren't Dr. Jefferson Potter and Senior Boatmaster James Eden the ones to do the job?"

Greenberg seemed upset. "Look, with all due respect to you two, I don't think you see the ramifications of the problem. First"—he counted on his fingers—"the trouble appears to lie deep within the Sun. Second, we don't have a vehicle that can penetrate deeper than about two miles; in fact, Jim"—he looked at Eden—"no one has ever equaled that depth you reached some years ago on that Anderson problem. Third, we can't even take measurements at those depths. Fourth, our theories of occurrences at those depths have never been proved out." He dropped his hands. "We are probably in a worse position than we were when we first approached the problem of Sun control as a means of weather control."

Potter and Eden stared reflectively at Greenberg. Then Potter said, "You know, he's just given us an overall breakdown." Greenberg wondered what he was talking about, then realized that Potter was talking to Eden.

Eden said, still looking at Greenberg, "Yes, and he's the man in the best position to make the judgment so far. Four main groups along those lines, with good cross liaison. He's come up with a great way to start out, at least."

Potter said, "Four scientific administrators, each with a cabinet of a dozen or so people with assigned responsibilities. Each of the four groups places its own R & D and hires its own people."

Eden said, "Each cabinet has a member responsible for cross liaison with the other groups. In fact, each cabinet member has sole responsibility for an assigned area. He'll have his own staff to help administer his group."

It was Potter's turn again. "Any overlapping can be minimized by frequent meetings of the big four. Ought to work. Now let's see. All the problems come together on the Sun, so I guess that's where you ought to be. I'll stay here to keep things on the track. We can get together every month or so if necessary. How's that sound to you, Bob?"

Greenberg had caught the drift of the discussion and had been following it, fascinated. He nodded. "Sounds fine to me. Where do the Advisors come into this?"

"Seems to me you should be standing by for any extraordinary computing problems, of which there will be plenty. Don't forget you will also have the day-to-day work going on as usual. You had better increase your staff here, don't you think?"

Greenberg nodded. "Yes, but I can see some problems in getting enough scientific personnel to do all the work on the overall project. We'll wind up with one of our groups bidding against another."

"Bound to happen. We'll try to keep it to a minimum."

Potter said, "All right. I'll get on the horn and we'll start the ball rolling. Wilburn ought to be explaining things to everybody right about now."

Only two of the two hundred councilmen were absent, and Wilburn knew those two were in the hospital. Furthermore, the councilmen sat on the edge of their seats, listening intently to the voices booming over their desk speakers. Wilburn looked down impassively from his desk, but he was deeply shaken. The debate had gone on for three hours with no interruptions for any reason, and the opposition to the proposed research program was surprisingly strong. What was worse, the mood of the Council was emotional to a degree Wilburn had never seen before. Even Councilman Reardon of 35-50 E 30-45 N, normally a cool speaker, ended his five minutes with his voice broken and quavering. Wilburn frantically tried to think of a way to break the spell, to interject somehow a rational appeal. But he could not prevent the councilmen from obtaining their five minutes to speak. Many of them were so carried away with what they were saying that they did not see the thirty-second warning light on their desks, and they were cut off in mid-sentence by the sergeant at arms when their five minutes were up, left sobbing at a dead microphone.

Wilburn quietly turned to his desk, checked his directory, and dialed the desk of the next speaker, Francisco Espaiyat, 60-75 W 15-30 N. "Frank," he said, "you getting ready to speak?"

"I certainly am, Wilburn. I've come up with some reasons that haven't been mentioned yet, so I hope to do some good here. You got any particular suggestions?"

Wilburn hesitated. "Yes, I have, Frank, but I don't know whether to ask you to do it or not. See what you think. When you come on, simply state that you are in favor of the program, and then leave the rest of your time empty. Give us four minutes and fifty-five seconds of golden silence for a little somber reflection along with a quick trip to the bathroom. I don't like to ask you to give up your speaking time, but nobody yet has got through to these hotheads. What do you think?"

Espaiyat thought about it and then said slowly, "I don't know if it will work, Jonathan, but I'm willing to give it a try."

Three minutes later, when the sergeant at arms announced the speech of Councilman Espaiyat, the Council was startled to hear, "I speak in favor of the program, but I hereby devote the balance of my time to rest and relief from this interminable speechmaking." Espaiyat got up and started down the aisle. Immediately Wilburn got up and went out the door nearest him. After a moment's looking around the chamber in puzzlement, every other councilman suddenly got up and headed for a door, and as they pressed out to the corridors, some of them began to laugh. A low chant of "Yay, Espaiyat" started up from a few members and quickly spread over the entire chamber and up to the galleries, which were also emptying.

When they poured back to their desks a few minutes later, the spell was broken. Men and women chatted and called to one another. The next speaker, Madame Iwanowski, 45-60 E 45-60 N, spoke against the program, but she tried to marshal some facts. She yielded after two minutes twenty-eight seconds. The crisis had passed. Other speakers disgorged their thoughts, but the tenor of the speeches was only mildly argumentative, for the sake of the constituency back home. In half an hour the question was called and the vote taken. The tabulation flashed on the great board. A small cheer broke out from the floor and gallery. The vote was 133 for, 65 against. Wilburn sat impassively, staring out over the floor, ignoring the numbness that had come back in his legs. They had the required two-thirds vote, but it was much, much too close. On a project of this size he needed all the support in the Council he could get, but about one-third of the group was against him. He sighed. This would not do. There were hard times ahead. If this program didn't work out, he saw clearly who the scapegoat would be. For the first time a President of the Weather Congress would not so much step down as be thrown out. Well, that was politics. Harriet would be waiting for him when it was over, and they could always take up a pleasurable retirement. Key West, now, there was a place he had always loved, and perhaps the same had come to— He caught himself and straightened his shoulders. No time for retirement thoughts yet. There was work to be done. He headed for his office to call Greenberg.

"The trouble is," Senior Boatmaster James Eden said matter-of-factly, "the film of carbon vapor begins to collapse at these pressures. The rate of carbon consumption goes up, the sessile effect dissipates, and the boat itself is consumed."

"Very interesting," said Dr. John Plant. "Now don't you think we ought to get the hell out of here before you demonstrate the point?"

Eden nodded and said into the intercom, "Up. Forty degrees. Now." He fingered the keys and took the boat up to within five hundred yards of the surface before he leveled off. He said to Plant, "Don't wash it out, though. Those limitations I just mentioned will allow these boats to be consumed, but there may be a way around them."

"I don't know what they could be. Those limitations seem pretty fundamental to me. I think we need a whole new approach to get down to the center. We'll never do it with this kind of equipment."

Eden shook his head and said, "I never thought I'd be sitting in a sessile boat on the Sun and hear someone say it was obsolete. Look here. The carbon toruses that surround the boat act as a mirror. They absorb all the radiation from infrared down to the hard stuff to a depth of a fraction of a millimeter and then reflect it with an efficiency of ninety-nine point nine nine nine nine eight. That's the turnaround effect we've been telling you about. Carbon vaporization protects against the balance of the radiation, and the power difference is supplied by our internal reactors. So look. If we can increase the efficiency of the turnaround effect by a factor of a few thousand, we could cope with the increased temperatures and radiative effects at great depths. What's wrong with that?"

"Well, just how do you—"

"We can still balance out the gravitational force by channeling additional power to the bottom toruses, to take advantage of the radiative pressure on the bottom of the boat. Right?"

"Well, just how do you—?"

"That's your problem. I've told you how to do it. You're the scientist. I'm just a boat captain. Now, stand by while we get this thing back to base. I'm going Earthside today."

Plant sighed and settled back in his harness while Eden picked up the beacon and followed it back to base, through the lock and into the bay. While they were stripping off their lead suits, Plant said, "Maybe a carbon alloy." .

"What?" said Eden.

"Maybe a carbon alloy would improve the efficiency of the turnaround effect."

"Sounds promising to me. Give it a whirl. Nice going."

Plant looked at him wryly. "Thanks. Glad you like my ideas." Eden was too busy to pay any attention to the slight emphasis on the word "my," so Plant smiled at Eden's back, shrugged and hung up his suit.

They found Base Commander Hechmer in the day room with some of the staff watching a teevee transmit Earthside. Wilburn was addressing the Weather Council, bringing the members up to date on the Sun program. He told them results were coming in. The Sun's core was behaving anomalously. Neutrino formation at the core had accelerated and apparently was going to accelerate even more. The Sun appeared to be moving out of the main sequence a billion years ahead of schedule. Hechmer said, to no one in particular, "Gives you a nice comfortable feeling, doesn't it?"

On the screen Wilburn said, "To finish my report to you, we should know in a few weeks exactly what is wrong with the Sun, and we should then be in a position to know what to do about it. In short, ladies and gentlemen of the Weather Council, this most massive of research efforts has borne fruit. It is isolating the problem, and it will arrive at a solution. Thank you." The applause was long and genuine, and Wilburn made a slight bow and quickly put his hand on the podium.

The Advisors had the jitters, so Greenberg called together his mathemeteorologists and said, "Now look. Just because we have the heavy artillery in the scientific world showing up here in a few minutes is no reason to get all upset. It's just a high-level meeting, and they're holding it here. After all, we've made an important contribution to the total research effort on this program."

"Yes, but why here? They going to change the Advisors?"

"I hear they're going to fire us."

"Yeah, clean shop and start again with a new group."

Greenberg said, "Oh, cut it out. They probably want our advice on the next steps in the program. You'll have to admit, we have a problem there. We may have accomplished everything we can in the program."

People began to drift in, and soon the room was full. Potter took over as chairman. "What we've got to do is see where we go from here. We've accomplished almost all the major objectives of the program. What's left?"

Kowalski said, "We've fallen down on boat design. We haven't been able to come up with a boat that will get us down to the center of the Sun and back up again. We don't know where to turn next. We've explored every alley we can think of, and we have some thirty thousand people working on the project, including some real bright ones, problem solvers. All we've done is improve the efficiency of the boats by a factor of a thousand. We don't know where to turn next."

Potter said, "You can get a boat down, but you can't get it back. That right?"

"Yes, and don't anybody here tell us about remote control or automation. Center-of-Sun conditions are such that we can't communicate twenty feet away. As to automation, we can't get into the boat a computer of the size we need to make a few critical decisions. The presence of the boat is going to change center-of-Sun conditions, so someone is going to have to make a quick evaluation. Well, let Frank Valko tell you what's there."

Dr. Frank Valko, senior scientist in charge of evaluation of the Sun's deep interior, smiled and rubbed his chin in embarrassment. "I wish I could tell you precisely what's there. Then perhaps we could automate. But here's what we have. Our Bomnak group came up with a neutrino detector of reasonable size, one we could get in a spaceship. This is a device we've been trying for a hundred years. If the program produced nothing else, the neutrino detector alone has been worth it. Well, we put it in a ship and orbited it around the Sun and did some scanning. This detector is adjustable—most remarkable. We ran the scale from the fastest neutrinos with the weakest interaction to the slowest with some slight interaction, and we were able to peel the core of the Sun like an onion. Each interior layer is a bit hotter than the one outside it. And when we got to the core—I mean the real core now—we found the trouble. We found the very center at a temperature of over half a billion degrees Kelvin. The neutrino energy was greater than the light energy. The electron-positron pairs do not annihilate back to high-energy photons completely. We get significant neutrino-antineutrino formation. There are also some neutrino-photon reactions. But the point is that with such neutrino formation, energy can escape from the core, right through the walls of the Sun. And there you are." He looked around at the others brightly.

The rest of them looked at him blankly, and Eden said it. "Where?"

"Why, the Sun is in the earliest stages of decay, unpredictably early. All we have to do is dampen the core, and we get our old Sun back."

Potter said sarcastically, "How do we do that? Throw some water on it?"

"Well, water might not be the best substance. We're working out the theory to improve on water. I think we'll come up with something."

Eden said, "From a practical point of view, wouldn't it take quite a bit of water?"

"Of course not. Oh, I forgot to tell you. The hot core —the troublemaking part—is only about one hundred feet in diameter right now. But it's spreading. We ought to do something within the next six months."

Potter sat back and rubbed his face. "All right. We know what the trouble is. We know where the trouble is. And we will soon know what to do about it. Fair enough?" He looked around the room. Most of those present nodded. Anna Brackney and two other mathemeteorologists shrugged. Potter glared at them for a moment and continued. "We can even get down there to quench it. But we can't get back. Is that what's left of our problem?" No one said anything, and there were no shrugs this time. Potter waited a moment, then continued. "Well, if that's really all that's left, then we may be all done. I'm certain we can find a volunteer to take the sessile boat down to the core. The question is, should we allow the volunteer to do it? Do we continue to try to find a way to get him back up?"

Eden started to speak, but before he could form the words Anna Brackney cut in. "Now, just you don't say anything here at all. There's going to be a lot more thought put in on this problem before we go setting up a hero situation." She turned to Kowalski and said, "You have six months. Isn't there a chance you can come up with a suitable boat design in that time?"

Kowalski said, "A chance, yes. But it isn't very likely. We've reached the point where we know we need a major breakthrough. It could happen tomorrow—we're trying. Or it might not happen in the next ten years of intensive work. We've defined the problem sufficiently so that we know what's needed to solve it. I am not optimistic."

Potter said, "Any ideas from any others? McCormick, Metzger?"

Metzger said, "I think you've summarized it, Jeff. Let's try for another, say, four months to get a boat design and to check out what we think we know. If we finish up right where we are now, we won't have hurt anything. We can then find someone to take a boat down, and we'll give him a great big farewell party. Isn't that about it?"

More shrugs from the mathemeteorologists, and Anna Brackney glared at Eden. Potter said, "I think I'll go call President Wilburn and tell him our conclusion. Can I use your office, Bob?" Greenberg nodded, and Potter said, "Be back in a minute. Work out the details while I make the call."

He left, and a desultory conversation went on in his absence as the group set up priorities and discussed the beginnings of the phase-out of the giant program. Ten minutes passed. Potter reappeared and stood in the doorway. Eden looked up, leaped to his feet and ran around the table toward him. Potter was pale and his face was drawn. He leaned against the door jamb and said, "President Wilburn is dying."

"I'm going with you, Jonathan," said Harriet Wilburn. She sat across from Wilburn, dry-eyed, in their breakfast corner.

He smiled at her, and the cosmetics on his face wrinkled, giving his face an odd, ragged appearance. He reached across and patted her hand. "You have to stay behind to protect my good name. There's a bitterness in some people. As long as my wife is alive, they won't go too far."

"I don't care about them." The tears were in her eyes now, and she looked down at the table to hide them. She wiped her cheeks in annoyance and said in a steady voice, "When do you leave?"

"In three days. The doctors want to make one more attempt to find out what's causing the central myelitis; there's got to be *some* reason for spinal cord deterioration. They hope they can come up with a cure someday, but first they have to find out what causes it."

Harriet Wilburn burst out, "I don't care about all this knowledge, all this good, all this benefit-of-man nonsense. I want you." She put her head down on the table and frankly sobbed. Wilburn reached over and patted the back of her head.

"I don't really believe all this, Boatmaster," said Technician O'Rourke. "When the first manlike creature put out the first fire something like a half million years ago, he almost certainly used water. Now here we are, quenching the core of a sun heading toward a nova, and what do we use? Water. I don't believe it."

Eden did not smile. His mind was on a sessile boat, now about thirty thousand miles deep within the Sun and heading deeper. He sat with Technician O'Rourke in front of the main viewer panel of the neutrino detector, monitoring the flux density at the various energy levels. Eden said, "The reaction we are trying to get back to is simply the high-energy reaction of two photons to produce an electron-positron pair. As it is now, in the core the temperature is so high that the electron-positron pair doesn't go back to two high-energy photons. Instead they are producing a neutrino-antineutrino pair, and these pour right out through the Sun and are lost to space. If we don't stop that energy loss, the core will collapse. Since all we have to do is reduce the temperature by absorbing photons, we have a choice of materials to use. Many substances will do it, but water is the safest to carry down there without decomposing or volatilizing and killing Wilburn. That's why the water."

"Well, thanks. I still say it's a mighty funny situation. Somebody's going to do a lot of philosophizing on it, I'll bet you. How deep is he now?"

"About forty thousand miles."

Wilburn thought, "You never know. You never know until you're there. I thought I'd be reflecting on my life, the few things I did right, the many things I did wrong, wondering what it all meant." He glanced at a depth gauge that read 46,000, and he continued thinking, "About ten percent of the way, ninety percent to go, many hours yet." He felt hungry, but his ability to swallow had deteriorated to the extent that it was no longer possible for him to eat normally. He sighed, and went about the business of hooking up a bottle of a solution of sugar and protein to the needle in his arm. There were other ingredients in the solution, too, so after the solution was all in, he took a long, painless nap. When he awoke, there were only forty thousand miles to go, and Wilburn realized with a shock that he had had his last meal.

He checked out the few gauges he was familiar with; his briefing period had been limited. He remembered once as a boy his father had taken him through a power plant, and the array of dials and gauges had been fantastic. There had been a large room, divided by a series of panels, and every square inch of the panels and walls of the room had been covered with dials and gauges. When the time came to kick in additional units, one of the operators had called him over and said, "Okay, son. Push that button." Wilburn did, and his father said to him, "Don't forget this.

All the sensing instruments and dials in the world don't mean a thing without one human finger."

Wilburn looked at the one gauge he didn't like—the one that recorded outside temperature. It read 678,000°K, and Wilburn looked away quickly. He was not a scientific man, and he was incapable of really believing that any living creature could exist in an environment of six hundred and seventy-eight thousand degrees. He thought of Harriet.

He had found it necessary to take steps to prevent her from using her rather significant influence to stow away on this boat. He chuckled and felt the wave of warmth he always felt when he thought of her. For her sake it would have been better to allow her to come, but there were times when one could not take the easy and most desirable path. A soft chime sounded through the boat.

He was approaching the core. He focused his attention on the two instruments directly in front of him. He could feel the deceleration of the boat as the toruses, top and bottom, became more nearly balanced. The temperature inside the cabin was one hundred and forty-six degrees Fahrenheit, but Wilburn was not uncomfortable. He had the feeling that everything was going very well, and he wished he could tell Harriet. The deceleration continued; several of the gauges on the periphery of his vision went off scale. He was very close to the core. Conditions seemed to be as predicted.

He continued to watch, and a chime softly began a beat that slowly increased in tempo. He did not know it, because there was no instrument to record it, but the temperature outside approached the one billion mark. He watched the neutrino flux direction indicator, knowing that the great quantity of water aboard was no longer in the form of a liquid, vapor or solid, and it crossed his mind to wonder how that could be. And when the neutrino flux direction indicator wavered, and changed direction to show he had just passed through the very center of the core, he placed his finger on the black button. The last thing he remembered were the words, still clear in his ears, "don't mean a thing without one human finger." Then the walls of the boat collapsed and released the water. And the electron-positron pairs appeared instead of the neutrino-antineutrino pairs. On the neutrino detector in the orbiting ship, Eden saw the tiny, hot core fade and disappear. The technician made an adjustment to bring in the neutrinos with slightly greater interaction, and the normal core showed up again, with its normal neutrino flux. But Eden, though he stared at the screen with eyes wide open, could see nothing but a blur.

GRAHAM CHARNOCK

THE CHINESE BOXES

The room was white. Its walls were like unmarked fields of snow, gleaming in the light of four fluorescent strips set in the ceiling. In the center of the room stood the Box, a huge cube of stainless steel ten feet on a side. It resembled some exquisite, ultimately formal piece of modern sculpture, although Carpenter, whose last visit to an art gallery had been as a freshman many years ago, preferred to think of it as a shiny, oversized sugar lump.

The surfaces of the Box were, with one exception, featureless, and this exception showed the outline of a flush-fitting door. In place of a latch there was a metal plate possibly five inches square and secured with four crosscut, countersunk bolts. Elleston, who relieved Carpenter at the end of his afternoon watch, had told him that the plate concealed something called a time lock.

Carpenter sat on a chair with his back to one of the room's white walls and facing the Box's door. He was a large man and the chair was rather too small to be comfortable. He'd asked Horden, the man who'd hired him, for a new chair. Carpenter thought that Horden, who was

165

a sedentary, oversized, florid man himself, would be sympathetic to his request, but three weeks had passed so far and the chair had not been replaced.

For four hours in the morning and four hours in the afternoon Carpenter was supposed to watch the Box. There was a red disk inset on the wall beside him and he was supposed to press this if anything untoward occurred. Untoward was Horden's word. Supposedly the red disk was some kind of alarm.

Anne had picked him up in her Volkswagen after his first day at Chemitect.

She was glad he had got the job. He was really very lucky. Had he seen the unemployment count, going up and up? This was really a job he should try to hold onto. How had it gone?

The Volkswagen purred into life. Carpenter was happy to let Anne drive. He didn't like the Volkswagen—its seats were too small for one thing—but it was cheap and it was economical to run and it was all they really needed.

He told her about the job, about how all it was was just sitting there, you see, and watching this . . . Well, he didn't know what it was. It was big and square and shiny. Like a big, square shiny box. Yes, he meant he just sat there, he really did. On a chair. Well, wasn't sitting in a clean room better than grease-monkeying? Yes, that was it, only this big square, shiny box, nothing else. What was in the box? Well, he didn't know. It had a door so . . . so he forgot about the door, just a door, nothing else. Well, it had a door, so he supposed there was something inside. Sure he'd asked. He'd asked Elleston . . . Who Elleston? He didn't know who Elleston. Elleston relieved him at the end of his afternoon watch, Cochran stood in for him for two hours at lunchtime and Levinson—yes he thought he was Jewish—was the one he relieved in the morning. Yes, he'd asked all three, but none of them knew. None of them knew what—if anything—was in the box.

And there was the alarm of course. . . .

Anne turned her head sharply. Blond, slightly greasy hair spun and whipped at him.

For Christ's sake watch the road! What are you doing
. . .

Anne turned into a side-street and pulled up.

Well, he was coming to the alarm wasn't he? Jesus, just a red button. Yes, red. Look, you can't stop here. He pushed the button if anything untoward happened. What untoward? He meant unusual. OK, he meant if anything went wrong. He didn't know what was likely to go wrong. Nothing. Nothing would go wrong. They wouldn't make him sit there if it was dangerous would they? He meant it wasn't likely to explode was it? He meant that if it exploded, then they wouldn't need an alarm, would they? Everybody would know about it, you bet. Yes, he realized it wasn't funny.

Anne said she didn't like it. Not at all. But she started up the car. Looking out of the window as the city swallowed the Volkswagen, Carpenter smiled so that she wouldn't see. She was pretty when she worried and wasn't it nice to have somebody worry about you? He'd marry her when things were better. This job was only the beginning. Hadn't he thought that about all the others? Sure but the gas station, the drugstore, all the no-hope jobs that anybody could get, that had a high turnover rate unemployment or no unemployment . . . losing those jobs had at least taught him the importance of keeping this one. Wait until they had enough money put by to go east. Everybody knew the best jobs were in the east. He'd marry her then, in the east.

Later that evening at his apartment she made him promise.

If you don't promise you don't get your reward. You *know* what I mean. Promise you'll find out what's in that box. Promise you'll find out if it's dangerous. I don't want you involved in anything dangerous. Please. You know I get worried about you.

She smiled and looked pretty.

He promised.

The cell was white, or had been once.

Its walls were blank, or had been once.

The prisoner slept on a discolored pallet that stank of decaying weeks and months. He wore a coarse shirt and trousers that itched upon his skin and caused rashes. Apart from the prisoner and the pallet, and the pail into which he urinated and defecated, there was nothing.

The light, which came from a small barred slit high on one wall of the cell, was dim and constant during the day, nonexistent during the night, which, like the dawn, always came on abruptly. If he jumped he could just reach the window slit with his fingers and, hanging there, could usually just manage to draw himself abreast of it for a few seconds. The slit was only a few inches high and possibly a foot deep in the wall. Through it he could see only blue sky. He never saw a trace of cloud, nor any birds.

The temperature was constant too. Constantly warm. At the window slit he never saw either rain or snow, or any manifestation of the seasons, although he assumed, as with the absence of clouds and birds, that this was merely bad luck. He seldom had the strength to hoist himself to the slit more than twice a day, usually after the meager warmth and sustenance of a meal.

A typical meal was a lukewarm soup with a little meat in it and two ounces of something spongy that might have been bread. It was served to him regularly through a narrow, hinged flap in the door, so regularly that his stomach had become attuned to it. He could tell if it was even thirty seconds late, and it never was. The food was served in a flat metal pan. Sometimes, when the pan was slid through the door, he would be kneeling there, waiting by the slit. He never managed to see the hand that fed him, however. Sometimes he would shout through the slit as his meal was pushed in—requests for small comforts, for a word, for a sight of his captors.

Once he refused to eat the food. He couldn't remember what his crime was or why he should be in prison. He was convinced they had done something to his mind to make him forget. He thought they might be using drugs in his food, slowly poisoning him, so for six days (he counted them with fecal smears on the wall) he starved. And remembered nothing.

After that he searched his scalp through his long matted hair for a surgical scar. He found nothing, but this didn't shake his conviction that somehow they had interfered with his mind: why had they taken his memory? Had they done it thinking it to be a kindness? Or had they done it in the hope that, not remembering, he would come to accept his guilt? He would never do that. He was sure that things like guilt and innocence transcended memory. They were qualities of mind, and wherever mind was, memory or not, they would be there. And innocence was there in his case, he was sure of it. He did not believe he had committed any crime. He could not believe he should be punished. "Give me a trial," he cried through the dinner slit. "Tell me what I am accused of." But his captors, whoever they were, gave no sign of having heard him.

He began to take food again. When he finished, he would fling the pan into a corner. The following day, when he awoke, the pan was always gone and a new pail (or perhaps it was merely the old one emptied and cleaned) had been placed there for his droppings. He assumed that, when he slept, one of his captors entered the cell to perform these duties. For three nights he tried to stay awake but succumbed eventually to the absolute womb darkness and the comforting warmth. Always the pan was removed, the pail changed.

The next night he succeeded, standing in a corner and scoring his arms against the stone wall to achieve additional discomfort, in staying awake until dawn came. He was certain that nobody had entered the cell, but once again saw that the pan had been removed and the pail changed.

By this time he had become obsessed with the pan and the pail and decided he would make it impossible for either to be removed without his knowledge. He ripped a sleeve from his shirt and, lacing it through the pail's handle, used it to secure the pail around his neck. The stench itself was enough to keep him awake that night. The pan formed an uncomfortable pillow for his head. In the morning both the pail and the pan were untouched. His captors, spying on him, had obviously noted his precautions and had refrained from entering the cell. The prisoner let out a cry of triumph. He had achieved communication of a sort; he had at least done something to influence the actions of his captors. He set the utensils down in a corner and went back to his pallet exhilarated. That morning, however, when he came to use the pail he found it clean and empty. He looked for the dinner pan but it had disappeared. He thought about this for a long time but was unable to find an explanation of the phenomenon.

Chemitect was a campuslike layout of small island structures surrounding a massive central hive. Anne dropped him at the entrance of the main building. On the raised piazza fronting the entrance, water dribbled over a chunk of shiny basalt in a concrete bowl. Beyond this, over the entrance itself, "Chemitect" was picked out in low relief. The whole hive was faced with a specially treated sandstone, like some Nubian desert fortress.

"What goes on in there anyway?" asked Anne.

Carpenter paused with his hand on the Volkswagen's door. "It's a research foundation," he said. "There are a lot of college kids about, too. I think its function is partly educational."

"But what do they do?"

"I asked Horden that and he said, 'Anything and everything.' He speaks like that. He's actually got a plaque with 'THINK!' on the wall of his office. It's probably a joke though."

"What does it mean, 'Anything and everything'?"

Carpenter shrugged. "It doesn't bother me as long as *they* know what they're doing."

"Do they though," said Anne and Carpenter threw a playful punch at her and closed the Volkswagen's door. Anne watched him until he had entered the building.

Horden's office was windowless, snug in the core of the building, along a mirror-sleek, waxed corridor that made Carpenter feel as though he were walking on ice. He knocked on the door once and went in. Inside it was cool and the air conditioner blew out an artificial scent of pine. Horden was checking typed columns of figures. He looked up from his papers and nodded Carpenter to a seat. Carpenter sat looking at the plaque which said "THINK!" and finally decided he didn't understand it. On the opposite wall there was a print of an "impossible object," a spiral staircase that ate its own tail and spiraled downward (or upward) forever. It was rather easier to understand.

Horden shuffled his papers together and shifted his weight in his chair.

"Carpenter, isn't it? How does it feel to be one of the team?"

"It's okay. It's a job and jobs are hard enough to get. I'd feel a bit better if I knew what I was doing though."

"I don't understand."

"Watching a shiny steel box isn't exactly taxing work, mentally or physically. I could feel a bit more interested if I knew the point of the exercise. What's in the box? What's it for?"

"I can't tell you that."

"You *can't*?"

"I mean I don't know myself. My job is to hire administrative personnel for this establishment. I'm an administrator myself, not a scientist." Horden leaned back in his chair and fixed his gaze on the "THINK!" plaque. When he spoke his tone was almost nostalgic. "Once I was curious about Chemitect's role in society too. When I first came here. I knew its business was research, the kind of research that only makes the headlines in the technical press, but I thought it would be interesting to know a little more. A general view is always more rewarding than a narrow one, and like everybody else, I thought it would be nice, too, to be able to point to some gadget or scientific achievement and say, I played a small part in that. So I went on a grand tour of the various departments. I asked what the processes involved were and what the end results were supposed to be. Most of the scientific staff were pleased for an opportunity to explain their work, and when they weren't available the students always proved equally willing. They told me everything, explicitly, in the minutest detail. And do you know what?"

"What?"

"I didn't understand a word of it. Not a fact, not a theory, not a concept, not an idea. I never thought I was an exceptionally intelligent man, just normal, but to have kids of nineteen and twenty run mental rings round you is a frightening experience. I could arrange it for you if you feel you'd fare any better than I did. Do you want a grand tour?"

"No, I'm not looking for godlike knowledge. All I want to know is one very simple thing: what's in that box?"

Horden smiled and sighed. "And I must tell you again that I can't help you." He swiveled in his chair and switched his gaze from the "THINK!" plaque to the impossible object. His eyes seemed to follow the staircase in its eternal descent/ascent. Carpenter left the office.

Levinson was reading a newspaper. He was a small man with black nervous eyes that seemed to be perpetually flinching away from something nobody else could see. They flinched as they wandered across the newspaper columns and they flinched as they looked up to greet Carpenter.

"I'm sorry I'm late," Carpenter said. "I went to see Horden."

Levinson looked at his watch and dropped his newspaper to the floor. "I hadn't noticed," he said. "What did you see Horden about?"

"I wanted to know what we're all supposed to be watching the Box for. Don't *you* ever get curious?"

"I never think about it." Levinson stood up, stretching himself.

"How long have you been here?"

"Three-four months. It's only temporary, though. My uncle's got a delicatessen out east. He's going to die soon and leave it to me. Then I'll pack up and take my family the hell out of here."

"What's wrong with your uncle?"

"Bad heart. He's just going to fold up someday."

"I'm sorry."

"No, he's been like it for years. I'm over that now. He's going to die soon though. Real soon."

He left and Carpenter settled himself awkwardly in the chair. He picked up Levinson's newspaper and began leafing through it. He glossed through articles on how the population growth curve was leveling out at last and on how the unemployment curve continued to skyrocket. There was an article on suicide as well but he didn't bother to read that.

After ten minutes he put the newspaper aside. His back was stiff from the chair and he stood and walked over to the Box. He put a hand on its side. It was pleasantly cool and he thought he detected a slight vibration. He put his ear to the Box but could hear nothing.

The fungus was a green patch about the size of a hand. It appeared one morning on the wall above the prisoner's pallet. The prisoner moved his pallet into the opposite corner of the cell and a cockroach fell from the bedding, scuttling about on the dusty floor of the cell, as trapped as he was. He watched it with interest. He formed barriers in its path, diverting it, making it trek from location to location in the cell. He shook his bedding and succeeded in dislodging a second insect. He picked a cotton thread out of his shirt and tied one end around the thorax of each of the cockroaches. The cockroaches circled about each other, weaving the cotton into complex knots, occasionally indulging in a comic, scrabbling tug-of-war that would leave them quiescent for a while, as if dazed.

The day passed quicker than usual. That night he allowed the insects to return to the safety of the bedding. He slept fitfully. It seemed colder than usual and he dreamt that cockroaches swarmed on his body. He wanted to run, to shake them off, but he was tied down and wore the insect bodies like a suit until it seemed to him that he himself had become an insect.

He awoke at dawn, sweating. When he shook his bedding seven chitinous bodies fell to the floor like dry leaves. He killed them all in a fit of disgust but regretted it almost immediately.

It was distinctly colder in the cell. The drop in temperature prickled his skin and made him shiver. He ate the warm soup greedily when it was served and hoisted himself up to the window slit. There seemed to be a change in the quality of the light outside. It was hazier, grey, the sky itself seemed colder. It was winter's initial foray into a long, timeless autumn.

Days passed and the cell became a beachhead for the cold's attack on his body. Everything he touched seemed dead and inert. Warmth drained quickly from the soup when it was served, and it was cold and unnourishing before he finished it. Only very rarely now could he muster the strength to pull himself up to the window slit, and when he did, the sight was never encouraging, merely the usual empty expanse of cold sky.

He begged through the dinner slit for extra clothing or a small stove to heat the cell, but there was never any response. The cold affected his feet worst of all. When he awoke in the morning, there was no sensation in them, and the skin always seemed pasty and colorless. He forced himself to walk to restore some feeling in them, dragging them across the icy stone floor until they bled.

Occasionally he heard the sound of rain blustering outside the cell. He would have liked to see it, to feel the water on his skin, but he had to save his strength for the endless automatic hobble from cell wall to cell wall.

Day followed day and he began to hope that during the night his frozen body would finally sink through the surface of sleep to death. He always awoke, however. There was always another day.

The fungus continued to spread. Now its mottled pattern covered one wall and half the ceiling.

Winter came suddenly, early, with a severe uncharacteristic blizzard that left the city snowbound for a day. The heating in his apartment was inadequate and Carpenter began to long for the controlled warmth of Chemitect. Anne called him to say she would come over. She lived on the other side of the city and he told her not to bother, traveling was impossible. But she said she had to see him. It was important.

She arrived two hours later with snow melting into beads of moisture on her hair. Carpenter kissed her. "You're cold," he said, touching her cheek. "You shouldn't have come. What was so important?"

He helped her off with her coat and she opened her handbag and took out a newspaper clipping headed "The Loneliest Man in the World." She gave it to him. "This."

"Where did this come from?"

"I was clearing out some old newspapers and it caught my eye. It's about six months old. Read it."

He read: "Today Richard Crofton Keller enters an eight-foot square cell at the Chemitect Research Foundation to become the loneliest man in the world. Keller, a thirty-four-year-old, unmarried ex-bartender, will spend eighteen months in voluntary solitary confinement in an attempt to discover the effects of prolonged periods of isolation. Dr. Thomas S. Maynard, in charge of the project, explained: 'Keller will be fed, nourished and cared for by completely automatic systems built into the cell and during the term of his confinement he will have no contact whatsoever with the outside world. Experiments of this nature have been carried out in the past, but we believe this will be the first time in which the subject will be isolated in any absolute sense. Keller won't even possess what is popularly termed a "chicken switch." He will have no means to curtail the experiment should he feel it is going badly. We are using body sensors and other devices to record his behavior and condition, but will have no means of monitoring these while the experiment is in progress. This may seem inhumane but we feel the step is psychologically necessary if the experiment is to have any validity at all. Because this is the first time anything like this has been attempted we're naturally reluctant to discuss the possible results of the experiment. It is, however, basically intended to provide information of use in the treatment of a wide range of schizophrenic and other mental disorders stemming from isolation and alienation in society.' "

Anne took the cutting from him when he had finished it. "I don't think you should go back there," she said.

Carpenter found himself shivering and moved nearer the orange glow of the apartment's electric heater. "What do you mean? I've got to go back. Horden *must* have known about this. He lied to me."

"The job's not important," Anne said. "Not a job like that."

Carpenter turned to her. "What do you mean the job's not important? A couple of weeks ago you were glad I'd got it."

"Don't shout at me, hon."

"I'm sorry," Carpenter said. "I'm upset about Horden

lying to me. Why would he do a thing like that?
Deliberately keeping me in the dark." He put his arms
around her, wrapping her slight figure in his body. "Do
you want me to quit the job?"

"It's the thought of that poor man," Anne said. "I don't
like the idea of you as some kind of jailer. I didn't think
you'd want to be used that way either."

For a moment they stood together wordless and sway-
ing slightly, enjoying the warmth of each other's body.
Then Anne broke away almost guiltily. "Think about it,
hon," she said.

"I will. I will."

One morning the prisoner awoke and knew it could not
go on. There was no purpose in remaining alive, in dragging his body through the torture of extreme cold or in
dragging his mind through the torture of exhausted
memories. The memories had sustained him at one time,
but they were scanty and largely morbid glimpses of a
childhood that had never seemed happy and of an adulthood that had so far been a chronicle of failure, of drifting from job to job and worthless relationship to worthless
relationship. The more he reran these scenes in his mind
the more unreal they seemed, like the less-than-credible
plot of a particularly melodramatic movie. The movie
faded out into mental blankness sometime before his im-
prisonment and picked up again sometime after, when existence was his cell and memory was no real memory at all
but merely days running out like identical grains of sand.
The terminal memory was a suitably bizarre one. He had
once run a bar, a dim basement grotto beneath a pawn-
broker's in the slum area of the city. He remembered a
poet, a young Jesus-haired character (who knows, he
might have thought himself the messiah of his age) who
used the bar's toilet to fix himself and then came to sit and
talk to him while the heroin worked in his blood, an untouched beer before him for appearances. He talked about
things the bartender could understand: disillusionment, a
lifetime of bad breaks and unkind people. He talked about
what it was like to poison yourself with heroin until the
kick began to kick you back, until it became a necessity

like air. It was a form of suicide, the poet said, suicide without real decision, an easy suicide for people with weak minds. The bartender asked him if it was really any different from drinking yourself to death or, for that matter, driving a car until statistics singled you out as one of the *x* percent killed every year in motor accidents. The poet merely smiled and said no, he supposed all life for everybody was one prolonged suicide, that you started killing yourself on the day you were born.

The poet had once given the bartender a book of poems. They were by T. S. Eliot and the bartender had put the book aside, saying he didn't read poetry. One morning he'd just opened up the bar when there was a scream of brakes outside. He went up to the road where a small crowd was already beginning to form. A big saloon was wedged diagonally across the road. Its rear fender had scraped paint from three cars parked along the opposite curb. Something was wedged under the rear wheels and the bartender saw it was the young poet. The driver, a plump man in a neat business suit, was leaning on the car's open door. His face was streaked with blood from a cut on his forehead and he was appealing to the bystanders. "The kid must have been crazy . . . He just stepped out in front of me. Did he want to get killed or something? What was I supposed to do? You saw it, didn't you? Didn't you?"

The bartender went back to the bar. He remembered the Eliot poems and found the book. He read one called "Rhapsody on a Windy Night," which ended:

> The lamp said,
> "Four o'clock,
> Here is the number on the door.
> Memory!
> You have the key,
> The little lamp spreads a ring on the stair.
> Mount.
> The bed is open; the tooth-brush hangs on the wall,
> Put your shoes at the door, sleep, prepare for life."
>
> The last twist of the knife.

He didn't understand the poem, except that it seemed black and pessimistic, somehow a suitable epitaph for the young poet.

Memory faded. . . .

Perhaps it was a suitable epitaph for him too, the prisoner thought. The cold would kill him eventually, he knew, but he was afraid of the discomfort and suffering and that it would take too long. He dwelt on the fear. Briefly it seemed to warm him, but soon it was just another stale taste in his mouth. He realized that he wasn't afraid, after all, and that he had come to an acceptance of what he had to do. It wasn't fear that led to suicide, he realized, but a lack of fear and a lack of any prospect of ever experiencing fear again.

He took off his shirt and tore it clumsily with numbed fingers into strips. He tied the strips together until he had formed a serviceable rope several feet long. He tied one end tightly about his neck.

He went to stand beneath the small barred window slit. It required an almost superhuman effort to pull himself up to the slit, but he reflected that it would be the last effort ever required of him and jumped, wedging one hand into the slit and grabbing a bar with his cold fingers. The stone lip of the window cut at his wrist, sending shooting pains along his arm, but he hoisted himself up until he came abreast of the slit. Quickly he tied the rope's other end around one of the bars. The strength was slipping rapidly out of his arms as he pulled the knot tight. He took a last look out of the slit. The sky was as cold and grey and hopeless as ever and with his last remaining strength he threw himself backward from the wall.

Carpenter dropped the cutting on Horden's desk. Horden glanced at it briefly and said: "I see."

"Why didn't you tell me, Horden? You must have known what was going on."

"Yes, I knew. But you're making it sound unnecessarily sinister. . . ."

"I've reason. You lied to me."

"I told you a harmless untruth, yes. I didn't see why such things should concern you. I still don't. Really, does it matter? You were happy enough doing the job when you didn't know about it. Does this really change anything?"

Carpenter went to the door. He felt confused by Horden's questions. "A job's a job," he said, "even if I don't particularly like myself for doing it. I don't like being lied to, that's all."

Horden waited until Carpenter had left the office; then he leaned forward and pushed a button on his intercom.

Carpenter went down to the Box to find Elleston on duty.

"Where's Levinson?" he asked. It disturbed him to find a familiar routine interrupted. "Is he sick?"

"More than sick," Elleston said. "He's dead."

"Dead?" For a second the word genuinely puzzled Carpenter, like a case of *jamais vu*.

"Yeah, the poor little kike. Apparently he collapsed in the street yesterday, in the snow. He should never have gone out, not in that sort of weather, not with a heart condition like his."

"He had a heart condition? I never knew that."

"Yeah, he'd had a bad heart for years. He must have known it would catch up with him sooner or later."

Carpenter felt a profound sorrow for the small, nervous Jew. He wondered if Levinson's uncle really owned a delicatessen out east. Probably not. There had probably never even been an uncle.

"Well, I'm going to grab some rest," Elleston said. "I sure hope they can get somebody to replace him soon."

"They will," Carpenter said. "There's always somebody."

Elleston nodded and left.

Carpenter approached the Box. He wondered what Keller was doing at this moment, what he was thinking. Perhaps he was asleep. He tried to imagine what six months in isolation would do to *him,* but it was unimaginable. Like trying to imagine death, he thought. Surely no man could endure such isolation and remain sane? What sort of man would volunteer for something like that anyway, something that would very likely destroy him? A disappointed man? An idealistic man? He remembered what he had told Elleston: "There's always somebody."

He ran his fingers along the seam of the Box's door. The man *had* volunteered, but there still remained a moral question. The full burden of it lay upon the scientists who had devised the experiment, but Carpenter carried some of it on his own shoulders. Ought Keller to be held to his voluntary decision, a decision almost certainly made without full knowledge of the consequences? Absently, experimentally, Carpenter took a coin from his pocket and tried it in one of the bolts that secured the door's time lock. He twisted and the countersunk bolt turned easily. He gave it several turns. He watched the bolt as it threaded smoothly away from the covering plate and felt suddenly dizzy. *What was he doing?* If he freed Keller, he possibly freed a man with no desire to be free. And he certainly lost a job that paid good, regular wages. Carpenter screwed the bolt back firmly and dropped the coin into his pocket.

He went back to his seat by the wall and noticed for the first time, with some irony, that Horden had at last replaced the chair. The new one was larger and fully upholstered. Carpenter settled himself into it comfortably. He had only been watching the Box for a few minutes when a stranger in a white lab coat arrived, accompanied by a tired-looking, disgruntled Elleston.

"Are you Carpenter?" the stranger asked. "Will you come with me?"

Carpenter looked questioningly at Elleston, who merely shrugged and took Carpenter's place in the chair. Carpenter followed the stranger along quiet corridors to an office practically identical to Horden's. Instead of an impossible object, however, there was a print of Brueghel's "Massacre of the Innocents" on the wall. The stranger sat behind the desk and Carpenter sat opposite.

"Cigarette?" The stranger offered him a box in which cigarettes and cigars lay partitioned and segregated. Carpenter declined and the stranger took a small cigar and lit it from a desk lighter that reminded Carpenter of a miniature version of the Box. It was shiny chromium. The stranger tapped its top and a lid opened automatically.

Automatically a second, smaller box rose from within the first. Its lid, in turn, opened to reveal a third box which rose up, its uppermost surface glowing like a hot plate. The stranger touched it to his cigar, smiling. "Chinese boxes. It's a favorite toy of mine. My name is Maynard. Horden has asked me to speak to you, to explain why we have to fire you."

"I don't understand."

"You've shown yourself to be disturbed by certain aspects of the work," Maynard said. "It would be dangerous to let you remain."

"Dangerous in what way?"

"Dangerous to the experiment and possibly dangerous to you. It would be a pity, for instance, if you got it into your head to try and release Keller."

"Why should I do that?"

"Not everybody has the mentality of a prison warden, Carpenter, which is in effect what you're expected to be. For certain people—I'd say for practically everybody these days—it goes against the grain. That is why Horden had to lie to you. He has standing orders to conceal the nature of the work whenever possible." Maynard looked at Carpenter through a haze of cigar smoke. "You see, we live in a liberal society, a society educated in the politics of freedom and human rights. It's not always possible to find people who will accept the role this particular job calls for." He smiled. "It's true of the job situation as a whole these days. Education is more than assimilating facts. It's acquiring a whole system of behavioral rules and values. At the present period of history people have been educated to expect a better deal than society can manage to give them. Hence unemployment and unrest. There are too many well-qualified people going after too few really worthwhile jobs.

"You look surprised, but I should have thought you'd have realized this yourself, Carpenter. You're no fool. You're smart. Not so many years ago you wouldn't have been chasing dead-end jobs. You'd have held some senior management post. Now, however, there are too many people like you. And everybody can't be in management."

Carpenter nodded. "Perhaps I did realize it all along. But it's not an easy thing to accept."

Maynard took a packet from his desk and gave it to Carpenter. "Here's a month's pay. What's the matter? You don't look too happy."

"It's just one thing that still puzzles me about the Box. You said in that article that Keller was going to be isolated for eighteen months, that he'd be taken care of by various gadgets inside the box and also that he'd have no way of curtailing the experiment himself. When Horden gave me the job, he said it involved watching for anything 'untoward,' but it seems to me you've got the untoward pretty well sewn up. What's the point of hiring people to watch a foolproof system? Is it just making jobs for the unemployed?"

"No. It's an essential safety measure. You see, there *is* one way Keller can curtail the experiment although not directly through an act of his own will. It's a way he didn't even know about. We don't monitor his life functions, but they're linked directly to the time lock. If, for some reason, they become critical or indeed, stop, then the door automatically opens."

Carpenter felt sick. "You mean the only way he could escape would be by committing suicide. Is that likely?"

"By no means likely, but possible. There are so many unknown factors in this experiment and we have to cover every eventuality. Almost certainly he'll fantasize and some of the fantasies may involve symbolic suicide. From that it's only a small step to the real thing."

Carpenter swore at Maynard, dragging up the most considered, unsubtle epithet he could think of. "There's another reason you employ people to watch that Box," he said. "You're the prison wardens, Maynard, you and your kind, but you need someone to take over your role. You hope it will absolve you of responsibility but it won't. And I think you know it won't."

He stood and went to the door. Behind him he heard a voice squawk from Maynard's intercom. It was Horden and he sounded overexcited. There was another voice in the background, possibly Elleston's. Carpenter didn't pause to hear what they were saying. He was afraid he knew and he hated himself because he knew he could have prevented it. He left the building, walking past the basalt fountain and across the campus to the highway. Above him the sky was grey and cold like the underside of a great steel lid.

GENE WOLFE

A METHOD BIT IN "B"

I suppose it was because I had attended a film just before
going on duty. I have the late tick—what we occasionally
call the "graveyard" tick—and that makes it possible for
me to visit the one cinema our little village boasts before I
go on. Since a new film comes not more than fortnightly, I
don't indulge myself in this way often.

The fog had been extraordinarily thick. We have a great
deal of fog in every month of the year; still, that night was
exceptional. I remember stepping in through the doors of
the station house and having it roll past me in great
billows as though it were being blown from behind me;
and that is strange, because now that this terrible business
at the manor house is over, or nearly over, that is the first
moment I can recall clearly. It's as if all my previous life
were nothing more than a preparation for holding the
dying girl in my arms out there on the moors, or looking
into the man's horror-ravaged face. When I try to recall
anything else, service experiences from the four years I
spent in the Glousters for example, or something that has
happened during the time I've lived here in the village

184

(Stoke-on-Wold is what we call it), nothing seems to have taken place at all.

You won't find our little village on any map. Too small, I suppose. So when the new guest came to the manor it created a great deal of foolish talk—and ever since I was sworn in as a constable (the proudest day of my life, I might add), I have considered it a part of my duties to listen to that sort of talk. He was a big man, with a face somewhat like a St. Bernard's that has worms, and would come into the public bar of the Royal James some nights just before closing and drink a glass or two of cognac and watch the moon through the big mullion window. It wasn't full then, but what they call gibbous, meaning between the half and the full, and growing with every turn of the clock, like a bad girl without a ring. Talbot was what they said his name was, and he was an American.

That night, the first night I can really remember, as I told you, nothing to speak of occurred until just a trifle after midnight. Then the 'phone rang, and it was Wilkes, the butler at the manor. The poor chap was so taken I could hardly make out what he was saying, but I could tell it was serious and I hopped on my bike and pedaled out there. The fog had lifted from the high ground but it was still as thick as porridge in the low spots and looked silver-white in the moonlight—not yellow like one of your London fogs.

Breakchain House is the manor's right name, though it isn't used much. The legend that goes with that name is ugly enough that most of us in Stoke-on-Wold don't want to be reminded of it. Except when we can afflict it on trippers. (But then you're a kind of tripper yourself, aren't you? Thumbing your way through the pages.) It's a castle, really, to which a Georgian wing—they call it the "new wing"—has been added. No one lives in the old part now; at least, no one the people in the new wing want to talk about.

Wilkes answered the door for me, still white as paste; I had him assemble everyone in the library in the usual way. Besides Lord and Lady Breakchain, there was a very pretty Yank girl named Betty, and Talbot, and a Prof. Smith. This Smith was a striking-looking gent who called himself "a student of the occult." I noticed that he carried a cane with a heavy silver knob shaped like a wolf's head; that was unusual, of course, since in a place like the manor one usually gives one's stick to the butler—although I had kept my cosh.

I won't bore you with what was said in the library that night about the unearthly howling that had been heard on the moor or the thing Wilkes and the girl had seen lapping water from the fountain in the garden at midnight, since none of that really bears on what's bothering me now. But when I left there and rode back to the village I saw lights at the James, and thinking of that does put me off a bit. You see, the bar was open, just like any roadhouse in the States, and the barmaid and the owner didn't seem to have any fear of losing the license either, not even when I walked in, even though it was hours after closing.

What was more, they'd quite a number of patrons, late as it was, as if everyone had known the place would be open. Just now I was on the point of saying the patrons were ordinary enough village people, but they weren't, really. Every person for miles around that had something odd or comic about him, something that perhaps might make a stranger laugh, was there. And none of the others were.

The girl behind the bar too. A big strapping blonde. You'd expect her to be sour at having to work late like that and miss her beauty sleep; but she was chipper as a wren, pulling the old Major's long mustaches and making jokes with everyone. I didn't say anything about closing, but took a place at the bar and ordered a pint of the dark. When she brought it, I thought for a second or two that I'd come to the bottom of it all, but afterward I was more at sea than ever.

You see, the stuff in the tankard she brought me wasn't beer at all, but a kind of foaming ginger drink or some such slop. When I tasted it first I nearly spit it out on the floor, but then, as I said, for a moment I thought I had the whole game. "Going to have a good 'un on the law," I thought to myself, "when I tries to tag 'em for servin' after closin' hours they'd give me the proper laugh and claim none of this stuff's alcoholic." But then I looked around, and so help me none of it was! I couldn't hardly believe my eyes, and when the Major left for a bit of a go at the WC, I took up his brandy and sniffed it and tasted it, and it was nothing but tea—nasty, bad, cold tea at that. It was the same with everyone. Those that was supposed to have beer had the same slops they'd served me, and those that was drinking whiskey or what-not had tea. Of course I should have piped up right then and said, " 'Ere now, isn't there a one of you blighters with more sense than to sit up drinkin' this 'ere sweet bilge at two o'clock in the mornin'?" But I didn't. For the first few minutes I didn't because I expected they'd have the laugh on me, and after that it was because I felt it in my bones they'd say I'd gone crackers and call the sergeant to have me locked up.

Talking to one and another I tried to hint around about it, but it was no go. Nobody wanted to talk about anything except Talbot and what was happening out at the manor. Finally I told them what I had heard out there that night, very official about it so they wouldn't think I was just spreading rumors, and, crikey! when I did, every one of them did just what it was he was famous for. The Major coughed and talked in his throat like a sheep so that no one could understand what he was saying, Harry Dorsey the barber swallowed so you could see the Adam's apple bounce in his long neck, the barmaid patted her hair and said something smart and tartish, and so on.

That was the beginning of it, I suppose. That and the cinema and the time I walked by the widow Perry's window and happened to glance in. Of course that wasn't until later, but then the whole month, the month between the first call out to the manor and the second one, seemed just to pass in a dream anyway. I suppose I performed my regular duties, but I don't remember it. All I was really thinking about was coming into the station house with all the fog blowing past me that time, and how the folk in the village never seemed to have anything to do but gossip now. Also—I know this is going to sound queer, but I can't explain it better—how badly all of us spoke. Some, I mean, as though they were cockneys right out of Cheapside although they were born and raised here. And others like Canadians or even Yanks. I found I was doing it myself.

What I'm getting at is that the film set me thinking about how those method actor chaps are supposed to take a part—create a role is what they call it—and really make themselves believe they're the person. As I understand it, if one of the method chaps is supposed to be a sea captain, for example, he'll bloody well force his mind to believe he fairly *is* that captain.

Now when he's the captain, if you take my meaning, how does he feel about it, eh?

Does he like thinking that when the film's over he's going to be that twirpy little method chap again, not knowing the tiller from the main brace? Or does he even know it?

You see, it seems to me that almost the only thing I'm good for in the village here is going out to the manor as I did tonight to sort of wrap things up officially when all the dust has settled, like tonight when this Prof. Smith winged poor old Talbot with one of his silver—and a rum idea that is if you ask me—bullets and I made my speech about how the best thing would be for me not to report the goings-on at all for fear there'd be a panic. What bothers me, you see, is not watching all that hair come off Talbot's face and his teeth shrink up to normal ones again —that seems right enough, now that the Professor's explained it all—but that when I looked into the widow Perry's window there wasn't any insides to her house. Just empty ground, if you understand me, and weeds.

Don't *you* ever get the feeling that there are things in the world—hydrogen bombs and Moon probes for example, and civilized people who paint flowers on their faces—which only belong in a "B" film? How do you know that we're both not in one? Now that things at the manor seem to be about wound up, I'm getting this rotten feeling that if I was to climb up onto the hill yonder to look out over the moors, I might see a palm tree.

R. A. LAFFERTY

INTERURBAN QUEEN

"It was the year 1907 when I attained my majority and came into a considerable inheritance," the old man said. "I was a very keen young man, keen enough to know that I didn't know everything. I went to knowledgeable men and asked their advice as to how I might invest this inheritance.

"I talked with bankers and cattlemen and the new oilmen. These were not stodgy men. They had an edge on the future, and they were excited and exciting about the way that money might be made to grow. It was the year of statehood and there was an air of prosperity over the new state. I wished to integrate my patrimony into that new prosperity.

"Finally I narrowed my choice to two investments which then seemed about of equal prospect, though you will now smile to hear them equated. One of them was the stock-selling company of a certain Harvey Goodrich, a rubber company, and with the new automobile coming into wider use, it seemed that rubber might be a thing of the future. The other was a stock-selling transportation com-

189

pany that proposed to run an interurban railway between the small towns of Kiefer and Mounds. It also proposed (at a future time) to run branches to Glenpool, to Bixby, to Kellyville, to Slick, to Bristow, to Beggs, even to Okmulgee and Sapulpa. At that time it also seemed that these little interurban railways might be things of the future. An interurban already ran between Tulsa and Sand Springs, and one was building between Tulsa and Sapulpa. There were more than one thousand of these small trolley railroads operating in the nation, and thoughtful men believed that they would come to form a complete national network, might become the main system of transportation."

But now the old man Charles Archer was still a young man. He was listening to Joe Elias, a banker in a small but growing town.

"It is a riddle you pose me, young man, and you set me thinking," Elias said. "We have dabbled in both, thinking to have an egg under every hen. I begin to believe that we were wrong to do so. These two prospects are types of two futures, and only one of them will obtain. In this state with its new oil discoveries, it might seem that we should be partial to rubber which has a tie-in with the automobile which has a tie-in with petroleum fuel. This need not be. I believe that the main use of oil will be in powering the new factories, and I believe that rubber is already oversold as to industrial application. And yet there *will be* a new transportation. Between the horse and the main-line railways there is a great gap. I firmly believe that the horse will be eliminated as a main form of transportation. We are making no more loans to buggy or buckboard manufacturers nor to harness makers. I have no faith in the automobile. It destroys something in me. It is the interurbans that will go into the smallest localities, and will so cut into the main-line railroads as to leave no more than a half dozen of the long-distance major lines in America. Young man, I would invest in the interurban with complete confidence."

Charles Archer was listening to Carl Bigheart, a cattleman.

"I ask you, boy, how many head of cattle can you put into an automobile? Or even into what they call a lorry or trook? Then I ask you how many you can put into an honest cattle car which can be coupled onto any interurban on a country run? The interurban will be the salvation of us cattlemen. With the fencing regulations we cannot drive cattle even twenty miles to a railroad; but the little interurbans will go into the deep country, running along every second or third section line.

"And I will tell you another thing, boy: there is no future for the automobile. *We cannot let there be!* Consider the man on horseback, and I have been a man on horseback for most of my life. Well, mostly he is a good man, but there is a change in him as soon as he mounts. Every man on horseback is an arrogant man, however gentle he may be on foot. I know this in myself and in others. He was necessary in his own time, and I believe that time is ending. There was always extreme danger from the man on horseback.

"Believe me, young man, the man in the automobile is one thousand times as dangerous. The kindest man in the world assumes an incredible arrogance when he drives an automobile, and this arrogance will increase still further if the machine is allowed to develop greater power and sophistication. I tell you, it will engender absolute selfishness in mankind if the driving of automobiles becomes common. It will breed violence on a scale never seen before. It will mark the end of the family as we know it, the three or four generations living happily in one home. It will destroy the sense of neighborhood and the true sense of nation. It will create giantized cankers of cities, false opulence of suburbs, ruinized countryside, and unhealthy conglomeration of specialized farming and manufacturing. It will breed rootlessness and immorality. It will make every man a tyrant. I believe the private automobile will be suppressed. *It will have to be!* This is a moral problem, and we are a moral nation and world; we will take moral action against it. And without the automobile, rubber has no real future. Opt for the interurban stock, young man."

Young Charles Archer was listening to Nolan Cushman, an oilman.

"I will not lie to you, young fellow, I love the automobile, the motorcar. I have three, custom-built. I am an emperor when I drive. Hell, I'm an emperor anyhow! I bought a castle last summer that had housed emperors. I'm having it transported, stone by stone, to my place in the Osage. Now, as to the motorcar, I can see how it should develop. It should develop with the roads, they becoming leveled and metaled or concreted, and the cars lower and lower and faster and faster. We would develop them so, if we were some species other than human. It is the logical development, but I hope it will not come, and it will not. That would be to make it common, and the commonality of men cannot be trusted with this power. Besides, I love a high car, and I do not want there to be very many of them. They should only be allowed to men of extreme wealth and flair. How would it be if the workingmen were ever permitted them? It would be murderous if they should come into the hands of ordinary men. How hellish a world would it be if all men should become as arroagnt as myself! No, the automobile will never be anything but a rich man's pride, the rubber will never be anything but a limited adjunct to that special thing. Invest in your interurban. It is the thing of the future, or else I dread that future."

Young Charles Archer knew that this was a crossroads of the world. Whichever turning was taken, it would predicate a certain sort of nation and world and humanity. He thought about it deeply. Then he decided. He went out and invested his entire inheritance in his choice.

"I considered the two investments and I made my choice," said Charles Archer, the old man now in the now present. "I put all I had into it, thirty-five thousand dollars, a considerable sum in those days. You know the results."

"I am one of the results, Great-grandfather," said Angela Archer. "If you had invested differently you would have come to different fortune, you would have married differently, and I would be different or not at all. I like me here and now. I like everything as it is."

Three of them were out riding early one Saturday morning, the old man Charles Archer, his great-granddaughter Angela, and her fiancé Peter Brady. They were riding through the quasiurbia, the rich countryside. It was not a main road, and yet it had a beauty (partly natural and partly contrived) that was as exciting as it was satisfying.

Water always beside the roadway, that was the secret! There were the carp ponds one after another. There were the hatcheries. There were the dancing rocky streams that in a less enlightened age might have been mere gutter runs or roadway runs. There were the small and rapid trout streams, and boys were catching big trout from them.

There were the deep bush-trees there, sumac, witch hazel, sassafras—incense trees they might almost have been. There were the great trees themselves, pecan and hickory and black walnut, standing like high backdrops; and between were the lesser trees, willow, cottonwood, sycamore. Catheads and sedge grass and reeds stood in the water itself, and tall Sudan grass and bluestem on the shores. And always the clovers there, and the smell of wet sweet clover.

"I chose the wrong one," said old Charles Archer as they rode along through the textured country. "One can now see how grotesque was my choice, but I was young. In two years, the stock-selling company in which I had invested was out of business and my loss was total. So early and easy riches were denied me, but I developed an ironic hobby: keeping track of the stock of the enterprise in which I did *not* invest. The stock I could have bought for thirty-five thousand dollars would now make me worth nine million dollars."

"Ugh, don't talk of such a thing on such a beautiful day," Angela objected.

"They heard another of them last night," Peter Brady commented. "They've been hearing this one, off and on, for a week now, and haven't caught him yet."

"I always wish they wouldn't kill them when they catch them," Angela bemoaned. "It doesn't seem quite right to kill them."

A goose-girl was herding her white honking charges as they gobbled weeds out of fields of morning onions. Flowering kale was shining green-purple, and okra plants were standing. Jersey cows grazed along the roadway, and the patterned plastic (almost as patterned as the grasses) filled the roadway itself.

There were clouds like yellow dust in the air. Bees! Stingless bees they were. But dust itself was not. That there never be dust again!

"They will have to find out and kill the sly klunker makers," said old man Charles Archer. "Stop the poison at its source."

"There's too many of them, and too much money in it," said Peter Brady. "Yes, we kill them. One of them was found and killed Thursday, and three nearly finished klunkers were destroyed. But we can't kill them all. They seem to come out of the ground like snakes."

"I wish we didn't have to kill them," Angela said.

There were brightly colored firkins of milk standing on loading stoas, for this was a milk shed. There were chickens squawking in nine-story-high coops as they waited the pickups, but they never had to wait long. Here were a thousand dozen eggs on a refrigeration porch; there a clutch of piglings, or of red steers.

Tomato plants were staked two meters high. Sweet corn stood, not yet come to tassel. They passed cucumber vines and canteloupe vines, and the potato hills rising up blue-green. Ah, there were grapevines in their tight acres, deep alfalfa meadows, living fences of Osage orange and white-thorn. Carrot tops zephyred like green lace. Cattle were grazing fields of red clover and of peanuts—that most magic of all clovers. Men mowed hay.

"I hear him now!" Peter Brady said suddenly.

"You couldn't. Not in the daytime. Don't even think of such a thing," Angela protested.

Farm ducks were grazing with their heads under water in the roadway ponds and farm ponds. Bower oaks grew high in the roadway parks. Sheep fed in hay grazer that was higher than their heads; they were small white islands in it. There was local wine and choc beer and cider for sale at small booths, along with limestone sculpture and

painted fruitwood carvings. Kids danced on loading stoas
to little post-mounted music canisters, and goats licked
slate outcroppings in search of some new mineral.

The Saturday riders passed a roadway restaurant with
its tables out under the leaves and under a little rock
overhang. A one-meter-high waterfall gushed through the
middle of the establishment, and a two-meter-long bridge
of set shale stone led to the kitchen. Then they broke onto
view after never-tiring view of the rich and varied quasiurbia. The roadway forms, the fringe farms, the berry
patches! In their seasons: Juneberries, huckleberries, blueberries, dewberries, elderberries, highbush cranberries, red
raspberries, boysenberries, loganberries, nine kinds of
blackberries, strawberries, greenberries.

Orchards! Can there ever be enough orchards? Plum,
peach, sand plum and chokecherry, black cherry, apple
and crab apple, pear, blue-fruited pawpaw, persimmon,
crooked quince. Melon patches, congregations of bee-
hives, pickle patches, cheese farms, flax farms, close
clustered towns (twenty houses in each, twenty persons in
a house, twenty of the little settlements along every mile
of roadway, country honkey-tonks, as well as high-dog
clubs already open and hopping with action in the early
morning; roadway chapels with local statuary and with
their rich-box-poor-boxes (one dropped money in the top
if one had it and the spirit to give it, one tripped it out the
bottom if one needed it), and the little refrigeration
niches with bread, cheese, beef rolls, and always the
broached cask of country wine: that there be no more
hunger on the roadways forever!

"I hear it too!" old Charles Archer cried out suddenly.
"High-pitched and off to the left. And there's the smell of
monoxide and—gah—rubber. Conductor, conductor!"

The conductor heard it, as did others in the car. The
conductor stopped the cars to listen. Then he phoned the
report and gave the location as well as he might, consulting with the passengers. There was rough country over to
the left, rocks and hills, and someone was driving there in
broad daylight.

The conductor broke out rifles from the locker, passing
them out to Peter Brady and two other young men in the

car, and to three men in each of the other two cars. A competent-seeming man took over the communication, talking to men on a line further to the left, beyond the mad driver, and they had him boxed into a box no more than half a mile square.

"You stay, Angela, and you stay, Grandfather Archer," Peter Brady said. "Here is a little thirty carbine. Use it if he comes in range at all. We hunt him down now." Then Peter Brady followed the conductor and the rifle-bearing men, ten men on a death hunt. And there were now four other groups out on the hunt, converging on their whining, coughing target.

"Why do they have to kill them, Great-grandfather? Why not turn them over to the courts?"

"The courts are too lenient. All they give them is life in prison."

"But surely that should be enough. It will keep them from driving the things, and some of the unfortunate men might even be rehabilitated."

"Angela, they are the greatest prison breakers ever. Only ten days ago, Mad Man Gudge killed three guards, went over the wall at State Prison, evaded all pursuit, robbed the cheesemakers' cooperative of fifteen thousand dollars, got to a sly klunker maker, and was driving one of the things in a wild area within thirty hours of his breakout. It was four days before they found him and killed him. They are insane, Angela, and the mental hospitals are already full of them. Not one of them has ever been rehabilitated."

"Why is it so bad that they should drive? They usually drive only in the very wild places, and for a few hours in the middle of the night."

"Their madness is infectious, Angela. Their arrogance would leave no room for anything else in the world. Our country is now in balance, our communication and travel is minute and near perfect, thanks to the wonderful trolleys and the people of the trolleys. We are all one neighborhood, we are all one family! We live in love and compassion, with few rich and few poor, and arrogance and hatred have all gone out from us. We are the people with roots, and with trolleys. We are one with our earth."

"Would it hurt that the drivers should have their own limited place to do what they wanted, if they did not bother sane people?"

"Would it hurt if disease and madness and evil were given their own limited place? But they will not stay in their place, Angela. There is the diabolical arrogance in them, the rampant individualism, the hatred of order. There can be nothing more dangerous to society than the man in the automobile. Were they allowed to thrive, there would be poverty and want again, Angela, and wealth and accumulation. And cities."

"But cities are the most wonderful things of all! I love to go to them."

"I do not mean the wonderful Excursion Cities, Angela. There would be cities of another and blacker sort. They were almost upon us once when a limitation was set on them. Uniqueness is lost in them; there would be mere accumulation of rootless people, of arrogant people, of duplicated people, of people who have lost their humanity. Let them never rob us of our involuted countryside, or our quasiurbia. We are not perfect; but what we have, we will not give away for the sake of wild men."

"The smell! I cannot stand it!"

"Monoxide. How would you like to be born in the smell of it, to live every moment of your life in the smell of it, to die in the smell of it?"

"No, no, not that."

The rifleshots were scattered but serious. The howling and coughing of the illicit klunker automobile were nearer. Then it was in sight, bouncing and bounding weirdly out of the rough rock area and into the tomato patches straight toward the trolley interurban.

The klunker automobile was on fire, giving off ghastly stench of burning leather and rubber and noxious monoxide and seared human flesh. The man, standing up at the broken wheel, was a madman, howling, out of his head. He was a young man, but sunken-eyed and unshaven, bloodied on the left side of his head and the left side of his breast, foaming with hatred and arrogance.

"Kill me! Kill me!" he croaked like clattering broken

thunder. "There will be others! We will not leave off driving so long as there is one desolate place left, so long as
there is one sly klunker maker left!"

He went rigid. He quivered. He was shot again. But he
would die howling.

"Damn you all to trolley haven! A man in an
automobile is worth a thousand men on foot! He is worth
a million men in a trolley car! You never felt your black
heart rise up in you when you took control of one of the
monsters! You never felt the lively hate choke you off in
rapture as you sneered down the whole world from your
bouncing center of the universe! Damn all decent folks!
I'd rather go to hell in an automobile than to heaven in a
trolley car!"

A spoked wheel broke, sounding like one of the muted
volleys of rifle fire coming from behind him. The klunker
automobile pitched onto its nose, upended, turned over,
and exploded in blasting flames. And still in the middle of
the fire could be seen the two hypnotic eyes with their
darker flame, could be heard the demented voice:

"The crankshaft will still be good, the differential will
still be good, a sly klunker maker can use part of it, part
of it will drive again—*ahhhiiii*."

Some of them sang as they rode away from the site in
the trolley cars, and some of them were silent and
thoughtful. It had been an unnerving thing.

"It curdles me to remember that I once put my entire
fortune into that future," Great-grandfather Charles Archer moaned. "Well, that is better than to have lived in
such a future."

A young couple had happily loaded all their belongings
onto a baggage trolley and were moving from one of the
Excursion Cities to live with kindred in quasiurbia. The
population of that Excursion City (with its wonderful
theaters and music halls and distinguished restaurants and
literary coffeehouses and alcoholic oases and amusement
centers) had now reached seven thousand persons, the
legal limit for any city. Oh, there were a thousand Excursion Cities and all of them delightful! But a limit must be

kept on size. A limit must be kept on everything.

It was a wonderful Saturday afternoon. Fowlers caught birds with collapsible kite-cornered nets. Kids rode free out to the diamonds to play Trolley League ball. Old gaffers rode out with pigeons in pigeon boxes, to turn them loose and watch them race home. Shore netters took shrimp from the semisaline Little Shrimp Lake. Banjo players serenaded their girls in grassy lanes.

The world was one single bronze gong song with the melodious clang of trolley cars threading the country on their green-iron rails, with the sparky fire following them overhead and their copper gleaming in the sun. By law there must be a trolley line every mile, but they were oftener. By law no one trolley line might run for more than twenty-five miles. This was to give a sense of locality. But transfers between the lines were worked out perfectly. If one wished to cross the nation, one rode on some one hundred and twenty different lines. There were no more long-distance railroads. They also had had their arrogance, and they also had had to go.

Carp in the ponds, pigs in the clover, a unique barn-factory in every hamlet and every hamlet unique, bees in the air, pepper plants in the lanes, and the whole land as sparky as trolley fire and right as rails.

KATE WILHELM

THE ENCOUNTER

The bus slid to an uneasy stop, two hours late. Snow was eight inches deep, and the white sky met the white ground in a strange world where the grubby black bus station floated free. It was a world where up and down had become meaningless, where the snow fell horizontally. Crane, supported by the wind and the snow, could have entered the station by walking up the wall, or across the ceiling. His mind seemed adrift, out of touch with the reality of his body. He stamped, scattering snow, bringing some feeling back to his legs, making himself feel the floor beneath his feet. He tried to feel his cheek, to see if he was feverish, but his hands were too numb, his cheek too numb. The heating system of the bus had failed over an hour ago.

The trouble was that he had not dressed for such weather. An overcoat, but no boots, no fur-lined gloves, no woolen scarf to wind and wind about his throat. He stamped and clapped his hands. Others were doing the same.

There had been only nine or ten people on the bus, and some of them were being greeted by others or were slipping out into the storm, home finally or near enough now.

200

The bus driver was talking to an old man who had been in the bus station when they arrived, the ticket agent, probably. He was wearing two sweaters, one heavy, hip-length green that looked home-knit; under it, a turtle-neck grey wool with too-long sleeves that hung from beneath the green sleeves. He had on furry boots that came to his knees, with his sagging pants tucked tightly into them. Beyond him, tossed over one of the wooden benches, was a greatcoat, fleece-lined, long enough to hang to his boot tops. Fleecy gloves bulged from one of the pockets.

"Folks," he said, turning away from the bus driver, "there won't be another bus until sometime in the morning, when they get the roads plowed out some. There's an all-night diner down the road, three-four blocks. Not much else in town's open this time of night."

"Is there a hotel?" A woman, fur coat, shiny patent boots, kid gloves. She had got on at the same station that Crane had; he remembered the whiff of expensive perfume as she had passed him.

"There's the Laughton Inn, ma'am, but it's two miles outsida town and there's no way to get there."

"Oh, for God's sake! You mean this crummy burg doesn't even have a hotel of its own?"

"Four of them, in fact, but they're closed, open again in April. Don't get many people to stay overnight in the wintertimes."

"Okay, okay. Which way's the diner?" She swept a disapproving glance over the bleak station and went to the door, carrying an overnight bag with her.

"Come on, honey. I'm going there, too," the driver said. He pulled on gloves and turned up his collar. He took her arm firmly, transferred the bag to his other hand, then turned to look at the other three or four people in the station. "Anyone else?"

Diner. Glaring lights, jukebox noise without end, the smell of hamburgers and onions, rank coffee and doughnuts saturated with grease. Everyone smoking. Someone would have cards probably, someone a bottle. The woman would sing or cry, or get a fight going. She was a nasty one, he could tell. She'd be bored within an hour. She'd have the guys groping her under the table, in the end booth. The man half-turned, his back shielding her from view, his hand slipping between her buttons, under the blouse, under the slip, the slippery smooth nylon, the tightness of the bra, unfastening it with his other hand. Her low laugh, busy hands. The hard nipple between his fingers now, his own responsive hardness. She had turned to look at the stranded passengers when the driver spoke, and she caught Crane's glance.

"It's a long wait for a Scranton bus, honey," she said.

"I'd just get soaked going to the diner," Crane said, and turned his back on her. His hand hurt, and he opened his clenched fingers and rubbed his hands together hard.

"I sure as hell don't want to wait all night in this rat-hole," someone else said. "Do you have lockers? I can't carry all this gear."

"Lock them up in the office for you," the ticket agent said. He pulled out a bunch of keys and opened a door at the end of the room. A heavyset man followed him, carrying three suitcases. They returned; the door squeaked. The agent locked it again.

"Now, you boys will hold me up, won't you? I don't want to fall down in all that snow."

"Doll, if you fall on your pretty little ass, I'll dry you off personally," the driver said.

"Oh, you will, will you?"

Crane tightened his jaw, trying not to hear them. The outside door opened and a blast of frigid air shook the room. A curtain of snow swept across the floor before the door banged again, and the laughing voices were gone.

"You sure you want to wait here?" the ticket agent asked. "Not very warm in here. And I'm going home in a minute, you know."

"I'm not dressed to walk across the street in this weather, much less four blocks," Crane said.

The agent still hesitated, one hand on his coat. He looked around, as if checking on loose valuables. There was a woman on one of the benches. She was sitting with her head lowered, hands in her lap, legs crossed at the ankles. She wore a dark cloth coat, and her shoes were skimpier than Crane's, three crossing strips of leather attached to paper-thin soles. Black cloth gloves hid her hands. She didn't look up, in the silence that followed, while the two men scrutinized her. It was impossible to guess her age in that pose, with only the dark clothes to go by.

"Ma'am, are you all right?" the agent asked finally.

"Yes, of course. Like the gentleman, I didn't care to wade through the snow. I can wait here."

She raised her head and with a touch of disappointment Crane saw that she was as nondescript as her clothing. When he stopped looking at her, he couldn't remember what she looked like. A woman. Thirty. Thirty-five. Forty. He didn't know. And yet. There was something vaguely familiar about her, as if he should remember her, as if he might have seen her or met her at one time or another. He had a very good memory for faces and names, an invaluable asset for a salesman, and he searched his memory for this woman and came up with nothing.

"Don't you have nothing with you that you could change into?" the agent asked peevishly. "You'd be more comfortable down at the diner."

"I don't have anything but some work with me," she said. Her voice was very patient. "I thought I'd be in the city before the storm came. Late bus, early storm. I'll be fine here."

Again his eyes swept through the dingy room, searching for something to say, not finding anything. He began to pull on his coat, and he seemed to gain forty pounds. "Telephone under the counter, back there," he said finally. "Pay phone's outside under a drift, I reckon."

"Thank you," she said.

The agent continued to dawdle. He pulled on his gloves, checked the rest rooms to make sure the doors were not locked, that the lights worked. He veered at a thermostat, muttering that you couldn't believe what it said anyways. At the door he stopped once more. He looked like a walking heap of outdoor garments, a clothes pile that had swallowed a man. "Mr.— uh—"

"Crane. Randolph Crane. Manhattan."

"—Uh, yes. Mr. Crane, I'll tell the troopers that you two are up here. And the road boys. Plow'll be out soon's it lets up some. They'll keep an eye open for you, if you need anything. Maybe drop in with some coffee later on."

"Great," Crane said. "That'd be great."

"Okay, then. I wouldn't wander out if I was you. See you in the morning, then. Night."

The icy blast and the inrushing snow made Crane start to shake again. He looked over at the woman who was huddling down, trying to wrap herself up in the skimpy coat.

His shivering eased and he sat down and opened his briefcase and pulled out one of the policies he had taken along to study. This was the first time he had touched it. He hoped the woman would fall asleep and stay asleep until the bus came in the morning. He knew that he wouldn't be able to stretch out on the short benches, not that it would matter anyway. He wasn't the type to relax enough to fall asleep anywhere but in bed.

He stared at the policy, a twenty-year endowment, two years to go to maturity, on the life of William Sanders, age twenty-two. He held it higher, trying to catch the light, but the print was a blur; all he could make out were the headings of the clauses, and these he already knew by heart. He turned the policy over; it was the same on the back, the old familiar print, and the rest a blur. He started to refold the paper to return it to the briefcase. She would think he was crazy, taking it out, looking at it a moment, turning it this way and that, and then putting it back. He pursed his lips and pretended to read.

Sanders, Sanders. What did he want? Four policies, the endowment, a health and accident, a straight life, and a mortgage policy. Covered, protected. Insurance-poor, Sanders had said, throwing the bulky envelope onto Crane's desk. "Consolidate these things somehow. I want cash if I can get it, and out from under the rest."

"But what about your wife, the kids?"

"Ex-wife. If I go, she'll manage. Let her carry insurance on me."

Crane had been as persuasive as he knew how to be, and in the end he had had to promise to assess the policies, to have figures to show cash values, and so on. Disapprovingly, of course.

"You know, dear, you really are getting more stuffy every day," Mary Louise said.

"And if he dies, and his children are left destitute, then will I be so stuffy?"

"I'd rather have the seven hundred dollars myself than see it go to your company year after year."

"That's pretty shortsighted."

"Are you really going to wear that suit to Maggie's party?"

"Changing the subject?"

"Why not? You know what you think, and I know what I think, and they aren't even within hailing distance of each other."

Mary Louise wore a red velvet gown that was slit to her navel, molded just beneath her breasts by a silver chain, and almost completely bare in the back, down to the curve of her buttocks. The silver chain cut into her tanned back slightly. Crane stared at it.

"New?"

"Yes. I picked it up last week. Pretty?"

"Indecent. I didn't know it was a formal thing tonight."

"Not really. Optional anyway. Some of us decided to dress, that's all." She looked at him in the mirror and said, "I really don't care if you want to wear that suit."

Wordlessly he turned and went back to the closet to find his dinner jacket and black trousers. How easy it would be, a flick of a chain latch, and she'd be stripped to her hips. Was she counting on someone's noticing that? Evers maybe? Or Olivetti? Olivetti? What had he said? Something about women who wore red in public. Like passing out a dance card and pencil, the promise implicit in the gesture?

"Slut!" he said, through teeth so tightly pressed together that his jaws ached.

"What? I'm sorry."

He looked up. The woman in the bus station was watching him across the aisle. She still looked quite cold.

"I am sorry," she said softly. "I thought you spoke."

"No." He stuffed the policy back in his case and

fastened it. "Are you warm enough?"

"Not really. The ticket agent wasn't kidding when he said the thermostat lies. According to it, it's seventy-four in here."

Crane got up and looked at the thermostat. The adjustment control was gone. The station was abysmally cold. He walked back and forth for a few moments, then paused at the window. The white world, ebbing and growing, changing, changeless. "If I had a cup or something, I could bring in some snow and chill the thermostat. That might make the heat kick on."

"Maybe in the rest room. . . ." He heard her move across the floor, but he didn't turn to look. There was a pink glow now in the whiteness, like a fire in the distance, all but obscured by the intervening clouds of snow. He watched as it grew brighter, darker, almost red; then it went out. The woman returned and stood at his side.

"No cups, but I folded paper towels to make a funnel thing. Will it do?"

He took the funnel. It was sturdy enough, three thicknesses of brown, unabsobent toweling. "Probably better than a cup," he said. "Best stand behind the door. Every time it opens, that blizzard comes right on in."

She nodded and moved away. When he opened the door the wind hit him hard, almost knocking him back into the room, wrenching the door from his hand. It swung wide open and hit the woman. Distantly he heard her gasp of surprise and pain. He reached out and scooped up the funnel full of snow and then pushed the door closed again. He was covered with snow. Breathless, he leaned against the wall. "Are you all right?" he asked after a few moments.

She was holding her left shoulder. "Yes. It caught me by surprise. No harm done. Did you get enough snow?"

He held up the funnel for her to see and then pushed himself away from the wall. Again he had the impression that there was no right side up in the small station. He held the back of one of the benches and moved along it. "The wind took my breath away," he said.

"Or the intense cold. I think I read that breathing in the cold causes as many heart attacks as overexertion."

"Well, it's cold enough out there. About zero by now, I

guess." He scooped out some of the snow and held it against the thermostat. "The furnace must be behind this wall, or under this area. Feel how warm it is."

She put her hand on the wall and nodded. "Maybe we can fasten the cup of snow up next to the thermostat." She looked around and then went to the bulletin board. She removed several of the notices and schedules there and brought him the thumbtacks. Crane spilled a little snow getting the tacks into the paper towel and then into the wall. In a few minutes there was a rumble as the furnace came on and almost immediately the station began to feel slightly warmer. Presently the woman took off her coat.

"Success," she said, smiling.

"I was beginning to think it had been a mistake after all, not going to the diner."

"So was I."

"I think they are trying to get the snowplows going. I saw a red light a couple of minutes ago. It went out again, but at least someone's trying."

She didn't reply, and after a moment he said, "I'm glad you don't smoke. I gave it up a few months ago, and it would drive me mad to have to smell it through a night like this. Probably I'd go back to them."

"I have some," she said. "I even smoke once in a while. If you decide that you do want them. . . ."

"No. No. I wasn't hinting."

"I just wish the lights were better in here. I could get in a whole night's work. I often work at night."

"So do I, but you'd put your eyes out. What—"

"That's all right. What kind of work do I do? An illustrator for Slocum House Catalogue Company. Not very exciting, I'm afraid."

"Oh, you're an artist."

"No. Illustrator. I wanted to become an artist, but . . . things didn't work out that way."

"I'd call you an artist. Maybe because I'm in awe of anyone who can draw, or paint, or do things like that. You're all artists to me."

She shrugged. "And you're an insurance salesman." He stiffened and she got up, saying, "I saw the policy you were looking over, and the briefcase stuffed full of policies and company pamphlets and such. I knew an insurance salesman once."

He realized that he had been about to ask where she was going, and he clamped his jaw again and turned so that he wouldn't watch her go into the ladies' room.

He went to the window. The wind was still at gale force, but so silent. With the door closed, the station seemed far removed from the storm, and looking at it was like watching something wholly unreal, manufactured to amuse him perhaps. There were storm windows, and the building was very sturdy and probably very well insulated. Now, with the furnace working, it was snug and secure. He cupped his hands about his eyes, trying to see past the reflections in the window, but there was nothing. Snow, a drift up to the sill now, and the wind driven snow that was like a sheer curtain being waved from above, touching the windows, fluttering back, touching again, hiding everything behind it.

She was taking a long time. He should have gone when she left. Now he had the awkward moment to face, of excusing himself or not, of timing it so that she wouldn't think he was leaving deliberately in order to dodge something that one or the other said or hinted. She had done it so easily and naturally. He envied people like her. Always so sure of themselves.

"Which face are you wearing tonight, Randy?" Mary Louise reached across the table and touched his cheek, then shook her head. "I can't always tell. When you're the successful salesman, you are so assured, so poised, charming, voluble even."

"And the other times? What am I these times?"

"Afraid."

Drawing back from her hand, tight and self-contained again, watchful, he said, "Isn't it lucky that I can keep the two separated then? How successful a salesman would I be if I put on the wrong face when I went to work?"

"I wonder if mixing it up a little might not be good for you. So you wouldn't sell a million dollars' worth of insurance a year, but you'd be a little happier when you're not working."

"Like you?"

"Not like me, God forbid. But at least I haven't given up looking for something. And you have."

"Yeah. You're looking. In a bottle. In someone else's bed. In buying sprees."

"*C'est la vie.* You can always buzz off, you know."

"And add alimony to my other headaches? No thanks."

Smiling at him, sipping an old-fashioned, infinitely wise and infinitely evil. Were wise women always evil? "My poor Randy. My poor darling. You thought I was everything you were not, and instead you find that I am stamped from the same mold. Number XLM 119543872—afraid of life, only not quite afraid of death. Someone let up on the pressure there. Hardly an indentation even. So I can lose myself and you can't. A pity, my darling Randy. If we could lose ourselves together, what might we be able to find? We are so good together, you know. Sex with you is still the best of all. I try harder and harder to make you let go all the way. I read manuals and take personalized lessons, all for your sake, darling. All for you. And it does no good. You are my only challenge, you see."

"Stop it! Are you crazy?"

"Ah. Now I know who you are tonight. There you are. Tight mouth, frowning forehead full of lines, narrowed eyes. You are not so handsome with this face on, you know. Why don't you look at me, Randy?" Her hands across the table again, touching his cheeks, a finger trailing across his lips, a caress or mockery. "You never look at me, you know. You never look at me at all."

He leaned his forehead against the window, and the chill roused him. Where was the woman? He looked at his watch and realized that she had been gone only a few minutes, not the half hour or longer that he had thought. Was the whole night going to be like that? Minutes dragging by like hours? Time distorted until a lifetime could be spent in waiting for one dawn?

He went to the men's room. When he returned, she was sitting in her own place once more, her coat thrown over her shoulders, a sketch pad in her lap.

"Are you cold again?" He felt almost frozen. There was no heat in the men's room.

"Not really. Moving about chilled me. There's a puddle under the funnel, and the snow is gone, but heat is still coming from the radiator."

"I'll have to refill it every half hour or so, I guess."

"The driver said it's supposed to go to ten or fifteen below tonight."

Crane shrugged. "After it gets this low, I don't care how much farther it drops. As long as I don't have to be out in it."

She turned her attention to her pad and began to make strong lines. He couldn't tell what she was drawing, only that she didn't hesitate, but drew surely, confidently. He opened his briefcase and got out his schedule book. It was no use, he couldn't read the small print in the poor lighting of the station. He rummaged for something that he would be able to concentrate on. He was grateful when she spoke again:

"It was so stupid to start out tonight. I could have waited until tomorrow. I'm not bound by a time clock or anything."

"That's just what I was thinking. I was afraid of being snowed in for several days. We were at Sky Mount Ski Lodge, and everyone else was cheering the storm's approach. Do you ski?"

"Some, not very well. The cold takes my breath away, hitting me in the face like that."

He stared at her for a moment, opened his mouth to agree, then closed it again. It was as if she was anticipating what he was going to say.

"Don't be so silly, Randy. All you have to do is wear the muffler around your mouth and nose. And the goggles on your eyes. Nothing is exposed then. You're just too lazy to ski."

"Okay, lazy I know this, I'm bored to death here. I haven't been warm since we left the apartment, and my legs ache. That was a nasty fall I had this morning. I'm sore. I have a headache from the glare of the snow, and I think it's asinine to freeze for two hours in order to slide down a mountain a couple of times. I'm going back to the city."

"But our reservation is through Saturday night. Paid in advance."

"Stay. Be my guest. Have yourself a ball. You and McCone make a good pair, and his wife seems content to sit on the sidelines and watch you. Did you really think that anemic blonde would appeal to me? Did you think we'd be too busy together to notice what you were up to?"

"Tracy? To tell the truth I hadn't given her a thought. I didn't know she didn't ski until this afternoon. I don't know why Mac brought her here. Any more than I know why you came along."

"Come on home with me. Let's pack up and leave before the storm begins. We can stop at that nice old antique inn on the way home, where they always have pheasant pie. Remember?"

"Darling, I came to ski. You will leave the car here, won't you? I'll need it to get the skis back home, and our gear. Isn't there a bus or something?"

"Mary Louise, this morning on the slope, didn't you really see me? You know, when your ski pole got away from you."

"What in the world are you talking about? You were behind me. How could I have seen you? I didn't even know you had started down."

"Okay. Forget it. I'll give you a call when I get to the apartment."

"Yes, do. You can leave a message at the desk if I don't answer."

The woman held up her sketch and narrowed her eyes. She ripped out the page and crumpled it, tossed it into the wastecan.

"I think I'm too tired after all."

"It's getting cold in here again. Your hands are probably too cold." He got up and took the funnel from the wall. "I'll get more snow and see if we can't get the furnace going again."

"You should put something over your face, so the cold air won't be such a shock. Don't you have a muffler?"

He stopped. He had crushed the funnel, he realized, and he tried to smooth it again without letting her see what he

had done. He decided that it would do, and opened the
door. A drift had formed, and a foot of snow fell into the
station. The wind was colder, sharper, almost deliberately
cutting. He was blinded by the wind and the snow that
was driven into his face. He filled the funnel and tried to
close the door again, but the drift was in the way. He
pushed, trying to use the door as a snowplow. More snow
was being blown in, and finally he had to use his hands,
push the snow out of the way, not outside, but to one side
of the door. At last he had it clear enough and he slammed
the door, more winded this time than before. His throat felt
raw, and he felt a constriction about his chest.

"It's getting worse all the time. I couldn't even see the
bus, nothing but a mountain of snow."

"Ground blizzard, I suspect. When it blows like this
you can't tell how much of it is new snow and how much
is just fallen snow being blown about. The drifts will be
tremendous tomorrow." She smiled. "I remember how we
loved it when this happened when we were kids. The drifts
are exciting, so pure, so high. Sometimes they glaze over
and you can play Glass Mountain. I used to be the
princess."

Crane was shivering again. He forced his hands to be
steady as he pushed the thumbtacks into the funnel to
hold it in place next to the thermostat. He had to clear his
throat before he could speak. "Did the prince ever reach
you?"

"No. Eventually I just slid back down and went home."

"Where? Where did you live?"

"Outside Chicago, near the lake."

He spun around. "Who are you?" He grabbed the back
of a bench and clutched it hard. She stared at him. He had
screamed at her, and he didn't know why. "I'm sorry," he
said. "You keep saying things that I'm thinking. I was
thinking of that game, of how I never could make it to the
top."

"Near Lake Michigan?"

"On the shores almost."

She nodded.

"I guess all kids play games like that in the snow," he
said. "Strange that we should have come from the same

general area. Did your milk freeze on the back steps, stick up out of the bottle, with the cap at an angle?"

"Yes. And those awful cloakrooms at school, where you had to strip off snowsuits and boots, and step in icy water before you could get your indoors shoes on."

"And sloshing through the thaws, wet every damn day. I was wet more than I was dry all through grade school."

"We all were," she said, smiling faintly, looking past him.

He almost laughed in his relief. He went to the radiator and put his hands out over it, his back to her. Similar backgrounds, that's all, he said to himself, framing the words carefully. Nothing strange. Nothing eerie. She was just a plain woman who came from the same state, probably the same county that he came from. They might have gone to the same schools, and he would not have noticed her. She was too common, too nondescript to have noticed at the time. And he had been a quiet boy, not particularly noteworthy himself. No sports besides the required ones. No clubs. A few friends, but even there, below average, because they had lived in an area too far removed from most of the kids who went to his school.

"It's only two. Seems like it ought to be morning already, doesn't it." She was moving about and he turned to see what she was doing. She had gone behind the counter, where the ticket agent had said there was a telephone. "A foam cushion," she said, holding it up. "I feel like one of the Swiss Family Robinson, salvaging what might be useful."

"Too bad there isn't some coffee under there."

"Wish you were in the diner?"

"No. That bitch probably has them all at each other's throats by now, as it is."

"That girl? The one who was so afraid?"

He laughed harshly and sat down. "Girl!"

"No more than twenty, if that much."

He laughed again and shook his head.

"Describe her to me," the woman said. She left the counter and sat down on the bench opposite him, still carrying the foam cushion. It had a black plastic cover, grey foam bulged from a crack. It was disgusting.

Crane said, "The broad was in her late twenties, or possibly thirties—"

"Eighteen to twenty."

"She had a pound of makeup on, nails like a cat."

"Fake nails, chapped hands, calluses. Ten-cent store makeup."

"She had expensive perfume, and a beaver coat. I think beaver."

She laughed gently. "Drugstore spray cologne. Macy's Basment fake fur, about fifty-nine to sixty-five dollars, unless she hit a sale."

"And the kid gloves, and the high patent-leather boots?"

"Vinyl, both of them." She looked at him for an uncomfortable minute, then examined the pillow she had found. "On second thought, I'm not sure that I would want to rest my head on this. It's a little bit disgusting, isn't it?"

"Why did you want me to describe that woman? You have your opinion of what she is; I have mine. There's no way to prove either of our cases without having her before us."

"I don't need to prove anything. I don't care if you think you're right and I'm wrong. I felt very sorry for the girl. I noticed her."

"I noticed her, too."

"What color was her hair, her eyes? How about her mouth, big, small, full? And her nose? Straight, snub, broad?"

He regarded her bitterly for a moment, then shrugged and turned toward the window. He didn't speak.

"You can't describe what she really was like because you didn't see her. You saw the package and made up your mind about the contents. Believe me, she was terrified of the storm, of those men, everything. She needed the security of the driver and people. What about me? Can you describe me?"

He looked, but she was holding the pillow between them and he could see only her hands, long, pale, slender fingers, no rings.

"This is ridiculous," he said after a second. "I have one

of those reputations for names and faces. You know, never forget a name, always know the names of the kids, the wife, occupation, and so on."

"Not this side of you. This side refuses to see anyone at all. I wonder why."

"What face are you wearing tonight, Randy?" Mary Louise touching him. "Do you see me? Why don't you look at me?"

Wind whistling past his ears, not really cold yet, not when he was standing still anyway, with the sun warm on him. But racing down the slope, trees to his right, the precipice to his left, the wind was icy. Mary Louise a red streak ahead of him, and somewhere behind him the navy and white blur that was McCone. Holding his own between them. The curve of the trail ahead, the thrill of the downward plummet, and suddenly the openmouthed face of his wife, silent scream, and in the same instant, the ski pole against his legs, tripping him up, the more exciting plunge downward, face in the snow, blinded, over and over, skis gone now, trying to grasp the snow, trying to stop the tumbling, over and over in the snow.

Had his wife tried to kill him?

"Are you all right, Mr. Crane?"

"Yes, of course. Let me describe the last man I sold insurance to, a week ago. Twenty-four, six feet one inch, a tiny, almost invisible scar over his right eyebrow, crinkle lines about his eyes, because he's an outdoor type, very tanned and muscular. He's a profesional baseball player, incidentally. His left hand has larger knuckles than the right . . ."

The woman was not listening. She had crossed the station and was standing at the window, trying to see out. "Computer talk," she said. "A meaningless rundown of facts. So he bought a policy for one hundred thousand dollars, straight life, and from now on you won't have to deal with him, be concerned with him at all."

"Why did you say one hundred thousand dollars?"

"No reason. I don't know, obviously."

He chewed his lip and watched her. "Any change out there?"

"Worse, if anything. I don't think you'll be able to use

this door at all now. You'd never get it closed. It's half covered with a drift."

"There must be a window or another door that isn't drifted over."

"Storm windows. Maybe there's a back door, but I bet it opens to the office, and the ticket agent locked that."

Crane looked at the windows and found that she was right. The storm windows couldn't be opened from inside. And there wasn't another outside door. The men's room was like a freezer now. He tried to run the water, thinking that possibly cold water would work on the thermostat as well as snow, but nothing came out. The pipes must have frozen. As he started to close the door, he saw a small block-printed sign: "Don't close door all the way, no heat in here, water will freeze up." The toweling wouldn't hold water anyway.

He left the door open a crack and rejoined the woman near the window. "It's got to be this door," he said. "I guess I could open it an inch or two, let that much of the drift fall inside and use it."

"Maybe. But you'll have to be careful."

"Right out of Jack London," he said. "It's seventy-two on the thermometer. How do you feel?"

"Coolish, not bad."

"Okay, we'll wait awhile. Maybe the wind will let up."

He stared at the puddle under the thermostat, and at the other larger one across the room near the door, where the snowdrift had entered the room the last time. The drift had been only a foot high then, and now it was three or four feet. Could he move that much snow without anything to work with, if it came inside?

He shouldn't have started back to town. She had goaded him into it, of course. Had she suspected that he would get stranded somewhere, maybe freeze to death?

"Why don't you come right out and say what you're thinking?" Red pants, red ski jacket, cheeks almost as red.

"I'm not thinking anything. It was an accident."

"You're a liar, Randy! You think I guessed you were there, that I let go hoping to make you fall. Isn't that what you think? Isn't it?"

He shook his head hard. She hadn't said any of that. He

hadn't thought of it then. Only now, here, stranded with this half-mad woman. Half-mad? He looked at her and quickly averted his gaze. Why had that thought come to him? She was odd, certainly, probably very lonely, shy. But half-mad?

Why did she watch him so? As if aware of his thoughts, she turned her back and walked to the ladies' room. He had to go too, but he remembered the frozen pipes in the men's room. Maybe she'd fall asleep eventually and he'd be able to slip into her rest room. If not, then he'd wait until morning. Maybe this night had come about in order to give him time to think about him and Mary Louise, to really think it through all the way and come to a decision.

He had met her when he was stationed in Washington, after the Korean War. He had been a captain, assigned to Army Intelligence. She had worked as a private secretary to Senator Robertson of New York. So he had done all right without her up to then. She had introduced him to the president of the company that he worked for now. Knowing that he wanted to become a writer, she had almost forced him into insurance. Fine. It was the right choice. He had told her so a thousand times. But how he had succeeded was still a puzzle to him. He never had tested well on salesmanship on aptitude tests. Too introverted and shy.

"You make other people feel stupid, frankly," she had said once. "You are so tight and so sure of yourself that you don't allow anyone else to have an opinion at all. It's not empathy, like it is with so many good salesmen. It's a kind of sadistic force that you apply."

"Oh, stop it. You're talking nonsense."

"You treat each client like an extension of the policy that you intend to sell to him. Not like a person, but the human counterpart of the slick paper with the clauses and small print. You show the same respect and liking for them as for the policies. They go together. You believe it and make them believe it. Numbers, that's what they are to you. Policy numbers."

"Why do you hang around if you find me so cold and calculating?"

"Oh, it's a game that I play. I know there's a room

somewhere where you've locked up part of yourself, and I keep searching for it. Someday I'll find it and open it just a crack, and then I'll run. Because if it ever opens, even a little, everything will come tumbling out and you won't be able to stop any of it. How you'll bleed then, bleed and bleed, and cry and moan. I couldn't stand that. And I can't stand for it not to be so."

Crane put his head down in his hands and rubbed his eyes hard. Without affect, that was the term that she used. Modern man without affect. Schizoid personality. But he also had a nearly split personality. The doctor had told him so. In the six sessions that he had gone to he had learned much of the jargon, and then he had broken it off. Split personality. Schizoid tendencies. Without affect. All to keep himself safe. It seemed to him to be real madness to take away any of the safeties he had painstakingly built, and he had quit the sessions.

And now this strange woman that he was locked up with was warning him not to open the door a crack. He rubbed his eyes harder until there was solid pain there. He had to touch her. The ticket agent had seen her, too, though. He had been concerned about leaving her alone with a strange man all night. So transparently worried about her, worried about Crane. Fishing for his name. He could have told the fool anything. He couldn't remember his face at all, only his clothes.

All right, the woman was real, but strange. She had an uncanny way of anticipating what he was thinking, what he was going to say, what he feared. Maybe these were her fears too.

She came back into the waiting room. She was wearing her black coat buttoned to her neck, her hands in the pockets. She didn't mention the cold.

Soon he would have to get more snow, trick the fool thermostat into turning on the furnace. Soon. A maniac must have put it on that wall, the only warm wall in the building. A penny-pinching maniac.

"If you decide to try to get more snow, maybe I should hold the door while you scoop it up," she said, after a long silence. The cold had made her face look pinched, and Crane was shivering under his overcoat.

"Can you hold it?" he asked. "There's a lot of pressure behind that door."

She nodded.

"Okay. I'll take the wastecan and get as much as I can. It'll keep in the men's room. There's no heat in there."

She held the doorknob until he was ready, and when he nodded, she turned it and, bracing the door with her shoulder, let it open several inches. The wind pushed, and the snow spilled through. It was over their heads now, and it came in the entire height of the door. She gave ground and the door was open five or six inches. Crane pulled the snow inside, using both hands, clawing at it. The Augean stable, he thought bitterly, and then joined her behind the door, trying to push it closed again. At least no blast of air had come inside this time. The door was packing the snow, and the inner surface of it was thawing slightly, only to refreeze under the pressure and the cold from the other side. Push, Crane thought at her. Push, you devil. You witch.

Slowly it began to move, scrunching snow. They weren't going to get it closed all the way. They stopped pushing to rest. He was panting hard, and she put her head against the door. After a moment he said, "Do you think you could move one of the benches over here?"

She nodded. He braced himself against the door and was surprised at the increase in the pressure when she left. He heard her wrestling with the bench, but he couldn't turn to see. The snow was gaining again. His feet were slipping on the floor, wet now where some of the snow had melted and was running across the room. He saw the bench from the corner of his eye, and he turned to watch her progress with it. She was pushing it toward him, the back to the wall; the back was too high. It would have to be tilted to go under the doorknob. It was a heavy oak bench. If they could maneuver it in place, it would hold.

For fifteen minutes they worked, grunting, saying nothing, trying to hold the door closed and get the bench under the knob without losing any more ground. Finally it was done. The door was open six inches, white packed snow the entire height of it.

Crane fell onto a bench and stared at the open door, not

able to say anything. The woman seemed equally exhausted. At the top of the door, the snow suddenly fell forward, into the station, sifting at first, then falling in a stream. Icy wind followed the snow into the room, and now that the top of the column of snow had been lost, the wind continued to pour into the station, whistling shrilly.

"Well, we know now that the drift isn't really to the top of the building," the woman said wearily. She was staring at the opening.

"My words, almost exactly," Crane said. She always said what he planned to say. He waited.

"We'll have to close it at the top somehow."

He nodded. "In a minute. In a minute."

The cold increased and he knew that he should get busy and try to close the opening, but he felt too numb to cope with it. The furnace couldn't keep up with the draft of below-zero air. His hands were aching with cold, and his toes hurt with a stabbing intensity. Only his mind felt pleasantly numb and he didn't want to think about the problem of closing up the hole.

"You're not falling asleep, are you?"

"For God's sake!" He jerked straight up on the bench and gave her a mean look, a guilty look. "Just shut up and let me try to think, will you?"

"Sorry." She got up and began to pace briskly, hugging her hands to her body. "I'll look around, see if I can find anything that would fit. I simply can't sit still, I'm so cold."

He stared at the hole. There had to be something that would fit over it, stay in place, keep out the wind. He narrowed his eyes, staring, and he saw the wind-driven snow as a liquid running into the station from above, swirling about, only fractionally heavier than the medium that it met on the inside. One continuum, starting in the farthest blackest vacuum of space, taking on form as it reached the highest atmospheric molecules, becoming denser as it neared Earth, almost solid here, but not yet. Not yet. The hole extended to that unimaginable distance where it all began, and the chill spilled down, down, searching for him, wafting about here, searching for him, wanting only to find him, willing then to stop the ceaseless whirl. Coat him, claim him. The woman belonged to the coldness that came from the black of space. He remembered her now.

Korea. The woman. The village. Waiting for the signal. Colder than the station even, snow, flintlike ground, striking sparks from nails in boots, sparks without warmth. If they could fire the village, they would get warm, have food, sleep that night. Harrison, wounded, frozen where he fell. Lorenz, frostbitten; Jakobs, snow-blind. Crane, too tired to think, too hungry to think, too cold to think. "Fire the village." The woman, out of nowhere, urging him back, back up the mountain to the bunkers that were half filled with ice, mines laid now between the bunkers and the valley. Ordering the woman into the village at gunpoint. Spark from his muzzle. Blessed fire and warmth. But a touch of ice behind the eyes, ice that didn't let him weep when Lorenz died, or when Jakobs, blinded, wandered out and twitched and jerked and pitched over a cliff under a fusillade of bullets. The snow queen, he thought. She's the snow queen, and she touched my eyes with ice.

"Mr. Crane, please wake up. Please!"

He jumped to his feet reaching for his carbine, and only when his hands closed on air did he remember where he was.

"Mr. Crane, I think I know what we can use to close up the hole. Let me show you."

She pulled at his arm and he followed her. She led him into the ladies' room. At the door he tried to pull back, but she tugged. "Look, stacks of paper towels, all folded together. They would be about the right size, wouldn't they? If we wet them, a block of them, and if we can get them up to the hole, they would freeze in place, and the drift could pile up against them and stop blowing into the station. Wouldn't it work?"

She was separating the opened package into thirds, her hands busy, her eyes downcast, not seeing him at all. Crane, slightly to one side of her, a step behind, stared at the double image in the mirror. He continued to watch the mirror as his hands reached out for her and closed about her throat. There was no struggle. She simply closed her eyes and became very limp, and he let her fall. Then he took the wad of towels and held it under the water for a few moments and returned to the waiting room with it. He had to clear snow from the approach to the door, and then he had to move the bench that was holding the door, carefully, not letting it become dislodged. He dragged a second bench to the door and climbed on it and pushed the wet wad of towels into the opening. He held it several minutes, until he could feel the freezing paper start to stiffen beneath his fingers. He climbed down.

"That should do it," the woman said.

"But you're dead."

Mary Louise threw the sugar bowl at him, trailing a line of sugar across the room.

He smiled. "Wishful thinking," he/she said.

"You're dead inside. You're shriveled up and dried up and rotting inside. When did you last feel anything? My God! You can't create anything, you are afraid of creating anything, even our child!"

"I don't believe it was our child."

"You don't dare believe it. Or admit that you know it was."

He slapped her. The only time that he ever hit her. And her so pale from the operation, so weak from the loss of blood. The slap meant nothing to him, his hand meeting her cheek, leaving a red print there.

"Murderer!"

"You crazy bitch! You're the one who had the abortion! You wanted it!"

"I didn't. I didn't know what I wanted. I was terrified. You made the arrangements, got the doctor, took me, arranged everything, waited in the other room writing policies. Murderer."

"Murderer," the woman said.

He shook his head. "You'd better go back to the ladies' room and stay there. I don't want to hurt you."

"Murderer."

He took a step toward her. He swung around abruptly and almost ran to the far side of the station, pressing his forehead hard on the window.

"We can't stop it now," the woman said, following him. "You can't close the door again now. I'm here. You finally saw me. Really saw me. I'm real now. I won't be banished again. I'm stronger than you are. You've killed off bits and pieces of yourself until there's nothing left to fight with. You can't send me away again."

Crane pushed himself away from the glass and made a halfhearted attempt to hit her with his fist. He missed and fell against the bench holding the door. He heard the woman's low laugh. All for nothing. All for nothing. The bench slid out from under his hand, and the drift pushed into the room like an avalanche. He pulled himself free and tried to brush the snow off his clothes.

"We'll both freeze now," he said, not caring any longer.

The woman came to his side and touched his cheek with her fingers; they were strangely warm. "Relax now, Crane. Just relax."

She led him to a bench where he sat down resignedly. "Will you at least tell me who you are?" he said.

"You know. You've always known."

He shook his head. One last attempt, he thought. He had to make that one last effort to get rid of her, the woman whose face was so like his own. "You don't even exist," he said harshly, not opening his eyes. "I imagined you here because I was afraid of being alone all night. I created you. *I created you.*"

He stood up. "You hear that, Mary Louise! Did you hear that? I created something. Something so real that it wants to kill me."

"Look at me, Crane. Look at me. Turn your head and look. Look with me, Crane. Let me show you. Let me show you what I see. . . ."

He was shaking again, chilled through, shaking so hard that his muscles were sore. Slowly, inevitably he turned his head and saw the man half-standing, half-crouching, holding the bench with both hands. The man had grey skin, and his eyes were mad with terror.

"Let go, Crane. Look at him and let go. He doesn't deserve anything from us ever again." Crane watched the man clutch his chest, heard him moaning for Mary Louise to come help him, watched him fall to the floor.

She heard the men working at the drift, and she opened the office door to wait for them. They finally got through and the ticket agent squirmed through the opening they had made.

"Miss! Miss? Are you all right?"

"Yes. I broke into the office, though."

"My God, I thought . . . When we saw that the door had given under the drift, and you in here . . . alo—" The ticket agent blinked rapidly several times.

"I was perfectly all right. When I saw that the door wasn't going to hold, I broke open the inner office and came in here with my sketch book and pencils. I've had a very productive night, really. But I could use some coffee now."

They took her to the diner in a police car, and while she waited for her breakfast order, she went to the rest room and washed her face and combed her hair. She stared at herself in the mirror appraisingly. "Happy birthday," she said softly then.

"Your birthday?" asked the girl who had chosen to wait the night out in the diner. "You were awfully brave to stay alone in the station. I couldn't have done that. You really an artist?"

"Yes, really. And last night I had a lot of work to get done. A lot of work and not much time."

Pelican Books
The Buddha

Trevor Ling is Professor of Comparative Religion
in the University of Manchester. He has previously
taught comparative religion at Leeds University,
during that time visiting India, Ceylon and
Thailand, and has also spent two years in the
University of Rangoon. He first became interested
in Asian religion when he was stationed in Bengal
for three years during the Second World War.

At the School of Oriental and African Studies his
doctoral research in Indian Buddhism was
concerned with the sociological significance of the
Buddhist symbol of Mara, the Evil One. Among his
publications are *Buddhism and the Mythology of
Evil*; *Buddha, Marx and God*; *A History of
Religion East and West* and *A Dictionary of
Buddhism*.

Trevor Ling

THE BUDDHA

BUDDHIST CIVILIZATION IN INDIA AND CEYLON

Penguin Books

Penguin Books Ltd,
Harmondsworth, Middlesex, England
Penguin Books Inc.,
7110 Ambassador Road, Baltimore, Maryland 21207, U.S.A.
Penguin Books Australia Ltd,
Ringwood, Victoria, Australia
Penguin Books Canada Ltd,
41 Steelcase Road West, Markham, Ontario, Canada
Penguin Books (N.Z.) Ltd,
182–190 Wairau Road, Auckland 10, New Zealand

First published by Temple Smith 1973
First published in the United States by Charles Scribner's Sons,
New York 1973
Published in Pelican Books 1976
Copyright © Trevor Ling, 1973

Made and printed in Great Britain by
Hazell Watson & Viney Ltd, Aylesbury, Bucks
Set in Linotype Baskerville

Dedicated with her permission to

SHRIMATI INDIRA GANDHI

Prime Minister of India
in the 25th Anniversary Year
of the Republic of India

Contents

10   *Contents*

Epilogue: Beyond the Present Horizons

Editor's Note

BY PROFESSOR S. G. F. BRANDON*

No founder of a great religion ever lived before his time. To win disciples, his message had to be relevant to current needs and presented in a contemporary idiom. Hence such a message drew upon a tradition of culture, and it cannot be truly understood apart from it. But it contained also something new, some fresh and dynamic insight into the nature and destiny of man that derived from a unique religious sensitivity, and was embodied in the personal being of the genius concerned. It is because of such factors that the emergence of a new religion marks the beginning of a process of change destined to affect the lives of untold generations of individuals and have incalculable cultural, and often political and economic, consequences. To that process of transformation many others in time contribute, possibly altering in varying degrees the founder's message or deflecting the development of his intention. Thus from the alchemy of the founder's own genius, which transmutes the cultural tradition in which he was nurtured, there gradually evolves a new culture and civilization. And so, to take a random example, a causal nexus of infinite complexity connects Jesus of Nazareth, a Galilean Jew of the first century, with the building of the Cathedral of Chartres, that supreme epitome of Western medieval culture.

It is the aim of this series of books to show something of the fascinating transformation of cultural traditions that the founders of the great religions have wrought in the course of history. Starting with the world into which such a founder was born, each volume will attempt to explain how, from the stimulus of his personality and teaching, a new cultural world eventually emerged.

*Professor Brandon, who died in 1973, was the Editor of the series Makers of the New World published by Temple Smith.

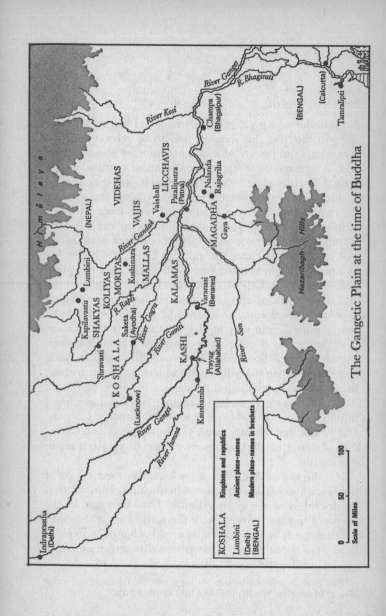

The Gangetic Plain at the time of Buddha

Part 1
Perspectives

1 Buddhism and Religion

To say that Gotama the Buddha founded a religion is to
prejudice our understanding of his far-reaching influence.
For in modern usage the word religion denotes merely one
department of human activity, now regarded as of less and
less public importance, and belonging almost entirely to
the realm of men's private affairs. But whatever else
Buddhism is or is not, in Asia it is a great social and cultural tradition. Born of a revolution in Indian thought it
has found sponsors in many of the countries of Asia outside the land of its origin. What is a particularly interesting fact about these sponsors is that very often they were
men concerned with *public* affairs, kings, emperors and
governors. Yet it was not only to rulers that Buddhism
appealed. Through its own special bearers, representatives
and guardians, the orange-robed *bhikkhus*,[1] it has found its
way into the common life of the towns and villages of
much of Asia. Especially in Ceylon and South-East Asia it
has continued to the present day to impart to the ordinary
people its own characteristic values and attitudes, and has
had a profound influence on the life of the home, as well
as of the nation.

Buddhism has its own long and noble tradition of
scholarship, and of education of the young, with the result
that some of the traditionally Buddhist countries of South-
East Asia have an unusually high rate of literacy for Asia.
It has encouraged equality of social opportunity but without frantic economic competition. Buddhist values have
inculcated a respect for the environment and a realistic
attitude towards the importance of material things, an
attitude which sees the folly of plundering and extrava-

gantly wasting what cannot be replaced. For Buddhism has not encouraged ideas of dominance, in the sense that man should, by some divine sanction, dominate either his environment, or his fellow men. Neither exploitation nor colonialism have any place in Buddhist civilization; the key word is cooperation, at every level of being. The values and attitudes implicit wherever Buddhist culture survives have proved resistant to the campaigns and the blandishments directed from the West towards Buddhist Asia. From the time of the first contacts with European culture represented by the sixteenth-century Portuguese, hungry for spices and Christian converts, to the more recent work of American, British and French missionaries, the people of Buddhist Asia have not seen in either the doctrines or the fruits of Christianity anything sufficiently compelling to cause them to abandon their own tradition and culture in any large numbers. In Burma in 1931, the year in which the last decennial census under British rule was taken, Christians were 2·3 per cent of the total population, and Buddhists were 84 per cent.[2] Christian missionary activity in Burma had begun in the early eighteenth century. In Thailand, to take another example, according to the official report for 1965 issued by the Department of Religious Affairs in the Ministry of Education, 0·53 per cent of the total population were Christians and 93 per cent were Buddhists.[3]

IS BUDDHISM A RELIGION?

It is clear that in entering the world of the Buddha we are confronted by something more than a religion, if by religion is meant a system of *personal* salvation. The question could also be raised, and in fact often has been raised, as to whether Buddhism is a religion at all. It is possible from the historical perspective to answer both 'yes' and 'no' to this question.

Some attempts to deal with it appear to end inconclusively, in a circular argument. If one asks, 'Is Buddhism a religion?' it is obvious that one needs to know what a religion is, in order to say whether Buddhism is one or not. And when one asks, 'What is religion?' the definition will frequently be found to include reference to belief in a god or gods. If this is to be regarded as an essential constituent of religion, and if the absence of such belief denotes something other than religion, then the objection is likely to be raised, 'But what about Buddhism?' By this is usually meant early Buddhism, which does not appear to *require* belief in a god or gods as an essential part of the belief system. Emile Durkheim ran into this difficulty in his attempts to define religion. He pointed out that early Buddhism was not covered by such a definition of religion as E. B. Tylor's: that religion consists of 'belief in Spiritual Beings'.[4] In his support he quoted Burnouf's description of Buddhism as 'a moral system without a god', H. Oldenberg's, that it is 'a faith without a god', and others of a similar kind.[5] Durkheim's argument is that Buddhism is in essence a non-theistic religion, and that in defining religion in general one should have this case in mind, and formulate a definition which will cover both theistic and non-theistic systems.

The assumption which Durkheim appeared to be making was that Buddhism must be regarded as a religion, that is, a particular example of a general category, 'religion', a word about whose meaning there is some common agreement. Or he may simply be saying, 'I have a feeling that Buddhism should be included in, rather than excluded from, any survey of religions, for if it is not a religion, then what is it?' It might in fact be more useful, as Melford Spiro has pointed out, to pursue the latter question 'If not a religion, then what is it?'[6] For it may be that no conclusive answer will be found, in terms of any of the other possible conventional categories. If early Buddhism was not a religion, this does not necessarily mean that it was therefore a philosophy, or a personal code of ethics, or anything else for which a category exists. Inability to find any satisfactory answer may have the effect of stimulating further research, not only into the nature of what is generally regarded as 'Buddhism', but into the nature of what is regarded as 'Christianity', or as 'Islam', and so on. It might be found that these titles merely serve to indicate large, complex structures whose constituent factors have to be studied by the psychologist, philosopher, sociologist, the political scientist, the historian, and the economist. If this were found to be the case, then, since the entities concerned ('Buddhism', etc.) are so comprehensive and at the same time so diffuse that they are virtually coextensive with human life itself, they should be known respectively as the Buddhist way of life, the Islamic way of life, and so on. Another way of dealing with the matter would be to speak, for example, of 'Buddhist civilization' or 'Islamic civilization'. In the next chapter it will be suggested that this is what they once very largely were, and that 'religions' as we know them are reduced civilizations.

BUDDHISM AND THE SACRED

First, there is the question of Durkheim's hunch, referred to a little earlier, the conviction which he seems to have had that Buddhism belonged in the category of community belief-systems of a certain kind. What distinguished such belief systems, said Durkheim, was *a sense of the sacred* which each of them manifested, and which differentiated them from secular belief systems. Furthermore, Durkheim suggested where the source of this sense of the sacred was to be found: it was in the human individual's awareness of his own dependence on the values and the collective life of the society to which he belonged, something which greatly transcended him, with his own short span of life, something to which he was indebted, which upheld him, and which provided the sanctions for his conduct. One might say that that which totally *sanctions* the life of the individual is the *sanctus*, the sacred. This need of the human individual for a collective with which he can identify, and which 'sanctions' his existence can be seen as underlying a good deal of what goes by the name of religion, and may be seen, also, as providing a powerful source of motivation for much of the activity which is called 'political'.

It was this, rather than belief in a spiritual, superhuman being or beings, according to Durkheim, which was the dominant strand in 'religion'. This very useful distinction provided by the concept of the sacred will be taken up later, in connection with the Buddhism of Ceylon, where the classical Theravada form exists in association with local beliefs in gods and spirits.

The answer to the question whether Buddhism is a religion is thus both Yes and No. It is not necessary to regard it as a religion if by that is meant a system of beliefs focusing in the supposed existence of a supernatural spirit being or beings, a god or gods. For in at least one of its major forms, the Theravada school, prominent in India in the early centuries, and still the dominant form in Ceylon and South-East Asia, Buddhism has no essential need of such beliefs. Later on in India a form of Buddhism emerged, alongside the Theravada, which was characterized by beliefs in, and practices associated with, heavenly beings who possessed superhuman spiritual power, and who were known as Bodhisattvas. This form of belief seems to be virtually indistinguishable in practice from polytheism (or trans-polytheistic monism), whether of India, or China, or Japan. In both senses of the word religion (belief in spiritual beings *and* belief in the sacred), the Bodhisattva school of Buddhism, sometimes known as Bodhisattva-yana, sometimes as Mahayana, was a religious system. The common element which it shares with the Theravada (the one survivor of eighteen schools of non-Mahayana, which collectively are called Hinayana) is the sense of the sacred. But even here an important distinction between the two schools has to be made. For Mahayana Buddhism the sacred has its special focus in the heavenly realm where dwell the Bodhisattvas, the superhuman spiritual beings who are said to exert their influence to help poor struggling mortals. In directing their attention to this supramundane heavenly community the Mahayanists showed themselves correspondingly less concerned with the need to order the earthly society of men in such a way that would facilitate the pursuit of the Buddhist life, and would enhance and encourage human effort. More reliance on heavenly power meant that less attention needed to be given to earthly factors. The Mahayanists became more concerned with devotions to the heavenly beings, with ritual and speculation, and less with the nature of the civilization in which they lived.

On the other hand there was the hard core of Buddhist tradition which never totally disappeared from Buddhist India even in the period when Mahayana flourished in such great citadels as Nalanda (in Bihar). This tradition was that reliance on the saving power of heavenly beings is contrary to the teaching of Gotama, the Buddha, who emphasized that men's supreme need was for sustained moral effort and mental discipline.[7] Where this point of view prevailed there was also a general tendency to realize Buddhist values as far as it could be done in the life of the society concerned; wherever possible this would be at the national level. In the areas where Theravada has been influential there has been a strongly developed sense of the need for a Buddhist state. It has been in the Theravada countries that Buddhism has most clearly expressed its character in this way, and that Buddhist civilization has been most strongly developed and has endured.

This should not, of course, be taken to mean that Mahayana Buddhism is of less significance for the sociological study of religion. In a sense a much greater refinement of approach is needed in dealing with the sociological interrelation of, say, economic factors with certain kinds of belief. That is an important task for the cross-cultural sociology of religion, but it is one which is not undertaken in the present work. The focus of the present study is in the idea of a Buddhist civilization, and the particular form this takes in the Buddhist state.

THE HISTORICAL PERSPECTIVE

There are various ways in which one can study the teaching of some outstanding figure such as Gotama the Buddha (or Jesus, or Muhammad). Ultimately, however, the various ways will be seen to resolve themselves into two main ones. The first of these may be called the literalist approach. The sayings of the Buddha are regarded as propositions to be understood literally without any necessary reference to the context in which they were spoken; as they stand they can be examined (if one is an historian of ideas), or thought about (if one is an interested inquirer), and acted upon (if one is a devotee). Usually it has been the devotee (of a certain type) who has been responsible for encouraging the literalist approach. For he who, in the first instance, has come to regard the total teaching of the founder of his religion, contained in the canon of scripture, as *the* truth will also very easily apply such an evaluation to this or that particular saying which he finds in the canon; such sayings become invested with the quality of 'eternal truths', propositions which are universally valid in all circumstances and under all conditions. The historian of ideas and the interested inquirer note this claim and proceed to work within these terms of reference: to be a Christian, or a Muslim, or a Buddhist, is to accept the canonical words of Jesus, or Muhammad, or Gotama as inspired, eternal truths. From such absolutist claims there follows all too easily the clash of rival 'absolutes', as well as the alienation of the more thoughtful.

The second approach may be called the historical–critical. In this case the teaching of the Buddha is related to the historical situation in which it was delivered, so far as it is possible to reconstruct and understand that situation. Attention is paid not only to the substance and meaning of the words spoken, but also to the fact that they were spoken to certain hearers in a given, concrete situation. In order to know what weight is to be given to a particular saying it is necessary to remember that the words were not uttered into the empty air, but to a specific audience. The nature of the audience, their level of understanding, their preconceptions or prejudices, and so on, all need to be taken into account in assessing how profound or how ephemeral the words are. In following such a method, difficult though it may be to apply in all cases, one is enabled to see that some aspects of the teaching have permanent validity because they are relevant to some enduring feature of the human situation, whereas others will be understood as having only limited validity since they refer in a very particular way to special situations which existed in the teacher's own day and which now no longer exist, or to beliefs which were current then but which are not held now. This second approach, like the first, may be adopted with equal appropriateness whether one is an historian of ideas, an inquirer, or a devotee.

Severe limitations attend the literalist approach. These show themselves specially clearly when one is attempting to evaluate the message of a teacher such as the Buddha in relation to the teachings of other prominent figures in the history of ideas. An extreme example will serve to highlight the difficulty. Karl Marx wrote a good deal concerning the alienation or estrangement (*Entfremdung*) which he saw as a feature of the human situation, but to search for a saying of the Buddha on this subject is to draw a blank, since Marx was dealing with industrial, capitalistic society in nineteenth-century Europe, and nothing of this sort existed in the India of the sixth century BC. To attempt to relate the teaching of the Buddha to that of Karl Marx purely in terms of propositions is likely to be an unprofitable exercise; it is like trying to get a telephone conversation going between two men who speak different languages, and one of whom cannot hear the other.

However, those who have by common convention been regarded as in some sense or other 'religious' teachers have this much in common, that they have all ultimately been concerned with a dimension to human existence other than the material and the temporal, a dimension which, in the interests of brevity, may be called the transcendental dimension. This applies to the Buddha, as to other so-called 'religious' teachers, even although, in his case, unlike most of the others, belief in the existence of a supreme divine being is not integral to his teaching. It is this transcendental dimension which invests the life of the human individual with a significance it would not otherwise have, and which it does not have in purely materialistic schemes of thought. 'There is, O monks,' the Buddha is reported to have said, 'that which is not-born, not-become, not-made, not-compounded. If that not-born, not-become, not-made, not-compounded were not, there would be no release from this life of the born, the become, the made, the compounded.'[8] Another feature of the teaching of the Buddha which, in general terms, is shared with the other great systems which have come to be called religions is the importance given to proper moral conduct and moral attitudes on the part of the individual. This may be seen as the counterpart, at the level of human response, of the importance accorded to the transcendental dimension.

After recognizing these two common features, however, one begins to be more aware of differences than of similarities. It is at this point that the historical–critical approach is particularly relevant. It has already been pointed out that the form and even the content of a particular saying may be due to the local historical factors which have to be known and understood if the saying is to be realistically evaluated. This principle, by which we recognize this or that *saying* to have been conditioned by the circumstances in which it was spoken and the audience to whom it was addressed, can be extended beyond the form and content of particular sayings. The possibility which has to be considered is this: that the form and content of the teaching *as a whole* may be the result of conditioning by local, historical and geographical factors. It is to the exploring of this possibility, in so far as it relates to the religious teaching of the Buddha, that the first part of this book is devoted (chapters 2–4).

It should perhaps be made clear at the outset that this is not a full-scale cultural history of Buddhism. It has a more limited, simple, two-fold aim: first, to show what were the historical conditions in India – environmental, economic, political, and social – out of which the Buddha emerged, and in terms of which his significance must be assessed; and second, to provide an account of the distinctively new phenomenon which resulted in due course from the Buddha's life and work, namely, Buddhist civilization. This will be examined first in principle (chapters 6–8) and then in practice (chapters 9–12).

Thus, in one sense of the word 'religion', denoting beliefs and practices connected with spirit-beings, Buddhism was in origin not a religion, but a non-religious philosophy. In the other, more sophisticated meaning of the word 'religion', which indicates awareness of that which is *sacred*, that which sanctions every individual existence, Buddhism in its Asian setting remains in certain respects what it was in origin, a way of attempting to restructure human consciousness and the common life of men in accordance with the nature of what it conceives to be the sacred reality. There are signs that in the modern period this important dimension of Buddhist civilization – the societal and political dimension – has been lost sight of, and that Buddhism is being reduced from a civilization to what the modern world understands by religion: that is, a system of 'spiritual' beliefs to be taken up by the minority in whatever country it happens to be who care for that sort of thing, a source of comfort to some, but in the last resort a private irrelevance, having little bearing on the real issues that shape human affairs. When Westerners have looked at Buddhism, too often they have seen only this, because this was all they were looking for. We shall examine this issue in general terms before we embark on our main purpose.

2 Religions and Civilizations

MODERN RELIGIOUS PLURALISM

In a brief but highly significant article on the role of Buddhism as a religion in modern, traditionally non-Buddhist societies, Elizabeth Nottingham indicates a number of important points for any comparative, sociological study of Buddhism.[1] One of these is the assimilation of Buddhism to the common pattern of 'religions' in urbanized societies. She observes that in contemporary situations in the United States and elsewhere 'Buddhism has had to accommodate itself to an existence as *one* religion among *a number* of other religions in a given country.' Introduced in the first place by Chinese and Japanese immigrants, Buddhism is now making itself at home in the United States and 'is already taking its place as *one* of the many organized "religions" of America ... While still remaining Buddhism it is beginning to take on forms of organization and congregational services modelled on the American pattern.'[2] The same kind of process appears to be going on in parts of Europe and non-Buddhist Asia, especially in urban situations. In Malaysia, to take a random example, an organization for Buddhists, mainly residents of the capital, Kuala Lumpur, was founded in 1962, known as the Buddhist Missionary Society. The local achievements of the Society include the development of a uniform system of worship in connection with regular religious services, a Sunday School attended by hundreds of adolescent boys and girls and school children, religious classes for youths and adults, sessions for the singing of Buddhist hymns and songs, services of blessing by monks for newly-wedded couples, after the civil ceremony, and the performance of last religious rites.[3] Growth in the numbers taking part in these activities since 1962 is said to have been remarkable. Equally remarkable to the Western observer is the degree of assimilation to the pattern of activities of urban religious groups, of all kinds, in the West. One important factor in the Malaysian case may be the number of Ceylonese Buddhist expatriates living there. Many of these are middle-class people in professional occupations who have imported urban assumptions about the proper pattern for Buddhist activities from Ceylon. These assumptions appear to be largely due to accommodation to Christian concepts, encountered in Ceylon.[4]

To take another example, Buddhism is represented in England by a number of local associations in cities, towns and universities in various parts of the country.[5] While these groups vary to some extent in the kind of activities they engage in, and to a minor extent also in the social stratum from which their members are drawn, they share a tendency to see themselves as part of the spectrum of local religious sects and churches. Anyone who is familiar with institutionalized English Christianity will find much that is similar here, only with Buddhist terminology substituted. One characteristic which this kind of Buddhism shares with conventional middle-class suburban Christian organizations is an extreme reluctance to become involved in, or even to allow discussion of, matters of a political nature.

Thus, the temptation grows to answer the question 'What is Buddhism' by conceding that, after all, it is merely one of the *religions*, that is, one of the many organizations in the modern world which cater for men's private 'spiritual' needs, and which, competing for recruits, regard the number of those gained as the measure of the organization's success. To accept this as an adequate answer to the question 'What is Buddhism?' would, however, be to take a short-sighted and simplistic view; short sighted because it would force Buddhism permanently into the perspective of the suburban religious situation of the West; and simplistic because it would ignore the implications which Buddhist values carry in the realms of politics, economics and social structure. It would be to underestimate the social-revolutionary potential of Buddhism if it were assumed that it is merely a message of private consolation, or spiritual uplift, and that its presuppositions, and the life-style which it implies, are ultimately indistinguishable from those of the suburban residents of London or Petaling-Jaya.[6]

This phenomenon of the recent growth of Buddhist groups in the urban middle-class sector of traditionally non-Buddhist societies may, however, represent a significant new cultural development. For it may be serving to channel what in the first instance are largely negative feelings of dissatisfaction with Western society, its norms and values. Aspirations towards an alternative type of society, dimly perceived and perhaps not consciously formulated, may be nourishing this growth of Buddhist groups in non-Buddhist countries, a growth which has been particularly noticeable, not only since the end of the Second World War, but in the last decade.[7] This is a possible explanation which will be considered again at the end of this book, when the nature of Buddhist civilization has been explored.

'GREAT RELIGIONS' AS RESIDUAL CIVILIZATIONS

For Buddhism is, and has been for more than two thousand years, something very much more significant, socially, economically and politically, than is allowed by the statement 'Buddhism is one of the religions'. So also were Judaism, Christianity (for at least 1200 years) and Islam (for 1300 years), although these also today find themselves being relegated to the league of those organizations which cater mainly for the private, 'spiritual' aspirations of individual citizens, whose lives are, at the same time, being moulded and determined in the public dimension by forces quite independent of the organized 'religions'. It was not always so. There was a time when at least the major representatives of what are today identified by the reductionist term 'religions' or even 'great religions' were considerably more than institutionalized systems of private comfort and salvation which have no business to concern themselves with 'politics'; but this is what they have become today in the eyes of the majority of their adherents, especially their lay adherents.

What all these 'great' systems have in common is that each in origin was a total view of the world and man's place in it, and a total prescription for the ordering of human affairs in all the various dimensions which in the modern world are separated and distinguished from one another as philosophy, politics, economics, ethics, law and so on. Such an undifferentiated view of things is characteristic of 'unsophisticated' tribal life. But when, for one reason or another, the structure of tribal life is upset, there eventually follows, perhaps after an interval of time and after the enforced mingling of originally separate tribal cultures, some attempt at reintegration, now in a wider context than before, and with considerably extended horizons. The old tribal integration would eventually be broken by the trauma which historical events were to bring about. The new integration is on the other side of the trauma; it recognizes the traumatic events, and goes beyond them. It is an integration which would not have been possible, or would have had no relevance, in the earlier situation.

HINDU CIVILIZATION

What is popularly known as Hinduism provides a good example of this. 'Hinduism' covers, in fact, a large family of cultural systems and theistic sects. The most important of these, historically and structurally, is the system properly known as brahamanism. Metaphysics, cult, ceremonial, social structure, ethical principles, political and economic prescriptions, all are to be found in brahman-ism. In this case the 'crisis' which brought it into being appears to have been the encounter of the incoming Aryan civilization with the culture which already existed in India when the Aryan immigrants arrived.[8] It was probably a fairly protracted crisis, extending over several centuries, but the result was an integrated civilization in which everything had been considered and provided for by the brahmans, the socially predominant priestly class, who were the architects of the system.[9] One of the most com-prehensive treatises on the nature and structure of brah-man civilization is the *Treatise on Government (Arthasas-tra)* of Kautilya. Another is the *Law Code of Manu (Manava Sastra)*, a work composed by brahmans but ascribed to Manu, the mythical father and lawgiver of the human race.

The word *artha* in the title of the first of these treatises represents an important concept of the brahmanical view of the world. The three principal concerns of man are, in this view, in order of importance: *dharma* (righteousness or duty), *artha* (the public economy) and *kama* (aesthetic pleasure). When these are properly regulated and wisely pursued it becomes possible for man to achieve *moksha*, the spiritual goal of life. Thus, rules governing the public economy are an essential feature of brahman civilization, and so are rules governing the whole realm of aesthetic pleasures. Both of these, however, are subordinate to *dharma*, a word for which there is no single English equivalent. It indicates the eternal principle of being, that which *is*, and upholds all things. It also means the mode of life which is in harmony with this eternal prin-ciple. And it can mean, too, the specific code of conduct proper to each group, or to each individual according to the stage of life he has reached. It is in this context that one has to place such a treatise as the *Arthasastra*, the treatise on public wealth, welfare or economy.

The *Arthasastra* of Kautilya deals first with the life of the king: how he should discipline himself by restraining the organs of sense, the principles which should govern the appointment of his counsellors, and the conduct of the meetings of king and counsellors. It then goes on to describe in detail the rural economy, the development of villages and the regulation of their life with a view to the quiet and uninterrupted pursuit by the villagers of their proper occupations. It deals also with legal contracts, disputes, sexual offences, marriage and heritance laws, property purchase and sale, personal assault, betting and gambling, and so on. Other sections of the treatise deal with public finance, the civil service, defence, foreign policy and diplomacy. The emphasis, it will be seen, lies fairly heavily on legal, economic and political matters. The other treatise, the Law Code of Manu, is wider in its scope. It is more than a legal treatise; as Keith says, 'It is unquestionably rather to be compared with the great poem of Lucretius, beside which it ranks as the expression of a philosophy of life.'[10] After a description of the creation of the universe, the text sets before us the brahmanical view of the hierarchy of living beings, of whom 'the most excellent are men, and of men [the most excellent] are brahmans'. The life of men is then covered in great detail, and regulations are laid down for every aspect of human affairs: sacramental initiation, student life, the life of the householder, marriage, types of occupation, duties of woman, rules for hermits and ascetics and rules concerning the king: how he should be honoured, how he should spend his time, when he should offer worship, and how he should conduct the public affairs of the kingdom. A considerable body of civil and criminal law is also included, covering such matters as recovery of debts, agreements in respect of sale and purchase, boundaries, defamation, assault, theft, violence, adultery, inheritance, and various other matters.[11]

These two are not the only brahman treatises governing religious, political, economic and social life, but they are the best known, most important, and have been influential in the shaping of Hindu civilization. It is clear that what is described in these texts, and what was envisaged by the brahmans as their legitimate field of concern, is not adequately described as *religion*, as that word is now commonly used, but *civilization*.

ISLAMIC CIVILIZATION

Islam provides an even better example. As D. S. Margoliouth wrote, 'We are apt to think of Islam as a religion, whereas the prophet probably thought of it rather as a nation.'[12] Early Islam was a complete prescription for human life as it then existed in the Arabian peninsula. A document known as *The Constitution of Medina*, together with the Quran, provided for every aspect of human needs in the early period – a view of the world and man's place in it, an account of man's destiny, the rules by which social relations and personal conduct were to be governed, how economic resources were to be used, what customs, ceremonies, festivals and so on, were to be followed. It was, in other words, the vision of a new civilization. At first it was believed that this vision was for the people of Arabia; then it came to be considered as one which had universal relevance, and which therefore could be applied to other situations outside Arabia. As Islam spread into the other lands of the Middle East, it was as a civilization that it spread and developed in the initial stages. Leadership in prayer and leadership in political control were alike the responsibility of the Prophet and, after him, of each *khalifa*, or successor of the Prophet. The community of Islam was, as *The Constitution of Medina* said, one community over against the rest of mankind; it was one in theology, in government, in economic life and in social *mores*. But when, in the course of time, political power and economic practice became independent issues, then 'Islam' was the residue: namely the theology, the ethic and the social customs. What was originally a civilization had now, by a process of reduction, become a 'religion'. In the case of Islam, however, the original vision has never been entirely lost, and even in the modern world there have been attempts to reconstitute Islam after the earlier fashion, as a nation-state based on a theology and an ethic. An example is the Republic of Pakistan – at least, this was the hope claimed by some of the Muslims of undivided India in 1947.

Judaism has had a similar history. Its earliest identifiable form is found in the tribal confederation, united by the common vision of the prophets, a vision of what human society should be, what were its sustaining values, what its norms of social and individual behaviour, what its proper political form. But when the confederation was politically disrupted, north from south, each half thereafter maintained a theologically diminished and politically distorted version of the original theocratic civilization. The two halves each adopted, instead of theocracy, the ancient Near Eastern pattern of government, which was that of a militarily maintained, city-based monarchy. Thus, Yahwistic civilization was in essence abandoned. The theological, social and ethical residue was preserved, however, in an uneasy coexistence and compromise with the urban monarchical system of government until at last, in the course of the political history of Palestine, the head of the Judaean state was overthrown by the empire of Babylon; and Judaism developed in its residual form as a civilization without political or economic dimensions, that is, as a 'religion'.

JUDAEO–CHRISTIAN CIVILIZATION

As in the case of Islam, so, too, in the history of Judaism there were attempts to reconstitute it as a totally integrated civilization, attempts to 'restore the kingdom to Israel'. This is not the place to examine them in detail. It may be noted, however, that yet another of the great 'religions' of the world – Christianity – may possibly have resulted from one of them. In this case, however, the early nature of the movement is now almost entirely unknown to us. Those early developments which took place in Palestine in a community of Aramean-speaking Jews are known to us only through a set of documents in Hellenistic Greek. In these not only the original words of Joshua (Hellenized as 'Jesus') of Nazareth have been translated into a foreign language, but the interpretation of the significance of the events themselves is given to us in terms of Hellenistic Jewish thought, much of it that of Saul (Paul) of Tarsus, a Jew of Roman citizenship, indebted to the Hellenes for a great part of his culture. It is evident from the evidence of these documents (known by Christians as The New Testament) that there were a number of partisan interpretations of the events which had taken place in Judaea in connection with Jesus, and that Paul's was one among others. Evidence from non-Christian sources concerning the movement is very scanty and tells us nothing more than that Jesus was put to death by the Romans for sedition. S. G. F. Brandon, in his examination of the available evidence, comments 'on the irony of the fact that the execution of Jesus as a rebel against Rome is the most certain thing we know about him'.[13] Professor Brandon goes on to examine the connection between Jesus and the Zealots. He points out that because the latter were rebels against an imperial power, they tended to have a poor press in the West, where they could too easily be assimilated with Russian, Irish or Indian revolutionaries, all groups who threatened the stability of Western capitalist, imperialist rule. Since the Second World War, however, with its change of sentiment towards 'resistance groups' there has, he notes, been some slight change of attitude to the Zealots among Western scholars. What is still hard for Christians, thinking of Jesus as the incarnate God is 'even to consider the possibility that Jesus might have had political views'.[14] He points out that

if theological considerations make it necessary to prejudge the historical situation and to decide that Jesus could not have involved himself in a contemporary political issue, the judgement must accordingly be seen for what it is . . . Such an evaluation of Jesus may be deemed theologically necessary and sound, but it will surely concern another Jesus than he who lived in Judaea when Pontius Pilate was procurator, under whom he suffered crucifixion as a rebel against Rome.[15]

The historical evidence concerning the period in which Jesus lived clearly points to the existence of widespread political discontent among the Jews of what had, by then, become a Roman province, and of various movements aimed at the overthrow of Roman power and the restoration of the Jewish theocratic ideal. Whether or not the movement associated with the name of Jesus of Nazareth was one such movement, aimed at the recovery of an integrated Jewish civilization, it is clear that by the time it had begun to win adherents in the Hellenistic world outside Palestine, it had lost any such total vision; in leaving Judaea it very soon became non-political. Its apologists were eager to make this very clear to the Roman authorities, and later Christian theologians neither understood, nor had any interest in understanding, Jewish politics of the time of Jesus.[16] Like later Islam, and Judaism after AD 70, the early Hellenistic Christian movement had the restricted range of interests of a religion rather than of a civilization. It is noteworthy in this case, however, that when Christianity had become combined with the state religion of Rome, in the time of the Emperor Constantine, it did take on the kind of characteristics which justify its being called from this time, and throughout the medieval period, a civilization. The old gods of Rome had lost their ability to legitimate the imperial power; but once the Roman political system had found for itself a new source of legitimation, in the Jewish–Christian idea of God, it was assured of continuity, in the form of the Roman Church and the Roman Christian civilization to which it gave rise. The system lasted until, in the modern period, the theistic belief which had provided it with its sanctions began to be eroded by the rationalism of the emerging modern cities. After passing through the transitional stage which characterized it in its modern urban–rationalistic milieu, the stage of Protestantism, Christian civilization may now be said to have disappeared almost finally into the sands of modern Western secularism.

MODERN SOCIETIES AND THEISTIC BELIEF

Each of the 'major religions' which we have considered, *as they now exist*, may be seen as theological, ethical and ritual deposits left behind when the civilizations of which they were part lost their distinctive political and economic features. In each case the original vision on which the civilization was based had some form of theistic belief as its legitimation. Islam was realized as a civilization because there were men who were persuaded that the God of whom Muhammad spoke was a living reality, the supreme being, whose commands could not be set aside. It was the work of persuading men of this which was in the first instance the prophet's great achievement, carried out as it was in the face of the opposition and scepticism of the Meccan merchants and their followers. Initially, the prophet's success must be attributed to the power of his personality, together, perhaps, with a predisposition on the part of some of his hearers to belief in a supreme, powerful and righteous being. Given such belief there could follow, detail by detail, the realization of the prophet's vision of a new structure for human society which would transcend tribal limits and individual self-interest. When the civilization thus created eventually lost its political cohesion and its economic integrity, the theistic belief which had been its sanction remained as its central feature. As modernization advances, and Islamic life becomes by degrees more and more secularized, it is the element of belief in Allah which remains as the final distinctive feature. When a Muslim living in Britain is encouraged or forced by circumstances to conform more and more closely to the pattern of life of his workmates, and can perhaps no longer even observe properly the fast of Ramadan, then what finally marks him out as a Muslim is the distinctive nature of his belief in God, differing as it does from that of both Jew and Christian. This then, this surviving shred of the whole civilization which once encompassed the life of his forefathers, is what in the end Islam may come to mean for him: one variety among others of belief in God. What was once a civilization has now become a man's 'religion' – as that word is frequently used and understood in the West today. Perhaps some ritual practices and ethical attitudes will be preserved, but their maintenance will be precarious, depending very largely on the continuance of belief in the God of Islam. In the case of the children of such a man, brought up in modern industrial Britain, when belief in Islam's God is no longer tenable, there would seem to be little justification for practices and attitudes which mark them off from their schoolfellows; such justification as there is will then consist almost entirely in the strength of the family's own tradition.

This situation is one which all the major religions of the West share now that they have been reduced to their present state of being little more than precariously held theistic beliefs with attendant ethical attitudes and a possible modicum of ritual practice. Their viability is thus limited; they will last as long as theistic belief can be maintained in a modern industrial society. This may, of course, be longer than the unbeliever expects, especially among politically, socially or culturally deprived or depressed classes of society for whom traditional theistic belief can be a major source of satisfaction and comfort.

ALTERNATIVES TO THEISM

It is often assumed in the West that theistic belief is the only possible way in which a man or a civilization can be spiritually orientated. A major refutation of this assumption is provided by Buddhism. It is possible that Marxism may provide another but, as yet, it has not had as long a period as Buddhism in which to demonstrate its capacity in this direction. What they have in common is that they both begin from a vision of a new civilization which will enable man to grow and develop into a quality of life beyond what he has known hitherto. In neither case, however, does this vision need to be legitimated by reference to belief in a supreme divine being. The sanctions in both cases are philosophical rather than theological; in the case of Buddhism they are also to some extent derived from what, for brevity, may be called psychological experience.

Thus, one view of the relationship between religion and civilization is that religions make civilizations – or that they have done so in the past. Another view is that what are seen today as the 'great religions' – Hinduism, Buddhism, Christianity, Islam – are vestigial remains of civilizations. Mere hummocks of what were once, so to speak, great mountain ranges, they now have a mild charm, standing out a little, as they do, from the flat alluvial expanse of secularism in which they are slowly being silted up. Perhaps, to continue the geological metaphor, they will be superseded by some upthrust of new rock from the depths. The first rumblings of this movement can already faintly be heard. Whether that will be so or not we cannot tell. What we can discern is the present shape of the so-called 'great religions', and their drastically reduced dimensions, compared with what once they were. In the process of erosion by which civilizations were reduced to religions, one of the severest stages was that which occurred about a century ago. It has been described by Louis Wirth: 'The atomistic point of view arising out of the biological and mechanistic tradition of the late nineteenth century led to the recognition of the individual organism as the solid reality constituting the unit of social life, and depreciation of "society" as a terminological construct or an irrelevant fiction.' [17] The idea that human society is nothing more than the aggregate of the individual members of which it is composed is reflected in the nineteenth-century view of religion as the wholly private affair of the individual, a view which is given concrete expression in the American 'secular' state, where what is public and official has to be kept from all contact with religion which is essentially the affair of the individual.[18]

What the Buddha initiated, therefore, was not a religion – at least not in any sense that has meaning in the twentieth century. The same is true of the civilizations initiated by Moses, and Muhammad and perhaps Jesus, and the anonymous brahmans of ancient India who are represented by the name of Manu. What these all initiated were more than 'religions' in the reduced, individualistic sense of today. What exactly the Buddha did initiate it is the purpose of this book to explore. When its full scope has been revealed and its essential features have been examined, we may then decide how best it may be characterized. To do this will lead us to consider the characteristics of the Ashokan Kingdom of India in the third century BC, territorially and in other ways one of the greatest India has ever known; it will require us to look at the subsequent fate of Buddhist civilization in India, and to consider the long history of Buddhism in the island of Ceylon as it has existed now for twenty-two centuries.

Part 2

North India in the
Sixth Century BC

3 The Physical, Economic and Social Environment

THE INDIAN 'MIDDLE COUNTRY'

Gotama the Buddha was born at a time when the main centre of Indian civilization was located in the Ganges plain.[1] Whether there were at that time other important centres of development elsewhere in India is an open question. Certainly less is known of the peninsula or the south for this period.[2] The only other area of India for which historical evidence is available is the Indus valley. One of the indications that the Ganges valley had become the focal area of development is that in the literature which dates from this period, both brahmanical and Buddhist, it was termed 'the middle country' (*Madhyadesa*, Skt; *Majjhimadesa*, Pali). The exact extent of the area to which this title was applied seems to have varied from one literary source to another but generally it designates the middle Gangetic plain. The Buddhist sources tend to regard the Majjhimadesa as extending farther to the east than do the brahmanical sources. For the Buddhists the eastern boundary was at a town called Kajangala, possibly the most easterly point reached by the Buddha in his travels. Kajangala was described by the Chinese Buddhist pilgrim, Hsuan Tsang, as being 400 *li* to the east of Champa (modern Bhagalpur). This would locate it at the point where the Ganges, at the eastern edge of Bihar, makes a major change of course towards the south, to flow through Bengal. In the other direction the boundary of the Majjhimadesa was a little to the west of the modern city of Delhi, along the western watershed of the Yamuna river, the major tributary to the Ganges, which flows parallel with it through most of the northern part of the Gangetic plain.

It was in this region, the 'middle' or 'central' country,

comprising the Ganges valley from its upper reaches as far as the approaches to the delta, which was regarded as the most important area of India by all the ancient writers. Wherever brahmanical or Buddhist literature deals with geographical description, great attention is devoted to 'the central country' and much less to the other four regions – namely, northern, western, southern and eastern India. One does not have to seek very far for a reason for this, as B. C. Law pointed out:

As with the brahmanical Aryans, so with the Buddhists, Middle Counry was the cradle on which they staged the entire drama of their career, and it is to the description and information of this tract of land (by whatever name they called it) that they bestowed all their care and attention. Outside the pale of Madhyadesa there were countries that were always looked down upon by the inhabitants of the favoured region.[3]

THE HEART OF THE MIDDLE COUNTRY

By the time of Gotama's birth in the sixth century B C, however, it is possible to identify, even within the territory of the Middle Country, an inner heartland of the developing civilization.[4] This heartland consisted approximately of the area comprised by the rival Kingdoms of Koshala and Magadha, to which further reference will be made in the next chapter. Roughly, the territory concerned was the Gangetic plain from just west of the modern city of Lucknow to Bhagalpur in the east. Another way of identifying it is to say that it consists of the south-eastern third of the modern state of Uttar Pradesh, a small part of Nepal, and the northern half of the state of Bihar. Apart from a relatively small proportion of upland – the southern slopes of the Himalayan foothills of central Nepal and some outliers of the Bihar hills in the neighbourhood of Gaya – the whole of this area of about 70,000 square miles consists of the broad, flat expanse of the middle Gangetic plain, which nowhere in this region rises abovè 350 feet.

Along the entire northern edge of this plain are the

steeply rising slopes of the Himalayan mountain range, whose peaks are the highest in the world; from plains level to a height of 20,000 feet is reached in a horizontal distance of about seventy miles. Issuing southwards from this mountain range are the many tributaries which flow south to join the Ganges. The Ganges river itself emerges from the mountains in the extreme north of Uttar Pradesh to flow 1300 miles south-eastwards through this great plain before turning southwards to enter the Bay of Bengal. From Kanpur, where the river has yet 900 miles to go before reaching the sea, its height above sea-level is only 360 feet, so low and level are the plains from here.

For four months of the year, from June to September, the monsoon pours heavy rain over the whole region; this is heaviest in the eastern part of the region, and over the forested slopes of the Himalayas along the northern boundary. Most of the great rivers which flow south-eastwards across the plain, eventually to join the Ganges, have their source in the Himalayas, and between them they carry down the vast volume of water which the monsoon discharges. Some of the larger rivers on the northern half of the plain, such as the Gandak and Kosi, cause great damage by flooding the countryside, changing their courses, and depositing sand and stones across the plain. Ninety per cent of the total yearly rainfall comes in these four months, with the result that during the remaining eight months many of the smaller rivers dwindle away almost to nothing. The Gumti, for instance, is more than two miles wide in the rainy season, but a mere two hundred feet in the hot season.[5] The larger rivers, however, are fed from another source during the burning heat of the summer, from February to May; having their sources in the heights of the Himalayas they receive their water from the melting snows and glaciers. The Ganges 'never dwindles away in the hottest summer'.[6] Thus the plains which surround these larger rivers have a year-round supply of water, and agriculture can be maintained by irrigation. The soil of the Gangetic plain varies in quality, but in many places,

especially where the Ganges, unlike the devastating Gan-
dek and Kosi rivers, deposits rich alluvium it is suitable
for intensive agriculture; 'the alluvial silt which it spills
over its banks year by year affords to the fields a top-dress-
ing of unexhaustible fertility'.[7] It is therefore not surprising that throughout the history of the region its people
have held sacred the source of such fertility and life.

Between the four months of monsoon rain and the four
months of burning sun and scorching wind comes the
season of winter, from October to the end of January: a
time of calm blue skies, when the days are warm, the
nights cool and the mornings fresh and dewy. There may,
however, be a period of light winter rain in January. This
is the time when the *rabi* (spring-harvested) crops are
grown, such as wheat and barley, and linseed and mustard
for their oil.

A LAND OF ABUNDANT FOOD

In the Buddha's day the situation was in some respects
very much more favourable for agriculture than it is today.[8] Much of the Gangetic plain was still forested, and
land could be had for the clearing, where virgin soil was
ready to produce abundant harvest. The Greek writers of
the period describe the agriculture of the Ganges valley
with great enthusiasm. Diodonis, who derived his knowledge of India from the work of Megasthenes, writes in this
way:

> In addition to cereals there grows ... much pulse of different
> sorts, and rice also ... as well as many other plants useful for
> food, of which most grow spontaneously ... Since there is a
> double rainfall in the course of each year, one in the winter
> season, when the sowing of wheat takes place as in other coun-
> tries, and the second at the time of the summer solstice which
> is the proper season for sowing rice and bosmorum as well as
> sesamum and millet, the inhabitants of India always gather in
> two harvests annually ... The fruits, moreover, of spontaneous
> growth, and the esculent roots which grow in marshy places

and are of varied sweetness, afford abundant sustenance for man. The fact is, almost all the plains in the country have a moisture which is alike genial whether it is derived from the river, or from the rains of the summer season which are wont to fall every year at a stated period with surprising regularity.[9]

A passage from Strabo tells the same story:

From the vapours arising from such vast rivers and from the Etesian winds, as Eratosthenes states, India is watered by the summer rains and the plains are overflowed. During these rains, accordingly, flax is sown and millet; also sesamum, rice and bosmorum, and in the winter time wheat, barley pulse and other esculent fruits unknown to us.[10]

Many of these fruits, then unknown to Europeans, were gathered by the people of India from the forests which at that time were far more extensive – fruits such as mango, jack-fruit, date, coconut and banana. Throughout the Buddhist and brahmanical literature one is constantly reminded of the thick growth of forest which still covered the greater part of the plains in the sixth century BC.[11]

The wagons that carried merchandise from one town to another had to pass through dense and sometimes dangerous forests where wild creatures, human or sub-human lay in wait for the unprotected traveller. But the forests were also lovely with flowering trees, especially in the cool season and early summer. Buddhist literature frequently refers to the sound of the birds 'there, where the forest is in flower'.[12] Banyan and bo-tree, palmyra, date palm, coconut, acacia, ebony and sal, all these and many other trees are mentioned in the contemporary literature as features of the everyday scene. When, in the pursuit of the spiritual life men wished to withdraw from the enclosed village area of houses and fields, it was into the all-encircling forest that they went. In a region so vast and with a population still relatively small there was plenty of space for all, whether they wished to cultivate the numerous crops the land would bear, or to withdraw into silence and solitude.

THE ARYANIZATION OF THE MIDDLE COUNTRY

Some of the inhabitants of the Gangetic plain may originally have come from the north and east, from the lands we now call Burma and Tibet. At its eastern end there were, at the time of the Buddha, a people called the Anga, whose capital was Champa (near modern Bhagalpur). Their name, as indeed that of the Ganges itself, has been identified as Tibeto-Burman, or Sino-Burman. The findings of linguists and archaeologists are summarized as follows: 'Heine Geldern believes that the south-eastern Asiatics (Austronesians), already having considerable Mongoloid mixture, who had come down into Assam and Burma, migrated westwards into India and introduced the tanged adze between 2500 and 1500 B C before the Aryan invasion. Percy Smith recognizes a Gangetic race in northern India before the Aryan invasion. He believes that a Himalayo-Polynesian race, allied to the Chinese and Tibetan formerly spread over the Gangetic basin from further India.' [13] What is generally regarded as certain is that there had, for some centuries before the time of the Buddha, been a considerable process of 'Aryanization' spreading south-eastwards from the Indus valley, down the Ganges plain. This may have been the consequence of an actual physical invasion by Aryan-speaking peoples from the north-west beyond India, which swept away the ancient city-civilization of the Indus valley, or it may have been part of a general cultural movement, like other cultural 'invasions' which have taken place over the same territory in the centuries since that time. The invasion of north India by Islam provides a clear example of the latter possibility. While there were, it is true, actual movements of Muslim invaders from the north-west, these were only a minority among the people whom they invaded. The spread of Islam (mainly from the eleventh century AD onwards) consisted largely in the adherence of large numbers of the original inhabitants of the territory to Islamic culture and Persian language. This kind of process may well have occurred in the course of the Aryanization of northern India which marked the centuries immediately before the time of the Buddha. In north India this period was, as Kosambi points out, one of transition from a pastoral, herd-keeping mode of life to one of cultivation of the soil. The land was at the 'crucial stage where soon the plough would produce much more than cattle' in the way of food supply.[14] The stages by which this would have come about are fairly clearly traceable.

RICE CULTIVATION AND POPULATION INCREASE

The situation in the Buddha's time can be seen as one of increasingly extensive agriculture in the middle Gangetic plain. The cost of this increase in agriculture was extensive deforestation. Round each village settlement was an area of cultivated fields, beyond this some pasture, and then the forest. As the bounds of the cultivated fields were pushed outwards, the forested area retreated before the agriculturist's axe and fire. New fields were to be had for the clearing and some of the more enterprising were opening up new settlements. There was consequently a continually spreading area of cultivated field. Where cattle raising, associated with a nomadic or semi-nomadic way of life, is the main occupation, there is not normally a high density of population. The increase in cultivation would, therefore, have entailed a sharp increase in the human population of the region. The land which was being brought under cultivation was pre-eminently suited to rice-growing, especially when advantage was taken of the all-the-year-round water supply from the Ganges in the development of irrigation. It is known that at the time of the Buddha this was, in fact, being done.[15] It was the rice of the Gangetic plain which became, and has remained, the major source of food supply in the eastern half of Uttar Pradesh, in Bihar and Bengal. The time spent in cultivating the land would have meant that less time and energy could be spent on herd-keeping. This, together with a decrease in the range of land available for herds, meant a gradual decline in the cattle population. In this way a change in the balance of the people's diet would have occurred, from one in which milk products and meat had a large place, to one in which the larger place was taken by rice and vegetables. It has been pointed out that the latter type of diet is a factor in further population increase. Rice, says Beaujeu-Garnier 'produces two to two-and-a-half times more grain to the acre than wheat, two thirds more than barley, and one third more than maize. Moreover, it is a food of high value, especially when consumed in the husk.'[16] In addition to this, whereas a high protein diet, such as that enjoyed by those whose diet consists in large measure of milk products and meat, appears to reduce fertility, a rice diet seems to have the opposite effect; rice provides 'women with a diet which predisposes them to fertility; furthermore it can be consumed by very young infants either as a gruel or as a pulp, enabling them to survive and thus to be weaned early so that the mother is ready to conceive again'.[17] The increase in human population, which had followed the beginning of the deforestation of the Ganges plain, would have resulted in a demand for yet more land to support the increasing numbers.

By the time of the Buddha a steady growth in the density of population of the Gangetic plain was taking place, and, together with this, there was probably a decline in the number of cattle being reared. To this fact has to be added another, as we shall see later: that cattle were a consumable commodity, so to speak, since they were required in considerable numbers for the brahmanical sacrificial system. Moreover, these sacrifices would probably have increased in number, if only slightly, with the increase in human population. This would have been the case especially in times of threatened shortage of cattle or food, since the sacrifice was supposed to ensure prosperity. The growth of monarchy and the aggressiveness of kings would have supplied another reason for an increase in the number of sacrifices, since success in battle was also held to be secured through priestly offerings. Over the whole area under cultivation the density of population would have remained reasonably uniform, without any very great unevenness anywhere, as is usually the case in rice-growing regions. There would, however, have been a natural and proportionate increase in size of the larger settlements. Towns or cities were certainly to be found throughout the Gangetic plain in the Buddha's day. The six great cities, named in Buddhist texts, were Savatthi, Saketa, Kaushambi, Kashi (Varanasi), Rajagriha and Champa. Apart from these a number of other large towns of the area are known to us by name, such as Kapilavastu, Vesali, Mithila and Gaya. With the rise in population and a general steady growth in the size of settlements, some of the small villages would have expanded into towns, wherever special factors were present to encourage such development, such as location at the junction of cara-van routes, or near to river crossings, at places of religious importance, and at points of strategic military or political importance, wherever a stronghold had been established.

DEVELOPMENT OF URBAN LIFE

It is therefore possible to see that one of the features of life in this region in the sixth century BC was a steady growth in the numbers of people who were beginning to experi-ence an urban way of life. They were then a small minor-ity; but then, as now, they were a minority with a consider-able social, cultural and political significance. The cities and towns were centres of industry and trade. Workers in the various industries were organized in guilds, and it is known from the brahmanical and Buddhist sources that these included guilds of wood-workers, iron-workers, leather-workers, painters, ivory-workers and others. These guilds appear from the sources to have been highly organ-ized autonomous bodies, recognized by the state, and able to exercise control over their members.[18] Most of the cities and large towns which have been mentioned by name were also political and administrative centres, in that they were capitals of kingdoms (Shravasti, Saketa, Kashi and Rajagriha are examples) or centres for the ruling assemblies of republics (as, for example, Vaishali). They would have become so owing to their strategic situation or the existence of resources for an industry, or both; these reasons together would also have encouraged their growth as centres of trade. Connecting the urban trade centres were established and recognized routes. For example, from Shravasti, the capital of the Kingdom of Koshala, there was a major route eastwards along the northern edge of the Gangetic plain. The route kept close to the Himalayan foothills because at that level the rivers flowing southwards and southeastwards towards the Ganges could more easily be forded or ferried than lower down in their courses, where they increased in size. The towns which lay along the line of this eastward route received an added importance from the caravan traffic which passed through them and made use of their facilities as halts. Such a town was Kapilavastu, the home of Gotama, the Buddha-to-be, one of the five recognized halts on the route. This continued eastwards to the crossing of the river Gandak, then turned southeastwards through Vesali, southwards across the Ganges at Pataligama, and thence to Rajagriha, the capital of the Magadhan Kingdom. From there another route led southwards to Gaya and beyond. In other directions, from Shravasti a route led southwards to the city of Ujjain and beyond, while yet another ran north-westwards to Hastinapura and the cities of the Punjab, including, most notably, the city of Taxila. There was a good deal of travel by river as well as by land routes, especially in the central part of the Gangetic plain, where the rivers were large enough to allow vessels of considerable size. They also provided a more convenient, safer, and sometimes quicker method of transporting goods, especially heavier ones, than the overland caravan routes. Kaushambi, Varanasi, and Champa would have been busy riverports and trade centres.[19]

The cities and towns of the Ganges plain thus began to

develop a style of life which was in certain respects fairly distinct from that of the country villages. As centres of business and trade they drew in the wealth of the country, and they also became centres of learning and culture, attracting, too, what Atindranath Bose describes as 'parasite professions like stage-acting, dancing, singing, buffoonery, gambling, tavern-keeping and prostitution'.[20] In contrast with the sophisticated and heterogeneous life of the towns is the style which the *Arthasastra* considers proper for the villages; provision is made in that treatise of government for the work of agriculture to be protected from disruptive and diverting influences:

No guilds of any kind other than local cooperative guilds shall find entrance into the villages of the Kingdom. Nor shall there be in villages buildings intended for sports and plays. Nor, with the intention of procuring money, free labour, commodities, grains and liquids in plenty, shall actors, dancers, singers, drummers, buffoons and bards make any disturbance to the work of the villagers.[21]

The existence of such a regulation, whether it was put into practice, or remained an ideal, is enough to indicate that there was felt to be a distinct difference between the relatively sophisticated life of the town, and that of the countryside. The villagers' awareness of this difference may have been the reason for their reluctance to visit the towns, observed by Megasthenes: 'husbandmen themselves with their wives and children live in the country and entirely avoid going into town'.[22]

THE SIX CITIES OF THE MIDDLE COUNTRY

Of the six great cities of the Gangetic plain at the time of the birth of Gotama, one had become particularly prominent: Shravasti, the capital of the Kingdom of Koshala. By the time of the Buddha's death, however, it was beginning to lose this position of superiority as Rajagriha, some 270 miles to the south-east, grew in importance. Nevertheless, throughout the sixth century BC Shravasti was the great centre of life and activity. In the Jataka literature, cities such as Varanasi (Banaras), capital of a kingdom which had by now been conquered and absorbed by Koshala, appear as places which had lost some of their former importance and had yielded in prestige to the large, lively and wealthy city of Shravasti. According to a tradition mentioned by the great Buddhist writer of the fifth century AD, Buddhaghosa, there were in the Buddha's day 57,000 families living in Shravasti.

The city was both the capital of the Kingdom of Koshala and the leading centre of commercial activity. It lay on the caravan route from north-west to south-east where this passed between the foothills of the Himalaya and the difficult terrain to the south, where the rivers became broad and difficult to cross and where there were still tracts of dense tropical jungle and marsh. Moreover, Shravasti was at the junction of this trade route with another which led southwards to the city of Kaushambi and beyond it to the Deccan. So Shravasti, as an important junction of trade routes, had become famous for its rich merchants. One such was Anathapindika, who, at a very high price, purchased from Prince Jeta of Shravasti a pleasant piece of ground outside the city in order to give it to the Buddha and his monks as a residence and a retreat.

The explanation of the name Shravasti which is given in later Pali Buddhist literature is itself evidence of the city's prosperity: the name, it is said, was derived from the common saying of those days that this was a place where everything was obtainable.[23] This is interesting as historical evidence of the standard of living in Shravasti, although it is questionable as etymology. A modern explanation of the name of the city, and of the river Ravati on whose bank it stood, connects them both with *Sharavati*, derived from the name of the sun-god, Savitri.

The city lay along the south bank of the Ravati; it was crescent shaped, with the concave side facing the river. Its 'walls and watch towers' are mentioned in one of the Jatakas, and even today, 2,500 years later, the ruins of these solid brick walls are forty feet high and the remains of the western watch tower, on the river bank, are fifty feet high. The site's modern name is Saheth Maheth, a corruption of the original name, and it is in Gonda district, in Uttar Pradesh, about ten miles by road from the railway station of Balrampur. The ruins were identified by General Cunningham in the course of his archaeological survey of India;[24] archaeological excavations were carried out in 1907–8 and in 1910–11, and today the place has become a well-frequented pilgrim centre. The original lay-out and character of the city can thus be fairly reliably reconstructed from both literary and archaeological evidence. The major routes entered the city through the principal gateways on the south-west, the south, and the south-east. The roads converged in an open square in the centre of the city. The larger and more important buildings were in the western half, while in the eastern half were streets and lanes where were the bazaars and houses of the common people.[25] In this eastern half were gathered all kinds of specialized trades, each street-bazaar specializing in one commodity:[26] in one street were the cooks, in another the garland-makers, in another the perfumers, and so on. One of the Jatakas mentions a group of about five hundred page-boys in the city, who were particularly adept at wrestling. Containing a royal court and the residences of opulent merchants, the city would have been the centre of attraction throughout the wide area served by the routes which converged here. It was undoubtedly the 'modern' city of the time, and had been so sufficiently long for this reputation to have been established by the time of the Buddha, even though it was by then nearing the end of its period of pre-eminence. The significance of these facts will be seen later, when we consider the special nature of the community founded by the Buddha.[27]

Most of the characteristic features of Shravasti were found in the other great cities, except Rajagriha, which in certain respects was distinct from the rest. But Saketa,

Kaushambi, Varanasi, and Champa had much in common with one another, and with Shravasti, the greatest of them all. Each had as its original *raison d'être* the fact of being both a political and a commercial centre. Each of the four had been the capital of a formerly independent kingdom, which, by the Buddha's time, had been absorbed by one or other of the two giants, Koshala and Magadha. These capital cities, which had by then lost their autonomy, had clearly been places of power and grandeur, and much of this would still have been apparent in the Buddha's day, in the impressive fortified walls and watch towers that each possessed, so massive that in some cases they still exist, like those of Shravasti, as substantial ruins even today.[28]

Situated in each case on a large river, at the junction of important trade routes, they were also prominent commercial cities. Since river boats carried a good deal of traffic, both in passengers and commodities, the cities were important *entrepôts* at the crossing of land and river routes. Their leading citizens were merchants and bankers, officials and princes from various places, who would travel about the city in horse-drawn chariots or by elephant. Within the wide extent of the city walls were contained, in addition to the houses of merchants and traders, a great variety of crafts and industries, 'perfumers, spice sellers, sugar-candy sellers, jewellers, tanners, garland-makers, carpenters, goldsmiths, weavers, washermen, etc'.[29] Like other large cities, ancient and modern, they had also the distinction of 'abounding in rogues'.[30] In one respect Varanasi (Banaras) was distinguished from the others, in that it was, in the Buddha's day, not only a wealthy and prosperous place noted for its textiles and ironware, but also a great centre of learning, with educational institutions which were among the oldest in India. Then, as for many centuries since, it was the most prominent intellectual and religious centre, certainly of northern India. Its city hall had become a place used not so much for the transaction of public business as for public discussions of religious and philosophical questions.[31] This intellectual pre-eminence of Banaras in the Buddha's day is a fact we shall refer to again in connection with the outline of the Buddha's public activity.

Rather distinct in certain respects from these other cities was Rajagriha, the capital of the growing Magadhan kingdom. This was situated to the south of the Ganges, in what is now Bihar, where the river plain meets the first line of hills, outliers of the greater upland region of Chota Nagpur and central India. Rajagriha was one of the oldest cities of India, with a history reaching back long before the sixth century BC.[32] The original site was a stronghold encircled by five low hills as a natural rampart, with walls and embankments filling the gaps between them. For this reason, the older name of the city was Giribbaja (mountain stronghold). A new city, just outside the northern hill, was built by Bimbisara, the king of Magadha, who was an older contemporary of the Buddha. Bimbisara's action would appear to reflect both the expanding population of the city, which could no longer be contained in the original area, and the growing strength of the Magadhan kingdom; and it may indicate, too, a confidence that the security of the new city was assured against any possible attack. Northwards from Rajagriha the major trade route was the one that led to Shravasti and thence to the north-west of India. Southwards the route led to one of the major sources of Magadha's strength, the iron-bearing hills of what is today south Bihar. As the capital of an expanding kingdom Rajagriha attracted travellers of all kinds; provision is said to have been made for these to be accommodated in a large building in the centre of the city. One such traveller was the rich merchant Anathapindika,[33] from the Koshalan capital, Shravasti, who, according to Buddhist tradition, first met the Buddha in Rajagriha. At night the outer gates were closed against possible enemy attack under cover of darkness, for in spite of the buoyancy of mood which led to the building of the new city, there was apparently still some fear of invasion from hostile neighbouring states. It is said that the sanitary conditions within the city left much to be desired because of the density of the population. The city was the venue for a famous festival [34] which attracted crowds of people of all social classes from the whole area of Magadha and Anga. Nautch dances formed a prominent part of the public entertainment, which was held in the open air, together with popular music, singing and other amusements. Special arrangements were made for the provision of food for the crowds. At other times troupes of players, acrobats and musicians used to visit the city and provide entertainment for days at a time.

This brief summary of some of the available information about the six major cities of the Buddha's day is enough to indicate certain common features which they shared. The life of each of these cities was conditioned by two major factors: first, a junction of trade routes, and second, a royal court. Each of these cities had been the capital of a kingdom, even though some of them (Saketa, Kaushambi, Varanasi and Champa) had been absorbed into more powerful kingdoms and had become vice-royalties. The crucial factor in the growth of each of them had been the development of monarchy in north India, although important subsidiary factors, such as a tradition of learning, had aided the original growth. Ultimately it was the presence of a royal court which seems to have determined their prosperity; it was essential to the security of a kingdom that the royal capital was strong and secure; as the kingdom grew and prospered so did the life of the city. When the kingdom became weak or lost its independence so, eventually, did the city and in some cases the end of a kingdom meant the end of the life of the city. The one exception is Varanasi (Banaras) where, in spite of the loss of political sovereignty, the city has survived to modern times. This must very largely, though not entirely, be attributed to the special sanctity which Varanasi possesses for Hindus. In addition, it had a strong tradition of brahmanical learning and the natural local advantages of its site. Since there is an important connection between the character of early Buddhist civilization and the life of the north-Indian city, and also between the latter and the growth of monarchy, it is necessary at this point to give attention to the political conditions in north India in the sixth century B C.

4 Monarchy, the City and Individualism

REPUBLICS IN DECLINE

At the time of Gotama's birth, two types of government were in competition with one another in northern India: republican and monarchical. Not only were the republics engaged in a struggle for survival in the face of the expansion of the monarchies; there were also minor feuds between different tribal republics, as well as major struggles between one monarchy and another. The general result of all this was a trend towards an increase in the size and power of the monarchies at the expense of the republics.

The republics occupied a belt of territory which ran across the middle of the Gangetic plain in a roughly north-west to south-east direction from the Himalayas to the Ganges. The most northerly of them was the Shakyan republic, in which Gotama himself was born. Adjoining its territory, to the south-east, was the Koliyan republic, and beyond this the Moriyan. To the east of these three was the territory of the Mallas, whose capital was Kushinara, where the Buddha's decease occurred. The republic of the Mallas, together with some other republics – the Licchavis, the Videhas, the Nayas, and the Vajjis – appear to have formed themselves into a loose confederation for joint action against common enemies; this was known by the name of the last one in the list, the Vajjis. It is unlikely that it was a federation in any permanent and formal sense.[1] Government by discussion was the keynote of the republics; that is to say, within these tribal groups the common life was regulated by discussion among the elders or noblemen of the tribe meeting in a regular assembly. These assemblies were known as *sanghas,* and

since this institution was the most characteristic feature of
the republics, this is the general term by which the republics themselves were known. Earlier in Indian history, in
the Vedic period, there appears to have been a somewhat
different practice, namely, the assembly of all the members
of the tribe to discuss matters of importance. The republican assemblies of the Buddha's day differed from these
older folk-assemblies in that it was the elders only who
assembled to discuss the affairs of the republic. They were
not elected by the rest of the people; rather, they were
leading men of the tribe, men belonging to the Kshatriya
clan. The form of government was aristocratic rather than
democratic. Final authority in all important matters lay
with the assembly of the 'fully qualified members of this
aristocracy'.[2]

The case of the Shakyan republic is particularly interesting. Here the form of government seems to have been a
mixture of the kind of republicanism which has just been
described, with features of monarchy. The Shakyas, probably for this reason, are not found in many of the lists of
typical *sanghas* (republics) found in the texts of this
period; the Shakya republic was recognized as being of a
somewhat different constitution. The case of the Shakyas
is interesting because of its possible bearing on the question of what stage of political evolution the *sanghas* may
be taken to represent. It has been suggested that their
aristocratic form of government was derived from monarchy, through the emergence of royal, princely groups
among whom power was shared. On the other hand, the
sanghas might be seen as an intermediate stage between
the earlier collectivism of fully popular tribal assemblies,
and the later, fully developed autocracy of the monarchical state. On one view of the matter, the constitution of
the Shakyas could be interpreted as a sign that they had
not yet progressed as far as the other *sanghas* from monarchy to republicanism, and that they still retained traces
of monarchy; on the other view, it might be held that they
were ahead of the others in their progress from some sort

of collective tribal rule towards a fully established monarchy.[3] The case is all the more interesting in that it was to the Shakyas that Gotama belonged, and one of his most common titles serves as a reminder of this: Shakya-muni, 'the sage of the Shakyas'. It is significant that in the Pali canonical texts both republican government and kingship are represented as subjects on which the Buddha had something relevant to say, as we shall see in more detail later (see chapter 8, p. 172).

The weakness of the republics is demonstrated by the fact that their collapse followed within a few years of the Buddha's decease, that is, by about the middle of the fifth century B C. While this was due partly to the aggression of the monarchies, it was also due in fairly large measure to internal disagreements among the republican nobles or elders, and to moral indolence, lack of discipline and justice, and an ill-founded pride.[4] In general, therefore, the collapse of the republics may be said to have been due to the prevalence of an *undisciplined individualism*.

Whether monarchy was a type of government superior to the republicanism of the Buddha's day is a question whose answer will depend on how other, prior questions are answered. For one must first ask, 'superior in whose view and for what purposes?' One needs to know how widely the effects of one form of government as distinct from another were actually felt throughout the societies concerned, and whether monarchy had more unpleasant and uncomfortable consequences for a greater number of people than republican rule. Was the condition of the people as a whole worse or better under a monarchy from the point of view of personal security, economic prosperity, social freedom, and spiritual satisfaction? To say that the aim of good government is the greatest good of the greatest number is simply to beg two questions: what *is* the greatest good, and how is agreement on this issue reached? Some forms of government are based on the claim that the governing élite knows what is best for the people; monarchical government may even be based on the claim of a totalitarian ruler that he possesses superior wisdom and insight, vouchsafed to him from some divine source.

On the other hand it may be that all such theoretical niceties are beside the real point, that power belongs to him who is successful in seizing it and keeping it. In this view of the matter people merely acquiesce in whatever form of government is thrust upon them until it becomes acutely intolerable, when they may be driven to rebel and overthrow the tyrant, hoping that out of the new situation will emerge a more agreeable alternative.

Such observations as these are, at best, only attempts to simplify what are, in actual historical situations, extremely complex mixtures of conscious evaluation and choice on the one hand, and environmental, economic and social determinants on the other.

With regard to India at the time of Gotama's birth, the kinds of considerations which have just been mentioned are very appropriate. How far the growth of a great monarchy such as Koshala or Magadha was accepted as an evil necessity, or perhaps a *fait accompli*, in the face of which the common people were powerless, and how far it was accepted for its own sake as providing more satisfactory solutions to problems connected with the common life than republicanism was able to offer, are questions to which no clear answers can be given. Such issues were certainly discussed in the Buddha's day, and various views were taken of the origins and respective merits of different systems of political organization.[5]

THEORIES OF KINGSHIP

One view of the origin of monarchy is found in the Buddhist Pali canon. The *Agganna Sutta*, or 'Discourse on Genesis', said to have been delivered by the Buddha at Shravasti, describes how the first king came to be instituted, in the early days of the human race. Men had become greedy, dishonest, quarrelsome and violent (for

reasons which are set out at length in the early part of
the Sutta). Recognizing this, they came together, and, be-
wailing the situation, reasoned in this way: 'What if we
were to select a certain being, who should be wrathful
when indignation is right, who should censure that which
should rightly be censured, and should banish him who
deserves to be banished?' In recognition of the role which
such a being would play in the interests of the common
good, they decided to 'give him in return a proportion of
the rice'. Thereupon, we are told, they 'went to the being
among them who was the handsomest, the best favoured,
the most attractive, the most capable' and put to him their
proposal. He accepted it, and, chosen by the whole people,
became their *raja*, or ruler. The text emphasizes that he
and his like (that is, other rulers among men) were in
origin of the same blood as other men: 'their origin was
from among those very beings, and no others; like unto
themselves, not unlike; and it took place according to
what ought to be, justly, and not unfittingly.' It was
assumed that there was a 'norm' or ideal, of a ruler, and
that actual rulers were selected according to their fitness
in terms of this ideal.[6]

The theory of kingship which is set out here is well
known in other contexts, where it occurs in roughly the
same form: it is the theory which sees the origin of kingship in a social contract. The way in which it is presented
in this early Buddhist text suggests that it was at that time
a commonly accepted view of the origin and proper function of the political ruler.

In his discourse on this occasion, the Buddha is represented as having gone on to describe the origin of the four
social classes – they were in ancient India believed once to
have existed in separation – namely, the landed ruling
class, the priestly class, the trading class and the hunters
(the lowest class of all). What is of interest at this point is
a view of kingship which, as Ghoshal says, 'imposes upon
the ruler the obligation of punishing wrong-doers in return for the payment of the customary dues by the people',

and the conception of 'the temporal ruler's quasi-contractual obligation of protecting his subjects'.[7] The relation of the Buddhist monk to such a ruler, and to the other classes of society, is the real crux of this discourse, but with that we shall be concerned at a later stage (see chapter 8).

Monarchy was, it seems, recognized as being preferable to anarchy, and the monarch was a mortal man as other men: that much can safely be affirmed on the basis of these words of the Buddha. In the theory of kingship found in the brahmanical writings, however, the king was a noble, semi-divine, and beneficent being, promoting the welfare of his people, who were his subjects by right. This was a somewhat different, and certainly more exalted view of kingship from that set forth in the Buddhist texts. In the brahmanical writings the king is represented as being in origin closely associated with the gods; from this fact some, at least, of his authority is derived. The Vedic hymns, and the slightly later writings known as the *Brahmanas*, which all belong to the pre-Buddhist period, set out a double theory of the origin of kingly authority: 'one theory is based upon his creation and endowment by the Highest Deity, and the other is founded upon his election by the gods in the interest of their external security.'[8] From this there developed the principle that it was his subjects' *duty* to honour and obey him. This idea is clearly affirmed in the *Law of Manu*, a treatise which, in its present form, is perhaps of roughly the same date as the Buddhist Pali texts, but may have existed in an earlier form.[9] There the divine origin of kingship is quite explicitly affirmed: 'When creatures, being without a king, were through fear dispersed in all directions, the Lord [i.e., Bhagavan, or God] created a king for the protection of this whole creation.' 'Even an infant King must not be despised, from an idea that he is a mere mortal; for he is a great deity in human form. Let no man, therefore, transgress that law which the king decrees with respect to those in his favour, nor his orders which inflict pain on those in disfavour.'[10]

In its ancient Indian form the theory of kingship had another aspect: the kingly office carried with it an obligation to act in accordance with the highest moral principles, the king's connection with the gods giving him no right to act arbitrarily or despotically. The great epic, the *Mahabharata*, contains a section called *Shantiparvan* (the Book on Peace), which sets out, among other things, the principle of the king's protectorship: 'One becomes a king for acting in the interests of righteousness and not for conducting himself capriciously. The king is, indeed, the protector of the world.' [11] The famous treatise of Indian statecraft, the *Arthasastra* of Kautilya [12] places the emphasis somewhat differently. Its author was a brahman priest and minister of state whose function was to instruct the secular ruler in his proper *dharma* or duty, and while in the course of doing so he makes formal acknowledgement of the idea of *righteous* rule, nevertheless, the real concern of this work is with the successful exercise of political power, the continual aggrandizement of the state, and the extension of its territorial empire. The tone of the work has been variously characterized as that of political realism, cynicism and Machiavellianism. It is perhaps significant that this treatise is more firmly connected with an historical person (Kautilya, or Chanakya, its brahman author) than either the *Law of Manu* or the *Mahabharata*. It is significant, too, that its prescriptions are known to have been closely related to the actual policy of the Mauryan empire (which grew out of the Magadhan Kingdom shortly after the lifetime of the Buddha). In other words, we may, in the severely practical aspect of this treatise of statecraft, have a more realistic picture of the actual policies and procedures of ancient Indian monarchical rule than is to be found in the somewhat idealistic accounts given in *Manu* and the *Mahabharata*.

These, however, may come nearer to the actualities of monarchical rule in India when they dwell on the shortcomings of kingship rather than when they describe its ideal merits. For the criticisms of kingly rule found in the ancient literature are more likely to have been prompted by real experience, than conceived in the abstract, as possibilities which might arise.

THE DISADVANTAGES AND ADVANTAGES OF MONARCHY

The malfunctioning of the monarchical system is again and again acknowledged. A Buddhist text makes the point that when a king becomes unrighteous, the fault soon spreads to the king's ministers, from them to the brahmans, and from them to the householders, townsmen and villagers. Before long even the environment is affected; the times are out of joint, the winds blow out of season, the rains fail, and the whole kingdom grows weak and sickly.[13] Conversely, when a king acts righteously, benefits follow in the same sequence. Unrighteousness in a king shows itself chiefly in pride, asserts the *Shantiparvan*, and this led many kings to ruin. He who succeeds in conquering pride becomes a real king.[14] Frequently mentioned among the snares to be avoided by a king are overindulgence in drink, gambling, hunting, women and music. In brahmanical theory of the seventh and sixth centuries BC, the king's *authority* was, as we have seen, vested in him by the gods and was exercised, in part at least, by virtue of his quasi-divine nature, but it is very clear, too, that he had no inalienable right to this kingly authority, should he by unrighteousness disgrace his office. Warnings against unrighteous conduct are too frequent for us to assume that real examples of kingly misrule were unknown. The fact that in the *Law of Manu* strong emphasis is placed on the need for the king to rule his own passions successfully if he is to be a successful ruler of his kingdom suggests that, by the time *Manu* was composed, the necessity had been very clearly seen from historical examples. 'Day and night he must strenuously exert himself to conquer his senses, for he alone who has conquered his own senses can keep his subjects in obedience.'[15] *Manu* also lists certain vices which kings must shun: hunting, gambling, sleeping by day, censoriousness, excess with women, drunkenness, inordinate love of dancing, singing and music, and useless travel.

Another disadvantage of monarchy is that it means the concentration of power in the hands of one individual, for an individual is more acutely vulnerable to violence, disease or some form of fatality than is a company of men such as a republican assembly. It was fully recognized in ancient India that this constituted a peculiar weakness of monarchy. In a hereditary system of monarchy, the king, especially as he grew older and his sons came to manhood, was always at risk from the latter's jealousy. Various safe-guards against this danger were set out in the Indian manuals of kingship. One of them declared cynically that any prince for whom his father felt no affection should be secretly killed in infancy. Another recommended that the king should deliberately encourage his sons to indulge in sensual pleasures, for in that way they would be too pre-occupied to plot against their father. Yet another advises the king to engage spies to instigate the princes to commit treason, and other spies to dissuade them from doing so. These and other similar prescriptions indicate a general agreement that the ambition of princes constituted a perennial danger to the security of the king, and that the protection of the king's person must be a fundamental aim of royal policy, for upon this rested the whole security of the state.[16]

However, the concentration of power in the hands of one individual was seen to have compensating advantages, too. One of the chief of these was the greater likelihood of uniform punishment for crime, since this was administered entirely by the king. The fact that punishment was meted out by one individual rather than by a number of different men was a guarantee of equity. The citizens of the state could depend on it that all would receive roughly the same treatment – assuming that the king administered justice impartially: so this, too, was a matter on which great emphasis had to be laid. Originally, the function of law enforcement was part of the king's military role. It was his duty to defend his territory and people by force of arms, and by the same kind of force to inflict punishment on wrongdoers; to restrain those who did not restrain themselves, to punish those who violated their prescribed duties. No one was exempt from the performance of his own special duty. The context of thought is of a strongly military kind. The stability and integration of the kingdom depended to a large extent on the manner in which justice was administered. Kautilya's manual of statecraft, the *Arthasastra*, though it may have been composed a century or so after the Buddha's death, nevertheless reflects the experiences of kings and their subjects in the earlier period when it declares that the king who is too harsh in administering punishment depresses and damages the whole realm, that the king who is too mild loses authority and may be overthrown, while the one who inflicts punishment justly gains the respect and support of all his subjects.[17] The great epic, the *Mahabharata*, makes the same point: if the king is too gentle and forgives too frequently, the ordinary people will overpower him, like the little elephant driver who climbs up on the head of that great and noble animal and makes it subservient;[18] the king should be neither too severe nor too mild, but like the spring sunshine, in whose rays one experiences neither excessive cold nor excessive heat. In general the manner of inflicting punishment seems to have been one of the major criteria by which a king's rule was evaluated. If punishment was well-judged, then, it was said, the people became wise and happy; when it was ill-judged and prompted by anger or desire, people were afflicted by a sense of injustice; when it was neglected altogether the whole realm fell into anarchy. In India this was described as the state of affairs in which the larger fishes devour the smaller.[19]

THE KING AS THE SUPREME INDIVIDUAL

This might lead one to suppose that at the time of the Buddha monarchy was expanding at the expense of the tribal republics because it was popularly held to be a preferable form of government. But that would be to think that the known examples of it were, on the whole, just and beneficent rather than otherwise, and such a thought is both naïve and historically unwarranted. It would be too ingenuous to imagine that monarchical rule had its origins in the free choice of the people; the king was where he was, in almost every case, largely because he had, so to speak, climbed up on the shoulders of others. Even in the case of a long-established dynasty, where a king had succeeded to his throne by hereditary right, he would almost certainly have had to deal with rival claimants, in the form of ambitious brother-princes, or powerful ministers who might easily become would-be usurpers. In India palace intrigue and the *coup d'état* were far from uncommon. They are, in fact, envisaged in the manuals of statecraft as possible courses of action to be followed when a king failed to rule in accordance with the traditional *dhamma*,* or law of righteousness laid down by generations of brahman priests. The king's quasi-divinity afforded him no protection if he defaulted in his role as the upholder of *dhamma*. It is clear that he ruled, in the first place, by virtue of his ability to protect himself from intrigue and attack. That he ruled by the grace of God or with the consent of the common people were, in reality, subordinate considerations. It was as the *de facto* solitary wielder of power that he inspired fear and reverence; to such a figure it would not be difficult to attribute divinity, especially in India, where the dividing line between men and gods is less sharply drawn than it is in some other cultures.

There was a special reason for the growth in power of one of these monarchies in particular, namely that of

---

* *Dhamma* is the Pali spelling of the Sanskrit *Dharma*.

Magadha. The territory of this kingdom covered approximately the area which today forms the adjacent administrative Districts of Patna and Gaya. To the south of this is an area containing vast iron-ore deposits, described by modern geologists as 'one of the major iron ore fields of the world, in which enormous tonnages of rich ore are readily available'.[20] It is noteworthy that this iron ore, which is of high grade, 'occurs usually at or near the tops of hill ranges' and that most of it 'can be won by open-cast methods'.[21] Of the kingdoms of the Gangetic plain it was Magadha which was best placed to benefit from this good supply of readily available iron. Since it was nearby, the trouble and cost of transporting the ore would not have been so great for it as for other more distant kingdoms. Moreover, supplies of ore to the other kingdoms of the north Indian plain would have had to pass through Magadha's territory and it would consequently have been able to exercise some kind of control of iron supplies to these other states. The iron was used for agricultural tools (and so aided the development of agriculture), and also for weapons of war. The kingdom which controlled the iron supply and had easiest access to it would obviously be in a position to develop agriculturally and militarily more rapidly than others. The shift in the balance of power among the north Indian kingdoms in favour of Magadha seems to have been taking place during the Buddha's lifetime, in the reign of the Magadhan king, Bimbisara, and his son. Ajatashatru, who was also king while the Buddha was alive. Ajatashatru, especially, appears in the early Buddhist literature as a very powerful, determined and ruthless monarch.

The old maxim that nothing succeeds like success appears to find support in the history of kingship in India. What seems to have been abhorred more than anything was political anarchy. The social evils of this are depicted in the ancient texts, brahmanical and Buddhist, in a way that suggests that the common view of society was one which saw it as an aggregate of aggressive, violently self-assertive individuals whose mutual destructiveness could be held in check only by a single controller possessing the authority and the power to punish. The violence of the many individuals was to be met and overcome by the violence of the one supreme individual.

THE EMERGENCE OF INDIVIDUALISM

A question which it is important to try to answer at this point is one concerning the causes of this individualism during these early centuries of Indian history. It was a period, we have seen, characterized not only by increasingly marked individualism but also by the growth of monarchy; together with these factors there appears to have been an intensification of urban life in some of the larger cities. These three features of the life of the period certainly seem to be in some way inter-related. What has to be considered is whether one of them developed first, independently of the other two, and, if so, whether this was because of some other prior condition. The possibilities are (1) that individualism was the primary factor, that is, that the trend towards individualism facilitated the growth of monarchical government, and that this entailed increased urbanization; or (2) it may have been that monarchy was the novel factor which, once introduced into the lands of the Gangetic plain, gave rise to urbanization, which in turn led to increased individualism; or (3) it may have been that the growth of cities was the primary factor: that is, that there were non-political reasons why certain cities grew in size and density of population, and that these cities then became the growth-points of an individualism, which, by gradually spreading through the whole region, paved the way for the advance of strong monarchical government as the only solution to the evils entailed in its increase.[22] There is something to be said for each of these possibilities, but on balance the known facts seem to favour the third.

We have already seen that a considerable growth of

population was taking place in the Gangetic plain at the time of the Buddha, due largely to the increased cultivation of what had formerly been forest (see p. 46). In the 'middle' country (*Madyadesa*) it was rice growing which predominated, but it is clear from the evidence of the Pali Buddhist texts that a variety of other crops and fruits were also grown. The result of this increased population *size* would have been a slight increase also in population *density* over the whole area, with, however, more acute increases in density in the cities of the plain. We have seen, too, that there was in the cities a considerable diversity of occupations, with a fairly refined degree of specialization. This was due partly to the needs of a royal court, which each of the great cities either was or had been at some stage in its history. But it was due too, and possibly in even greater measure, to the diversification of the economy which would have followed as a consequence of the growth of population, the development of agriculture, the growing differentiation in methods of production (such as herd-keeping, fishing, the raising of rice and other cereal and vegetable crops, fruit-growing, forestry and mining) and a general increase in the economic wealth of the region. Moreover, the continual extension of the area of society which was under monarchical rule, as opposed to tribal republican government, would have meant a growing complexity in modes of social organization.

All this accords well with the general line of argument developed by Emile Durkheim, that the development of the division of labour has for its principal cause an increase in the density of a society.[23] An increase in the overall density of population brings with it an increase in what Durkheim calls 'moral density'. By this he means increased facilities for transportation and communication throughout the area, and thus an increase in the extent to which, and the area over which, social contacts take place. Durkheim summarizes his argument at this point in the following proposition: 'The division of labour varies in direct ratio with the volume and density of societies, and, if it progresses in a continuous manner in the course of social development, it is because societies become regularly denser and generally more voluminous.'[24] This would appear to fit very well what was happening in the Ganges valley in the period we are concerned with. Among the consequences of such a development of diverse specialist occupations, according to Durkheim, is the growth of individualism: 'far from being trammelled by the progress of specialization, individual personality develops with the division of labour'.[25] He points out that in more primitive societies each man resembles his companions; there is little differentiation of tasks and statuses and it is the corporate life of the tribe which, so to speak, occurs in each and every man. But with the development of specialization there is increasingly for each man 'something in him which is his alone and which individualizes him, as he is something more than a simple incarnation of the generic type of his race and his group'.[26]

More recent work in the field of sociology confirms this view of the development of individualism in societies characterized by developed occupational specialization, particularly where this is found in an urban milieu. Louis Wirth points out that 'in contrast with earlier, more integrated societies, the social life of the city provides much greater *potentials* for differentiation between individuals'.[27] One passage in particular from Wirth's writings may be quoted here for its relevance to our study of early Indian urban life:

The superficiality, the anonymity, and the transitory character of urban social relations make intelligible, also, the sophistication and the rationality generally ascribed to city dwellers. Our acquaintances tend to stand in a relationship of utility to us in the sense that the role which each one plays in our life is overwhelmingly regarded as a means for the achievement of our own ends. Whereas the individual gains, on the one hand, a certain degree of emancipation or freedom from the personal and emotional controls of intimate groups, he loses, on the other hand, the spontaneous self-expression, the morale, and the sense of participation that comes with living in an integrated society. This constitutes essentially the state of *anomie*, or the social void, to which Durkheim alludes in attempting to account for the various forms of social disorganization in technological society.[28]

This agrees with what is known of urban society in the early Buddhist period. In the Jataka stories and in the many dialogues between the Buddha and various different individuals, it is precisely this sophistication, this rationality of the urban dweller that we recognize. Moreover, there was also at that time a considerable degree of what Durkheim called *anomie*, or moral and social dislocation. To be more specific, the transition which many people were then experiencing from the familiar, small-scale society of the old tribal republics to the strange, large-scale and consequently more impersonal, bleaker life of the new monarchical state, was accompanied by a psychological *malaise*, a heightened sense of dissatisfaction with life as it had to be lived. It was this *malaise* which the Buddha was to take as the starting-point of his analysis of the human condition, calling it *dukkha* (see chapter 7, p. 134). Erich Fromm, too, has drawn attention to the association between the developing sense of individuality in the human person and a sense of *growing aloneness*.[29] He refers to the separation which the growing person experiences from the world which was familiar to him as a child. 'As long as one was an integral part of that world, unaware of the possibilities and responsibilities of individual action, one did not need to be afraid of it. When one has become an individual, one stands alone and faces the world in all its perilous and overpowering aspects.'[30]

INDIVIDUALISM AS A CONSEQUENCE OF URBANISM AND MONARCHY

There are thus good reasons for saying that *the development of urban life*, as a result of population increase, and the political innovation of *monarchical rule* were both responsible for the development of an awareness of individuality and the sense of personal isolation and psychological *malaise* which accompanies such awareness. What is more, monarchical rule had the further effect of giving the development of urban life an extra stimulus, over and above the general incentive towards the development of cities which the extension of agriculture and the accelerating growth of population provided.

But kingship, as it had emerged in early Indian civilization, was itself a consequence of the specialization of functions which had developed in Aryan society in the Vedic period. The primary differentiation of functions was between the brahman priest and the kshatriya nobleman. In the earlier, nomadic period of the Aryans' history, as in the early stages of other societies, political, cultic and judicial functions appear to have been performed by the same person or class. It has been suggested that 'the tribal priests who antedated the brahmans and were not always distinguished from the kshatriya warriors developed some sort of secret organization as a preparation for sacrificial purity.' [31] It is possible, too, that changing conditions, from the more violent and insecure conditions of nomadic life to those of settled agricultural communities, deprived the kshatriya warrior of his superior authority just at a time when the development of ritual and sacrificial ideas was enhancing the authority of the brahmans. Perhaps, indeed, the stimulus for the development of these new sacrificial ideas was the need for a new source of authority in the changed conditions of life, and the need to legitimate that new authority – the authority of the brahman priest. This, certainly, is what appears to have happened: on the one hand an increasing specialization in the sacrificial *cultus* and the esoteric mysteries connected with its performance, and on the other an increasing specialization in the business of secular government, now no longer by the kshatriyas as a class, but by kings, as individual specialists in the technicalities of political administration, diplomacy and so on.

So, by the time Aryan civilization reached the Gangetic midland plain it was already characterized by the first stage in the specialization of functions and an incipient trend towards urbanism,[32] in the sense that its political structure required an administrative capital. The nature of the terrain and its resources were such that these characteristics soon developed, in the way we have seen, into an increasingly diversified political and economic structure. From this situation there then emerged, as a consequence of the increasing complexity of life – especially in the cities – a growing awareness of personal differentiation, or individualism.

5 The Religious and Ideological Environment.

It was suggested at the outset (see pp. 15 f. and 28) that we merely prejudice our understanding of the Buddha's historical significance if we think of him as the founder of a religion in the customary modern sense of the term. A more useful way of approaching the matter is to examine the nature of the early Buddhist community – its principles, its purposes, and its social implications – and then to consider whether it is not more appropriate to regard the Buddha as the founder, in effect, of something more approaching a type of civilization. We shall not, therefore, begin by regarding the Buddha as one who was consciously a religious reformer or innovator. It is possible that his role is better understood as that of the opponent or critic of religion, who had no intention of founding yet another example of what he criticized. This is, of course, to assume that 'religion' could already be identified in the Buddha's day as a more or less distinct set of phenomena, and not as an aspect of a civilization. We have suggested that what are now identified as 'religions' may be seen as surviving elements of civilizations which tend to seek re-embodiment in some new, integrated system. This is, broadly, how the situation in the Buddha's day may be interpreted. The old Vedic society of the Aryans was in a state of dissolution as a consequence of the movement of Aryan peoples into a new geographical environment (that of the middle Gangetic plain), and as a result of their having settled into a new kind of economy, one which was predominantly agricultural rather than pastoral and nomadic. The brahman priests had merged as a distinct social class and were, consciously or unconsciously, engaged in redefining their own position in society, and the position of other classes in relation to their own. The reconstituted civilization which was centred on kingship, brahmanically consecrated and legitimized, was only just beginning to emerge. Religion, as a phenomenon of the transitional period of flux between one civilization and another, a vestigial remnant of the old which had not yet been re-integrated in a new, emerging culture, seems to have existed in the Buddha's day in a number of characteristic forms.

With regard to these, and to the religious element in classical Hindu civilization [1] it may be useful at this point to correct a fairly common Western misconception. One of its best-known exponents was Albert Schweitzer. He worked out a broad contrast between Eastern and Western religions, using as a basis for differentiation their respective attitudes to the empirical world. Western religion, declared Schweitzer, was, in general, world- and life-affirming, while Eastern religion was world- and life-negating. Like all generalizations of such magnitude, Schweitzer's is open to many objections and qualifications. For instance, there are and have been examples of Western religious belief and practice which are very good candidates for inclusion in Schweitzer's world- and life-negating category. It is true that there are and have been some minor systems of thought and practice in Asia, especially in India, which do virtually deny the reality of the life of the senses and the physical, historical world, and which do direct men's attention away from the realm of sensory existence, which is regarded as ultimately unreal, to a realm of pure bliss which is to be attained through the realization of the idea that this world and its life are illusion. ·

But in the Buddha's time, however, such a world- and life-negating attitude was *not* a prominent characteristic of religious belief in India. It was not entirely unheard-of, however, and was found in embryonic form in a few places in the Upanishadic literature. The Upanishads can be described in the most general way as philosophical writ-

ings. Most of the principal Upanishads are regarded as
products of the period between about 800 BC and the time
of the Buddha. The name 'Upanishad' indicates teaching
which is given to a few select initiates, those who are
'sitting round, near': that is, near to the teacher who is
imparting his esoteric doctrines to them. This interpretation of the title is confirmed by the contents and the style;
the language used is often cryptic, requiring the possession
of some kind of key for its elucidation, one which is not
now always available. The reason for its cryptic nature
appears to have been that the teaching was given only to
those whom the teacher regarded as sufficiently mature
spiritually. Unlike the later Sutra literature, the Upanishads are not systematic treatises; they contain a variety of
ideas, some of which are, in fact, in contradiction to one
another. But certain central themes may be said to be
common to all the Upanishadic literature. Of these the
most outstanding is the idea that 'underlying the exterior
world of change there is an unchangeable reality which is
identical with that which underlies the essence in man.' [2]
This identity is obscured from the vast generality of men,
each of whom follows the devices and desires of what he
imagines to be his 'true' self: namely, the empirical ego,
which is subject to all the conflicting impressions and impulses that make for confusion and turmoil rather than
peace. Deceived as he is by the passing, illusory world of
the physical senses, each man's 'true' welfare is, rather, the
realization of the identity of his own inner, essential being
(*atman*) with the world-soul (*brahman*). It was in connection with this teaching of the Upanishads that there developed a view of the material world as something to be
rejected and renounced in the interests of the *atman*, or
true self. In any case, however, the Upanishads represent
the attitude of an élite few, and at the time of the Buddha
such teaching was still largely esoteric. [3]

In order not to neglect anything which could conceivably be included under the heading of 'religion' at the

time of the Buddha, it is appropriate to consider all phenomena which may possibly be relevant, even borderline candidates from the realm of the ideologies of the time. Three major areas can be identified: first, there was the sacrificial *cultus* of the hereditary priestly class, the brahmans; second, there was the vast range of popular cults and beliefs of the ordinary people, mostly villagers, who constituted the majority of the population; and third, there was the variety of ideas and practices expounded by various non-brahmanical teachers, who were known collectively as *shramanas*.

THE SACRIFICIAL SYSTEM OF THE BRAHMANS

The brahman or, properly, *brahmana*, was so called because of his claim to be the specialist in dealing with *brahman*, the impersonal absolute which was held to be the source of the world and its life. The word *brahman* referred also to the sacred word, the chant, which was the essence of the sacrificial ceremony. The knowledge of this sacred chanting was confined strictly to the priestly class, its guardians and preservers. In brahman theory, the world had come into existence through a primeval sacrifice, and was maintained in existence by the further performance of sacrifices by the brahmans. Although brahmanistic theology envisaged a large number of deities, prominent among whom were Agni and Indra, even these were held to be subject to the power of the sacrifice, and thus, ultimately, to the controller of the sacrifice, the brahman priest. The stage of development which had been reached by the early Buddhist period was one in which, as S. N. Dasgupta puts it, 'sacrifice is not offered to a god with a view to propitiate him or to obtain from him welfare on earth or bliss in Heaven; these rewards are directly produced by the sacrifice itself through the correct performance of complicated and interconnected ceremonials which constitute the sacrifice.'[4] Thus, in the time with which we are concerned, the sacrifice, which the brahman controlled, had come to be regarded 'as possessing a mystical potency superior even to the gods'.[5]

With this claim for the mystical supremacy of the sacrifice, in which the brahmans were specialists, went a corresponding claim for the social supremacy of the specialists themselves. The line of argument which the brahmans used was simple, and if the first claim were accepted, the second had to be, inevitably. The world, ran the argument, was kept in existence, and the important aims of human life were achieved, by the operation of the sacrifice; the brahmans were the sole possessors of the knowledge of how the sacrifice was to be performed, and it was their *dharma*, or duty, and theirs only, to perform it. The second claim was that the brahmans, consequently, were the most essential class in society. By their due and wise control of *brahman*, the sacred force, the world continues in existence.

Both these claims were rejected by the Buddha, according to the early tradition of the Buddhists. The Buddha's attitude to the brahmanical sacrifice is evident in many of the early texts, and is set out in detail in a discourse known as the *Kutadanta Sutta*, which deals explicitly with this subject. It recounts a conversation which is supposed to have taken place between the Buddha and a brahman named Kutadanta or 'Sharp-tooth', who lived at a place called Khanumata, where he owned some land which had been presented to him by the king. T. W. Rhys Davids captures the spirit of the situation by rendering this brahman's title as 'the Very Reverend Sir Goldstick Sharp-tooth, lord of the manor of Khanumata'.[6] In this rather ironical story he is 'represented as doing the very last thing any brahman of position, under similar circumstances, would think of doing. He goes to the Samana Gotama for advice ...' This highly improbable action on the part of the brahman is a device which enables the storyteller to set forth the Buddhist attitude to sacrifice in the words of the Buddha to this imaginary brahman. In what the Buddha says to him there is no direct criticism of the brahmanical theory of sacrifice; only an indirect allusion to its practical aspects. Kutadanta asks the Buddha how a sacrifice should be performed, and in reply the Buddha tells an ironical story of a great sacrifice that had once been offered by the brahman chaplain of a very prosperous king.

At that sacrifice neither were any oxen slain, neither goats, nor fowls, nor fatted pigs, nor were any kinds of living creatures put to death. No trees were cut down to be used as posts, no dabbha grasses mown to strew around the sacrificial spot. And the slaves and messengers and workmen there employed were driven neither by rods nor fear, nor carried on their work weeping with tears upon their faces . . . With ghee, and oil, and butter, and milk, and honey, and sugar only was that sacrifice accomplished.[7]

The irony consists in the fact that nothing could be more unlike a brahmanical sacrifice of the late Vedic period. The descriptive details are precisely the reverse of what would in fact have happened at a normal sacrifice. As Rhys Davids comments, all 'the muttering of mystic verses over each article used and over mangled and bleeding bodies of unhappy victims, verses on which all the magic efficacy of a sacrifice had been supposed to depend, is quietly ignored'.[8] The narrative continues with an account of the surprising decision of the king who had ordered the sacrifice not to make a levy on the people of his realm to pay for it, but to use his own wealth. This, moreover, after the people had *asked* to be taxed for the purpose. 'Sufficient wealth have I, my friends, laid up, the produce of taxation that is just. Do you keep yours, and take away more with you!' Thereupon the people, baulked in their desire to be taxed, made voluntary contributions which were to pay for the performance of three other great sacrifices, as well as that offered by the king. The tale is, of course, entirely ludicrous, and one can imagine the delight with which the Buddha's contemporaries would have responded to its humour. What emerges as the point of the story is a critique of brahmanical sacrifice on the grounds of economic wastefulness, cruelty to animals, forced labour, with harsh treatment of the labourers, and oppressive taxation of the people in order to pay for it all. It is clear, too, that the supposed efficacy of the sacrifice is being quietly dismissed. By implication, this heightens the objection to the lavish expenditure, cruelty and social oppression.

That there are, however, forms of 'sacrifice' which are worth making, in the Buddhist view, is made clear in the second part of the narrative. Kutadanta asks the Buddha, 'Is there, O Gotama, any other sacrifice less difficult and less troublesome, with more fruit and more advantage than this?' The Buddha replies that there is. In fact there are six other preferable forms of sacrifice, and these the Buddha describes to Kutadanta. The first five are all 'sacrifices' which are open to ordinary householders. Better than the offering of the brahmanical sacrifice is an offering of alms to wandering holy men (*shramanas*). The second form of sacrifice, which is open to all, and better than the first, is to build a dwelling place, a Vihara, for members of the Buddhist Order. Even better than this is the third kind of sacrifice, which is to go with a trusting heart to the Buddha as guide, and to the Doctrine which he teaches, and to the Order which he founded and in which the Doctrine is preserved. Such devotion is referred to in the regularly repeated formula which anyone making the humblest claim to be a Buddhist still uses, in private and in public: 'To the Buddha I go for refuge, to the Dhamma I go for refuge, to the Sangha I go for refuge.' Even better than this, however, is to take the five precepts of Buddhist morality upon oneself.

When a man with trusting heart takes upon himself the precepts – abstinence from destroying life; abstinence from taking what has not been given; abstinence from evil conduct in respect of lusts; abstinence from lying words; abstinence from strong, intoxicating, maddening drinks, the root of carelessness – that is a sacrifice better than open largesse, better than perpetual alms, better than the gift of dwelling places, better than accepting guidance.[9]

This is the fifth and highest form of 'sacrifice' for a house-holder, in the Buddhist view. Beyond this there is only the sixth and greatest sacrifice, namely to give up the house-hold life and become a member of the Buddhist Order, the *Sangha* (see chapter 7).

POPULAR CULTS AND BELIEFS

The significance of such teaching on the subject of sacrifice has to be seen in the context of the times when it was first given. For, as we have said, the Vedic sacrificial system was something which concerned the specialist, the brahman priest, and the man who was, at the very least, fairly well-to-do and able to meet the cost of such sacrificial offerings. For the common people, the villager, the peasant, the craftsman and the tradesman, there was a great variety of popular magic to which they might have resort for comfort, guidance, peace of mind, protection from evil, and so on. A list of these magical practices is given in one of the discourses of the Buddha.[10] They are described by the Buddha as 'low arts', and are of the kind practised by certain of the brahmans and *shramanas*. They included, apparently, such activities as palmistry and fortune-telling; determining lucky sites for houses by a knowledge of the spirits of the place and how to propitiate them; prophecies of various kinds, concerning such matters as rainfall, the nature of the harvest, pestilences, disturbances, famines and so on; divining, by the use of signs, omens and celestial portents; the provision of charms and spells; the obtaining of oracular answers from gods by various means; the interpretation of dreams; the propitiation of demons; and the offerings of oblations of various kinds, such as grain or butter, to Agni the god of fire. That such practices are forbidden to members of the Buddha's Order is emphasized in a number of places. 'You are not, O *bhikkhus*, to learn or to teach the low arts [literally "the brutish wisdom"] of divination, spells, omens, astrology, sacrifices to gods, witchcraft and quackery', the Buddha is reputed to have charged the members of the Order.[11] On another occasion, in answer to the question of how a member of the Buddhist Order is to achieve perfection and be entirely unattached to any worldly thing, the Buddha lists the many requirements; one of these is as follows: 'Let him not use Atharva-Vedic spells, nor things foretell from dreams or signs or stars; let not my follower predict from cries, cure barrenness, nor practise quackery.'[12]

The account of these magical practices or 'low arts' given in the Buddhist texts agrees well with the picture of priestly magic practised mostly on behalf of the common people which is found in the brahmanical text compiled probably a little before the time of the Buddha, known as the *Atharva-Veda*. This is the fourth of the Vedic collection of hymns, and the last to be accorded official recognition. It stands somewhat apart from the other three Vedic hymn-collections[13] on account of the very much more popular, local, indigenous material which it contains, compared with the more Aryan and priestly-class concerns of the earlier collections. Nevertheless, it did eventually gain general recognition as a brahmanically composed text,[14] and this fact is itself further evidence that some brahmans were engaged in this kind of popular magical activity, possibly having taken over the role of earlier, pre-Aryan, non-brahmanical priests; in return for the provision of priestly-magical services the brahmans would expect from the villager recognition of their authority, and of the Vedic tradition they represented.

For our purpose the *Atharva-Veda* is important as evidence of popular attitudes and practices with regard to such matters as sorcery and magic at the time of the Buddha. A mention of some of its contents will illustrate the point. By far the greater part of the text consists of charms. These include charms against various diseases, and disease-causing demons; the diseases range from fever in general, through coughs, headaches, jaundice, excessive bodily discharges, constipation and internal pain, to heart disease and leprosy. There are charms against snake-poison, charms to promote the growth of hair, or virility, or long life, or for general exemption from disease. Another section contains imprecations to be used against sorcerers, demons and enemies. Yet another is devoted to the needs of men and women – charms for such varied purposes as obtaining a husband, or a child, or to prevent miscarriage, or to obtain easy childbirth, charms by which a man may secure a woman's love, or arouse her passion, or allay jealousy, or deprive a rival of his virility. One whole section consists of charms pertaining to the needs of a king: for his success as a ruler, for victory in battle and so on. Yet another contains charms to ensure political and social harmony while other sections are devoted to domestic and mercantile affairs. There is, significantly for the status of the text as Vedic, a section devoted to prayers and imprecations in the interests of the brahmans. The collection ends with a group of hymns to various gods and goddesses, such as Mother Earth, Kama (the god of sexual love) and Kala (time personified as a deity).

These, then, were the popular magical practices which had come within the sphere of interest of some brahman priests, sufficiently so for them to be regarded as at least marginally 'Vedic', once the Atharvan collection had gained recognition. It is interesting that the Buddha's attitude to these practices, in which brahmans had taken an interest, and which had thus passed, at least partially, under the aegis of the priests, was one of only moderate disapproval. His criticism of practices which were partly popular, partly priestly, was not so vigorous as his criticism of the brahmanical animal sacrifices, but it is clear enough that he wished to discourage the members of his own order from any interest in them.

More ambiguous is the Buddha's attitude to a popular-priestly form of belief, namely, in Brahma, the supreme creator-deity. At a later period of Indian religious history, Brahma as Creator became the somewhat shadowy first figure in the Hindu theistic trinity, the other two great deities being Vishnu the Preserver, and Shiva the Destroyer. But at the time of the Buddha, Brahma had recently emerged as the spirit of the universe (*Brahman*) conceived of as a personal god. In the priestly texts called the *Brahmanas*, which belong to a period some centuries before the time of the Buddha, the creator-deity, to whom sacrifice is offered, is known as Prajapati. In the Upanishadic literature, the supreme reality is represented as impersonal, and is referred to by the neuter noun *brahman*. But in the popular epic-poem, the *Mahabharata*, the composition of which can be dated a century or so after the time of the Buddha (that is, from about the third century B C onwards), we find that Brahma (masculine) appears as a divine personal being, the god of creation. The earlier creator-deity, Prajapati, had it seems, come to be identified with the impersonal world-soul (*brahman*)[15] of the Upanishads, and been given the new name, Brahma. It is uncertain just how important belief in Brahma had become by the time of the Buddha, or what place this creator-god held in the religious ideas and practices of the people. Some have argued that Brahma was never a very important god in popular belief. This is the view of the Indian historian, R. C. Majumdar: 'Although Brahma is theoretically acknowledged to be the creator of man and even of gods he never occupies a prominent place in the actual religious devotion of the people. Vishnu and Shiva overshadow him from the very beginning ...'[16] On the other hand, it has been argued that the worship of Brahma, the creator-god, was in pre-Buddhist times very important and widespread, and that it only subsequently suffered eclipse, partly because of the rise in the rival cults of Vishnu and Shiva, and partly because of the spread of Buddhist and Jain belief and practice.[17]

What is clear from the early Buddhist sources is that Brahma was, so far as the Buddha was concerned, a fairly prominent feature of the celestial scenery of the time, and a figure whom one should not take too seriously. The notion that Brahma is the prime being, and creator of all other beings was treated with somewhat less than respect by the Buddha. A story attributed to him, tells how in the course of time this world-system passes away. Then, after a further period, it begins to re-evolve. At an early stage in this process Brahma's 'palace' (that is, his abode, or place in the celestial set-up) happens to be vacant. It is, however, soon filled by some being or other who, until then, had been living in the superior 'World of Radiance' but who finds himself, his merit having been exhausted, descending to the lower realm and coming to rebirth as Brahma. Newly arrived, and feeling lonely there in Brahma's palace, he wishes that he had some companions. It so happens that some more beings whose merit has run out just at that moment also descend from the World of Radiance and appear in Brahma's realm, as though in response to his wish. At this, the one who was first reborn thinks to himself,

I am Brahma, the Great Brahma, the Supreme One, the Mighty, the All-seeing, The Ruler, the Lord of all, the Maker, the Creator, the Chief of all, appointing to each his place, the Ancient of Days, the Father of all that are and are to be. These other beings are of my creation. And why is that so? A while ago I thought. 'Would that they might come!' And on my mental aspiration, behold the beings came.[18]

In a similar fashion the new arrivals conclude that the one who was there first must be their creator: 'This must be Brahma, the Great Brahma, the Supreme [etc.]. And we must have been created by him. And why? Because, as we see, it was he who was here first, and we came after that.' Finally, the Buddha suggests that when one of the beings in Brahma's realm, by reason of his poor stock of merit, suffers yet a further fall and arrives on earth, he reflects that while he is a fallen being, Brahma dwells for ever in his heaven: 'He by whom we were created, he is steadfast, immutable, eternal, of a nature that knows no change, and he will remain so for ever and ever.'

One can safely assume that the Buddha was making light of contemporary belief in an eternal creator-god called Brahma. There would be no point in making fun of a belief which nobody held. In another of the discourses, Brahma, in the midst of his great retinue of subordinates, is represented as being asked a question by a member of the Buddhist Order: 'Where do the four great elements – earth, water, fire and wind – cease, leaving no trace behind?' In reply Brahma answers, 'I, brother, am the Great Brahma, the Supreme, the Mighty, the All seeing ... the Ancient of Days, the Father of all that are and are to be!' 'But,' replies the Buddhist, 'I did not ask you whether you are indeed all that you now say. I asked you where the four great elements cease, leaving no trace behind.'[19] The fact is, of course, that this is a question Brahma cannot answer. In order to save face, and not display his ignorance before all his retinue, Brahma takes the Buddhist brother by the arm, leads him aside and says, in effect: 'I didn't wish to say so in front of them, for they think I know everything, but I don't know the answer. You really should not come to me with a question like that. You should ask the Buddha. I'm sure he will be able to tell you!' The attitude of deference towards the Buddha which is attributed to the god Brahma in this instance is shown elsewhere in Buddhist literature. The most famous example, perhaps, is the occasion when the Buddha, immediately after his Enlightenment, was pondering whether the *dhamma*, or truth, to which he had won could possibly be made known to other men. Brahma, perceiving what the Buddha was thinking, lamented the possible great loss to the world that might ensue if the Buddha did not proclaim to men his *dhamma*. He then left the Brahma-realm and immediately manifested himself before the Buddha, and having saluted him with joined palms, said 'Lord, let the Lord teach *dhamma*; let the well-farer teach *dhamma*; there are beings with little dust in their eyes who, not hearing *dhamma* are decaying, but if they are learners of *dhamma* they will grow.'[20]

The contemporary view of Brahma which is reflected in these and other references in the early Buddhist writings is that he was the Creator of the universe, the highest of all beings, union with whom, through prayer and sacrifice, was the highest possible good for men. It is a view which is gently and ironically set aside in the Buddhist sources. The god who was the product of brahmanism mixed with popular mythology is represented as by no means the supreme being that his devotees believed him to be, but as deluded, somewhat ignorant, slightly pompous but nevertheless benevolent, and on the whole well-intentioned – a slightly larger-than-life-size human being. In fact Brahma is, in the Buddhist view, a *type* of being, rather than a single unique being; there are many Brahmas; they inhabit the heavenly region known as the Brahma-world, and rebirth in this realm is quite favourably regarded, even though, in the cosmic hierarchy, it is considerably inferior to the supreme state of Nirvana, just as the Brahmas are in all things subordinate to the Buddha.

Just as tolerant on the whole is the Buddha's attitude towards belief in the many supernatural beings who were respected, venerated, propitiated or worshipped by the mass of the common people; such beliefs and practices have remained, throughout the centuries, major elements in the folk-lore of village India. Buddhist tolerance towards folk beliefs (shown by the Buddha himself and subsequently by Buddhist monks) may be seen to have had educative effects; it made easier a gradual and gentle infusion of Buddhist notions, in such a way that the original folk-beliefs were, over a long period, imperceptibly transformed and made to nourish Buddhist attitudes and to serve Buddhist religious goals.

Belief in evil spirits provides a good illustration of this process. There was at the time of the Buddha widespread belief in numerous demons, evil spirits, ogres, goblins and the like. These were thought of as acting capriciously and at random, and mostly in ways that were inimical to human welfare. They were often referred to as 'flesh-devourers', and this suggests that they were thought of as horrific beings, akin to beasts of prey, cannibals, or as agents of wasting diseases. They were frequently, though not always, creatures of the night, or of lonely places, who by their wild, weird or loud cries caused alarm or dread to humans who encountered them. They could in their malice assume all sorts of deceptive shapes and disguises in order to seduce men or lead them astray. According to popular belief, one of the ways they could be placated was by offering of sacrifices.

Beliefs of this kind appear to have been tolerated by the Buddha, and it is this kind of imagery which is used in some of his discourses to the more unsophisticated of his hearers. Some of the members of the Order, monks and nuns, are recorded as using such popular notions to describe their own experiences, in the *Songs of the Brethren* and the *Songs of the Sisters*, for example.[21] The Buddha, however, appears to have made a new contribution to the demonology of his day. Out of the notion of the common-place hostile demon, in conjunction with one or two other major concepts, such as that of *Mrtyu* (Death, personified) and *Namuci*, another great demon hostile to human welfare, there emerges in the teaching of the Buddha, the figure of Mara, the Evil One, the supreme head of all the forces that militated against human well-being and holy living. Instead of the experiences of evil being regarded as happening at random, they now begin to be seen as all part of the total evil in human experience which is brought into focus as having a unitary character. That is to say, all human experience of evil is seen as having a common root and source, and as having common, shared effects. To put it in these terms, however, is already to have moved on into the realm of abstract thinking and analysis. And this is precisely how the Buddhist notion of Mara, the Evil One, was used – to serve as a bridge-concept, a transition from the popular demonology on the one hand, which saw only chaos and random evil attacks from demons, to the idea of a common moral root for the ills which all humanity suffers, on the other. The importance of the concept lay in its use in religious practice. Whereas a peasant woman who encountered something terrifying in the darkness of the night might exclaim: 'How terrible for me! There is a demon after me!' [22] a Buddhist sister would in similar circumstances react by saying: 'Now who is this ...? It is that foolish Mara!' (for Mara's power, as every Buddhist knew, had been conquered once for all by the Buddha). As the present writer has dealt with this subject at length elsewhere it will be sufficient at this point to quote briefly from that other source certain words which have a bearing on the Buddha's attitude to popular, unsophisticated beliefs: '[The teaching of the Buddha] does not close the frontier of thought where it touches animism and popular demonology; it allows it to remain open, but controls it from the Buddhist side, and for Buddhist purposes.' [23]

So it can be seen that there is something of a contrast between the Buddha's attitude towards the brahmanical system of costly sacrifices on the one hand, and the popular beliefs and practices of the common people on the other, with a middle ground of moderate disapproval of popular magical practices, which had been adopted as 'Vedic' by some at least of the brahman priests. There were, however, at that time others beside the Buddha who were opposed to or indifferent to the priestly sacrificial system. But this was not enough in itself to provide a guarantee of any further common ground among them; there were, in fact, considerable differences between these various other teachers and their schools, and to these we must now turn our attention.

THE MENDICANT PHILOSOPHERS

It was mainly opposition to the brahmanical sacrificial and social system which the Buddha shared with other contemporary Indian teachers, or *shramanas*. The term *shramana* refers mainly to non-brahmans, but among these 'non-conformist' mendicant philosophers there were some brahmans by birth who also rejected the authority of the Vedic scriptures and the caste system of their day. Each *shramana* with his disciples constituted what may be loosely referred to as a 'sect' and between them these sects covered a variety of views, or philosophical positions, from materialism to mysticism. There seems, however, to have been an earlier stage, when there was practically no sectarian organization, but only a large number of individual ascetic, homeless wanderers, known in a broad sense as *ajivakas*. This later became the name of a particular sect, but in the earlier period, just before the time of the Buddha, the term can be applied to all who had adopted the *ajiva*, or 'special way of life which was the alternative to an ordinary trade'.[24] This alternative way of life was embraced, says A. K. Warder, 'by many who wished to escape the need to work, or the responsibility of family life, not to speak of conscription, forced labour or slavery, and was a carefree existence very different from the life of strenuous asceticism, complicated discipline, and intensive study required of members of most of the organized sects afterwards'.[25] This opting-out of the social and economic life of the time seems to have been the one feature common to men of otherwise widely varying viewpoints, all of whom, however, were sceptical or critical of the accepted religious philosophy of the brahmans. As individuals such men were known also as 'homeless ones', or *Parivrajakas*, men who had 'gone forth', forth, that is, from the life of the ordinary householder. There was, apparently, a recognized ritual connected with the initial act of 'going forth', a ritual which demonstrated the man's complete renunciation 'of the whole system of Vedic social practice and religious culture and all its signs and symbols'.[26] All external signs or marks which a man possessed, indicating his householder's status, kinship, and caste, he ceremonially removed, and the implements and symbols of the Vedic brahmanical sacrifice were consigned to the fire.[27] By the time of the Buddha wandering, mendicant ascetics in considerable numbers were a familiar feature of the social scene.[28]

After a while, however, their originally anarchic way of life came to be modified in the direction of rudimentary forms of organization. One of the factors which aided this development was the need, which such homeless wanderers could not avoid, for some kind of temporary shelter during the period of the monsoon rains. At about the beginning or the middle of June the thunderclouds gather and torrential rain beats down for long periods at a time; river channels, which in the dry weather a few weeks earlier are 'broad expanses of sand with small streams trickling down the centre', become full rivers, broad and deep, rising every hour until they over-top their banks and inundate the surrounding countryside.[29] Rivers everywhere throughout the Gangetic plain become wide, rapidly flowing torrents, which it is very difficult, if not impossible, to cross by ferry; so, since bridges are in most cases out of the question, and cross-country roads are either washed away or have become morasses of mud when any use is made of them, travelling is difficult and hazardous, as well as unpleasant. This state of affairs continues in most parts of northern and eastern India until the latter part of September. During this season of the year, therefore, the almsmen had to give up their wandering life for about three months and congregate in various temporary retreats from the rains – possibly caves or forest-shelters made specially for the purpose.

The other factor in the development of some degree of organization was the increasing power of the state. The monarchies of Koshala and Magadha, in particular, were extending their bounds and also intensifying the degree of control which was exercised over the lives of the people within their territories. If the wandering almsmen were not as a class to become objects of the king's displeasure and hostility they would have to organize themselves, and then, as organized schools of 'philosophers', show that they had some contribution to make to the public good. It became necessary for them to find leaders who would be able, as Warder says, to 'confront the kings as powerful and respected heads of organized sects ... and convince them of the importance and usefulness of the *Shramanas* in the new society (in comparison with other occupations)'.[30]

THE AJIVAKAS

So, out of what was possibly in the beginning a very broad category of homeless wanderers, 'drop-outs', or men of the 'alternative life' (*ajivakas*), there developed a number of separate and distinct philosophical schools, committed to various different viewpoints. One of the best known of these inherited the name *Ajivakas* as a special designation; the school so named adhered to the teaching of a man named Makkhali Gosala, who was one of the most prominent of the earlier leaders in the process of systematization. The doctrines of the Ajivakas may, however, have been taught somewhat earlier by two other wandering philosophers whose names have been preserved, Purana Kassapa and Pakudha Kaccayana, and then have been co-ordinated or further developed by Gosala.

These doctrines are known to us mainly from the criticisms of them which are found in Buddhist and Jain literature. The Ajivakas appear to have denied the notion of *karma*, namely, that a man's lot in his present existence is held to be the consequence of actions performed in previous existences and that his actions in this existence will determine his condition in future existences. The Buddhist understanding of the doctrine of *karma* carries with it the implication that a man can affect his own destiny for better or worse by his moral choices, and by the performance of morally wholesome or unwholesome acts. This principle the Ajivakas rejected. In their view, it seems, the supposed choice of action had no real effect whatever on men's condition of life, here or hereafter. All that happened within the universe took place within a totally closed causal system in which all events were completely and unalterably determined by cosmic principles over which there was no control. The doctrine that men do not act in any real sense seems to have been the contribution of Purana; what appears as the act of a man, who is the supposed actor, is no act at all, and there is therefore no question of choice of action and, therefore, no moral choice.

The teaching of Purana Kassapa is represented in the Buddhist Pali canon in the following terms:

To him who acts, O king, or causes another to act, to him who mutilates or causes another to mutilate, to him who punishes or causes another to punish, to him who causes grief or torment, to him who trembles or causes others to tremble, to him who kills a living creature, who takes what is not given, who breaks into houses, who commits dacoity, or robbery, or highway robbery, or adultery, or who speaks lies, to him thus acting there is no guilt. If with a discus with an edge sharp as a razor he should make all living creatures on the earth one heap, one mass of flesh, there would be no guilt thence resulting, no increase of guilt would ensue. Were he to go along the south bank of the Ganges striking and slaying, mutilating and having men mutilated, oppressing and having men oppressed, there would be no guilt thence resulting, no increase of guilt would ensue. Were he to go along the north bank of the Ganges giving alms or causing them to be offered, there would be no merit thence resulting, no increase of merit. In generosity, in self-mastery, in control of the senses, in speaking truth, there is neither merit nor increase of merit.[31]

Nevertheless, the Ajivakas practised an ascetic life. This fact they explained as being due, like everything else, to the wholly impersonal mechanism by which the universe operates. One of the inevitable stages in human destiny was the practice of asceticism. Every individual's destiny was unalterably fixed; men must pass through innumerable different kinds of existences, and last of all the ascetic life of the Ajivaka wanderer. Then came final peace. The whole process had an unimaginably long duration; the number of years for its completion was reckoned as 'thirty million million million multiplied by the number of the grains of sand in the bed of the River Ganges'.[32]

The Ajivaka doctrine would appear to be that 'all beings, all lives, all existent things, all living substances attain, and must attain, perfection in course of time.'[33] There is a fixed, orderly mode of progression through which all beings must pass, and through this transformation and constant change all, in the end, reach perfection. In the Ajivaka scheme it was laid down that there were fixed numbers of beings in the various categories of existence at any one time: there were, for instance, fourteen hundred thousands of species of being, six classes of men, forty-nine hundred kinds of occupation, forty-nine hundred Ajivakas, and forty-nine hundred (other) homeless wanderers.[34]

By such arguments the Ajivakas would assert the necessity of their mode of existence to any inquiring monarch. Such questioning of *shramana* teachers and ascetics by Ajatashatru, the King of Magadha, who was contemporary with the Buddha, is described in the Pali *sutta* entitled 'The Fruits of the Life of a Recluse'.[35] The king takes the line that since every other known occupation is profitable to society generally, as well as to the man who practises it, it is appropriate to ask what contribution is made by the life of the *shramana*.

The attempted justification by the leader of the Ajivakas of their position does not appear to have impressed King Ajatashatru greatly: 'I neither applauded nor blamed what he said,' recalls the king, 'and though dissatisfied I gave utterance to no expression of dissatisfaction, and neither accepting nor rejecting that answer of his, I arose from my seat and departed thence.'[36] One has to bear in mind, of course, that this is the Buddhist version of the matter.

THE JAINS

A somewhat similar position was maintained by the Jains. Mahavira, the leader of the Jain community at the time of the Buddha, appears to have been associated originally with Gosala, the leader of the Ajivakas. Which of the two was the 'pupil' seems uncertain; possibly each was indebted to the other in certain respects. The tradition is that they were associates for six years and then parted company. They met again, sixteen years later, only to disagree with one another. The major point on which the Jains differed from the Ajivakas was with regard to the freedom of the will. In opposition to the Ajivakas they asserted that every living being (human and non-human) was a transmigrating soul, and that by choosing morally wholesome actions it was possible for the soul to wear out its bad *karma* and eventually, after sustained moral improvement of this sort, to gain release altogether from the mortal realm into the highest heaven, a pure, eternal, non-material state of being. Like the Ajivakas, the Jains practised very severe austerities, but in their case as a means of neutralizing bad *karma*, and of their own free choice.[37] They laid great emphasis also on the necessity to avoid the acquisition of further bad *karma* through violent deeds, and they therefore made it a principle to avoid taking life in any form.

THE MATERIALISTS

A completely different philosophical position was maintained by the school of *shramanas* known as Lokayatas, or materialists. Their name indicates that their principal concern was with *loka*, the material, common, or natural *world*. In the light of a long list of references to the Lokayatas in Indian literature from the time of the Buddha to the fourteenth century, T. W. Rhys Davids came to the conclusion that

the best working hypothesis ... seems to be that about 500 BC the word Lokayata was used in a complimentary way as the name of a branch of Brahman learning, and probably meant *Nature-lore* – wise sayings, riddles, rhymes, and theories handed down by tradition as to cosmogony, the elements, the stars, the weather, scraps of astronomy, of elementary physics, even of anatomy, and knowledge of the nature of precious stones, and of birds and beasts and plants.[38]

On the basis of this rudimentary, folk-loristic view of the natural world there appears to have developed a theory of life whose principal exponent at the time of the Buddha was a man named Ajita of the hair-blanket (*kesa-kambalin*). In his own words, as they are represented in the Buddhist source,

A human being is built up of the four elements [earth, air, fire and water]. When he dies the earthy in him returns and re-lapses to the earth, the fluid to the water, the heat to the fire, the windy to the air, and his faculties pass into space [by the 'faculties' are meant the five senses, and the mind]. The four bearers ... take his dead body away; till they reach the burn-ing-ground men utter forth eulogies, but there his bones are bleached, and his offerings end in ashes ... Fools and wise alike, on the dissolution of the body, are cut off, annihilated, and after death they are not.[39]

A Buddhist commentator, Candrakirti, asserted that in the Lokayata view, consciousness was the product of the chemical interaction of the four elements of which the human body was composed, just as alcohol, with its inebri-ating power, is the product of ingredients which separately and by themselves are not inebriating. The Lokayatas appear to have rejected the idea of any moral causation: that is to say, the view that moral action produces one kind of consequence, and immoral action another kind of consequence. Every substance has its 'own nature' (*sva-bhava*) – it is self-determined. Translated into the realm of human action, this meant a doctrine of complete free-dom of will. In the Lokayata view men were entirely free to act as they chose. The only proper criterion of action, in their view, was whether it increased human pleasure.

By 'pleasure' was meant both the pleasures of the senses, and the mental pleasure of human relationships. Their ethic was therefore characterized as that of 'do-as-you-like' (*yadrccha*). On balance, life was potentially more full of pleasure than of pain; what was needed was the discrimination to seek pleasure in the ways in which it could most profitably be found, and this, no doubt, provided the Lokayata wanderers with the justification for their adoption of the 'alternative life'.

THE SCEPTICS

Finally, there was among the *shramanas* one more major position or school, generally known as the Agnostics, or Sceptics. These appear to have been men who rejected the traditional way of life, the Vedic doctrines, and the priestly system on the grounds that the speculative doctrines of priests and teachers were contradictory of one another, and that no final position of 'truth' could ever be reached. They avoided all argumentativeness, which, they said, was productive only of ill-temper. Their positive emphasis was on the cultivation of friendship and of peace of mind. These agnostics were criticized in the Buddhist sources as 'eel-wrigglers' because they wriggled out of every question that was put to them and refused to give any firm answer. Their leader, Sanjaya, is represented as saying,

If you ask me whether there is another world – well, if I thought there were I would say so. But I don't say so. And I don't think it is thus or thus. And I don't think it is otherwise. And I don't deny it. And I don't say there neither is, nor is not, another world. And if you ask me about the beings produced by chance; or whether there is any fruit, any result, of good or bad actions; or whether a man who has won the truth continues, or not, after death – to each or any of these questions I give the same reply.[40]

What was common to these various schools of thought found among the *shramanas*, of whom the Buddha also was one, was their rejection of the practices, beliefs and social system of the hereditary Vedic priesthood. But, as we have seen, they differed among themselves, and the Buddhists certainly differed, to greater or less degree, from all of them. We shall be in a better position to appreciate the points of difference between the doctrines of these other *shramanas* and the doctrine of the Buddha when we have considered the circumstances of the Buddha's life. It will then be possible to evaluate his role in relation to the religious, ideological, political and economic conditions of the time.

Part 3
Buddhist Civilization in Principle

6 Profile of the Buddha

Evidently, the Buddha belongs in the company of the *shramanas*, the non-brahman teachers who were critical of the brahmanical sacrificial system and who rejected the religious and social claims of the brahmans. How the Buddha's teaching differed from the other non-brahman schools of thought is considered later (see chapter 7). Meanwhile, there are other questions to be answered. We have to inquire about the characteristic concerns of the Buddha, the nature of his public activity, what kind of people he met with and what his relations with them were, how he was regarded by others, and so on. In this way, as the pattern of the Buddha's life is examined, and some sort of a profile emerges, it may be possible to determine a little more closely how he is to be characterized: that is, as religious innovator, or reformer, or as philosopher, or what.

First, we have to note that for the earliest Buddhists it was the *word* of the Buddha rather than the *life* of the Buddha which seems to have been of paramount importance. It was the discourses which were remembered, rehearsed at his death, and carefully preserved and transmitted in the community of his followers. His life-story was not in itself a matter of such intrinsic interest apparently, since the canon of scripture of the Theravadin school, which is representative of early or 'primitive' Buddhism (though not necessarily exclusively representative) contains no continuous narrative of his life. It was not until later in Buddhist history that full-length biographies of the Buddha were produced, such as the Sanskrit work of perhaps (at the earliest) the second century BC, entitled *The Great Event* (*Mahavastu*) or the more elaborate work by the Sanskrit poet of the second century AD, Ashvaghosha, entitled *The Acts of the Buddha* (*Buddhacarita*). Because of this apparent pre-occupation of the earliest followers of the Buddha with his doctrines rather than his life, the idea has been suggested by some Buddhists that possibly the doctrine is all that matters. It is the doctrine, they urge, which has eternal validity; the disciples' concern is to accept it, apprehend it and practise it; the Buddha-figure is simply the personification of a spiritual principle. 'The existence of Gotama as an individual,' writes Edward Conze, 'is, in any case, a matter of little importance to Buddhist faith.'[1] To some extent this attitude may have been provoked by the suggestions of Western scholars (at a time when it was fashionable to question the historical existence of any cult hero) that the Buddha who is described in even the earliest Buddhist literature is pure invention. H. H. Wilson, for instance, argued that the Buddha's life as it has come down in the traditions, is nothing more than an allegorical version of the Sankhya philosophy; others, such as E. Senart and H. Kern, suggested that the Buddha was a solar symbol and the story of his life, a solar myth.[2] The Indian scholar, T. R. V. Murti, while not denying the historical existence of Gotama, regards it as unimportant for the Mahayana form of Buddhist religion – that is, the form which he regards as the most fully developed and most adequate as a religion. 'The Mahayana religion escapes the predicament of having to depend on any particular historical person as the founder.'[3]

It is worth noting, in passing, that the late-nineteenth-century wave of scepticism about the historicity of the Buddha has now receded. As André Bareau has said, nowadays, as a result of greater knowledge of the philological and archaeological sources, scientific study admits that in the case of the Buddha there really existed an historical personage the principal traits of whose life and personality can be known.[4] It is important to notice, too, that while the Buddha's earliest disciples seem to have had no interest in recounting the entire life of the Buddha *seriatim*, they were nevertheless concerned to record carefully what they appear to have considered the most important events, events relating to certain crucial or significant moments in the pattern of the Buddha's life, such as his renunciation of the life of a prince, his enlightenment, the inauguration of his public activity as a teacher, and his decease.

These four events provide a convenient framework within which to examine the personality and role of the Buddha; they indicate four historically important aspects of the Buddha's relation to the life of his time: (1) his particular social and cultural milieu; (2) the experience of spiritual unrest, and subsequent enlightenment which he underwent; (3) the nature of his public activity; and (4) the significance of the ceremonies connected with his decease.

GOTAMA'S SOCIAL AND CULTURAL MILIEU

The man who was to become known as the Buddha (and who until his enlightenment at Bodh-Gaya is properly known as the *Bodhisattva*, or one who has the essence of Buddhahood, or enlightenment) was, says the tradition, the son of Suddhodana, the leading citizen of Kapilavastu. This was a busy town on the north-west to south-east trade route which ran along the foot of the Himalayan mountains, amid the thick forests at the extreme northern edge of the Gangetic plain. It lay due north of Banaras, and a few miles within the border of what is now Nepal. The town was the capital of the Shakyas, a people who had, as we have seen, an aristocratic republican form of government. Their territory probably extended about fifty miles from east to west, and about thirty or forty from north to south, from the foot of the Himalayas.[5] Apart from Kapilavastu, the capital, the region contained a number of market towns. The Buddha-to-be belonged to the clan of the Gotamas, and it is by this name that he is often known, as if it were a surname. His given, or personal name was Siddhartha. Later Buddhist literature magnifies the position of his father to that of a very great king and depicts the life-style of the young prince as one of extreme grandeur, luxury and wealth. It is more probable that his father was the elected head of an aristocratic hereditary ruling class, having some of the rank, status and prestige of the ruler of a small kingdom, but nothing more. As might be expected, the Buddhist sources provide a certain amount of information about the Shakyas, although it is mostly of the kind that has to be pieced together from scattered references. With regard to the ancestry of the Shakyas, for example, there is an interesting allusion to the progenitors of their tribe having had their dwelling 'on the slopes of the Himalayas'.[6] In the present form of the story, as it is told in the Pali canon, although it is explained that these progenitors *went* to the Himalayas when they were banished from the court of their father, a legendary Indian raja of ancient times, named Okkaka, the explanation could well be a device to account for the fact that the ancestors of what was now a north-Indian tribe had at an earlier period lived in the Himalayas, if this were a strongly established tradition among them. It would, in fact, be more in accordance with the natural course of migration for a Himalayan tribe to have moved southwards towards the sun and the plains than *vice versa*, for, in general, this has been the predominant direction in which migration of peoples occurred throughout north India and continental South-East Asia. The *Ambattha Sutta*, in which the story occurs, suggests that the Shakyas were a non-brahman tribe. The brahman Ambattha, in conversation with the Buddha, referring to the division of society into those who were brahmans and those who were not, reminded the Buddha that it was the duty of the latter to serve the former, and to honour them. The Shakyas, he compained, appeared to be lacking in this sense of respect for brahmans.

Once, Gotama, I had to go to Kapilavastu on some business

or other . . . and went into the Shakya's Congress Hall (*Santha-gara-sala*). Now at that time there were a number of Shakyas, old and young, seated in the hall on grand seats, making merry and joking together, nudging one another with their fingers; and for a truth, methinks, it was I myself that was the subject of their jokes; and not one of them even offered me a seat. That, Gotama, is neither fitting, nor is it seemly, that the Shakyas, menials as they are, mere menials, should neither venerate, nor value, nor esteem, nor give gifts to, nor pay honour to Brahmans.[7]

Such lack of respect for brahmans which is attributed to the Shakyas in this tale may possibly reflect the attitude of the developed Buddhist community towards the brahmans. It is also possible that this was known by the Buddhists to have been the attitude of the Shakya people. If the Shakyas were Himalayan hill people who had migrated to the edge of the plains, it is likely that they would have been of a sturdy independent spirit, and well disposed to reject the social pretensions of the Aryan brahman class. That they were of such a spirit is suggested by one or two other casual references.[8] Their sturdy spirit is shown too in their relations with the neighbouring great monarchy of Koshala (see chapter 3, pp. 53 f.). The king of Koshala, Pasenadi, a great admirer of the Buddha, and benefactor of the Buddhist Order, wished to strengthen his relationship with the Shakyas. He sent to the Shakyan elders a polite request that he might be allowed to marry one of their daughters. They, however, considered that such a marriage would be degrading to them; it would, they said, destroy the purity of their race and be contrary to their tradition. But they could not afford to risk the anger of this very powerful neighbouring king, so they sent him the illegitimate daughter of one of the chiefs, born of a slave-woman, passing her off as pure Shakyan. The attitude of the Shakyans is referred to in the course of the story (the *Bhadda-Salu Jataka*) in the words of king Pasenadi's messengers: 'These Shakyas are desperately proud, in matters of birth!'[9] Another interesting fact about the Shakyas is that they were fond of sports, and especially archery. They had an established school of archery, run by a family who specialized in this sport.[10] It is said, too, that the Buddha, as a young man, had to prove his prowess as an archer before any Shakyan nobleman would consider him as a future son-in-law.[11] While Kapilavastu, the capital of the Shakyan republic, was not one of the recognized six great cities (*mahanagara*) of the time, it was certainly a place of importance and some affluence. It is described as a city where there were crowds of people and plenty of food, a place whose streets were full of traffic, in the form of elephants, horses, chariots, carts and pedestrians, and where, with their hubbub and jingle and clatter, was mingled the sound of street musicians, singers and traders.[12] The general pattern of Indian cities of this period has already been described (see chapter 3, pp. 53 f.), and Kapilavastu would no doubt have conformed generally to this pattern. The Buddhist sources mention the council hall, the *Santhagara-sala*, which stood at the centre of the town, and where public business, administrative and judicial, was carried out. Mention is made, too, of the massive ramparts surrounding the city, said to have been eighteen cubits high. It was as the leading citizen of such a city, and as one who carried the responsibility for presiding over the affairs of the small state of which Kapilavastu was the capital, that we have to see the father of the Bodhisattva. It is appropriate to think, not so much in terms of the idle ostentation of the court of some great oriental emperor, as of the material comfort and well-being of a cultured upper-class townsman in a prosperous commercial and administrative centre: of urbanity and sophistication, rather than of luxurious imperial grandeur.

The background of the Buddha's youth and early manhood is represented, therefore, as having been one of urban life, comfortable and easy by the standards of the time, and made more so by the privileges that went with superior social class; Shakyan society was certainly not classless, as the story of king Pasenadi's bride makes clear.

The fact that the Shakyan state was not a monarchy may be significant in connection with the problem which was raised in chapter 4, namely, which came first – individualism, monarchy, or urbanism? Gotama's milieu, to the time of his manhood, was that of urban life, but it did not include experience of a developed monarchical society. The problem which he seems to have felt most keenly and which set him on his spiritual quest, was that of the suffering of *the individual*. This suggests that it was primarily urban life which precipitated individualism, rather than monarchy, or, at any rate, that this is how it was understood by the early Buddhist community. Moreover, it was a concern with the pain and the unsatisfactoriness of ordinary, common mortal existence which stirred Gotama; this can be seen as both a consequence of his upbringing and· a determining factor in the shape of the solution which he discovered for the ills of human existence. For the milieu in which he probably grew up is that of a traditional ruling class, one occupied with the practical aspects of public life, with the smooth functioning of the machinery of society and perhaps at least some general concern with, and feeling of responsibility for, human welfare.

It is meaningless to say, as some have done,[13] that the Buddha, a child of his time, was heir to the Hindu religious tradition. In the first place, it is an anachronism to ascribe a Hindu religious tradition to this early period; the characteristic set of beliefs and practices which came to be known as 'Hindu' (the word itself being a product of the Muslim period) was yet to be developed. Moreover, it is difficult to see how the Buddha can be described as an heir to the brahman religious tradition. One who did not believe in God, nor in theories of creation, and who did not accept the authority of the Veda, was about as much an heir to the Hindu tradition as Karl Marx was a Zionist.

It has been suggested that if Gotama was indebted to any earlier figure in the cultural history of India, the most likely candidate is Kapila, to whom is attributed the atheistic Sankhya doctrine. It is very likely, writes R. C. Majumdar, that Gotama, since he came from Kapilavastu, 'had some knowledge of the Sankhya doctrine'.[14]

The affinity between the teaching of the Buddha and the Sankhya philosophy was hinted at by Ashvaghosha (the Buddhist writer mentioned on page 106) in his full-length biography of the Buddha, the *Buddhacarita*. Those who hold the view that the Buddha was influenced by Sankhya attitudes point to the fact that one of the teachers to whom he resorted in the course of his wanderings, before his own 'awakenment' at Bodh-Gaya, was Alara (or Arada) Kalama. Alara's philosophy seems to have borne some slight resemblance to the Sankhya system, although there seem also to have been significant differences. The fact that Gotama stayed only a short while with Alara and then left him, because he was not satisfied with his teaching,[15] could mean that Gotama found Alara either insufficiently Sankhyan in his views, or too much so. A modern Indian writer takes the view that it would be a serious error to overlook the major similarity between the Sankhya system and Buddhism – the atheistic position which is common to them: 'since the Sankhya was undoubtedly much older than the rise of Buddhism, we are left with the strong presumption that at least for his atheism the Buddha was directly indebted to the Sankhya, though he evidently differed much from Kapila in his main interest.'[16] But this is to assume that Gotama was incapable by himself of arriving at an atheistic view, or adopting an atheistic premise as his starting-point. The likelihood that Gotama, living in Kapilavastu, might have been familiar with the Sankhya view, has to be taken in conjunction with the suggestion of Dandekar that the origin of the Sankhya is to be found in a 'pre-Vedic, non-Aryan thought complex'.[17] So it is an open possibility that Gotama's atheism also had its origin in the pre-Vedic, non-Aryan, non-Brahmanical culture of north-eastern India in general, and of the Shakya people in particular.

The notion that Gotama was a 'religious' man evidently

needs careful scrutiny. That he has come to be so regarded may be partly because of the assimilation of Buddhism with theistic systems of belief and practice as a 'religion', and partly because of the ill-founded idea that the inhabitants of India are, and always have been, more religiously inclined than the peoples of the West. In this way the Buddha has been subsumed under the general category of religious teachers or leaders. The Buddha's teaching, and the life of the early Buddhists is often regarded as an answer to personal spiritual *malaise*, a doctrine of personal salvation. The possibility which is being raised here is that it was something other than this. It has to be admitted, however, that the story of Gotama's enlightenment does, on the face of it, look very like a personal salvation story of a purely religious kind. But this may be because the modern understanding of 'religion' is being projected back into the time of the Buddha and made the criterion of his experience. We need to inquire what is said in the tradition of early Buddhism about the whole complex of events leading to the enlightenment at Bodh-Gaya.

THE ENLIGHTENMENT

According to tradition, Gotama was twenty-nine years of age when the decisive events occurred which led to his enlightenment. Various accounts are available, and they differ considerably, especially with regard to the circumstances of the renunciation. According to the later, more elaborate accounts, written in Sanskrit, the Bodhisattva, while he was out driving his chariot, was confronted successively by a very old man, then by a very sick man, and finally by a corpse being carried out to the burning *ghat*. These sights disturbed him profoundly, for they raised questions which he had apparently not considered before. Finally, the sight of a holy man stirred in him the desire to live the ascetic life and strive for spiritual enlightenment.

On the other hand, an early Pali text gives an account

which suggests that it was as a result of long reflection upon the human condition that Gotama decided to devote himself to a disciplined quest for spiritual satisfaction. In this account of the matter, the Buddha, some years after the event, makes known to his followers the two possible ends to which men may devote their lives, in terms of his own earlier experience. He identifies these two ends as the noble or holy quest (*ariya-pariyesana*) and the ignoble or unholy quest. Briefly, the human situation is seen as one in which, because of belief in self (*atta* or *atman*), men are vulnerable to the process of ageing, decay and dying, and hence to sorrow. The word translated as sorrow (*dukkha*) in fact carries a much deeper and stronger connotation than the English word, and implies a sense of utter unsatisfactoriness, weariness and pain of mortal existence. The ignoble quest, to which many devote their lives, consists in seeking after things which are liable to ageing, decay and death, the very conditions from which deliverance is needed.

'And what, monks, is the noble quest? That someone, being liable to birth because of self, and knowing the peril in whatever is liable to birth, seeks the unborn, the uttermost security from bonds – *nibbana*.' The same formula is then repeated for each of the other conditions of mortal existence. The noble quest is that in which someone, who because of self is vulnerable to ageing, decaying, dying, stain and sorrow, and who knows the peril in whatever is liable to the same things, seeks the unageing, the undecaying, the undying, the stainless, the unsorrowing – that which is itself freedom from all constraints: *nibbana*. The Buddha then goes on to say that when he was still the Bodhisattva, it was considerations such as these which stirred him, and made him ask 'Why do I seek what is liable to birth ... to ageing ... to decay ... to death ... to stain ... to sorrow? Being myself liable to birth, to ageing, to decay, to death, to stain, to sorrow, I should seek the unborn, the unageing, the undecaying, the undying, the stainless, the unsorrowing.' [18]

It is understandable, as E. J. Thomas pointed out, that this kind of account of personal experience and reflection should have been developed into the story of encounters with an old man, a sick man, and a corpse; it is less understandable, on the other hand, how, if these encounters had been real events the story could subsequently 'have been converted into this abstract form'.[19] On the day on which he saw these three manifestations of the human condition, so the tradition asserts, another event took place – the birth of Bodhisattva's son. On hearing the news, he pronounced his son's name, 'Rahula'. The commentators suggest the presence of a pun: the word 'rahula' means, they say, 'a bond', and so the Bodhisattva's utterance had a double meaning: 'Rahula is born. A bond is born.' Thus, it is very interesting to notice that of the six conditions of human existence mentioned in the Buddha's discourse – birth, ageing, decay, dying, stain and sorrow – *four* illustrative examples have been found in what are represented as the events surrounding the great renunciation. Finally, there is the further curious incident concerning a Shakya maiden named Kisagotami. It is said that from her balcony she saw Gotama returning home in his chariot after the news of his son's birth had been announced to him. She saw Gotama's 'beauty and glory' and 'she was filled with joy and delight', and began to sing: 'Happy is the mother, happy is the father, happy is the wife who has such a husband!' The word which she used for 'happy' (*nibbuta*) meant also 'cool' or 'healthy'. The Bodhisattva, upon hearing her song, took the word to mean 'cool', and, says the tradition, 'with aversion in his heart for lusts, he thought, "When the fire of passion is cooled, the heart is happy; when the fire of illusion, pride, false views and all the lusts and pains are extinguished it is happy".' In gratitude for the lesson she had taught him, the story continues, he sent the maiden a very costly pearl necklace. 'She thought that prince Siddhattha (Gotama) was in love with her, and had sent her a present, and she was filled with delight.' But a few hours later, in the quietness of the night, awakening to the sight of the dancers who had been entertaining him, and were now asleep in all kinds of disgusting and unseemly postures, he renounced the life of sensual pleasures, and took the crucial step of leaving his home, to set out on the life of the homeless wanderer, in search of spiritual peace.

Perhaps both the abstract analysis of the human situation, and the picturesque account, with its various personal illustrations, of the kind of 'fetters' or constraints from which Gotama felt he had to escape, indicate in their contrasting ways the nature of his quest. The abstract version emphasizes that it is 'the self', the *atman*, which is the ultimate root of the human experience of sorrow. It is because of the idea of 'self' that men are vulnerable to birth, ageing, decay, death, stain, and sorrow; it is this notion of 'self' which causes men to experience life as sorrowful. The stories of Gotama's encounters with old age, disease, death, birth and the taint of passion may have been the kind of characteristic experiences which brought a young man to see that it is the unending search for the satisfaction of the desires of the individual which leads to spiritual disenchantment. It was from this condition, from these constraints, that he sought some way of deliverance.

We return, therefore, to the point which was made earlier, that it was the ultimate unsatisfactoriness, the sorrowfulness of life, which set Gotama on his spiritual quest. How this quest was fulfilled, what was the nature of the 'salvation' which he found, we shall consider in detail in the next chapter. What we now have to take account of is the typical environment, the *locale* for his public activity after the enlightenment, after the great discovery had been made.

THE NATURE OF THE BUDDHA'S PUBLIC ACTIVITY

If we are correct in thinking that the problems of human life with which the Buddha was primarily concerned were the kind of problems which arise with the development of individualism, and if this was a feature which was more characteristic of urban than of rural life, then it is reasonable to expect that those in greatest need of his teaching, of his prescription for freedom and peace, would be found in the urban centres rather than in the countryside. It was, in fact, precisely there, in the cities, that most of the Buddha's public activity took ploce.

The profound experience he underwent at Bodh-Gaya was his awakening to the truth; it was itself an end of all the constraints of which he had previously been aware, and it was therefore described as *vimutti*, release, or *nibbana*, the state of 'coolness' or 'health after fever'. The tradition represents him as at first uncertain whether this truth which he had apprehended could ever be conveyed to other men. 'This *dhamma*, attained to by me is deep, difficult to see, difficult to understand, tranquil, excellent, beyond dialectic, subtle, intelligible to the learned. But this is a creation delighting in sensual pleasure, rejoicing in sensual pleasure ... [and for them] this were a matter difficult to see ...' The Buddha recalls that, as he was pondering and deciding against the attempt to communicate his discovery of truth to the generality of men, it occurred to the god Brahma that the world would be lost, would be destroyed, if the Buddha now refrained from teaching his doctrines (*dhamma*). He thereupon manifested himself to the Buddha in the way we have already seen.[20] The intention of this story may have been to show that even the gods were dependent on the eternal *dhamma* which the Buddha had perceived, and were therefore subordinate both to the *dhamma* and to him who was its bearer. The story has the effect, too, of showing that the relationship between the Buddha and the gods of popular belief was one of tolerant co-existence.

Now that he was persuaded that he should attempt to communicate the truth to others, the Buddha began to consider how this might most effectively be done. It is significant that the place he then made for was Varanasi, or

Banaras, which, as we have seen, was at that time the intellectual and philosophical metropolis of northern India (see p. 56). To some extent this significant fact is concealed by the ostensible reason given for his choice of Banaras – that he knew that he would meet there a group of five men whom he had known earlier, when he and they had been seeking spiritual satisfaction. It was to them that he now hoped to make known the truth. What has to be noticed is that their spiritual quest had led them to Banaras: it is almost as though, in ancient India, it was the case that all religious and philosophical seekers must at some time or other find their way to that ancient and holy centre of worship and philosophy. There, in a park a little way outside the city, he found them; and there he expounded to them in systematic, developed order, the *dhamma*, the truth by which release from the problems and constraints of mortal existence might be gained.

The account of this exposition is the famous *Dhamma-cakka-ppavattana Sutta* – the discourse (or Sutta) concerning the putting into motion of the wheel of *dhamma*. The Buddha remained with the five at Banaras and, a few days later, after another session of teaching, the five achieved the state of wisdom, dispassion, and release from all the bonds of empirical mortal existence, a state known technically in Buddhism as *arahant*-ship, a term which will be explained later. It is appropriate to call the occasion 'a session of teaching', for this is the nearest, in the writer's view, that one can get to a satisfactory description of the method used by the Buddha. To say that he preached a sermon (although this terminology has been used by Western writers to describe the Buddha's activity) would be rather misleading, for, to Western ears at least, it suggests a wholly passive role for the hearers, and for the preacher a position which is sometimes described as 'six feet above contradiction'. This was not so in the kind of teaching-sessions which are recorded in early Buddhist literature. The hearers frequently interject, or raise questions, or supply answers to questions addressed to them by the Buddha, and sometimes the Buddha engages them in what is almost a catechism. Even 'discourses' suggests something rather stilted, formal, and humourless, and it is clear that they were far from being addresses of that sort. It was, in fact, almost always a session of teaching, with the Buddha suiting his words to the occasion, and taking advantage of incidents happening at the time, adapting himself to the mood or condition of the hearers and allowing them to take a good deal of the initiative. In some ways these sessions might suggest, as the closest parallel, an academic seminar or tutorial, but the resemblance is only partial. On occasions the Buddha was addressing very large numbers of people, and apart from the fact that one is unlikely to meet tutors of his quality, there seems, in addition, to have been something of what today would be called a 'charismatic' quality about his teaching.

At Banaras the Buddha remained throughout the rainy season which then followed: that is to say, for about four months. His teaching won further adherents. The first was Yasa, a young man who, according to the Pali sources, came to the Buddha by night, feeling distress and disgust at the sordid sight presented by his own attendants who were asleep in unseemly postures. This disgust at the physically sordid aspects of human life was only the occasion for his flight from home; other, earlier experiences had conditioned him for it. He is represented as having been, like Gotama, one who had enjoyed a comfortable life; his father was one of the most wealthy financiers of Banaras. The Buddha, seeing his distressed state, called him and said 'Come, Yasa, here you will find neither distress nor danger'. There followed a session of teaching, as with the five, and at the end of it Yasa, too, apprehended the truth which the Buddha had been expounding and achieved the state of release, or *arahant*-ship. His father, alarmed by his absence, had followed the marks of Yasa's slippers, and now he, too, arrived on the scene. Not seeing Yasa at first, but only the Buddha, the father engaged him in conversation. After a time the father also came under the power of the Buddha's words, and there and then declared himself a follower. He is remembered in Buddhist tradition as the first lay-follower, or *upasaka*. The next day Yasa's mother and another woman became the first female lay-followers, when the Buddha, in response to an invitation from Yasa's father, visited the family at home and had a meal with them. Four of Yasa's companions, sons of leading families in Banaras, also became disciples of the Buddha. These, with the five former associates of the Buddha who had been the first to receive his teaching, now constituted the nucleus of what was to become the *Sangha*, or assembly of disciples, sometimes called the Buddhist Order. Later, fifty more citizens of Banaras, who had heard the Buddha's teaching, became *arahants* and entered the Order. So there came into being at Banaras a community of disciples of some size. Its members, having understood the doctrine taught by the Buddha, were sent out in different directions to teach the *dhamma* to others. The result is represented as having been a great number of further candidates who were, from this time onwards, ordained into the Order by the monks, rather than by the Buddha himself.[21]

THE BUDDHA IN RAJAGRIHA AND SHRAVASTI

At the end of the rainy season the Buddha set out from Banaras eastwards, towards another of the six great cities of the time, Rajagriha, the Magadhan capital. On the way he visited the site of his enlightenment, staying there for a while and making converts to his doctrine. At Rajagriha more converts were made, including Sariputta and Moggallana, who later became, with Ananda, the most prominent members of the Order. The then king of Magadha, Bimbisara, became interested in the Buddha's teaching; he, too, was convinced of its value, and became a lay-follower.

No consecutive narrative of the public activity of the Buddha was constructed by the early Buddhists, but from the account of the travels and teaching which is contained

in the Pali canon, it is possible to suggest, as Malalasekere
has done,[22] an outline for at least the first twenty years.
Then comes a period of a further twenty-five years when it
is impossible to trace any consecutive chronology, until
the last few weeks of the Buddha's life, when there is the
very detailed account of the last journey in the *Maha Parinibbana Sutta*, the *Sutta* concerning the great event of the
entry by the Buddha into complete nirvana *(pari-nib-
bana)*.

What is significant, however, from the evidence contained in the vast collection of discourses of the Buddha in
the Pali canon, is the large proportion of these which were
delivered in two major cities, Rajagriha and Shravasti. In
almost all cases the discourse is introduced by a short note,
indicating the place where it was delivered, and the occasion. From the evidence of these contextual notes it is possible to see that the Buddha lived more in the city of Shravasti than anywhere else. Until the later part of his life,
when it lost its pride of place to Rajagriha, Shravasti, the
capital of Koshala, was the most important city of the
Gangetic plain, commercially and politically. The Buddha
first went there at the invitation of a rich merchant named
Anathapindika, whom he met at Rajagriha on the visit
which has just been described. Anathapindika was visiting Rajagriha on business, and like so many others in the
city, came to hear of the new doctrine which was being
taught by the Shakya-sage. He, too, was converted and became a lay-follower. He invited the Buddha to spend the
next rainy season at Shravasti, and when the invitation
was accepted, he set off back to the Koshalan capital. Having arrived, he bought a piece of land on the outskirts of
the city, at considerable cost, and had a suitable *vihara*,
or retreat-house, built in readiness for occupation by the
Buddha and his company.

From the time when the Buddha and his companions
first went to live in Shravasti it became virtually their
headquarters. Twenty-five rainy seasons were spent there
by the Buddha; the remaining twenty were spent in

various other towns and cities, mainly Rajagriha. Of the discourses of the Buddha which go to make up the *Sutta-Pitaka*, 871 are said to have been delivered in Shravasti. Of 498 canonical *Jataka* stories, the telling of which is attributed to the Buddha, 416 are said to have been told in Shravasti.

Kapilavastu, the Buddha's home city, was visited by him more than once in the course of the years. On the first visit, in the year of his enlightenment, Gotama's little son, Rahula, was ordained as a novice. Thirteen years later, when he had come of age, Rahula was given *upasampada*, or higher ordination, this time in the city of Shravasti.[23]

Rajagriha, the other major city with which the Buddha's work was most closely associated, was the capital of the Magadhan kingdom, which was increasing in power and prestige throughout the Buddha's lifetime. The expansion of the city beyond its old bounds during this period was a sign of its increasing population. Its king, Bimbisara (see p. 120), remained a firm friend and supporter of the Buddha throughout his life. He entertained the Buddha and his companions and presented them with a place of residence. Even during the years when Shravasti was mainly his headquarters, the Buddha seems to have paid frequent visits to Rajagriha. Many important discourses are connected with the Magadhan capital, and it was from here that the Buddha set out on his last journey. By that time there were in Rajagriha eighteen large monasteries for members of the Buddhist Order.[24] This concentration of Buddhist houses in a large capital city shows the kind of milieu in which early Buddhism flourished and was most at home.

THE BUDDHA'S LAST JOURNEY

The Buddha's last journey is described in some detail in one of the longest of the Pali texts, the *Sutta of the Great Decease* (*Maha Parinibbana Sutta*). The events which are related cover a period of some months, and the narrative has many facets, each having its special value to this or that reader or hearer. What is unmistakable is the portrait of the Buddha which emerges: the portrait of the discoverer, initiator and exponent of a social, psychological and political philosophy, who takes his place among the great leaders and rulers of the world (a *Chakravartin*, or *world-ruler*).

The narrative of the *Sutta* begins in the city of Rajagriha. Bimbisara, the Buddha's helper and admirer, is no longer king of Magadha; he has been succeeded by his son, Ajatashatru. We are told that he was about to launch an attack on one of the remaining republican federations, the Vajjians, whose territory was to the north of Magadha, across the Ganges. He is represented, rather curiously, as sending a messenger to the Buddha, who at that time was in Rajagriha, to ask his advice on the matter. 'Tell him,' the king instructs his brahman messenger, 'that Ajatashatru, the king of Magadha ... has resolved, "I will strike at these Vajjians, mighty and powerful though they be, I will root out these Vajjians, I will destroy these Vajjians, I will bring these Vajjians to utter ruin!"' [25] The messenger is instructed to listen carefully to what the Buddha has to say by way of comment, and to come and repeat it to the king. The Buddha's comment turns out to be rather cryptic. He declares that so long as the Vajjians continue to observe their traditions properly, and to meet regularly in their republican assembly, seeking agreement in all matters, so long as they honour their elders, and maintain their customary rites and ceremonies as a republic, no harm can come to them; their prosperity is assured. The brahman messenger takes the meaning of the prediction to be that the Vajjians cannot be overcome in battle; they will be overcome only by diplomacy and internal dissension. Having drawn this conclusion, he hurries back to his royal master.

The Buddha then repeats to his companions word for word what he had said concerning the Vajjians, but applying his prediction, now, to the Buddhist *Sangha*. So long as the *Sangha* members continue to observe their traditions properly, and to meet regularly in their assembly, seeking agreement in all matters, and so on, no harm can come to the *Sangha*: it can only prosper. The crucial fact in the interpretation of this utterance of the Buddha is that the Vajjians were destroyed very shortly after this incident. According to tradition, spies and infiltrators succeeded in sowing the seeds of suspicion among the leaders and elders of the ruling assembly, and soon there was a rich crop of dissension and internal conflict which Ajatashatru was able to turn to his advantage. The Vajjian republic was conquered, and absorbed into the Magadhan monarchy. So, by the time this prediction of the Buddha was being repeated and transmitted in the oral tradition of the monks, it was known that, as a fact of history, the Vajjians had *not* succeeded in meeting the conditions required for their survival. It would have been clear to the monks who passed on these words of the Buddha that there must be some other, more permanent value in this utterance than simply an oblique prediction of the ruin of a people who were now only of historical interest. The point of the discourse lay in the application to the Buddhist *Sangha* of the same conditions for survival. The old republican *sanghas* or assemblies had now almost all disappeared, victims of historical circumstances in the form of expanding monarchical power. If that were a matter for regret, it had to be remembered that the *sangha* tradition was nevertheless being perpetuated and preserved in a new form – in the life of the Buddhist community, the new *Sangha*; we shall take up this point again later, when we come to examine the life of the *Sangha* (chapter 8). Meanwhile, what emerges from this opening section of the *Sutta of the Great Decease* is the evident and real interest of the Buddha in forms of social and political structure.

Soon after the incident concerning the Vajjians, according to the narrative, the Buddha and his companions left Rajagriha and began travelling northwards. They reached the southern shore of the Ganges at a place which at that time was called Pataligama, but which a century or so later was to be known as Pataliputra, when it became the new capital city of the expanding kingdom of Magadha; today it is Patna, the chief city of Bihar State. At this place the Buddha talked through the night with some local people who had assembled specially at the rest-house for travellers, where the Buddha was staying. These were lay-followers, who, while acknowledging the outstanding value of the Buddha's teaching, still continued their household life. In the Buddha's view, they too had an important place in the scheme of things, and it was for this reason that he undertook to instruct them in detail in the matters of social morality, pointing out to them the various advantages of moral uprightness and integrity. The morning after he had spoken with these householders, the Buddha observed that some ministers of the Magadhan state were supervising the construction of a new fortress at Pataligama. He then, it is said, uttered a prediction concerning this new stronghold. 'As far, Ananda, as Aryan people resort, as far as merchants travel, this will become the chief city, Pataliputra, a centre for the interchange of all kinds of wares. But three dangers will hang over Pataliputra, that of fire, that of water, and that of dissension among friends.' [26] The event referred to, the transfer of the royal capital of Magadha to Pataliputra, took place probably during the reign of Ajatashatru's son; the significance of the reference for our present purpose lies in the fact that the Buddha is represented as being keenly interested in a matter of this sort – the founding and growth of what was to become a great city.

After crossing the Ganges, and passing through two smaller towns, the Buddha and his companions came to the city of Vaishali, the capital of the Licchavi republic. Here the Buddha accepted the invitation of Ambapali, the chief courtesan of the city, to take a meal at her house after she had heard him teaching and been gladdened by his words. The chief citizens of Licchavi, hearing of the acceptance from Ambapali herself, asked her to be so good as to give way in deference to them, so that they might enter-

tain the Buddha. But although they offered her a large
sum of money, on this occasion her favour was not to be
bought. 'My lords,' she replied, 'were you to offer all Vaishali with its subject territory, I would not give up so
honourable a feast!' [27]

The Buddha remained in Vaishali for some time. It was
a place which he had visited several times before in his
travels, and for which he seems to have had a special liking. It contained a number of splendid shrines dedicated
to popular local deities, and the Buddha particularly enjoyed their beauty. 'How delightful a spot, Ananda, is
Vaishali. How charming the Udena Shrine, and the Gota-
maka Shrine, and the Shrine of the Seven Mangoes, and
the Shrine of Many Sons, and the Sarandada Shrine, and
the Chapala Shrine.' [28] The Sutta tells that after this visit,
when the time came for him to leave the city, knowing that
it would be the last time he would see Vaishali before he
died, the Buddha turned and took a long, full look at the
city, and then continued on his journey.

THE VILLAGE OF KUSHINARA

The place in which his entry into final *nibbana* occurred
was a small, insignificant village called Kushinara. A little
while before, it had become clear to the Buddha's companions that the end of his mortal existence was now very
near; not only was he eighty years of age, but he had become physically very weak. They had asked what ceremonies would be appropriate after his death, and had been
instructed that the remains of a Tathagata, or Buddha,
should be treated in the same way as it was customary to
treat the remains of a *Chakravartin*, a universal emperor.
They were to be wrapped in cloth, and soaked in oil,
placed on a funeral pyre made of all kinds of fragrant
wood, and burned; the relics were then to be enshrined in
a great memorial cairn, or *stupa*, built at the centre of a
crossroads. This was how the funeral rites of a *Chakra-*

vartin were carried out; the memorial cairn would be built at some important crossing of routes, in a major city.

The Buddha's companions were surprised when they realized from their master's severely weakened condition that it was in Kushinara that his life was to end. Ananda expressed their feeling:

> Let not the Exalted One die in this little wattle-and-daub town, in this town in the midst of the jungle, in this branch township. For, lord, there are other great cities, such as Champa, Rajagriha, Shravasti, Shaketa, Kaushambi and Banaras. Let the Exalted One die in one of them. There there are many wealthy nobles and heads of houses, believers in the Tathagata, who will pay due honour to the remains of the Tathagata.[29]

Perhaps Ananda really did feel such dismay at the prospect of the Buddha's life ending in Kushinara and of the cremation of his remains having to be carried out in so remote a spot. Perhaps Buddhists of a later age were embarrassed by, or at least surprised at, the lowliness of the place where, as a matter of historical fact, the death of the Buddha had occurred. The word which is used here to describe Kushinara as a town 'in the midst of the jungle' (*ujjangala*) may mean what in India would be called a 'jungly' place: that is, as the commentator Buddhaghosa understood it, a lawless, heathen, pagan sort of place; or it may mean simply a barren, waste place. In either case, Ananda's objection seems to indicate that the appropriate place for the Buddha to end his life would be a great city, an urbane and civilized place, the kind of place with which he was most properly associated.

An attempt to remove the objection and the embarrassment is made by the insertion at this point in the narrative of a tale of the ancient splendours of Kushinara in some former age when it was the capital city of a great emperor, Maha Sudassana. In those days the royal city, Kushavasti (as it was then known), 'was mighty and prosperous and full of people, crowded with men and provided with all things for food'. This description of the former glories of Kushinara is elsewhere expanded into a full-length discourse, contained in a separate *Sutta*, called the *Maha Sudassana Sutta*,[30] and it is found also as a Jataka story.[31] The account of the city which is given in these longer versions is highly idealistic; even if no such city ever quite existed in Indian history, the description allows us to see what was obviously the Buddhist notion of an ideal city, and to this aspect of the matter we shall return later on (see chapter 8, pp. 172 ff).

THE URBANITY OF THE BUDDHA

Whether appropriately or inappropriately, then, it was in this little town in the jungle that the Buddha's life ended. There his body was cremated, and the relics were divided, a portion being given to each of eight legitimate claimants: the king of Magadha, the people of Vaishali, the people of Kapilavastu, the people of Kushinara, three other tribes, and a brahman named Vethadipaka. In each of the respective towns or cities to which the relics were taken a memorial cairn was built. Over the vessel in which the remains had been collected another cairn was built, and yet another over the remaining embers. According to the tradition, therefore, ten *stupas*, or places where the Buddha was remembered and honoured, came into being immediately after his death. Some of these were in great cities – Rajagriha, Vaishali, and Kapilavastu – and so the dishonour which Ananda felt was incurred in the Buddha's life ending outside a great city, where no worthy memorial could be maintained, was removed.

This brief survey of the pattern of the Buddha's life, the milieu from which he came, and the characteristic features of his public activities, shows that the setting of his life, from the first to the last days, was predominantly urban. It was a life spent in great centres where people came together to trade and to deliberate, to study and to practise their special crafts and industries, to discuss and to be entertained, to seek justice, to make money, or to find the truth. The appeal of his doctrines was primarily to men of an urban background. Among the things which, tradition suggests, might be said in praise of him was that he abstained from 'village ways' (*gamadhamma*),[32] a term which could also be translated 'vile conduct'. T. W. Rhys Davids suggests that the phrase means 'the practice of country folk ... the opposite of *pori*, urbane'.[33] Later in the same passage it is said, in fact, that the words of the Buddha are 'pleasant to the ear, reaching to the heart, urbane (*pori*)'. The point here seems to be that the Buddha's urbanity of speech was consistent with the rational quality of the ideas which he expressed.

Towards contemporary forms of religion, it is clear that the Buddha adopted a generally tolerant attitude, with the exception of his criticism of the brahman hereditary priesthood and the sacrificial system. Towards folk beliefs and practices, except for those which came within the scope of priestly magic, he showed the urbane man's understanding of the proper place which mythology and ritual hold in the lives of unsophisticated people. He was not a religious reformer of the iconoclastic kind. Nor was he a prophet, if by that is understood one who comes as the messenger, servant or spokesman of the deity, for to the extent that Brahma may be taken as the supreme deity for the men of the sixth century BC in north India, the Buddha's relation to him is certainly not that of a servant, but rather that of one who has superior knowledge and insight. The Buddha's insight is represented as being, not that of the dogmatist, who asserts that such and such is the case and demands men's acceptance of his assertion in faith, but rather that of the analyst. And the analysis which is offered is both logical and psychological; its appeal is in its self-authenticating quality. Urbanity of manner and speech were wholly consistent with the rationality of what was expressed. It is to an examination of the doctrines themselves that we must now turn, in order to demonstrate this consistency.

7 The New Wisdom

The nature of the change which took place when Gotama
sat meditating under the bodhi * tree on the bank of the
Nairanjana river is traditionally described by saying that
he became the Buddha, that is, the Awakened. In later
Buddhist literature, the transition is described in terms
which make it literally an earth-shaking event, but the
earlier literature gives a more prosaic and analytical account, and one which makes the event described extremely
difficult to fit into the categories of 'religious' or 'spiritual'
experience. This was no 'inaugural vision', such as the
prophets of Israel underwent. There was no sense of awe
at the realization of the presence of the divine being, such
as Isaiah felt; no ecstatic experience like that of Jeremiah;
no voice from heaven accompanying the descent of the
holy spirit as Christian tradition represents happening in
the case of Jesus; no archangel as in the case of Muhammad, coming down to announce 'Thou art God's apostle',
making the chosen one to fall upon his knees and tremble.
The account given in a Pali *Sutta* called *Discourse on the
Ariyan Quest* [1] is represented as being the Buddha's own
version of the matter given years later to some of his disciples at Shravasti. Having described his wanderings in
search of the truth, he tells them how in due course he
arrived at Uruvela (the ancient name for the place that
has become known as Bodh-Gaya). 'There I saw a delight-

Ficus religiosus, the sacred tree of India. The tradition that it was
beneath such a tree that Gotama gained enlightenment has no strong
historical foundation. See the article, 'Bodhi-tree' by T. O. Ling, in
A Dictionary of Comparative Religion ed. by S. G. F. Brandon (1970),
p. 145.

ful stretch of land and a lovely woodland grove, and a clear flowing river with a delightful ford, and a village for support near by.' Seeing what a suitable place this was for earnest and strenuous meditation, he sat down there.[2] What follows is an account of the intellectual penetration into the nature of the human situation which the Buddha then achieved, in which the notion of the individual 'self' (*atman*) is seen as the root of mankind's troubles (see chapter 6, p. 114).

DISCOVERY BASED ON ANALYSIS

Another early Buddhist text from the same collection describes in rather more detail the process by which the Buddha became 'awakened' to the truth. This consisted first of his entry into and progress through four successively deeper stages of meditation; the emphasis here lies upon the purification of the mind which was necessary. In this way he is said to have achieved concentration, equanimity and dispassion. There then followed three further stages, one in each of the three watches of the night. First, says the Buddha, 'with the mind composed, quite purified, quite clarified, without blemish, without defilement . . . I directed my mind to the knowledge and recollection of my former habitations [existences].' In the second watch of the night, 'with the mind composed . . . I directed my mind to the knowledge of the passing hence and the arising of beings', that is, to the working of the law of Karma, or moral retribution. 'I comprehended that beings are mean, excellent, comely, ugly, well-destined, ill-going, according to the consequences of their deeds.' Finally, in the third watch, he discovered the four noble truths concerning the human situation. 'I understood it as it really is: suffering, the arising of suffering, the stopping of suffering, and the course leading to the stopping of suffering.' Knowing this, he says, his mind became free.

In freedom the knowledge came to be: I am freed; and I comprehended: Destroyed is birth, brought to a close is the

Brahma-faring, done is what was to be done, there is no more of being thus. This was the third knowledge attained by me in the last watch of the night; ignorance was dispelled, knowledge arose, darkness was dispelled, light arose even as I abided diligent, ardent, self-resolute.[3]

In yet other versions of these events it was the theory of 'Conditioned Origination' (*Pratitya-Samutpada*) which the Buddha is said to have discovered during this critical night, and so became fully 'awakened' to the truth of human existence. This is a basic Buddhist doctrine which has become best known, perhaps, through its pictorial representation, particularly in Tibetan art, as the Wheel of Existence. In its verbal form it is found, with slight differences, in various places in early Buddhist literature. It is regarded as so fundamental a truth that it is represented as being the vital discovery made by all 'Buddhas'. Its discovery by a former Buddha, Vipassi, is described in the *Mahapadana Sutta*.[4] We are told that he was meditating in seclusion (at the point in his life story which Gotama had reached in his when he sat down on the bank of the Nairanjana river), and reflected thus: 'Verily this world has fallen upon trouble; one is born, and grows old, and dies, and falls from one state, and springs up in another. And from this suffering, moreover, no one knows of any way of escape, even from decay and death. When shall a way of escape from this suffering be made known, from decay and from death?'[5] He then went on to seek an answer to the question: What is the antecedent cause or condition of decay and dying? The answer he reached was that birth was the antecedent cause. What then, he asked, conditions birth? The answer to this, he found, was that 'becoming' conditions birth. Similarly, the antecedent cause was sought for each link in the chain of causation: becoming was conditioned by the attitude and activity of 'grasping'; grasping arose out of craving; craving out of feeling; feeling out of sense-contact out of the six-fold field of the senses;[6] the six-fold field of the senses arose out of the physical body, or 'name and form'; and the physical body is conditioned by, or arises out of, cognition. At this point the recession ends in the particular text; elsewhere in Buddhist literature there are two more antecedent causes: the impulses, and ignorance.

The significance of this relentlessly pursued analysis is found when the series is reversed, and it is affirmed that when ignorance ceases, the impulses cease; when the impulses cease, cognition ceases; and so on, to the final stage – when birth (i.e. rebirth) ceases, then 'decay and dying, grief, lamentation, ill, sorrow and despair cease'. As D. L. Snellgrove has commented, 'Attempts have been made to discover a logical sequence of ideas from this ill-sorted list, both by early commentators and by European scholars. But no general relationship between the terms can be found which will relate in the same manner any two consecutive terms. The list is best understood as it is first presented to us, as a spontaneous searching back and back into the origins of death and rebirth.'[7] A further difficulty lies in the fact that the English translations of the various terms are in some cases little more than attempts to put a name to what, even in the original, is somewhat obscure. But although we may have to be content with an imperfect understanding of the series itself, we can at any rate perceive the nature of the Buddha's approach to the problem of the human condition. It was based on analytical reasoning; what was discovered was discovered by strenuous effort of the mind. But it was in the Buddhist view no 'ordinary' mind which put forth this almost super-human effort of understanding; it was essentially a mind purified, calmed, and cooled from all evil passion. It would be incorrect to say that this was *merely* an intellectual approach, for moral values obviously play a primary and absolutely indispensable part, too. Even so, in the last resort, Buddhist wisdom is to be regarded as a discovery of the human mind; it is in no sense a revelation to Gotama given by a non-human spirit or divine being.

There are a number of ways in which the Buddha's analysis of human existence can be set out. There is, as we have seen, the twelvefold causal chain, or circle of causes and effects. There is also the presentation of the essentials in the form of the 'four noble truths'. Again, there is a well-known and frequently used characterization of all life in terms of the 'three marks of existence' – suffering, impermanence and non-individuality. In every case the starting-point, the datum, is *dukkha*, the suffering, pain or grief which is the common lot of *all living beings*. For the Buddha, this is what constituted the problem to be solved; it was from here that all his thinking started and it was to the curing of this condition that all his effort was directed.

THE THREE MARKS OF EXISTENCE

Of the three 'marks' or characteristics of existence the first, then, is suffering; this is the most immediately obvious of the three, and possibly the one which is most readily comprehended. According to the Buddhist view, however, even this aspect of existence is not always fully apparent; men may be deluded by temporary and superficial experiences of pleasure into thinking that through the pursuit of selfish interests, pleasure can be a permanent possession. The teaching of the Buddha consisted in showing how the life of the unenlightened individual was permeated by suffering. This is emphasized in the exposition of the first of the 'four noble truths', the truth concerning suffering: 'Birth is suffering (*dukkha*), decay is suffering, death is suffering; sorrow, lamentation, pain, grief and despair are suffering.' This means, as a modern Buddhist writer comments, 'that all forms of existence whatsoever are unsatisfactory and subject to suffering (*dukkha*)'.[8] The same writer adds that this does not refer only to actual suffering – suffering which is felt as such, but 'in consequence of the universal law of impermanency, all the phenomena of existence whatsoever, even the sublimest states of existence, are subject to change and dissolution, and hence are miserable and unsatisfactory: and that thus, without exception, they all contain in themselves the germ of suffering'.[9]

The second mark or characteristic of existence is *anicca*, or impermanence. 'Impermanency of things is the rising, passing and changing of things, or the disappearance of things that have become or arisen. The meaning is that these things never persist in the same way, but that they are vanishing and dissolving from moment to moment.'[10] At the physical level continual flux is not difficult to discern: the human body is a continual flowing in and out of various substances; dead skin is constantly being removed and new skin forms; old cells are worn out and replaced by new cells; the waste products of the body's metabolism are disposed of in various ways. What is more, the physical pattern or structure is itself subject to constant, though slower, change: from infancy to childhood, through youth and adolescence to maturity, and then on into middle and old age, the physical size and shape of the components which go by the name of John Smith do not remain the same for long. According to Buddhist thought, even more impermanent are states of mind or consciousness. But this all-pervading impermanency may not always be discerned; the workings of 'commonsense' may serve to obscure it. 'The characteristic of impermanence does not become apparent because, when rise and fall are not given attention, it is concealed by continuity ... However, when continuity is disrupted by discerning rise and fall, the characteristic of impermanence becomes apparent in its true nature.'[11]

Related to this second mark of existence, according to the Buddha, is the third – *anatta*: that the idea of a permanent, unchanging ego as the basis of individual personality is a fiction. Nevertheless, it is this idea that there is a permanent ego whose interests must be served and protected, and whose power must be magnified, which ensures that suffering will continue to characterize existence.

THE FOUR NOBLE TRUTHS

The other method used by the Buddha in setting forth his analysis of the human situation was that of the four noble truths. Here again, the universal fact of suffering, or the unsatisfactoriness of life, its pain, its *malaise*, its inherent 'ill'-ness, is the starting-point. This is the first noble truth. The second identifies what is, so to speak, the motive power which keeps this universal suffering going, the fuel which prevents the fire from going out, and that is craving or desire. This same factor has occurred in another connection: it is one of the twelve links in the chain of conditioned origination which has already been mentioned. In that context it is seen as arising out of feeling, and in its turn giving rise to the activity of selfish 'grasping'. The third noble truth concerns cessation (*nirodha*), and it is that the cessation of suffering is a consequence of the cessation of craving. The word used in this connection – *nirodha* – is a synonym of *nibbana* (in Sanskrit, *nirvana*), the best-known name for the goal which Buddhist teaching has in view. Nirvana is the cessation of all evil passion, and because evil passion is regarded in Buddhist thought as a kind of fever, its cessation may be thought of as a 'cooling' after fever, a recovery of health. In fact, in the Buddha's time the associated adjective *nibbuta* seems to have been an everyday term to describe one who is well again after an illness. It is evident from this that the original Buddhist goal, *nirvana*, was the restoration of healthy conditions of life *here and now*, rather than in some remote and transcendent realm beyond this life. It will be seen that the Buddhist way is essentially a therapy. But the subject of the cure is not the individual. It would be more accurate to say that individualism is the disease for which a cure is needed. To this point we shall return later.

The fourth noble truth was the declaration that a way existed through which the cure might be achieved; this was the way delineated by the Buddha, which consisted of morality, meditation and the attainment of wisdom. These three constituents of the Buddhist way are all essential. There is an amplified description of the way in terms of eight rather than three constituent features. In this, the single item 'morality' becomes right speech, right bodily action, and right means of livelihood.[12]

This insistence on morality, and the giving of specific guidance on morality, are wholly characteristic of the Buddha's teaching. Morality is not a secondary matter; in the prescription offered by the Buddha it is a *sine qua non*. And just as the single requirement, 'morality', was given fuller expression, in terms of the three major forms of moral conduct which have just been mentioned, so these three are also given fuller expression in other contexts. One of the most commonly used summaries of what moral living meant for Buddhists, from the earliest days, is the list of five precepts: to abstain from taking the life of any being; to abstain from stealing; from unlawful sexual intercourse; from speaking falsely; and from the use of drugs, including alcohol. These are the basic moral precepts for the whole of human society, as we shall see in connection with actual societies or civilizations of Asia which reckon themselves to be Buddhist. For members of the professional order, the *Sangha*, there is a more elaborate code of morality (see chapter 8, note 23) but this, with its two hundred and seventy or so rules, is also an elaboration of those same basic principles of morality, and has the same aim and intention as the five precepts.

INDIVIDUALITY AND THE HUMAN MALAISE

In its simplest form, the intention of Buddhist morality can be said to be the undermining, erosion or withering of the idea of one's own permanent individuality. For each human being commonly feels this to be supremely important to him, and since it was this attachment of importance to individuality which, in the Buddha's view, was the root of human *malaise*, its destruction was the essential feature in the cure of that *malaise*. Of the three characteristic marks of existence, suffering, impermanence, and the fictional quality of the ego, the first two are relatively easy to comprehend, even if they are not accepted; in any case, Buddhism shares them to some extent with other systems of thought. But the third, the assertion that the individual ego is a pure fiction or illusion, is one which will ordinarily be found more difficult to accept because it seems to run counter to commonsense. It is, moreover, an assertion which Buddhism does not share with any other system of the time; indeed it belongs almost wholly and uniquely to early Buddhism, at least until recent times and the development of modern psychological theory. It was the one feature of Buddhism which other Indian philosophers regarded as its characteristic *par excellence* for they labelled it 'the no-soul doctrine' (*nairyatmavada*).

MORALITY, MEDITATION AND WISDOM

Since this popular notion of a permanent individual ego has so firm a hold generally, special measures are required to deal with it. These are connected with the Buddhist practice of meditation. The purpose of this, in the earliest period at least, seems to have been to enable others to follow the Buddha along the path of release from the confined consciousness of being an individual, an ego, to consciousness of a wider, fuller kind. Step by step with meditational practices aimed at the cooling down of the passions which kept the notion of the ego alive went the practice of intellectual analysis of human existence. One 'practised' the analysis which the Buddha had set forth, even though at first it was very difficult. With continual practice, accompanied by constant moral purification, came a degree of mastery of this way of seeing things. The moral purification was of necessity *impersonal*, since it was the notion of individuality which was being dissolved;

what was happening was described as the encouragement of morally good states of being (states which were, however, not confined to any one individual centre of consciousness) and the discouragement of morally unwholesome states of being. It follows that meditation, in its intention and scope, ranged over a much wider area of being than the one encapsulated within one human body.

More than this concerning Buddhist meditation it is not appropriate or even profitable to say in the present context. It is hoped, however, that this will give the reader sufficient understanding of the general point of view and method of early Buddhism to enable him to decide to what extent and in what sense it was a religion.

When the practice had been faithfully followed, then, there would follow, almost immediately in the case of some people, or more slowly in the case of others, that realization of the truth which the Buddha himself had first won. This was the third and final state of the Buddhist schema, after morality and meditation, and was characterized either as 'wisdom', or as the state of enlightenment, or liberation from the state of being bound to the ego-idea. The notion of the individual ego having been dissolved, with it inevitably disappeared the whole burden of individual *karma* or retribution and the prospect of the continually repeated experience of the sufferings of the individual ego. This, however, was only the negative aspect of the matter, the condition of ill from which human existence needed to be cured. There was also the positive aspect, the new, wider, fuller consciousness of being which was opened up when the walls of individualism were broken down. This was the new community, and without careful examination of what this entailed, any attempt to understand early Buddhism is bound to be unsuccessful. It is because some Western descriptions of early Buddhism have left out this social dimension that they have failed to make sense. We must examine the new community which Buddhism entailed very soon, but first, however, it is appropriate to consider the nature of the Buddhist analysis in relation to other systems of thought.

EARLY BUDDHIST DOCTRINE IN THE CONTEXT OF THE TIMES

One way of characterizing the Buddhist system is to say that it is a form of rationalism.

By rejecting animism and ritualism and emphasizing a rational outlook which treats reality as a causally and functionally determined system of plural synergies (*samskaras*), the emergence of Buddhism marks an important event in the history of Indian thought. The most distinctive feature of Buddhist ethics is its freedom from theism, which leaves room for rationalism and rules out submission to some superhuman power controlling the world-process.[13]

The 'rational outlook' which was certainly a very marked feature of early Buddhism had, as G. S. P. Misra's words imply, two aspects. On the one hand there was the rejection of dogmatic theistic presuppositions. On the other, there was the attempt to analyse, that is to reveal, the *basic* data of human existence. The Buddha himself is represented as making a clear distinction between these two contrasting attitudes: 'I am,' he said, 'an analyst, not a dogmatist.'[14] By dogmatist he meant one who made categorical statements which were to be accepted simply on the authority of the one who made them. The Buddha insisted that all propositions must be tested, including his own. The testing of these had to take the form of the living out of the disciplined life of morality, meditation and the systematic cultivation of insight. The propositions, as such, were not to become objects of attachment, any more than anything else in life, but were to be regarded simply as pointers or guides.

One of the most important characteristics of the Buddha's teaching, therefore, was the attitude of non-acceptance of traditional orthodoxy of any kind and, instead, a very marked 'intellectualism' as Max Weber called it.[15] This differentiates Buddhism from the orthodox theistic religion of the brahmans of his day, but it does not, of course, mark off the Buddha's teaching in any distinct way from the teachings of other *shramanas*, who likewise rejected traditional orthodoxy. What most clearly differentiated the Buddha's teaching from theirs was his theory of the absolute impermanence of all things (*anitya*) and, above all, his denial of permanent individuality (*anatta*). The Jains, for instance, reacted very strongly to the latter aspect of the Buddha's teaching; it was, they said, a 'pernicious view'.[16]

On the other hand, the Buddha's insistence on the real possibility of human choice and freedom of action, and his opposition to fatalism differentiate his teaching from that of the Ajivakas. His rejection of asceticism, and his constant avowal of the importance of the middle way between it and hedonism mark his teaching off from that of the Jains and the Ajivakas (see pp. 96–9) on the one hand, and the materialists, the Lokayatas (see p. 99) on the other.

It is not necessary to go farther in indicating the general outlines of the Buddha's teaching, and in pointing to those features of it which are indisputable and unmistakable. The main purpose has been to show, first, that the teaching of the Buddha cannot justifiably be described as 'religious', if by that we mean having reference to or depending on belief in any superhuman being or spirit. Such beliefs are not affirmed in the teaching of the Buddha, nor are they seen to be a necessary part of his scheme of thought. How is this view of life to be characterized, if not as a religion? We are left with only one possibility. In its original form Buddhism is best described as a theory of existence, an ideology, or possibly as a philosophy. But even in the simplest form known to us, it is, by its own terms of reference, not a *personal* philosophy. This point is important, and calls for a little elaboration.

EARLY BUDDHISM AS A PSYCHO-SOCIAL PHILOSOPHY

The Buddha, it was acknowledged in the early Buddhist tradition, was a *shramana*. The nearest equivalent which modern English can give us is, perhaps, 'philosopher', although this is not altogether satisfactory, as the basic meaning of the word, which its usage preserves, is 'one who strives, or labours hard'. Karl Marx observed that 'The philosophers have only interpreted the world, in various ways; the point, however, is to change it',[17] and one imagines that the Buddha would have agreed with the observation. What is certain, on the other hand, is that the Buddha was not regarded by the earliest generation of Buddhists as a superhuman figure of any kind. He had no religious role, such as that of the chosen revealer of divine truth, nor was he regarded by the early Buddhists as in any sense a superhuman saviour. As a modern Buddhist writer puts it, 'The Buddha exhorts his followers to depend on themselves for their deliverance, since both defilement and purity depend on oneself. One cannot directly purify or defile another. Clarifying his relationship with his followers and emphasizing the importance of self-reliance and individual striving the Buddha plainly states: You yourselves should make the exertion. The Tathagatas are only teachers (*Dhammapada*, v.276).'[18] The Buddha, or Tathagata, does not direct the attention of his disciples away from himself to some higher, holier being; he directs their attention to human nature, with which he is concerned and with which they, too, must be concerned. His words are in the spirit of the philosopher, whose attention is upon the human condition, and the right ordering of human affairs. As the son of the leading citizen of Kapilavastu, Gotama had the equality of status which enabled him throughout his long public life to meet with the kings of northern India on equal terms, but he did so also as one whose philosophy was of particular interest to those who dealt with the ordering of human affairs. The city with its royal court was the characteristic *locus* for his teaching activities. When he died we are told that he was honoured and his mortal remains disposed of after the manner of a king. If one asked whether the Buddha had the greater affinity with the priest or with the king, and whether it was to religion or to secular affairs that his characteristic concerns were closer, there can be no doubt about the answers which would have to be given.

The rigorously logical and scientific method of the discourses which are preserved in the Pali canon has been fully and competently expounded by other writers.[19] G. S. P. Misra concludes his account of the matter with these words: 'It can truly be said that Buddhism appeared in the intellectual arena as a harbinger of a new trend in the realm of thinking. The empirical and analytical outlook of the Buddhists led them to found a system of psychology and logic which had great influence on Indian thought as a whole.'[20] The early Buddhist period in India was, writes A. K. Warder, 'one of the supreme ages of rationalism in human history', and he adds that 'we have not yet outlived its repercussions'.[21]

This, then, was the new wisdom; it can hardly be called a religion. What has to be asked, therefore, is why, before many centuries had passed, it had begun to assume the characteristics of a religion (in the terms in which religion has been defined in chapter 1), with the result that in modern Asia it is unequivocally as a religion that Buddhism appears in the analyses of social scientists.

It is possible, even from what has been discovered so far in the course of our investigation, to see how this came about. The Buddha was not hostile to the religious ideas and practices of the ordinary people. He did not endorse these ideas and practices, but neither did he, in general, oppose them. From his time and throughout the subsequent history of the tradition, the Buddhist attitude appears to have been based, whether consciously or not, on the recognition that a man's view of the world can only be modified, not radically changed. That is all that can be expected immediately, and in the short run. In the long run it is possible that a radical shift of viewpoint may take place, but with the generality of men it will be a very long run before this happens. A distinction is sometimes made between men of traditional, or pre-industrial, societies and men of modern, industrialized ones in terms of a contrast between irrationality and rationality. It is assumed that in pre-industrial societies the processes of thought are a-rational or non-rational, or even, it has been suggested, follow a different kind of rationality from the one characteristic of men of Westernized, industrial society. But, as Malinowski pointed out with reference to the rationality of primitive people, 'a moment's reflection is sufficient to show that no art or craft however primitive could have been invented or maintained, no organized form of hunting, fishing, tilling or search for food could be carried out without the careful observation of natural processes and a firm belief in its regularity, without the power of reasoning and without confidence in the power of reason; that is without the rudiments of science.' [22] The process of reasoning will in principle be the same for men of primitive and of more advanced societies; in both cases it will be a systematic tracing out of causal sequences. The significant difference between the two will be in the premises from which each respectively starts. Given certain premises, the logical development will be one line of thought; given different premises, it will be another. What, therefore, distinguishes one man's world-view from another's is not necessarily the rationality or irrationality of his processes of thought but the premises from which his reflections upon the world begin. They are usually bequeathed to him in a general way by his culture; they may be determined more particularly by his economic circumstances, or perhaps by his social status, or his role-relationships, and so on. If the conditioning factors are changed, then it is conceivable that a man will abandon one premise and adopt another. The *rationality* of a man when he is a wholehearted Protestant may not differ in any significant way from his rationality when he decides to convert and become a Catholic; what is likely to have happened is that he has come to adopt a different premise as the basis for his reasoning about the world and about his part in the whole scheme of things. Rationality, remaining constant throughout, may have a part to play in convincing him that the explanatory value of a process of reasoning based on premise A is superior to the explanatory value of the process which is based on premise B. He may therefore change his premise, from B to A. Or the change may be due to rational choices less evident and conscious, to more indirect and unconscious influences, like a change in any of the other determining factors which have been mentioned – economic or social status, role-relationships, and so on.

The Buddhist method appears to have been not to make a frontal attack on the premise which was responsible for a man's world-view. The approach was rather one or other of the two which have been outlined: that is to say, either the use of rational means to persuade men to alter their premises, by a demonstration of the evidently superior explanatory value of basing thought on premise A rather than premise B; or by conditioning them through a new regime of life. In this latter case, men were to adopt the new way of life because of certain evident, inherent attractions which it had for them. At this stage, however, the premises on which they based their world-view were still those, let us say, of the artisan of a north Indian city in the sixth century BC. Buddhist monks do not all become masters of the Buddha's philosophy overnight, by the act of entering the Order. But in the course of following out the day-to-day and year-to-year requirements of life in the Buddhist Order, there ensues for such monks a slow and subtle shift in their view of the world. The adoption of this kind of policy might seem to leave Buddhism open to too great a danger of corruption. To some observers this is how it has seemed; for Buddhism has been tolerant, and has countenanced beliefs and practices which are fundamentally alien to its own central affirmations, beliefs, for instance of a polytheistic nature. Nevertheless, the principle has never altogether been lost sight of, that the Buddhist world-view is not dependent in any way upon belief in a god or gods or upon practices associated with such beliefs.

The phrase 'Buddhist world-view' has just been used, but only in the sense of a general view of human life and of the human situation, and not in the more technical sense of a systematically worked-out cosmology or cosmic geography. Such a world-view can, however, be found in Buddhism as it developed after the lifetime of Gotama; to be more accurate, there were three main Buddhist variations of Indian cosmology.[23] In all of these the major features of general Indian cosmology appear. There are sufficient references in the discourses of the Buddha to suggest that he is to be regarded as making use of traditional ideas about cosmic geography, although sometimes in a light-hearted and sometimes in a noncommittal way. It certainly does not appear to be a subject which, in the view of the early tradition, he regarded as of sufficient importance to deserve serious attention, or the elaborate systematic formulation which it received later on, in the *Abhidhamma* literature,[24] produced mostly after the Buddha's death.

We are now nearer to being able to offer at least a tentative answer to the question which was raised at the outset of this study: What is Buddhism? It will be evident that Buddhism is essentially *a theory of existence*. It is, however, a theory which consists of both diagnosis (of the human *malaise*) and prescription for a cure. Since the practical steps which need to be taken to put the prescription into effect are also part of Buddhism, it is certainly more than a theory. And it is more than a theory of *human* existence only, since the whole of life, human and non-human, comes within the range of its scrutiny and analysis. It is a theory of existence which is principally characterized and distinguished from other theories by the fact that it dis-

countenances and discourages the concept of the individual, and regards the boundaries between one so-called
'individual' and others as artificial. Moreover, it is a theory
of existence which is in no way dependent on the idea of a
divine revelation to which, ultimately, all men must sub-
mit in faith. Although it is a view of life which the Buddha
is said to have gained at his enlightenment, that event is
not thought of as having been brought about by some
supra-human or supra-natural power; nor is it thought of
as being beyond the ability of any other human being to
achieve. True, the achievement does not come through
intellectual effort alone; it presupposes great moral striving and purification, but this, too, is something which men
are regarded as able to achieve without needing to resort
to supernatural aid.

Buddhism is, therefore, in a certain sense, secular. It is
certainly secular, if the sacred is defined in theistic terms,
for neither the Buddhist diagnosis, nor the putting into
effect of the Buddhist prescription – morality and meditation – is in any way dependent on belief in a god or gods,
or in a personal power of any kind, and Buddhism does
not necessarily or in principle entail any practices of a traditional religious kind, cultic or ritualistic, such as sacrifices to the gods, reading the holy scriptures, sacred meals,
prayers and so on. Indeed, in such matters, it was in origin
anti-religious if anything. In matters of dogma it was non-
theistic, except in the sense that the gods were accepted as
part of the cosmic scenery; but they were also regarded
as having no ultimate priority or significance. However,
if the new wisdom had a certain relative secularity it was
not secular in an absolute sense, for there appears to have
been, from the earliest stage that can be identified, an
awareness of a transcendental dimension, a sense of that
which is sacred, although it is not expressed in terms of
belief in a god. There is, in the early formulation of Buddhist teaching, a sense of necessary loyalty to that which
transcends immediate personal gain or satisfaction, to
values which lie beyond the interests of human indivi-

duals or the interests of the contemporary societies and political organizations of India in the sixth century BC. In broad terms, the new wisdom consisted of an invitation to men, even an appeal to them, to discover and recognize that the structure of being was different from what was commonly supposed, and that the human individual was *not* the key concept to the understanding of the human situation. It was an appeal also to realize this in the actual reorganization of human affairs, a reorganization directed towards a new, non-individualistic society. It is this aspect of early Buddhism which has often been ignored in modern, Western accounts, and it is to this, the social dimension of Buddhism, that we must now turn our attention.

8 The New Society

In the words of a great Indian of modern times, Rabindranath Tagore, the way of the Buddha is 'the elimination of all limits of love', it is 'the sublimation of self in a truth which is love itself'.[1] Tagore has, in these words, identified the essence of what has come to be called Buddhism. For Buddhism is not, as so many Westerners have imagined, a private cult of escape from the real world. The word 'imagined' is used deliberately because such a view of Buddhism can proceed only from the exercise of the imagination, not from knowledge of the Buddha's teaching, or of the nature of the Buddhist community, the *Sangha*, or of Buddhist history. To speak of Buddhism as something concerned with the private salvation of the individual soul is to ignore entirely the basic Buddhist repudiation of the notion of the individual soul. The teaching of the Buddha was not concerned with the private destiny of the individual, but with something much wider, the whole realm of sentient being, the whole of consciousness. This inevitably entailed a concern with social and political matters, and these receive a large share of attention in the teaching of the Buddha as it is represented in the Pali texts. Moreover, as we have seen, the context of the Buddha's own spiritual quest was the increasing individualism which accompanied the growth of cities and monarchies, and the problems attendant upon this growth. To attempt to understand Buddhism apart from its social dimension is futile. Individualism places limits on love, and if Buddhism is an attempt to deal with what it sees as the disease of individualism, and is primarily a method of eliminating these limits, as Tagore realized, then it will entail a concern with the social and political dimension.

The primary form which this process takes is the life of the Buddhist community, the *Sangha*. The members of this community were in India called *bhikkhus* (Pali) or *bhikshus* (Sanskrit). In Western languages they are most usually referred to as 'monks' or the equivalent, and the *aramas*, or local institutions which provide the physical setting for their common life are often referred to as 'monasteries'. But this terminology, borrowed from European practice, is misleading.[2] The word 'monk', derived from the word *monachus*, 'originally meant a religious hermit or solitary'; later on it came to mean 'a member of a community or brotherhood living apart from the world'.[3] In neither of these senses can the word be applied appropriately to a member of the Buddhist *Sangha*.

The word *bhikkhu* means, literally, a 'sharesman', that is, one who receives a share of something. The Buddhist *bhikkhus* were, in fact, a special case of what had been a common feature of Indian civilization from a very early period. In general, as Sukumar Dutt has pointed out, the almsman or sharesman in India is 'differentiated from an ordinary beggar by the sacramental character of his begging. His begging is not just a means of subsistence but an outward token'[4] – an outward token of his renunciation of private or personal sources of livelihood or ownership of wealth, and his dependence instead on the 'common wealth', the public resources of the society in which he lives. Certainly the Buddhist 'sharesman' has not contracted out of society. The life he leads and the goal he seeks is not for his own private benefit, for this would be directly contrary to the Buddhist repudiation of individualism. By being what he is and by following the life he does, society will benefit. The nature of the role-relationship between the *bhikkhu* and the householders clearly demonstrates that the Buddhist professional is integrally involved in society.

The 'share' which the *bhikkhu* received and which gave

him his name was, primarily, the portion of food which was set aside for him by those householders who supported him. But it was more than this that he received; the share of food was representative of other things – the robes he wore, the shelter in which he lived, and the other material necessities of life, all of which were provided by the lay-people of the neighbourhood. His acceptance of those things from the 'common wealth' so to speak, was a symbol of his own renunciation of private property. In return the Buddhist *bhikkhus* had important contributions to make to the common life of society, as we shall see. These were not material or economic contributions but they were sufficiently important for the *bhikkhus* to be able to accept the material support which they were offered as something which was their proper 'share'. If what they received is sometimes referred to as 'alms', it must be remembered that these were offered in a spirit of deference and grati-tude; the *bhikkhus* were not, and are not, 'beggars' in any sense of the word. The *bhikkhu* was certainly *not*, there-fore, someone who lived apart from the world, like the Christian monk. One of the important achievements of early Buddhism was that it developed a new context for the spiritual quest. Traditionally in India, the search for salvation from the evils of human existence meant a life of solitude. For the Buddhist it meant a life in the com-munity. For a time, however, in the earliest period of Buddhist history, the old idea seems to have survived. So strong a hold did the Indian tradition of solitude have that even among Buddhists there were those who tried to practise the Buddha's teaching by the old method and, as an ancient text puts it, 'fare lonely as rhinoceros'.[5] But it was among the Buddhists that there soon emerged, for the first time in Indian history, an ordered community of those who were seeking for salvation from the human *malaise* as they saw it.

THE BEGINNINGS OF THE BUDDHIST ORDER

The *reasons* for having an ordered community, organized in local settlements, in close touch with the neighbourhood, are to be found in the nature of the new wisdom itself. The *occasion* for the actual coming into existence of such organized local settlements was, as it happens, a phenomenon peculiar to ancient India. We shall look at each of these aspects in turn.

The reason for the Buddhist community life is inherent in the nature of the Buddha's teaching. We have seen that this teaching consists of diagnosis and prescription: diagnosis of the human *malaise* as consisting essentially of the disease of individualism, and prescription for its cure as consisting primarily of the undermining or erosion of the notion that individuality is something permanent and of great importance. It is in the life of the *Sangha* that the prescription can most effectively be applied. Here is the community of being which comes into existence when the walls of individuality are completely and permanently broken down. And here, too, are found the optimum conditions for those who are seeking to achieve that state of life and consciousness where individuality is no more, but who have not yet arrived at that state.

The process of meditation which is prescribed in the early texts gives something of a glimpse of the community of consciousness which was aimed at in the *Sangha*.[6] The method was one which began from the recognition that, in its normal state, the mind, and particularly the surface of the mind, is constantly being fretted and distracted; it is in a state of continual upheaval, like the surface of the sea, tossed into countless waves by the buffeting of the wind. The first stage of meditation, or the first *jhana*, to give it its technical name, is the calming of the mind by detaching it from the bombardment of the senses, and from discursive thinking. This makes possible the second stage in the process, namely concentration: that is, the concentration of the consciousness upon one point. When this has been achieved, and only then, the next stage can begin, the stage of experiencing clarity and equanimity. Consciousness, thus purified and calmed, is then able to expand, and the experience becomes that of 'unbounded space'. The final stages of the process do not concern us here. What is of interest at this point is the sequence: a narrowing down of consciousness, followed by expansion. The underlying theory seems to be that when consciousness, normally restless, wild or even uncontrollable, is brought to a single point, it can then be dealt with effectively (like the bringing under control and harnessing of a wild horse). Thus controlled, by concentration, it then begins to exhibit the pure qualities which are always waiting to be manifested, namely joy and equanimity. In this way the concentration of consciousness produces, of itself, a subsequent broadening out into unbounded dimensions of the inherent qualities which are now given their rightful place.

Now, it is evident that the process of meditation carried on by more than one 'individual' will begin, in each case, from a state where each is conscious of a multiplicity of sense objects and desires, and that it will lead to a state where all are sharing in the same consciousness of joy and equanimity, which is infinite and the same for all. When the impurities have been removed, then there can be a fusion. Incidentally, this raises the question of the Buddhist view of the fundamental moral nature of man. In Buddhist philosophy, human nature is seen as fundamentally good rather than evil. The discipline which the life of the *bhikkhu* entails is likened by the Buddha to the process of refining gold. Stage by stage impurities are purged away: first the coarse dust and sand, gravel and grit; then the finer grit, then the trifling impurities like the very fine sand and dust. At last 'the gold-dust alone remains', and this is placed in the crucible and melted together, until it can be run out of the crucible. 'Then that gold is melted, molten, flawless, done with, its impurities strained off. It is pliable, workable, glistening, no longer brittle; it is capable of perfect workmanship ... Just in the same way in a monk who is given to developing the higher consciousness there are gross impurities of deed, word and thought.' These, too, are gradually purged out, first the coarser impurities, and then the finer, subtler impurities, until there comes a time when all this dross has been removed and the basic pure state of consciousness is reached.[7] According to the Buddha, this level of permanently pure consciousness is achieved when all the common distinctions and ways of differentiating human beings have been purged away – such considerations, for example, as family pride, national pride and personal reputation. 'We note here,' writes a modern Buddhist, commenting on this passage, 'how our preoccupations with thoughts concerning our race or state are considered harmful to the concept of a common humanity.'[8]

The stage at which purified consciousness begins to broaden out has also a social structure: this is the life of the *Sangha*. The experience of new purified consciousness, beginning with the experience of the Buddha, is, in this theory, to expand continually through human society in the form of the new community, the *Sangha*. Moreover, it is not only that the *Sangha* provides the right conditions for the practice of meditation – the restructuring of consciousness along non-individualistic lines; it also provides the maximum facilities for continued conditioning of consciousness away from individualism in all the ordinary, everyday actions of life. Both Buddhist meditation and Buddhist ethics have the same end in view.

This can be seen in connection with the ownership of property. One who becomes a member of the *Sangha* ceases to own any private property whatsoever. This has been a feature of *Sangha* life from the earliest times. Even those few articles of personal use, the robe, the alms-bowl and one or two other requisites, were in theory vested in the *Sangha*, and made available for the use of its members.[9]

However, it is interesting to notice that while the *Sangha* was, from a juristic point of view, the corporate person in whom property was vested, and while no *bhik-khu* had legal property rights, nevertheless, as K. N. Jaya-tilleke pointed out, 'some rights such as the right to life, to free speech, to personal freedom, etc., cluster round the notion of individual personality'.[10] He acknowledged that this would seem to be an inconsistency, for the doctrine of *anatta* would appear to be incompatible with the notion of personal responsibility. But since the psycho-physical processes of human life maintain a relative and temporary 'individuality', it is useful to distinguish one of these rela-tively individual series of processes from another, and to refer to each by the term 'person'. Where the Buddhist analysis differs from most other views of human nature is in denying any absolute and permanent substratum, 'soul', or 'person', in these temporary psycho-physical processes. In the Buddhist view of things it seems that the concept of individuality which is primarily and most emphatically denied is that of the private-property-owning individual. This is a practical, institutional expression of the basic doctrine that greed or grasping (*tanha*) is the root of human ills.

The *Sangha*, therefore, provides the environment in which a new dimension of consciousness becomes possible as a result of the denial, not only in theory but also in practice, of the idea of absolute and permanent individu-ality.

In the earliest period of Buddhist history the *Sangha* seems to have existed as a wandering sect, a movement with which a man identified himself with the minimum of formal ceremony, 'a unitary organization of monks hailing from all quarters irrespective of regional provenance'.[11] If European terms are to be used at all, such a wandering brotherhood was more like an order of friars than of monks. But this very fluid stage of its history seems to have been brief and transitional. The nature of the doctrine combined with historical circumstances soon resulted in the development of settled, local communities of *bhikkhus*. We have already seen that it was necessary in the conditions which prevail in the monsoon period in India for wandering sects of all kinds to seek shelter during the rainy season (see chapter 5, p. 95). But where Jains, Brahmanical wanderers, and other such schools neither required nor (in the case of the Jains) allowed any specially set apart 'retreat-houses' or lodgings in which all the members of the school in a given locality were to reside together for the period of the rains, in the case of the Buddhists it was precisely this which came to be prescribed. 'The Buddhist idea of rain-retreat seems to have been not to live [just] anywhere, or alone and companionless, or in promiscuous company, but to settle in a congregation of fellow-monks.' [12] The fact that this was the practice of no other sect of *shramanas* may be connected with the other feature which was unique to the Buddhist order – their adherence to the doctrine of *anatta*, or non-individuality. Perhaps the local settled communities were bound to have come into existence, the Buddhist view of life being what it was. Nevertheless, it happened that historically it was a particular feature of Indian life which precipitated the matter, and provided the actual occasion for the formation of local communities.

It is noteworthy that these were not established in remote places, in the depths of the forest and far from the busy centres of travel and trade and government; this was the environment which Brahmanical ascetics sought,[13] but not the Buddhists. The latter, on the contrary, established their typical settlements on the edge of a town or city, partly, as we have already seen, because it was from among the growing urban population of the time that the Buddhists found most of their recruits, and partly, too, because the size of the Buddhist communities required a substantial number of householders near enough to provide the necessary economic support. This, therefore, soon became the normal location for a Buddhist *arama*, as the local institutional settlement was called, although there was a minority of *bhikkhus*, of more conservative disposition, who preferred to have their dwellings in forest glades, and who were known by the general designation, *Aranyakas* (Forest-dwellers). They were in this way conforming to the more traditional Indian view of the proper setting for a life of meditation; but the majority of Buddhist *bhikkhus* was characterized by the more radical attitude, one which was more consistent with the special nature of Buddhist ideas, and which recognized that close proximity to the important centres of the world's business was where the communities belonged.[14]

THE POLITICAL AFFINITIES OF THE SANGHA

One point which is frequently emphasized in the early tradition is that the Buddha had firmly rejected the notion of authoritarian rule in the new community which he had brought into existence. The Buddhist *Sangha*, whatever else it might resemble, would not resemble a monarchy. The Buddha himself was not in any sense a personal ruler, nor was any member of the community to think of himself in this way after the Buddha's death: 'Surely, Ananda, should there be anyone who harbours the thought, "It is I who will lead the brotherhood", or "The Order is dependent upon me", it is he who should lay down instructions in any matter concerning the Order. Now the Tathagata [the Buddha], Ananda, thinks not that it is he who should lead the brotherhood, or that the Order is dependent on him. Why then should he leave instructions in any matter concerning the Order?'[15] The implication for the members is clear: 'Therefore, O Ananda, be ye lamps unto yourselves ... Hold fast to the *Dhamma* as a lamp.'[16]

In this respect the Buddhist community was perpetuating the tradition of the tribal republican *sanghas* (see chapter 4, pp. 60 f.), which 'knew nothing of personal rule', as S. Dutt points out: 'they deliberated and acted together, were communistic in their property-relationships, republican in their conduct of affairs, and had the tribal council as their organ of Government.'[17]

As another recent and more specialist study of the

tribal republics of this period observes 'each member of the assembly was called a *raja* (ruler), but none had the individual power to mould the decisions of the assembly.' [18]

It is clear that the Buddhist community inherited certain forms and methods of organization from the tribal republics. The question which was raised earlier must now be considered more fully, namely, whether the Buddhist *Sangha* was simply a reproduction of the old tribal collective or *sangha*, or whether it was a conscious and deliberate improvement on the older model, which was in the Buddha's day disappearing before the advance of the great monarchies, Koshala and Magadha. Was the Buddhist *Sangha* organized in imitation of the older political *sanghas* for no other reason than that the Buddhists were politically behind the times, or was it done, perhaps, in order to preserve something which was felt to be of value but which could be preserved in no other way (just as private enthusiasts in Britain today get together to preserve as a going concern some local steam railway)? On the other hand, was the Buddhist community organized as a new-style *Sangha*, one in which the defects which had made the old political model obsolete were corrected; was it a new and improved version which was being put forward as a serious contribution to political experimentation and development? Was it a version which would remedy, too, the weaknesses and disadvantages apparent in the monarchical system (just as, to continue the analogy, a reorganized and rationalized railway system of diesel locomotion might be seen as the most effective solution to the traffic and transportation problems of a country which is being slowly stifled by private motor cars)? [19]

The questions resolve into two main issues. The first concerns the *internal* government of the Buddhist community, the *Sangha*. The second concerns what form of government was regarded by the Buddha as desirable for society in general, outside the *Sangha*.

The answer to the first part of the question is relatively straightforward. The pattern which is represented as being laid down by the Buddha for the regulation of the affairs of the new community was one which has been loosely described as 'democratic'. Democracy is an ancient word, but as it is now understood, it is, of course, a political concept which emerged somewhat later in history and implies the existence of certain political institutions. The *Buddha-Sangha* has been described as democratic largely because there was no monarchical head, no authoritarian chain of command and responsibility, and because a recognized procedure existed for decision-making by the whole community corporately. Certainly every member of the *Sangha* was regarded as having equality of rights in any deliberations concerning the life of the community. K. N. Jayatilleke has argued that 'even the cosmic perspective is for the Buddhist democratic, for any man of his own free will may aspire to and attain to the status of a Buddha',[20] and that democracy was of the essence of the early community. The *Sangha* has been described, also, as a 'system of government formed by the *Bhikkhus*, for the *Bhikkhus* and of the *Bhikkhus*',[21] and therefore a democracy. But the principles of government in the *Sangha* differed from those of a modern democratic state in one important respect, which needs to be carefully considered.

The ideal for the government of the new community is described by the Buddha, as we have seen, in connection with the Vajjian confederacy. 'So long, O *bhikkhus*, as the brethren foregather oft, and frequent the formal meetings of their *Sangha*, *so long as they meet together in concord, and carry out in concord the duties of the Sangha* ... so long may the brethren be expected not to decline but to prosper.'[22] It is expressly stated that 'concord' or unanimity is essential for the proper functioning of the *Sangha*, otherwise its life will decline. The corpus of rulings on its life and organization and the conduct and discipline of its members, known as the *Vinaya-pitaka*,[23] contains similar injunctions for the community.[24] The principle which seems to have been regarded as of supreme importance was that of the maintenance of unity of view within each *local*

company or *sangha*. For as soon as permanent local settlements had been developed each of these was regarded as a
sangha in itself, a complete microcosm, so to speak, of the
whole *Sangha*. And while it was accepted that differences
of opinion were likely to develop, what was regarded as of
greatest importance was that each local fellowship, which
provided the actual, day-to-day experience of common life,
was to be a unity, undivided by any controversial issues. If
controversy did arise – and it was recognized that it could
and would – the method laid down for dealing with the
situation was that the dissenting group should remove itself and form a new settlement.[25] This 'law of schism',[26] as
it was called, was a matter of discussion at the second Buddhist Council, held at Vaishali a century after the Buddha's death; it was very important that this procedure
should be agreed upon because the maintenance of the
essential principle of unity in the *sangha* depended on it.
It was recognized that honest differences of opinion had
to be allowed for, but not at the expense of the structural
unity of the local *sangha*. As Sukumar Dutt has put it, the
unitary character of the local *sangha* was 'the basic principle of its functioning'.[27] All other considerations were
subordinate to this basic principle of local structural unity.

In view of what was said earlier concerning the *sangha*
as the necessary context for living the new life of non-
individualism, it will be easily understood why unity was
so important. It is this aspect of the *sangha*'s constitution,
therefore, which in the final analysis distinguishes it from
a democratic body. A democratic organization is one in
which the majority opinion is honoured and prevails. The
advantage of this method is that, if it can be followed
consistently, the formation of schismatic, dissenting groups
is avoided; but the price is the subordination of minority
views. The Buddhist method is one which allows minority
views to be held, and not disregarded, but the price to be
paid is the multiplication of bodies with different points of
view. The Buddhists, like others, had to choose between
the two principles; that the choice was a very difficult one

to make is seen from the fact that the matter was not settled until a hundred years after the Buddha's decease.
However, once a principle has been agreed upon, allow-
ances can be made for the fact that certain advantages
accruing from the opposite decision have been surrendered. In this case, what was surrendered was ideological
solidarity. Other political and religious institutions faced
with a similar choice have sometimes chosen the totalitarian way: formal organizational unity has been maintained at the expense of the rights of self-expression on the
part of minority groups. The history of Catholicism in
Europe, which is as much a matter of politics as of religion,
demonstrates what ensues when total institutional unity
is evaluated more highly than arrangements for the tolerance of dissent. Any group which threatens the formal
unity of the total organization has to be regarded as something alien to the true nature of the organization itself;
it is a sect, rather than true church. In the Buddhist case,
the inevitability of sectarian differences has been acknowledged, with the result that Buddhism has not experienced
the internecine wars of religion that have characterized
some other traditions, where dissent or 'heresy' has been
something to be stamped out.

This should not be taken to imply that the Buddhist
Sangha recognized no canons or orthodoxy. The matter is
represented as having been explicitly dealt with by the
Buddha himself, who set out certain criteria by which
authentic Buddhist doctrine could be recognized.[28]

In the matter of the relationship between the *sangha* of
the Vajjian confederacy and the Buddhist *sangha*, it
emerges that the latter was modelled very closely on the
former. It is not properly described as democratic in the
modern sense; its characteristics were those of the old
tribal republic, in which unanimity among the assembled
elders was the supreme requirement. Now, it is clear that
where this was the underlying principle of government,
lack of unanimity would produce dysfunction of the system
and possibly its breakdown, more quickly than any other

single factor; the Buddha implied as much in the observations he made on the prospects of the Vajjian confederacy's continued well-being.[29] Events showed that the Vajjian system was fallible. The reason adduced for this, in
the Buddhist view, was the disease of individualism, which
had now spread to the tribal republics, and was proving
too much for the strength of republican solidarity. J. P.
Sharma sees the collapse of the tribal republics, which took
place soon after the Buddha's decease, as due to the intru-
sion of individualism. The old understanding was that no
individual member of the republican assembly had the
power to mould the decisions of the assembly; nevertheless, by the time that the Buddha was called upon to give
an opinion on the prospects of the republican *sanghas*, a
situation had developed in which it is probable, says
Sharma,

> that some councillors or leaders of the republic either wished
> to rise above the rest and become virtual rulers ... or that some
> preferred to betray the republic for their selfish interests, thus
> becoming lieutenants of a king. The latter could offer these
> betrayers substantial rewards either in the form of material
> gains or by entrusting them with important state offices which
> they could not expect while the republic continued and pros-
> pered.[30]

The downfall of the republics was thus closely connected
with the spread of monarchy and of the spirit of individualism, or, as Sharma describes it, of 'personal ambition'.
  If the *malaise* which had afflicted the tribal republic
system could be identified as individualism, then the
remedy for individualism could serve as the remedy, or as
means of reviving the *sangha* system – assuming that in all
other respects it was worth restoring. That it was appears
to be the assumption implicit in the organization of the
early Buddhist Community as a *sangha*. What was being
said, in effect, was this:

> The tribal republican system of organization is preferable
> to monarchy, but lately it has been infected by the spread of

individualism; this is the evil factor in the situation. Buddhist practice can remedy this evil, and so the *sangha* system of solid organization can and will be restored. The *sangha* system which is needed now is the new *Buddha-Sangha*.

The Buddhist *sangha* might be seen, then, in the context of the fifth century BC, as the prototype social organization of the future. But there were serious difficulties in the way of such a prescription for the welfare of human society. Between the prototype, even as it could be seen in existence here and there, and the transformation of the whole of human society into a universal *sangha*, there was, so to speak, a large practicability gap. To organize what was still a relatively small sect or cult-association as a republican *sangha* was one thing; to propose that this form of politico-social organization could, by means of the therapy which Buddhism offered, become once again the norm for Indian society as a whole was quite another. Such a proposal would, in the circumstances of the time have been entirely impracticable, for a number of reasons. There is evidence to suggest that they were fully appreciated by the Buddha or at least in early Buddhist tradition, and that an interim scheme was envisaged which would make the best of the existing situation and encourage the development of a political and social climate more favourable to the full adoption of Buddhist attitudes and principles.

The two major reasons against the idea of the whole of contemporary Indian society becoming a universal Buddhist *sangha* were, first, the existence of powerful monarchies, and second, the unreadiness of the mass of the people for participation in the kind of society envisaged in Buddhist teaching. The Buddhist mission to society, if one may call it that, appears to have had both of these problems in view, and to have developed appropriate policies in each case.

THE BUDDHIST ATTITUDE TO THE
COMMON PEOPLE

The common people, or, more precisely, 'the ordinary man', is referred to by a word which occurs with relative frequency throughout the Pali literature – *puthujjana*. The basic meaning of *puthu* is 'widespread' and this meaning is carried into the usage of the word composed from it by the addition of *jana*, a person or a man. The word has thus been translated appropriately into English as 'the ordinary man', 'the common man' or 'the average man'.[31] From the various occurrences of the word in the early literature, it appears that the Buddha used it to refer to the generality of man distinct from brahmans and recluses.[32] It has to be remembered that the Buddha gives the word 'brahman' a new meaning, apart from its technical caste connotation. The priestly class who had in the Buddha's day appropriated the term had no special, innate right to it, according to the Buddha. A brahman is a brahman by character, and not merely by some hereditary right. In the conversations of the Buddha with brahmans the latter are often represented as being led by the course of the argument to admit this point. Perhaps some real brahmans of the Buddha's day did so, in fact. In any case it is clear that this was the Buddhist view of the matter. So 'brahmans and shramanas' becomes a phrase virtually equivalent in meaning to those who, from a Buddhist point of view, are genuinely in pursuit of the truth and of a righteous life. The generality of men who are thus distinguished from them are, in effect, the mass of mankind who are not members of the Buddhist community.

It is possible to construct from the references in the Pali texts a fairly detailed picture of the average man, or, literally, man as he is commonly found, from the point of view of the Buddha, or of the early Buddhists.

The ordinary man, we are told, 'is addicted to pleasure', and is at the mercy of his senses.[33] He is enthralled by the eye with objects that charm, by the tongue with savours that charm, etc.[34] He follows his natural desires, 'uncontrolled in the six-fold sense sphere, and eats his fill with ravenous delight among the five sensual pleasures'.[35] He welcomes personal fame and praise but resents obscurity and blame.[36] He is easily provoked to deeds of a morally unwholesome kind; he will murder his own father or his mother, inflict wounds on a saintly man, and cause dissension within the Buddhist *sangha*.[37] He is greedy [38] and lustful.[39] On the other hand, he resents any ill fortune; when afflicted with pain he is distressed and overcome with bewilderment about it; [40] he finds that those things on which he sets his hopes frequently turn out to be a disappointment; [41] he dislikes the sight of disease, or old age or death; [42] when old age comes upon him he mourns and pines and is tormented by sorrow,[43] and finally he goes to Purgatory.[44] All this is because he is lacking in wisdom, and in knowledge of the truth. Not only does he adhere to popular superstitions,[45] but he knows not, he sees not things as they really are,[46] he takes no account of those who are holy, those who are true, he does not comprehend which things should and which things should not be attended to; [47] he knows nothing of the origination of compounded things, and so is not set free from the power of ill; [48] he fails to reflect adequately and to understand the experiences of life for what they really are.[49]

The fact that he is described in the singular should not be allowed to disguise from us that this is the Buddha's view of the mass of mankind. Such being the case, J. P. Sharma is justified in his conclusion that the Buddhist *Sangha*, like the Greek oligarchies, was based on a belief in the 'unwisdom of the multitude'.[50]

BUDDHIST SOCIAL ETHICS FOR THE LAYMAN

Such belief did not lead, however, in the Buddhist case at least, to an attitude of cynicism towards the multitude. Far from it: the common people have an important part in the Buddhist scheme of things, for their present condition is not accepted as permanent or final. Indeed, between them and the *Sangha* there exists an important relationship, not of reciprocity exactly, but of complementariness. This relationship is set out formally in an early Buddhist text, the *Sigala* homily,[51] which remains today one of the best-known portions of Buddhist literature among the Buddhists of Ceylon and South-East Asia.

The *Sigala* homily is presented as being the extended answer given by the Buddha to a question from a young householder regarding his moral duties. The comprehensive nature of the advice which the Buddha gives him with regard to domestic and social relationships would by itself be sufficient to dispose of any assertion that the early Buddhist community's concerns were entirely 'other-worldly', 'spiritual' or 'selfish'. As a Buddhist of a later age, commenting on it, said, 'nothing in the duties of a householder is left unmentioned'.[52] It was, added the same writer, for the householder what the *Vinaya*, or code of discipline, was for the members of the *Sangha*.

The duties are set out in an orderly way, intended, no doubt, as T. W. Rhys Davids observed, to assist the memory. Six sets of reciprocal role expectations, or duties, are enumerated: first, those between parents and children; next, between pupils and teachers; then, husband and wife; followed by friends and companions; masters and servants; and finally householders and members of the *Sangha*. In each category, five duties are enumerated, with the exception of the *Sangha*'s duties to householders, and in this case there are six.

Children are to support their parents, who once supported them; they are to perform the proper family duties, to maintain the family line; to uphold the family tradition; (meaning, perhaps, not dissipating the family property and maintaining the family honour); and they are to show themselves worthy of their heritage. Parents are to restrain their child from wrongdoing, to inspire him to virtue; to train him for a profession, to contract a suitable marriage for him; and in due time to make over to him his inheritance.

Pupils are to serve their teachers by showing respect to them, by waiting upon them, by showing eagerness to learn, by supplying their needs, and by paying attention when they are being taught. Teachers in return are to give their pupils moral training, they are to inspire in them a love of learning, they are to instruct them in every subject, are to speak well of their pupils, and to protect them from any danger.

A husband is to cherish his wife by treating her with respect, by being kind to her, by being faithful, by allowing her her proper due rights, and by providing her with suitable ornaments. In return, a wife is to show her love for her husband by maintaining a well-ordered household, by being hospitable to their relatives and friends, by being faithful, by being thrifty, and by being diligent.

A man should recognize his obligations to his friends by making them gifts, by courtesy and benevolence towards them, by treating them as his equals, and by keeping his word to them. In return he may expect that they will take care of him or of his interests when he is unable to do so himself (for example, says the commentator, if he falls down in the street after too much drinking, his friend will stay with him until he sobers up, so that his clothes are not stolen), they will provide him with refuge when he needs it, they will stand by him in times of trouble, and will be kind to his family.

A good master (i.e., employer) is one who may be relied upon to show consideration towards his employees by allotting each one work suited to his capacity, by supplying them with good food and pay, by providing care for them when they are sick, by sharing with them any unusual delicacies which he receives, and by granting them regular time off from work. In return, employees or servants should show their affection for their master by being out of bed betimes and not going to bed until he has done so, by being contented with the fair treatment they receive, by doing their work cheerfully and thoroughly, and by speaking well of their master to others.

Finally, the reciprocal duties of householders and members of the *Sangha* are set out. A good householder ministers to the *bhikkhus* by showing affection for them in his actions, in his speech, and in his thoughts, by giving them a warm welcome and ample hospitality and by providing generally for their material needs. In return, the members of the *Sangha* are to show their affection for the householder by restraining him from evil courses of action, by exhorting him to do what is honourable, by entertaining kindly feelings towards him, by imparting knowledge to him, by dealing with his difficulties and doubts, and by revealing to him the way to heaven. The last is the sixth duty. Every other class of citizen named has been given five duties, but for the *bhikkhu* there is this one extra, which thus stands by itself in a position of special emphasis.

'We can realize,' commented T. W. Rhys Davids, 'how happy would have been the village or the clan on the banks of the Ganges, where the people were full of kindly spirit of fellow-feeling, the noble spirit of justice, which breathes through these naïve and simple sayings.' [53] Those who have been acquainted with the life of a country like Burma, where Buddhist culture was still a living force [54] will know that this is true, for the reality has existed. There is evidence that in India something approaching such a state of society existed wherever Buddhist culture or civilization was able to establish itself.

Here the crux of the matter is reached: the ability of Buddhism to establish and maintain itself. The 'practicability gap' which was mentioned a little earlier, between the Buddhist vision for human society and the realization of it in any actual society, was not quickly or easily bridged. There were, and are, certain essential conditions to be fulfilled before a Buddhist form of civilization can come into being anywhere. These necessary conditions have two primary focal points: (1) the *Sangha,* and (2) the governing power. In India at the time of the Buddha, the latter meant, of course, the monarchy. These will now be considered in a little more detail.

THE SOCIAL FUNCTION OF THE SANGHA

In the first place, it was essential that the *Sangha* should function within the wider society in the kind of way that was outlined in the *Sangha* homily. The duties there envisaged for the *bhikkhu* in his relations with the householder require constant, day-to-day contacts between the two. That is why the word 'monk', if it means a man who lives apart from the world, is in the strict sense inappropriate as a translation of *bhikkhu*. The *bhikkhu* has to exhort the householder, restrain him when necessary, instruct him, clear up his doubts, and constantly direct his attention to the path he should follow in order to reach 'heaven'.[55] This he would do most effectively if he himself was following that path and was providing an example and an inspiration to the householder, who otherwise, as we have seen, was all too prone to aim at the short-term goal of sensual pleasure. From the point of view of an anthropological analysis of Buddhism in modern Ceylon, Obeyesekere points out a principle which is inherent in early Buddhism also. The life of the *bhikkhu*, who has given up the comforts of household life as something which he no longer needs, has an important social function. His life 'exemplifies in exaggerated form the inhibition of natural drives, and such inhibition is a prerequisite for the conduct of all social life'. The effect of the example of an ascetic life was pointed out by Durkheim in terms which exactly fit the Buddhist situation:

... it is ... a good thing that the ascetic ideal be incarnated eminently in certain persons, whose specialty, so to speak, it is to represent, almost with excess, this aspect of the ritual life, for they are like so many models, inciting to effort. Such is the historic role of the great ascetics. When their deeds and acts are analysed in detail, one asks himself what useful end they can have. He is struck by the fact that there is something excessive in the disdain they profess for all that ordinarily impassions men. But these exaggerations are necessary to sustain among the believers a sufficient disgust for an easy life and common pleasures. *It is necessary that an élite put the end too high, if the crowd is not to put it too low. It is necessary that some exaggerate, if the average is to remain at a fitting level.*[56]

Whether these words of Durkheim are true for any other system or not, they are certainly true of early Buddhism. A passage from a canonical text reflects exactly the kind of attitude on the part of the lay-follower that Durkheim has depicted.

As long as they live, the *Arahants* . . . are abstainers from the slaying of creatures; . . . they are modest, show kindness, they abide friendly and compassionate to all creatures, to all beings. So also do I abide this night and day . . . abstaining from such actions, showing kindness to all beings. As long as they live the *Arahants* . . . abstain from stealing . . . they abide in purity free from theft. So also do I myself also abide . . .

The same formula is repeated for each of the eight precepts which were observed by those lay-followers or *upasakas* who were aiming at a somewhat higher level of moral attainment, in imitation of the example of the *bhikkhus*, and especially of the *Arahants*, who were regarded as having fully conquered selfish passions.

As long as they live the *Arahants* dwell observing chastity . . . abstaining from falsehood . . . abstaining from fermented liquor, which gives occasion to sloth . . . living on one meal a day . . . refraining from going to exhibitions of dancing . . . from the use of luxurious beds . . . So also do I abide. I also this night and day do likewise. By this observance I imitate the *Arahants* . . . and I shall have kept the sabbath.[57]

The particular occasion for the recital of these words was, as the last sentence indicates, the lay disciple's observance of a higher standard of moral discipline during the night and day of the sabbath, a practice which is still followed in Buddhist countries today. The householder who, once or twice a month, undertook this somewhat stricter rule of life would naturally be more disposed to follow the normally required five basic precepts more carefully than if he were not disciplining himself from time to time at a more advanced level. And from his example other householders might also be encouraged to take the Buddhist moral code more seriously. There was thus a widening circle from each local Buddhist *sangha*, a radiation of heightened morality, whose influence would, as time went by, penetrate more and more deeply into the surrounding society.

In this way, what was referred to above as the unreadiness of the mass of people to participate in, and make a success of, the kind of society envisaged in Buddhist teaching, would gradually diminish. Meanwhile, however, there would still be many who were not likely to respond to these influences, and whose attitudes and actions would have socially destructive effects if they were not held in check. In other words, there was the problem of how to deal with potentially violent or anti-social elements, even though it was only for an interim period while the Buddhist prescription became more widely effective in raising the level of moral life and eliminating social conflict and violence. There were, moreover, the monarchies, decreasing in numbers as the larger swallowed up the smaller, but not decreasing in the extent or degree of their power. These would constitute the most serious obstacle of all in the way of any hopes for the gradual establishment of a universal republic with the Buddhist *sangha* as its heart.

It may be useful at this point to remind ourselves that the Buddha, when he had achieved Buddhahood, does not appear to have abandoned the interest, which his family tradition and milieu had given him, in public affairs and the concerns of government. We may remind ourselves, too, that it was perfectly natural that the public world should come within the scope of the Buddhist prescription. This was not due merely to the need to guarantee the *Sangha* with political freedom and a sound

economic basis, necessary pre-conditions for its un-
tramelled existence and security though these were. It was
due equally to the fact that the private world of the individual, as the 'real' or important world, was denied legi-
timacy in Buddhist doctrine. Salvation was the movement
away from this private, separate and ultimately false
existence to a wider, non-egotistical sphere of being. Here,
then, we have three very important reasons why there
developed in early Buddhism so strong a concern with the
wise and beneficent government of human society: the
Buddha's own background, the need to ensure optimum
conditions for the Buddhist prescription for society to take
effect, and – most important – the fact that by its very
nature, unique among the ideologies of the time in its
denial of the individual soul, Buddhism could never be a
'private' salvation, 'the flight of the alone to the Alone' or
any other kind of world-rejecting escapism; by its very
nature its concerns were with the *public* world.

THE BUDDHIST ATTITUDE TO MONARCHICAL GOVERNMENT

The *Sangha* was to provide the growth point, or, rather, a
multiplicity of growth points, from which would spread
the new pattern of humanity, the social restructuring of
human life, which had as its aim the elimination of individualism with all its human ill effects. While this process
was going on, it would be folly to disregard the large areas
of society which were as yet untouched by the influence
of the *Sangha*, for unchecked individualism and violence
in these areas would threaten the peaceful growth of the
Sangha, and of what may be called the Buddhistically
oriented areas of society. Social stability appears to have
been recognized by the Buddha as a necessary condition
for the success of social and moral reconstruction. In the
existing situation in north India in the fifth century BC
the surest guarantee of social stability appeared to be in
the direction of a strong and benevolent monarchy. More-

over, a really enlightened monarchy, sympathetic to Buddhism, might have the further important, positive function of providing those conditions and of helping to create those attitudes among the people which would facilitate the widespread acceptance of the Buddhist prescription. This appears to have been the logic underlying the attitude of the Buddha towards the contemporary monarchs of Koshala and Magadha, as it is represented in the Pali canon.

Throughout his life, as we have seen, the Buddha was closely associated with the royal courts of his day. Pasenadi, the king of Koshala, and Bimbisara, the king of Magadha, were his life-long personal friends and supporters. Pasenadi, it is said, frequently visited the Buddha to have discussions with him.[58] It may be recalled that it was in Pasenadi's capital, Shravasti, that the majority of the Buddha's discourses were delivered. Bimbisara, from the time when he first entertained the Buddha, in his palace at Rajagriha, until his death thirty-seven years later, was a firm supporter of the Buddhist *Sangha*, and himself a disciple or *upasaka*, practising the layman's higher eightfold morality six times a month.[59] It may be recalled, too, that by this time Koshala and Magadha between them covered most of the territory of the lower Gangetic plain, that is, roughly the whole extent of the plain between the Himalaya and the Chotanagpur plateau, from modern Lucknow eastwards to Bhagalpur. The Buddha can hardly be said to have been out of contact with the important centres of political power of his day. He may justly be described as a social and political theorist, and indeed this aspect of his historical significance has been so generally ignored that it needs heavy emphasis. But he was not only a theorist; in addition to the familiarity with the concerns of government, which his upbringing in Kapilavastu would have given him, he was in constant touch with current problems of government, through the two kings who were his supporters and disciples. Nor was this indirect involvement simply a matter of *ad hoc* problem-solving;

the early Buddhist literature represents the Buddha as one who frequently had something to say on matters of policy.

It is not surprising, therefore, to find one of the most outstanding of historians of Indian political thought, U. N. Ghoshal,[60] observing that 'the most important contribution of the early Buddhist canonists to the store of our ancient political thought consists in their "total" application of the principle of righteousness to the branches of the king's internal and foreign administration.'[61]

The unwisdom of the multitude, the need for social and economic stability as a prerequisite of the prescription to overcome this unwisdom, the emergence of powerful monarchically ruled states – these things together provide an explanation of why the Buddha, who seems to have regarded the republican *sangha* as the ideal form of government, nevertheless gave a large place in his teaching to the important role of the righteous monarch. A number of the Jataka stories contain descriptions of the ideal king, and exhortations concerning good government.[62] The realm of the wise king is one which is free from all oppression, not ruled arbitrarily but with equity, where good men are honoured[63] and where the king and his officials exhibit qualities of selflessness, rectitude, mercy, political wisdom and a sense of equal respect for all beings, including different classes of society, townsmen, countrymen, religious teachers, and even birds and beasts.[64] The importance of the personal righteousness of the king is strongly emphasized.[65] A figure of speech frequently used is the bull who leads the herd aright: 'so should a king to righteous ways be true; the common folk injustice will eschew, and through the realm shall holy peace ensue.'[66]

When kings are righteous, the ministers of kings are righteous. When ministers are righteous, brahmans and householders also are righteous. Thus townsfolk and villagers are righteous. This being so, moon and sun go right in their courses. This being so, constellations and stars do likewise; days and nights, months and fortnights, seasons and years go on their courses regularly; winds blow regularly and in due season. Thus the *devas* are not annoyed and the sky-*deva* bestows sufficient rain. Rains falling seasonably, the crops ripen in due season. *Bhikkhus*, when crops ripen in due season, men who live on those crops are long-lived, well-favoured, strong and free from sickness.[67]

Figs, oil, honey, molasses, root-crops, fruits all taste sweeter and better in a country where the king rules righteously, according to another Jataka story.[68]

The economic welfare of the people should, in the Buddhist view, be a special concern of the wise king, who is exhorted to take positive, specific measures which will benefit the country, together with or in addition to the effects of his own personal righteousness. In the *Kutadanta Sutta* (see chapter 5, p. 82) we are told of a great king who, conscious of his good fortune hitherto, thought it advisable to offer a great sacrifice, and thereby ensure the continuance of his prosperity. His chaplain, however, tried to dissuade him, and pointed out that there would be greater wisdom in taking preventive action against possible occurrences of crime. This could be done, suggested the chaplain, by removing the economic causes of discontent. To farmers the king should issue a subsidy of food and of seed-corn. To merchants and tradesmen he should make available sources of capital which they could invest in their businesses. To those in government service he should give adequate wages and supplies of food. If this were to be done there would be no danger of subversion of the state by malcontents, but on the contrary, 'the king's revenue will go up; the country will be quiet and at peace; and the populace, pleased one with another and happy, dancing their children in their arms, will dwell with open doors.' [69] The king followed his chaplain's advice and all happened as the chaplain had predicted. It will be noticed that the advice given by this 'chaplain' is of a kind that would be offered by a Buddhist rather than by a brahman. Sacrifice is a waste of time; the king should concern himself instead with ensuring full employment in the country. The same principle is emphasized in another well-known *Sutta*, which tells the story of the city of Kushinara in its former days of prosperity, under the Great King of Glory.[70]

On the other hand, another *Sutta*[71] tells of a king who failed to make provision for the poor, and of the serious consequences in the life of the state. This king, we are told, instead of going to a holy man to ask advice concerning the proper duty of a king, as his prosperous and wise predecessors had done, followed his own devices. 'By his own ideas he governed his people; and they so governed, differently from what they had been, did not prosper as they used to under former kings.'[72] The one thing he had failed to do, apparently, was to make provision to remedy the condition of the poor in his realm. 'And because this was not done, poverty became widespread.'[73] This led to cases of theft. At first the king had dealt with the offenders by making them grants of money, on the grounds that they had stolen because they were poor men and this was the best way to remedy the situation. But in a short time this suggested itself to others as an easy way of making money, and the incidence of theft increased rapidly. The king thereupon changed his policy, and began cutting off the heads of those who were caught stealing. But this violent measure only engendered further violence. Thieves now began to say among themselves, Let us also resort to violence: 'Let us also now have sharp swords made ready for ourselves, and [as for] them, from whom we take what is not given us – what they call theft – let us put a final stop to them, inflict on them the uttermost penalty, and cut their heads off.' And so, we are told, 'they got themselves sharp swords, and came forth to sack village and town and city, and to work highway robbery. And them whom they robbed they made an end of, cutting off their heads.'[74] Such also, was the sad end of the state itself, whose ruler had failed to make adequate and wise provision for the relief of poverty. From stealing and violence there followed murder, lying, evil-speaking, adultery, false opinions, incest, and perverted lust, until the physical condition of the people deteriorated to the point where their life span was only a fraction of what it had once been.[75]

In these and similar early Buddhist stories, a great responsibility is laid upon the sovereign ruler of the state to act righteously, as far as his own life and conduct of affairs is concerned, and wisely, too, in terms of a social and economic ethic concerning which, it is emphasized, he needs to take advice from 'brahmans'. In the Buddhist literature, as we have seen, 'brahmans' are classed with *shramanas* and are recognized as such by their character and holy life, not by any hereditary right from having been born of a priestly family. The advice the righteous king needs to take, in other words, is that which, ideally, he will be offered by the Buddhist *sangha*.

There is a significant difference between the ethics of the state, with which the early Buddhist tradition was concerned, and the brahmanical idea of the moral responsibilities of the king. As U. N. Ghoshal has observed, the brahmanical royal ethic was the king's own personal *dharma* or duty, 'conceived in sufficiently elastic terms to provide for the needs of the kingdom and to permit in *Manu* and still more in the *Mahabharata* (after Bhishma) the wholesale incorporation of the *Arthasastra* categories'. On the other hand, 'the Buddhist *dharma* in its relation to the king involves the application of the universal ethics of Buddhism to the state administration.'[76] The king, in brahmanical theory, is working out his own personal *moksha*, or salvation, by doing his proper duty, or *dharma*, as a king, just as any other man works out his salvation by doing his own proper duty. The performance of one's personal *dharma* is the dominating principle in the brahmanical theory. But in the Buddhist view, the king is the agent or instrument through which the eternal, universal *Dharma* is made effective.

The point is made explicitly in a collection of sayings concerning kings found in the Pali *Anguttara-Nikaya*. The Buddha is represented as saying to the members of the *Sangha*, '*Bhikkhus*, the king who rolls the wheel of state, a

Dhamma-man, a *Dhamma-king*, rolls indeed no unroyal wheel.' One of the *bhikkhus* then asks, 'But who, Lord, is the king of the King?' The answer given by the Buddha is 'It is *Dhamma*, O *Bhikkhu!*' [77] The Buddhist king – the *Dhamma-king* or *Dharma-raja* – that is, the kind of king whose rule is envisaged as necessary for the implementing of the Buddhist scheme for society, is the king who rules in subordination to one power only – that of the eternal, universal *Dharma* (*Dhamma*). It is this which gives his rule a unique quality; in so far as he rules in accordance with universal *Dharma*, his rule itself has a quality of universalism; it is not appropriate to any one locality or region or period of time. The corollary of this would appear to be that neighbouring *Dhamma-kings* will find themselves ruling by the same eternal universalist principles and therefore in harmony with one another. The notion of a single universal *Dharma-raja* is already to be found in the early Buddhist tradition, as the idea of the one universal monarch, the *Chakravartin*. In Sanskrit literature *Dharma-raja* is another name for the Buddha.

THE CHAKRAVARTIN AND THE BUDDHA

It is significant that in Pali Buddhist literature also there is, in many of the references to the *Chakravartin*, a clear and conscious parallelism between this universal world-ruler and the Tathagata, or Buddha. Beside or behind the *Chakravartin* there stands the Buddha: the two are so closely linked that they almost appear to be one and the same in different roles. There was a strong tradition that Gotama's Buddhahood was seen as an *alternative* to his being a *Chakravartin*. But there is also a suggestion, in many passages, that the Buddha is in every respect virtually identical with the *Chakravartin*.

Bhikkhus, these two persons born into the world are born to the profit and happiness of many, to the profit, happiness and welfare of many folk. What two? A Tathagata, an *arahant* who is a fully Enlightened One (Buddha), and a world-ruling mon-

arch ... *Bhikkhus*, these two persons born into the world are
born as extraordinary men. What two? A Tathagata ... and a
world-ruling monarch. *Bhikkhus*, the death of two persons is
regretted by many folk. Of what two? A Tathagata ... and a
world-ruling monarch. *Bhikkhus*, these two are worthy of a
relic-shrine [*stupa*]. What two? A Tathagata ... and a world-
ruling monarch.[78]

Ghoshal interprets the parallel drawn here and elsewhere
in Buddhist canonical texts between the Buddha and the
World-ruler as meaning that the World-ruler 'is the temporal counterpart of the spiritual World-teacher, resem-
bling him not only in his outward bodily form (the
so-called thirty-two bodily signs of the superman) and the
extraordinary incidents of his birth, death, cremation and
commemoration, but also in the jointly unique role as
universal benefactors.'[79]

It is this close resemblance, amounting to virtual identity, between the World-ruler and the World-teacher
which has the effect, by implication, of distinguishing the
Buddhist conception of an emperor or world-ruler from
the brahmanical conception of the emperor, as the latter
is set out, for instance, in the *Arthasastra* of Kautilya. The
political philosophy which this treatise embodies, and
with which political practice corresponded fairly closely,
is that might is right, or that what is expedient is right.
The Buddhist political philosophy was founded, as K. N.
Jayatilleke pointed out, on the principle that 'the wheel
of might turns in dependence on the wheel of righteousness.'[80] The conflict between the two philosophies was
one which, as we shall shortly see, was experienced as a
conflict of conscience by the emperor Ashoka.

Certain clear inter-relationships can thus be seen within
the structure of society envisaged in early Buddhist tradition and practice. Three major elements can be distinguished: the *Sangha*, the king, and the mass of the people.
Three relationships can also be distinguished.
(1) The *Sangha*, as the realization in practice, or visible
embodiment, of the new wisdom, stood in a special re-

lationship to the king which was a continuation of the relationship which had existed between the Buddha in his day and the kings of Koshala and Magadha. This relationship was in principle of the same kind as that between the World-teacher and the World-ruler.

(2) In the other direction the *Sangha* was related to the mass of the people. The community of the *Sangha* arose out of the common people who both provided its recruits and ministered to its needs. Moreover, what the community of the *Sangha* was now, all humanity was eventually to become; proleptically, the common people were members of the *Sangha*.

(3) Meanwhile, it was necessary that until all should have fully apprehended the Buddha-Dhamma and have entered into the wider realm of consciousness to which life in the *Sangha* led, there should be a centre of political power to bring an interim unity into what would otherwise be the chaos of multiple units, to maintain law and order and promote the common welfare. From the people, in the Buddhist view, the king derived his authority rather than from any divine source; in their name and for their good he exercised it (see chapter 4, p. 65).

This triangular relationship, *Sangha*, king and people, provides the basic structure of Buddhist civilization. The introduction of Buddhism into a country meant, therefore, the attempt to establish this structure, and Buddhist civilization may be said to exist where this structure can be found. It will be the purpose of the second part of this book to trace the expansion of Buddhist civilization in these terms, first in India, and then, by way of confirmation, in Ceylon too.

Part 4

Buddhist Civilization
in Practice

9 The Ashokan Buddhist State

RELIGION: THE BUDDHIST AND THE MARXIST CRITIQUES

The reordering of human consciousness, and the reordering of human society – these, we have seen, were the two complementary aspects of the Buddha's teaching. If, in the Pali canon, it is the reordering of human consciousness which receives greater emphasis and has the greater amount of teaching devoted to it, this is because it was the primary concern of the Buddhist Order, the *Sangha*, while the second was regarded as the proper concern of the enlightened political ruler, acting in accordance with the general principles of the Buddha's teaching, and in co-operation with the *Sangha*, in order to promote what can be called a Buddhistic society. These two complementary concerns constituted the Buddhist prescription for the curing of the ills of the human condition. Now, there is nothing to prevent anyone from using the word 'religion' to describe this programme of action, just as there is nothing to prevent anyone from applying the same word to the philosophy, political and economic revolution proposed by Karl Marx, but in each case it would be a highly specialized and somewhat bizarre usage. The two ideologies, as it happens, are not dissimilar, in so far as both are prescriptions which owe nothing to supernatural or theological beliefs, and both are critical of contemporary religious practice. In the Buddhist case, this criticism is milder, and the general attitude, so far as popular beliefs and practices are concerned, is somewhat more tolerant, although even here there is a strong similarity between the early Buddhist attitude to popular religion and that of Karl Marx, expressed in his famous characterization of religion as 'the sigh of the oppressed creature, the heart of a heartless world, just as it is the spirit of the spiritless situation'.[1]

The Buddha's attitude to popular, as distinct from priestly, religion was one of mildly tolerant disapproval, coupled with an acknowledgement of the fact that unless other, basic factors in the situation were changed, it was futile merely to try to argue people out of their prejudices and superstitions. The Buddhist prescription was a plan for dealing with those other factors, psychological, social and political. Similarly Karl Marx insisted that it was the disease of which nineteenth-century European religion was the symptom which had to be dealt with, not merely the symptoms themselves. Both Buddhism and Marxism are based on a philosophical rather than a theological view of the human situation,[2] and both envisage the solution in terms of 'cells' or growth-points, characterized by the respective principles of corporate existence which each sets out, and devoted to the dissemination of these principles in theory and in action. Both envisage a stage at which the growth of these revolutionary cells will enable the centre of political and economic power to be brought within the revolutionary sphere. In the Marxist case this is a clearly defined aim and constitutes 'the revolution' *par excellence*, to be achieved if necessary by violence; in the Buddhist case it is less clearly defined as a conscious aim of the *Sangha*'s existence and growth, but the conversion of the political ruler to the attitudes entailed in the Buddhist revolution is obviously regarded in the early texts as highly desirable.

THE ASHOKAN REALIZATION OF THE BUDDHIST STATE

It took about two and a half centuries from the decease of the Buddha for this to come about in India. It is true that the two great kings of the Buddha's own day, Pasenadi and Bimbisara, were very sympathetically inclined towards the Buddha, his teaching, and his new community, but there does not appear to have been, either in Koshala or Magadha, a serious and systematic effort during the Buddha's lifetime to make the life of the state conform to the principles of the *Dhamma* like that subsequently made in the Mauryan empire under the emperor Ashoka in the third century BC. For the *Sangha* so to grow in influence and public esteem that eventually a monarch was entirely convinced of the rightness of Buddhist social and ethical principles, and dedicated himself to their practical realization, took two and a half centuries, but this was, nevertheless, the logical and proper consummation of the *Sangha*'s growth in popularity and influence during that period. Inherent in the Buddha's prescription for society was the Buddhistic world-ruler, or *Chakravartin*, and the adherence of Ashoka to Buddhism was not just an unexpected and unhoped-for stroke of luck; it had, since the Buddha's day, clearly been potential in the situation in north India, given the gradual growth and influence of the *Sangha*.

The intervening period had been for the Buddhist *Sangha* one of gradual expansion in spite of difficulties and, occasionally, hostility. In the kingdom of Magadha dynasty had succeeded dynasty, and the power and extent of the kingdom gradually increased. About a hundred and sixty years after the decease of the Buddha, a man named Chandragupta Maurya established himself as ruler of Magadha, displacing the Nanda dynasty.[3] The Nanda kings had, during the previous forty years, built up an empire in northern India that extended up to the frontiers of the Punjab.[4] The empire of Chandragupta was even more vast. He began by fighting a war of liberation in the north-west of India, to rid the Punjab and Sind of the Greek army of occupation left by Alexander the Great. He then marched south-eastwards to attack and slay the rich, proud and tyrannical king of Magadha, Dhana Nanda, in his capital at Pataliputra (Patna). Contemporary Greek writers testify to the vastness of the empire which Chandragupta established in India, from the borders of Persia to as far south as modern Goa, and as far east as the edge of the Ganges delta. This empire was inherited by his son, and later by his grandson, Ashoka. It was left to Ashoka during the early years of his reign, which began about the year 268 BC,[5] to extend the empire's boundaries south-eastwards to the Bay of Bengal by a violent campaign against Kalinga, an area roughly corresponding to modern Orissa.

Chandragupta had been guided and advised by a brahman minister, Chanakya. This brahman is identified with Kautilya, the author of the treatise on statecraft known as the *Arthasastra*. It was he who was the architect of the Mauryan empire. In the principles of government which he had laid down, and in which he had first instructed Chandragupta, the latter's son and grandson, Bindusara and Ashoka, were also trained. Ashoka thus entered upon his career as emperor of the greater part of the Indian sub-continent, heir to a brahman tradition of statecraft, in which he, as a young prince, had been educated, first in theory and then in practice, since the age of about ten.[6]

He was exposed, however, to other traditions. The new movements of thought and practice, of which Jainism and Buddhism were the two major representatives, were particularly strong in eastern India, and brahmanism as a social and ceremonial system was, as yet, correspondingly weaker. There is evidence that Chandragupta was an adherent of Jainism, at least towards the end of his life. Ashoka's mother, according to a Buddhist tradition, was strongly attracted to the doctrines of the Ajivakas. His first wife, Devi, was a lay-supporter of the Buddhist *Sangha*, and the two children he had by her, Mahinda, his son, and Sanghamitra, his daughter, entered the *Sangha* themselves, as *bhikkhu* and *bhikkhuni* respectively, in the sixth year of Ashoka's reign, according to the Pali canonical tradition. It was inevitable, too, that Ashoka himself, as he grew up, would have become familiar with the doctrines and practices of the Buddhist fraternity, which had by then been in existence and growing steadily in eastern India for more than two hundred years.

The turning-point in Ashoka's life appears to have come immediately after the conquest of Kalinga, where victory had been gained only at the price of a great human slaughter, which in Ashoka's own account of it ran into many thousands. In the Kautilyan theory of statecraft it was the monarch's duty to expand the bounds of his realm by military conquest. The difference between the brahmanical concept of kingship and the Buddhist was, as we have already noticed (chapter 8, p. 177), that in brahmanical theory, the king was working out his own personal salvation or *moksha* by the correct and due performance of his own personal *dharma*, that which was proper to him personally as king, whereas in the Buddhist conception of monarchical government, the king was the necessary instrument through which universal *Dharma* or righteousness, found expression. The enlargement of his domain by violent conquest was not required of a king in the Buddhist conception of monarchy, but rather the cultivation of peace, both with his neighbours and within his own realm.

ASHOKA ADOPTS THE BUDDHIST VIEWPOINT

It was from the brahmanical, Kautilyan theory of statecraft to the Buddhist conception that Ashoka turned, after the awful human massacre which his campaign against Kalinga had entailed. Exactly how this change of heart came about is unclear. There is the possibility that this third-generation member of the Mauryan dynasty was already predisposed to react against the brahmanical statecraft of his father and grandfather by the time he succeeded to the throne. Other philosophies were prominent in his empire and, as we have seen, were probably well-known to him, personally and through his own family. It may therefore have been as the result of his own knowledge of the Buddhist social ethic that Ashoka, reflecting on the necessary consequences of the kind of statecraft in which he had been trained, came to the decision to forsake the path of violent conquest and personal royal aggrandizement and devote himself instead to the realization of the Buddhist ideal of the righteous and peaceful monarch. A recent study of Ashoka [7] suggests that, while he had fully mastered the Kautilyan theory of statecraft, he felt it to be inadequate for the needs of his own situation and his own time. 'For Ashoka the state was not an end in itself but rather a means to an end higher than the state itself, namely, *dharma*, or morality ... If for Kautilya the state was a primitive instrument, for Ashoka it was an educative institution. For the dichotomy between force and morality, between Kautilya and Buddha, had existed for a long time. Ashoka felt that his most glorious mission was to resolve this dichotomy and endow the mechanism of the Kautilyan state with a moral soul.' [8] Professor Gokhale has, in these words, indicated that the perspective in which the Buddha-Dharma is properly seen is that of a 'public' (that is, an ethical-political) philosophy rather than merely a private cult of religious satisfaction or 'salvation'. Exactly at what point in his career Ashoka consciously arrived at this decision is, however, difficult to establish. It is not impossible, or even improbable, that it was reached as the outcome of his own reflection.

On the other hand, we have to remember that while Ashoka may have found himself in the position of an emperor in search of a new ethic, there is also the fact that the Buddhist movement had been for two centuries a potential civilization, pragmatically oriented towards monarchy, but needing a Buddhist monarch to convert the potential into the actual. Circumstances until then had not been favourable. Chandragupta, in so far as he was not entirely of orthodox brahmanical outlook, had been inclined towards Jainism. What little is known about Bindusara suggests that he was conventionally brahmanical in his policies, although an inquiring mind may be indicated by the story told of him, that he wished to purchase a philosopher from Greece, but was told that it was not the Greek custom to sell philosophers. Ashoka may from the time of his accession have appeared to the Buddhist

Sangha as an altogether more promising candidate for the role of Buddhist king. Certainly the traditions suggest that some initiative in the matter of securing Ashoka's adherence was taken by members of the Buddhist fraternity. According to the Theravada tradition preserved in Ceylon, Ashoka inherited from his father the practice of a daily distribution of food to large numbers of brahmans, 'versed in the Brahma-doctrine'. After a while, however, Ashoka became disgusted at the greedy manner in which they grabbed at the food and decided that in future he would find other, more worthy recipients. Standing at his window he saw a *bhikkhu*, Nigrodha, passing along the street, and, impressed by his grave and peaceful bearing, sent for him to come at once. Nigrodha came calmly into the king's presence. The king, still standing, invited the *bhikkhu* to sit down. Since there was no other *bhikkhu* present, says the narrator (that is, since there was no one present who was superior in rank to him) Nigrodha sat down on the royal throne. When he saw this, we are told, Ashoka was glad that he, being uncertain of the order of precedence for a king and a *bhikkhu*, had not made the mistake of offering Nigrodha an inferior seat. 'Seeing him seated there king Ashoka rejoiced greatly that he had honoured him according to his rank.'[9] The episode is interesting as an illustration of the evidently accepted principle that any member of the *Sangha* takes precedence over the king, and that the king, therefore, is, in Buddhist theory, subordinate in status to the *Sangha*. The chronicler then goes on to tell how Nigrodha, after he had received the king's gift of food, was questioned by Ashoka concerning his doctrine, and how, in response, he expounded to Ashoka some verses on the subject of 'unwearying zeal'.[10] Ashoka was greatly impressed by this exposition of Buddhist doctrine, and undertook to offer food regularly to Nigrodha. The next day, accompanied by other *bhikkhus*, Nigrodha again received food from the king, and again expounded the doctrine. As a result, Ashoka thereupon became a Buddhist lay follower.[11] Another account of the

manner in which Ashoka became an adherent of Buddhism is found in a collection known as the *Divyavadana*;
one of the sections of this is 'The Book of King Ashoka', a
work which possibly originated in Mathura, in north
India, in the second century BC. According to this source,
it was a *bhikkhu* named Upagupta who was the agent of
Ashoka's conversion.

The evidence of the Buddhist Chronicles, in the form
in which we now have them, however, dates from the sixth
century AD.[12] They do, of course, embody material which
had been transmitted from generation to generation of
bhikkhus with that scrupulous accuracy which is characteristic of Indian memorizing. The tradition which is embodied in the Pali chronicles may very well go back to
within less than a century after Ashoka's time. But Ashoka
himself provided contemporary evidence of the events of
his life in the imperial edicts which he caused to be inscribed on rock faces and on specially erected stone pillars
at various important centres throughout his realm. A
number of such edicts were promulgated throughout the
course of the reign, and each was inscribed in a number
of different places.[13]

In one of the earliest of them, Ashoka expresses his desire that serious moral effort should be made by all his
subjects:

Thus speaks *Devanam-piya* [beloved of the gods], Ashoka: I
I have been an *upasaka* [Buddhist lay-follower] for more than
two-and-a-half years, but for a year I did not make much progress. Now for more than a year I have drawn closer to the
Sangha, and have become more ardent. The gods, who in India
up to this time did not associate with men, now mingle with
them,[14] and this is the result of my efforts. Moreover, this is
not something to be obtained only by the great, but it is also
open to the humble, if they are earnest; and they can even
reach heaven easily. This is the reason for this announcement,
that both humble and great should make progress and that
the neighbouring people also should know that the progress is
lasting . . .[15]

The inscription from which the above is an extract is known as the Minor Rock Edict, 'From Suvarnagiri' (the first words of the inscription), the southern provincial capital of the empire, in Hyderabad.[16] The inscription includes a reference to the wide extent of its publication: it is to be inscribed 'here and elsewhere on the hills, and wherever there is a stone pillar it is to be engraved on that pillar'. Moreover the officers of the state are directed to 'go out with [the text of] this throughout the whole of your district'. The words which have been quoted raise a number of interesting questions. Ashoka refers to himself here, as in every of the thirty-two inscriptions except three,[17] by the title *Devanam-piya*, 'Beloved of the gods'.[18] This might suggest that he was consciously asserting the importance of the gods in whom he believed and whose special instrument he felt himself to be. But it is unlikely that the title held this kind of significance; it was a conventional epithet, meaning roughly 'His Gracious Majesty', and was used by other kings of the time without apparently implying any distinctively religious attitude.[19] So far as Ashoka's moral attitude is concerned, this inscription is of interest in the present context for the evidence which it provides concerning his own progress towards his present state of moral zeal. What is not clear is whether the war of conquest which Ashoka waged against the Kalinga came after his first, rather formal, adherence to Buddhism as a lay-follower, (i.e. the first year, concerning which he says 'for a year I did not make much progress') or before it. If he had already become a lay-follower it might seem strange that he should then embark on such a violent and bloody campaign of conquest. On the other hand, if one adopted the view that he first became a lay-follower after the Kalingan war, out of a feeling of revulsion for war and an attraction towards Buddhism, some explanation would then be necessary for what would have to be regarded as the subsequent change in his attitude, from moral luke-warmness to zeal. No event is known to have occurred and no experience is mentioned by Ashoka which would account for the sudden zealousness. However, Ashoka has left a record of the profound moral impression made on him by the Kalinga campaign:

When he had been consecrated eight years *Devanam-piya* Piyadassi [20] conquered Kalinga. A hundred and fifty thousand people were deported, a hundred thousand were killed and many times that number perished. Afterwards, now that Kalinga was annexed *Devanam-piya* very earnestly practised *Dhamma*, and taught *Dhamma*. On conquering Kalinga *Devanam-piya* felt remorse, for, when an independent country is conquered, the slaughter, death and deportation of the people is extremely grievous to *Devanam-piya*, and weighs heavily on his mind. What is even more deplorable to *Devanam-piya*, is that those who dwell there, whether brahmans, shramanas, or those of other sects, or householders who show obedience to their superiors, obedience to mother and father, obedience to their teachers and behave well and devotedly towards their friends, acquaintances, colleagues, relatives, slaves, and servants all suffer violence, murder and separation from their loved ones. Even those who are fortunate to have escaped, whose love is undiminished [by the brutalizing effect of war], suffer from the misfortunes of their friends, acquaintances, colleagues, and relatives. This participation of all men in suffering, weighs heavily on the mind of *Devanam-piya*. Except among the Greeks, there is no land where the religious orders of brahmans and shramanas are not to be found, and there is no land anywhere where men do not support one sect or another. Today if a hundredth or a thousandth part of those people who were killed or died or were deported when Kalinga was annexed were to suffer similarly, it would weigh heavily on the mind of *Devanam-piya*.[21]

Undoubtedly, the Kalingan war brought about a decisive change in Ashoka, and set him in active pursuit of the Buddhist goal of morality: 'afterwards ... he *very earnestly* practised *Dhamma*' (emphasis added). This agrees well with the statement he makes in the Minor Rock Edict, quoted above, that after making no moral progress for a year (after he had become a Buddhist *upasaka*), he has now 'for more than a year' been very ardent in his practice of morality. Since he tells us that the total length of time since he became a *upasaka* was 'more than *two-and-a-half years*' (emphasis added), and his account of his 'lack of progress' followed by 'much progress' covers altogether ('a year' plus 'more than a year') something over *two* years, this leaves a period of about six months during which, presumably, he was engaged in the Kalingan war.

This reconstruction of the story from the evidence provided by Ashoka's own words carries with it the implication that his advance towards full and enthusiastic acceptance of what it entailed to be a Buddhist was gradual. This accords with what we have already observed concerning Ashoka's background. It is difficult to say that he was ever entirely ignorant of Buddhism; he did not suddenly turn to it after the Kalingan war, as to something unknown to him before; he had known of it, had been sufficiently attracted by it to become a lay-follower and to take the first steps in the direction of the renunciation of self and the interests of the self. But Buddhist teaching takes account of the fact that men usually advance by degrees towards this goal, even after they have set out in its pursuit; and so it was, apparently, with Ashoka.

THE PUBLIC POLICIES OF ASHOKA AS A BUDDHIST RULER

What is presented to us in the evidence of most of the inscriptions, however, is the picture of an emperor who is now seriously, actively and effectively pursuing the kind of policies which are appropriate to a convinced Buddhist ruler.[22] It is interesting to notice where the emphasis was laid. In order of the frequency with which they are mentioned, Ashoka's principal preoccupations in the creation of a Buddhist realm appear to have been, first, exhortation of all the citizens of the state to moral effort, and, second, the implementing of measures designed to improve the quality of public life and facilitate the universal pursuit of Buddhist moral principles. Ashoka himself declares, in the Seventh Pillar Edict that 'The advancement of *Dhamma* amongst men has been achieved through two means, legislation and persuasion. But of these two, legislation has been less effective, and persuasion more so. I have proclaimed through legislation, for instance, that certain species of animals are not to be killed, and other such ideas. But men have increased their adherence to *Dhamma* by being persuaded not to injure living beings and not to take life.' [23]

'*Dhamma*' is mentioned frequently in Ashoka's edicts, and it is to this that he seems to be devoted. At an earlier stage of historical study of Ashoka's India, doubt was sometimes expressed whether the *Dhamma* to which he so often refers was identical with the Buddha-Dhamma, or Buddhist doctrine, as it is found in the canonical texts. The word *dhamma* was used widely, not only by Buddhists, and could bear a quite general meaning, such as 'piety'. But when the whole range of the Ashokan inscriptions is taken into account, there seems little room left for doubt that when Ashoka used the word he meant Buddha-Dhamma. In the First Minor Rock Edict he says, after greeting the *Sangha*,

You know, Sirs, how deep is my respect for and faith in the *Buddha*, the *Dhamma*, and the *Sangha*. Sirs, whatever was spoken by the Buddha was well spoken. And, Sirs, allow me to tell you what I believe contributes to the long survival of the Buddhist *Dhamma*. These sermons on *Dhamma*, Sirs . . .,

and then he gives a list of Buddhist discourses which he considers the most vital; 'These sermons on the *Dhamma*, Sirs, I desire that many *bhikkhus* and *bhikkhunis* should hear frequently and meditate upon, and likewise laymen and laywomen.' [24] His reverence for the Buddha is also clearly testified in the Second Minor Rock Edict, set up at Lumbini, the birthplace of Gotama, 'the Shakya-sage'; this edict records the fact that in the twentieth year of his reign, Ashoka 'came in person and reverenced the place

where Buddha Shakyamuni was born', and how 'he caused
a stone enclosure to be made and a stone pillar to be
erected.' [25]

In view of the fact that it is very clearly the Buddha,
Gotama, whom Ashoka regards as the great teacher,
supremely to be reverenced, and the Buddhist *Sangha* to
which he pays special and most frequent respect, it might
seem surprising that, in his exposition of what he understands to be the essence of the *Dhamma*, which he mentions so much, there appears to be very little in the way of
specifically Buddhist doctrine.

For the *Dhamma*, says Ashoka, is 'good behaviour towards slaves and servants, obedience to mother and father,
generosity towards friends, acquaintances and relatives,
and towards shramanas and brahmans, and abstention
from killing living beings.' [26] There are broadly two kinds
of virtue mentioned here: first, various role-responsibili-
ties: to servants, to parents, to friends and relatives, and
to shramanas and brahmans; and second, abstention from
killing. This basic pattern in the exposition of *Dhamma*
occurs elsewhere in the inscriptions. For example: 'It is
good to be obedient to one's mother and father, friends
and relatives, to be generous to brahmans and shamanas;
it is good not to kill living beings ...' This is how the
Dhamma is expounded in the Third Major Rock Edict.
But in this instance, a further item is added, concerning
economic activity: 'It is good not only to spend little, but
to own the minimum of property.' [27] Again, in the Fourth
Major Rock Edict, Ashoka reminds his subjects of the
'forms of the practice of *Dhamma*': they are, he says,
'abstention from killing, and non-injury to living beings,
deference to relatives, brahmans and shramanas, obedience to mother and father, and obedience to elders'.[28]
Non-injury of living beings, and abstention from killing
are mentioned in the Seventh Pillar Edict as the characteristic ways in which public adherence to *Dhamma* has
shown itself in Ashoka's realm: 'Men have increased their
adherence to *Dhamma* by being persuaded not to injure

living beings and not to take life.' [29] In two other contexts
in the inscriptions Ashoka explains *Dhamma* in slightly
different terms. The opening sentence of the Second Pillar
Edict reads: 'Thus speaks *Devanam-piya*, the king *Piya-
dassi*: *Dhamma* is good. And what is *Dhamma*? It is
having few faults and many good deeds, mercy, charity,
truthfulness, and purity.' [30] Again, in the Seventh Pillar
Edict, he says, 'The glory of *Dhamma* will increase
throughout the world, and it will be endorsed in the form
of mercy, charity, truthfulness, purity, gentleness and
virtue.' And he adds that 'Obedience to mother and father,
obedience to teachers, deference to those advanced in age,
and regard for brahmans and shramanas, the poor and the
wretched, slaves and servants, have increased and will
increase.' [31] If these various ways of expounding what
Ashoka meant by *Dhamma* are set out synoptically,[32] it
becomes clear that the item which occurs most frequently
is abstention from killing; this is mentioned as a way of
practising *Dhamma* in four of the five inscriptions which
explicitly explain what *Dhamma* is. The other most frequently occurring items are obedience to parents (four out
of five), generosity towards shramanas and brahmans (four
out of five) and good behaviour towards friends and relatives (three out of five). Taken together, the catalogue of
social responsibilities mentioned in the inscriptions cor-
responds closely to the well-known list in the 'layman's
code of ethics' the *Sigala-vada Sutta* of the Buddhist Pali
canon (see chapter 8, p. 166). Together with the prominence of the injunction to avoid taking life, this gives an
unmistakably Buddhist flavour to the Ashokan *Dhamma*.
The important point to notice is that this is laymen's
Buddhism; it is not Dhamma as *doctrine*, or philosophical
analysis of the human situation, for that is the concern of
the professionals, the *bhikkhus*. This, rather, is an ethical
system whose primary characteristic principles are non-
violence and generosity. As we shall see later, this code of
ethics has remained, down to modern times, the essence
of Buddhism for lay people.

If non-violence and generosity are the essence of Buddhist morality for the common people, they are also, in the Buddhist state, the minimum requirements of morality for the king and for the corps of professional Buddhists, the *Sangha*. Buddhism has no clear-cut, two-fold standard of morality, one for laymen and one for religious orders or priests; such differences as are recognized are of levels of attainment, the transition from one level to another being gradual and imperceptible rather than clear and distinct. The over-all structure is one of progression through a continuum.

Certainly Ashoka himself appears to have accepted his own ethical obligations. Both in matters concerning himself and his court, and in those concerning the public welfare, he appears to have undertaken in various ways to fulfil his responsibilities as he understood them, as a Buddhist ruler.

Non-violence to living beings was interpreted to mean that, as far as possible, the slaughter of animals for food should cease. 'Formerly in the kitchens of *Devanam-piya Piya-dassi* [Ashoka] many hundreds of thousands of living animals were killed daily for meat. But now, at the time of writing this inscription on *Dhamma*, only three animals are killed, two peacocks and a deer, and the deer not invariably. Even these three animals will not be killed in future.' [33] In another inscription, he records that 'the king refrains from [eating] living beings, and indeed other men and whosoever [were] the king's huntsmen and fishermen have ceased from hunting ...' [34] In yet another, much longer, inscription he records the ban which he has introduced on the killing of a wide variety of animals, birds, and fish, and even on the burning of forests without good reason. [35] As a result of his instructions to the people, 'abstention from killing and non-injury to living beings', as well as various forms of generosity and piety, 'have all increased as never before for many centuries'. [36]

The time which kings had formerly spent in hunting 'and other similar amusements' Ashoka devoted instead to the promotion of the moral condition of the realm. In the past, he records, kings used to go on pleasure tours. But in the tenth year of his reign, the year after he had begun to be a more ardent follower of the Buddhist way, he visited the scene of Gotama's Enlightenment at Bodh-Gaya.

From that time arose the practice of tours connected with *Dhamma*, during which meetings are held with ascetics and brahmans, gifts are bestowed, meetings are arranged with aged folk, gold is distributed, meetings with the people of the countryside are held, instruction in *Dhamma* is given, and questions on *Dhamma* are answered.[37]

He adds that he finds this more enjoyable than any other kind of activity.

But as well as the royal entourage's use of time in this way, in the interests of public ethical instruction and philanthropy, the resources of the state were devoted to various works for the common good. Throughout the entire realm, records the second Major Rock Edict, two medical services have been provided. 'These consist of the medical care of man, and the care of animals.' Moreover, 'medicinal herbs, whether useful to man or to beast, have been brought and planted wherever they did not grow.' Other public works mentioned in this inscription include the introduction of root crops and fruit trees where they were not grown formerly; the provision of wells at points along the roads, and the planting of trees for shade, to make travel easier for man and beast.[38] These things are recorded in the Seventh Pillar Edict too, where it is mentioned that provision of wells and of rest houses was made at regular intervals of eight *kos*[39] along the main roads, and the trees which were planted to provide shade are specified – banyan trees. The purpose of these public works is here said to have been 'that my people might conform to *Dhamma*'.[40] That is to say, it was considered that the improvement of the general quality of public life and health in these ways, and the enhanced trade that would follow, would help to create the conditions in which the Buddhist ethic could best be practised. Another measure taken by Ashoka with this end in view was the appointment of welfare-officers, known as 'commissioners of *Dhamma*'.[41] This new office was instituted by Ashoka in the twelfth year of his reign; appointments to the office were made throughout the whole realm.

Among servants and nobles, brahmans and wealthy house-holders, among the poor and the aged, they are working for the welfare and happiness of those devoted to *Dhamma* and for the removal of their troubles. They are busy in promoting the welfare of prisoners should they have behaved irresponsibly, or releasing those that have children, are afflicted, or are aged.[42]

ASHOKA'S ATTITUDE TO RELIGION

In the extracts from the Ashokan inscriptions which have been considered so far there has been virtually nothing that could unequivocally be called 'religious' in the emperor's concerns and policies. That is to say, there has been no mention of the sacred, or of sanctions for behaviour derived from the sacred, unless *Dhamma* may be held to fill the place of the sacred. But we are not altogether without evidence of Ashoka's attitude to contemporary beliefs and practices associated with belief in gods and sacred beings. His total opposition to the sacrificial offering of any living being is clearly expressed in the First Major Rock Edict, and his disapproval of the kind of assemblies associated with such sacrifices.[43] In another of the rock edicts he deals with various kinds of rites, practised by the common people on such occasions as the birth of a child, or at the start of a journey. Women, in particular, he says, 'perform a variety of ceremonies, which are trivial and useless'. The one 'ceremony' which is of great value is the practice of *Dhamma*.[44] The attitude which is revealed here – strong opposition to animal sacrifice, mild disapproval of useless and superstitious rites, together with commendation of the practice of the *Dhamma* – is characteristically Buddhist, and recalls, in particular, some of the Buddha's discourses in the *Digha Nikaya* (see chapter 5).

Ashoka appears to have shared contemporary cosmological belief, with notions of various layers of existence one upon the other. Below the earth were various hells; the surface of the earth was the abode of men, and above the surface of the earth were realms of increasingly refined and rarified atmosphere, the various heavens, where lived the spirit beings or *devas*, sometimes called 'gods'. These denizens of the upper regions were regarded as a 'natural' feature of the universe, as natural as any other beings, and subject to rebirth, but they enjoyed a more blissful present existence in heaven as a result of good *karma* in previous existences, according to the prevalent Indian view. Improvement in moral conditions on earth could attract them, however, and it was believed that in such happy circumstances the *devas* appeared from time to time among men. Such a condition of things Ashoka believed to have been brought about as a result of his strenuous efforts on behalf of *Dhamma*. Referring to his own increased moral ardour during the year that he had been a more active Buddhist he comments that 'The gods, who in India up to this time did not associate with men, now mingle with them'.[45] The same inscription endorses the contemporary popular idea that by living a good moral life any man could achieve a more blissful existence on some higher plane: 'This is not something to be obtained only by the great, but it is also open to the humble, if they are earnest; and they can even reach heaven easily.'

One further point of interest which arises from a study of the inscriptions is that Ashoka looked with strong disfavour upon sectarianism when it led to the disparagement of the views and attitudes of others. Like other rulers, before his time and since, Ashoka had a powerful interest in peace within his realm, in harmony among his subjects. True progress in essential truth, he says, will enable a man to control his speech 'so as not to extoll one's own sect or disparage another's on unsuitable occasions'; rather, 'one should honour another man's sect, for by doing so one increases the influence of one's own sect and benefits that of the other man; while by doing otherwise one diminishes the influence of one's own sect and harms the other man's.' In Ashoka's case, this concern with social harmony is all of a piece with his very evident and earnest concern for the general welfare of his subjects. He himself honoured with gifts and attended to the affairs of Ajiva-kas, Jains, and brahmans as well as Buddhists.[46]

From this survey of the evidence of Ashoka's fairly numerous inscriptions, what emerges is the picture of a ruler who was converted from one ideology of government to another. He was, throughout his life, both before and after his adherence to Buddhism, first and foremost a king; he did not give up the affairs of government for the affairs of some other, spiritual realm. He became a Buddhist be-cause it seemed to him that to do so was to become a better king; pursuit of the *Dhamma* would ensure that the realm over which he ruled was a better, happier and more peaceful place.

Ashoka has been compared to the Emperor Constan-tine, who made the Christian religion the official creed of the Roman Empire, and established the Church as the ecclesiastical arm of the state. If we start out with the idea that there is such a correspondence, that Ashoka was an Indian Constantine, then we soon find ourselves referring to the *Sangha* as the 'Buddhist Church',[47] and calling *bhik-khus* not merely 'monks', but even 'priests'. But what Ashoka promoted was a system of public morality and social welfare which was itself the logical working-out in the socio-political sphere of a sophisticated and radical analysis of the human situation. The basis of the appeal of this ideology was not to be found in any theistic sanctions, but in the self-evident attractiveness and value of the kind of life which it tended to produce when it was seriously adhered to and practised over a sustained period. The corps of professionals set the ethical and existential goal so high (*nibbana*) that in their pursuit of it, they enhanced the moral quality of the life of those around them. To support such men, to heed their philosophy, to facilitate the realization of their ideal by the proper ordering of society – this was Ashoka's primary concern from the time he became an enthusiastic Buddhist. As far as 'religion' was concerned, if by that were meant priesthood and sacrificial system, Ashoka was, like any other Buddhist, opposed to such institutions, as socially dangerous and intellectually deceptive. If by religion were meant popular rites and ceremonies other than sacrifice, he saw no great harm in these, nor any great usefulness either. Occasionally a ceremony or an ancient custom might have something to be said for it, as inculcating reverence for good traditions. But one should never be too dogmatic about such things, Ashoka held; certainly not if it were at the cost of fraternal goodwill and social harmony. Nevertheless, it was in the general area of mildly beneficial ancient customs that 'religious' forms of activity prospered in Ashoka's reign. The indigenous, non-brahmanical elements of popular belief were stimulated by the tolerance which they enjoyed, and so, together with the growth and influence of Buddhism there went a growth of non-priestly beliefs and customs. Perhaps the most significant of these was the cult of veneration of *stupas*, the stone or brick cairns in which were enshrined the reliquary remains of great men and heroes. The growth of this cult during Ashoka's time is clearly attested by the number of *stupas* in India which have been identified as dating from this period. It was this, associated as it was with Buddhism, which more than anything else marks the beginning of the characterization of the Buddhist movement in religious terms. By Ashoka's time the seeds of the attitude of *bhakti*, or reverential, loving devotion, had been sown, seeds which in later centuries were to bloom luxuriantly in the worship by lay people not only of the Buddha Gotama, but of countless other potential Buddhas, or Bodhisattvas, heavenly beings of such exalted and potent spirituality that they were in function and status indistinguishable from gods.

But in Ashoka's time all this lay in the future. Ashoka was no Constantine, discerning the growing popularity and power of the cult of a divine saviour; nor did Ashoka, as Constantine did, hasten to identify himself and his realm with the name of a new god that before long would be above every divine name, throughout the Roman Empire. Nor did he, as Constantine, graft this new faith on to the old religion of the state, continuing himself to function as *pontifex maximus* of the old priesthood. In contrast to all this, Ashoka was attracted to a social philosophy, and was attracted all the more strongly as his awareness of the problems that attend an emperor's task grew. The more he was drawn to this philosophy of the restructured society and restructured consciousness, the farther he moved from the old, priestly statecraft of the brahmans, while still paying respect to popular traditions. If there is any useful historical parallel with the Buddhism of Ashokan India, it is not the Constantinism of imperial Rome but the Confucianism of imperial China. And it has long been doubted whether that can be called a religion.

THE EFFECT OF INDIAN RELIGIOSITY UPON BUDDHISM

The fact remains that by the end of Ashoka's reign, Buddhism had come to be very much more closely and intimately associated with popular religious practice than had formerly been the case. It may be useful at this point to remind ourselves that the essential features of Buddhist practice, as they are portrayed throughout the Pali canon, are morality and mental discipline, leading ultimately to wisdom, or enlightenment. At the higher levels of the Buddhist movement both morality and mental discipline were equally important and equally emphasized as the proper concerns of the Buddhist professional – the *bhikkhu*. But at the lower levels of engagement, among those who were living the lives of householders and workers, it was expected that the major preoccupation would be with morality. This is implied, too, in the Ashokan inscriptions, as we have seen. Morality, or, in Ashokan terminology, *Dhamma*, consisted of generosity, expressed in various social relations, of non-violence, and simplicity of life. So far as any cultus of worship is concerned, there would appear to be nothing in the nature of Buddhism itself to require it or justify it. It was on aesthetic grounds, apparently, that the Buddha admired the various shrines in the city of Vaishali;[48] his words to Ananda on each occasion when they visited these shrines had to do with the practice of mental discipline. The value of such shrines appears to have consisted in the opportunity which they provided, as the text of the *Maha Parinibbana Suttanta* has it, for developing, practising, dwelling on, expanding and ascending to the very heights of the four paths to *iddhi*. *Iddhi* is a word which had various connotations, according to the context[49] for which the most general or comprehensive translation is 'glory' or 'majesty'. The 'glory' to which the 'four paths' here mentioned lead is that of the Buddhist who has attained the goal of emancipation from bondage to 'self-hood'. The four paths are those of will, moral effort, thought and analysis in the context in each case of the struggle against evil.

So, while there was nothing in the nature of early Buddhism to require worship as an essential activity, as there is in theistic religions like Judaism, Christianity, Islam and Vaishnavism, there was a tendency, dating back apparently to the earliest period, to associate mental discipline, in certain circumstances, with the aesthetically helpful setting provided by an already existing shrine. Beyond this use of a shrine early Buddhism had no reason to go: certainly not in the direction of any kind of public ceremonial or cultus. So far as the *bhikkhus* were concerned, the Buddha was represented as having explicitly forbidden them to engage even in the reverencing of his mortal remains after his death. That, he said, could be left to pious men among the nobles and householders; *bhikkhus* should concentrate on making progress in moral and mental discipline.[50] It was for noblemen and householders who were supporters of the Buddhist movement to supply the land, the resources and the labour for the building of *stupas*, so that the remains of the Buddha should be treated in the same way 'as men treat the remains of a *Chakravartin*',[51] or universal monarch. The cremation of the Buddha's body and the enshrinement of the bones and ashes was, as we saw earlier (chapter 6, p. 128), carried out in exactly the manner that was used for the cremation and enshrinement of the remains of a great emperor. We saw also (chapter 8, pp. 178–9) that this was one of a number of ways in which the Buddha and the *Chakravartin* are regarded as counterparts, spiritual or philosophical on the one hand, and political on the other.

It has been suggested that the building of a mound or *stupa* in which to enshrine relics was, in fact, an old custom put to new use in early Buddhism.[52] The old custom, says the exponent of this view, was the veneration of certain hemispherical mounds as sacred, and was a feature of ancient religious practice in a number of cultures. This custom was then given a new meaning by the use of such solid brick or stone mounds as receptacles for Buddhist relics; thus, what was originally simple *mound-worship* developed into *relic-worship*. There is no certainty about this, however, and the argument is based largely on the existence of 'traces of mound-worship in the Vedic age among the Aryans of India'.[53] While it is conceivable that *some* kind of cult of sacred mounds may have preceded their use in the early Buddhist period as reliquary shrines, there is no clear evidence of this. What is clear is that in the Ashokan period, large numbers of Buddhist *stupas* were constructed, in the course of what appears to have been a widespread popular movement. What was expressed by this practice was devotion to the Buddha, and the desire to reverence him. It is possible that Ashoka himself

was responsible for making the cult into a popular movement.[54] It must be emphasized that in the Ashokan period
the 'Buddha-image' or 'Buddha-statue' (properly called a
Buddha-rupa) had not yet appeared on the scene; this was
a devotional usage which did not develop until about the
first century BC, somewhere in north-western India. Until
then it was the *stupa* which served as a focus of reverential
feelings for the great man who had first gained supreme
enlightenment, who had first taught the eternal truths of
Dhamma, and had founded the Order of those who
guarded, practised and transmitted this eternal *Dhamma*.
In India the tendency to pay elaborate respect and reverence to great men, to the point of deifying them, is well
attested, from the modern period back to antiquity.[55] It
combines with another well-attested and widespread emotional attitude – the desire to surrender oneself in self-
abnegating adoration. In India this attitude is known as
bhakti, well described as the experience in which 'mind
and body are flooded with an overwhelming sweetness, the
Rasa, or *Raga*, which is the experience of being in love
not with a human lover but a divine'.[56] This religious
mood of utter surrender of the self to one who is thought
of as saviour or lord, makes its appearance in a variety of
forms and in diverse cultures outside India, from the
Amida-cults of medieval Japan to the Jesus-cults of
modern America. In India the cult of the *bhagavata*, the
beloved or adored one, has often focussed itself round an
historical figure whom subsequent generations have invested with divine qualities.

This merging of various strands of folk-religion was
made considerably easier by the encouragement which
Ashoka gave to it by his insistence on the meeting and
mingling of the adherents of different religious and philosophical sects; the Twelfth Major Rock Edict commands
that different sects should listen to one another's principles, honour each other, and promote the essential doctrine of all sects, and adds that the carrying out of this

policy was a special responsibility of the state-appointed 'commissioners of *Dhamma*'.[57]

That the Buddha had come to be the object of a popular *bhagavata*-cult in the Ashokan period is clear from the opposition expressed by those *bhikkhus* who adhered to the earlier, simpler concept of the Buddha. The *Kathavathu*, one of the seven books of the Abhidhamma collection in the Pali canon, is generally regarded as having been compiled during Ashoka's reign. Its main purpose appears to have been the correction of various errors which had developed with regard to the Buddha, and the Buddhist way; the very production of such a work by the more orthodox *bhikkhus* of Ashoka's time is itself an important piece of evidence regarding Buddhist development during that period. As Sukumar Dutt has pointed out, there would have been no need for a work of this kind unless grave misconceptions regarding the Buddha and his teaching really had developed, and unless, too, there existed in the community a sense of the importance of preserving the earlier tradition in its pure form, and a feeling that this was now being seriously threatened.[58] Among the points dealt with in the *Kathavathu* was the idea that the Buddha had not really lived in the world of men, but in the 'heaven of bliss', appearing to men on earth in a specially created, temporary form to preach the *Dhamma*.[59] Together with this virtual deification of the Buddha there went also a tendency to deny him normal human characteristics,[60] and on the other hand to attribute to him unlimited magical power.[61]

Such views of the Buddha were still being refuted by the Theravadins when 'The Questions of King Milinda' was composed, probably in the first century of the Christian era.[62]

THE DEVELOPMENT OF A RELIGIOUS BUDDHISM

It is possible to see that during the Ashokan period a number of different but related factors were at work in Indian

society, which, interacting upon one another, were tending
to produce an amalgam of philosophy, meditational practice, ethics, devotional piety and folk-lore which can justifiably be described as 'religious Buddhism'. In this process
the cult of the *stupa* was possibly the crucial item. Royal
support for the Buddhist movement meant the devotion of
royal resources for the meritorious work of *stupa*-building.
The general economic prosperity which Ashoka's internal
policies helped to foster, by providing a reasonable degree
of peace within the empire and good facilities for communication and transport, meant that other prosperous
citizens could afford to follow the royal example of *stupa*-
building. The growth in the number of *stupas* would,
among the mass of the people, lead very easily in the
Indian cultural atmosphere to a cult of the *bhagava*, the
blessed one, the Buddha, in whose honour these *stupas* had
all been raised. Given this virtual deification of the Buddha as the blessed one, the Lord, there would be no difficulty at all in relating him to the pantheon of Indian folk-
religion as one of the great beings, possibly the greatest, to
whom adoration and worship were offered. Nor would the
members of the *Sangha* be likely to discourage the building of *stupas* and their use as popular shrines, since there
was as we have seen, a tradition that the Buddha himself
had spoken of the value of the shrines as places for fruit-
ful mental discipline.

It is possible that it was the development of Buddhism
from a socio-political philosophy to a popularly based religious cult which was one of the chief causes of its eventual decline and virtual disappearance from India. Once
it had come to be regarded as a religious system it could be
thought of – and indeed was thought of – as a rival by
those who adhered to, and whose interests were vested in,
another religious ideology, notably the brahmans. Ashoka
himself seems to have moved his position in this respect
during the course of his roughly forty-year reign, from the
earlier attitude of equal tolerance and encouragement of
all sects and ideologies, to a more pronounced affinity for

the Buddhist movement in his later years. His prohibition of the slaughter of animals would not have been altogether welcome to those who were the guardians of a tradition of sacrificial ritual. His measures aimed at restricting or banning popular festivals of which he did not approve would also have diminished to some extent his public image as a man of complete religious tolerance. When, in addition, during the latter part of his reign, it was seen that the emperor was increasingly associated with the Buddhist *Sangha* and its affairs, at a time when Buddhism was taking on the characteristics of another, rival religious system – rival, that is, to the system of ideas and practices which the brahmans believed it was their sacred duty to uphold and preserve – some kind of conflict between the two would appear inevitable. There has been some debate among scholars regarding the extent to which the opposition of the brahmans was responsible for the decline of the Ashokan Buddhist state.[63] Those who deny that there was such opposition have not, in the opinion of the author, produced reasons for this view sufficiently convincing to match the strength with which they appear to hold it.

Without doubt, Ashoka's rule was autocratic. The Ashokan state was in no sense a democracy. Within the *Sangha* itself there was, as we have noted, a democratic system of self-government, but so far as the general run of men were concerned the Buddhist view was that men who by nature were dominated by passion needed strong, morally wholesome, autocratic rule. It was such a rule that Ashoka saw it to be his duty to exercise. In doing so, while he must have had the tacit consent of the mass of the people, he would also have incurred the dislike and even enmity of any sections of the community whose interests were not compatible with the public promotion of *Dhamma*. Ashoka suppressed what he believed was not in accordance with *Dhamma*. In doing so, he incurred an intensified opposition to *Dhamma*, as well as to himself and his dynasty. The Mauryan dynasty declined rapidly after his death, and survived him by barely half a century before it was super-

seded by the re-established brahman state under the Sun-
gas. Buddhism managed to survive, partly because of its
now increasingly popular basis and its marriage to folk
religion, and partly because the political power of brahmanism was not everywhere sufficiently great to allow the
enforcement of that policy towards Buddhism which is
stated clearly and unequivocally in what the Law of Manu
has to say concerning the treatment of heretics: 'Men belonging to an heretical sect [classed here together with
gamblers, dancers and singers, cruel men, those following
forbidden occupations, and sellers of spirituous liquor] let
him [the king] instantly banish from his town.'[64] Similarly, 'ascetics' (of heretical sects) are lumped together with
'those born of an illegal mixture of the castes' and
'those who have committed suicide' as classes of men to
whom no honour should be given.[65]

By the end of Ashoka's reign, the structure of dual relationship which the *Sangha* had evolved, between the king
on the one hand and the people on the other, was beginning to display some of the inherent disadvantages which
it entailed, particularly in the Indian situation. The close
ties between king and *Sangha* which Buddhist polity
seemed to require had, as an inevitable effect, the antagon-
izing of the brahmans. In order to function properly, the
Buddhist political arrangement which was pragmatically
to be preferred, namely the securing of the king's adherence to Buddhist values, had also to exclude his adherence
to brahman values and policies. By implication the scheme
had to be exclusive to the *Sangha*. Ashoka's occasional
declarations of goodwill towards the brahmans could not
ultimately disguise the facts of the situation. The hostility
of the brahmans, which exclusion from their former position of political influence would engender, gave the
Sangha a vested interest in the continuance of royal
patronage.

On the other hand, the *Sangha* did not and could not
rely entirely on royal support, for this by itself was not
sufficient. It is true that Ashoka, and after him, in a similar

manner, Buddhist kings of Ceylon, gave generously for the supplying of the *Sangha*'s needs, of food, clothing and housing. But these donations were, in the total perspective, symbolic and exemplary. Economically, the major support for the *Sangha*, on a day-to-day basis, would have come from the local people of the towns and cities of the Ashokan empire. Hence, there was a strong economic motive for an attitude of tolerance towards popular cults and beliefs, in order not to antagonize unnecessarily those on whom the *Sangha* depended for their daily needs. This attitude of tolerance was not difficult to accommodate for, as we have seen, it accorded well with the Buddhist view of the operation of reason and argument. But such an attitude towards popular belief and practices, arising out of both theory and economic requirement, had as its penalty the danger of the subversion of the *Sangha* by the all-pervasive popular cults of India, and particularly by the *bhagavata* cult.

The end of the Mauryan dynasty and the restoration of brahmanical statecraft of the Kautalyan kind to its former position of dominance might have seemed to signal the end of the Buddhist experiment to which Ashoka and, with less distinction, his successors, had devoted themselves. It might look as though Buddhism was now to survive in India merely as another of the many *bhagavata*-cults of which India seems never to have had any shortage. Gotama the Buddha and his teaching, the quiet social and ideological revolution which had for three centuries been making steady progress in northern India and beyond, were now, it seemed, destined soon to be forgotten as men gave themselves instead to a cult of a heavenly lord, while brahman priests who advised the rulers of the state took good care that Buddhism should never again be allowed to achieve the political and social influence which it had under Ashoka.

That is how it might have seemed, and to some extent that is how it was; but not entirely so. For while, in some places, the *Sangha* was swayed by the increasingly influential cult of the heavenly lord and its diverse developments, in other places it maintained the tradition of Gotama, the Sage of the Shakyas, the man who had completely destroyed all attachment to the notion of the individual self, the man who was 'cooled' from all passion, and fully awakened, the *Samasambuddha*, who had also inaugurated the company, the *Sangha*, of those who followed him on this path, the company which, as the embodiment of that same selflessness, was to be the prototype for humanity as a whole. So long as there was a stream of *Sangha* life where *this* tradition was maintained, even though the actual structure of a Buddhist state had been dismantled, there was always the possibility that what had happened when Ashoka succeeded to the throne of Magadha could happen again, and that another monarch, adhering fully and confidently to the Buddhist tradition, might, in cooperation with the *Sangha*, bring back into being the Buddhist pattern of society. So long as the *Sangha* survived, somewhere, in its earlier form and with its earlier perspectives, that tradition would be preserved out of which the Buddhist state and the Buddhist ordering of the common life might once again emerge.

The *Sangha* did so survive, in the school of the Theravadins, or those who adhere to the doctrine of the elders, and it was this school which preserved the tradition of the Buddhist state, in south India, north-east India, and most notably and most continuously, in Ceylon. It is to the story of the planting of Buddhist civilization in Ceylon that we now turn our attention.

10 The Buddhist State in Ceylon

ASHOKAN BUDDHISM IN A SINHALESE SETTING

It has been suggested in the course of this outline of Buddhist civilization that the structure of Buddhism which is presupposed in the discourses of the Buddha and his public activities is that of a triangular relationship between the *Sangha*, the king and the people. It has been suggested further that this is precisely the structure of the Ashokan Buddhist state, the first sustained realization of the Buddhist ideal. The *Sangha*, the new community of those who have abandoned the individualistic notions which nourish so much 'commonsense' understanding of life, and which produce so much envy, hatred, sorrow and conflict, constitutes the growing point – or growing points – of the restructured humanity. Meanwhile, the large remaining area of society outside the *Sangha*, which is nevertheless proleptically *Sangha*, potential but not realized, must have its own appropriate forms of organization and control, which will both discourage the violent and morally unwholesome elements, and encourage the pursuit of peace and morally wholesome action. In ancient India this task had to be performed by a Buddhist king, and this is the task that Ashoka appears to have accepted and endeavoured to fulfil, with notable success. So long as the ordinary people of such a society are being schooled in Buddhist ways and Buddhist attitudes, particularly those of generosity in thought and action, and so long as they are as yet only at the elementary stage of schooling, so to speak, they are not to be harangued or castigated for holding ideas and practising customs which belong to a pre-Buddhist stage of society. This appears to be the accepted Buddhist view, and so an open frontier is allowed, between

Buddhist attitudes and practices and those of the earlier folk culture. In the Ashokan Buddhist state this principle can be seen at work, in particular, in the widespread growth of the *stupa*-cult, and in the use of folk practices and ideas in the service of Buddhist teaching and devotion.

That this is a fairly accurate outline of what Buddhism was understood to be in the Ashokan period is confirmed by the fact that this is precisely the shape in which it was exported from India to Ceylon during Ashoka's reign.

The story is told in the Pali chronicles of Ceylon, namely, 'The Island Chronicle' (*Dipavamsa*), and 'The Great Chronicle' (*Mahavamsa*) and in a work by Buddhaghosa called *the Samanta-Pasadika*,[1] written in the latter half of the fifth century AD. As we have already seen, the chronicles were not compiled until about the fifth and sixth centuries respectively, of the Christian era, or roughly the tenth and eleventh centuries of the Buddhist era. This was eight or nine centuries after the events which were described. Nevertheless Buddhaghosa and the chroniclers made use of the traditions which had come down to them, and which had been transmitted with that meticulous care in reproducing exactly what is repeated which characterizes Indian oral tradition. A modern Sinhalese Buddhist, Dr G. P. Malalasekere, has put it in this way:

Even today [in Ceylon] great respect is shown to the man who carries all his learning in his head; for 'who knows whether books may not get lost or destroyed and become not easy to lay hands on?' And the person who trusts to books for reference is contemptuously referred to as 'he who has a big book at home, but does not know a thing'. Anyone visiting a village monastery in Ceylon at the present time will find the *ola* leaf books carefully wrapped up in costly silk cloths and reverently packed in beautifully carved bookcases, that the faithful devotees may offer to them flowers and incense and thus pay honour to the Buddha's word. The monk is expected to carry all his learning in his head.[2]

The account which the chronicles give us of Buddhism as it existed in the third century BC, and as it was taken to Ceylon, agrees very well with what has already appeared from the evidence of Ashoka's stone inscriptions, and with the profile of Buddhism in the canonical writings. The story of the coming of Buddhism to the island is told in a number of clear, successive stages.

THE ESTABLISHMENT OF BUDDHIST KINGSHIP AND SANGHA

The first was the establishment of very cordial relations between Devanam-piya Tissa, who had just succeeded to the throne of Ceylon, and Ashoka. This came about, according to the chronicler, in the following way. At the accession of Devanam-piya Tissa a great quantity of precious stones of all kinds was discovered in the island and its surrounding waters: sapphire, beryl, ruby, pearls, and many other 'priceless treasures' were found. Tissa's immediate response was to send a magnificent gift of these jewels to the emperor of India, 'to my friend, *Dhamma* Ashoka', for he 'and nobody else is worthy to have these priceless treasures', said Tissa. We are told by the chronicler that 'the two monarchs, Devanam-piya Tissa and *Dhamma* Ashoka had already been friends a long time though they had never seen each other.'[3] Four officials of Tissa's court were appointed as envoys, and with the support of a body of retainers, they carried the precious stones to Pataliputra, Ashoka's capital. Ashoka received both the jewels and the envoys with enthusiasm; upon the latter were bestowed appropriate titles of honour.

What is more significant, however, is the further response which was made by Ashoka in assembling and sending to Tissa all that was necessary for an Indian royal consecration. The list of the requisites of royalty given in the chronicle reads as follows:

a fan, a diadem, a sword, a parasol, shoes, a turban, ear-ornaments, chains, a pitcher, yellow sandalwood, a set of garments that had no need of cleansing, a costly napkin, unguent brought by the nagas, red-coloured earth, water from the lake Anotatta and also water from the Ganges, a spiral shell winding in auspicious wise, a maiden in the flower of her youth, utensils as golden platters, a costly litter, yellow and emblic myrobalans and precious ambrosial healing herbs, sixty times one hundred waggon loads of mountain-rice brought thither by parrots, nay, all that was needful for consecrating a king, marvellous in splendour . . .[4]

With these things Ashoka sent Tissa envoys

with the gift of the true doctrine, saying, 'I have taken refuge in the Buddha, the *Dhamma*, and the *Sangha*. I have declared myself a lay-disciple in the discipline of the Shakyan. Seek then even thou, O best of men, converting thy mind with believing heart refuge in these best of gems!' and saying moreover [to the envoys]: 'Consecrate my friend yet again as king.' [5]

On their arrival back in Ceylon the gifts were delivered, and the consecration of Tissa was carried out in accordance with Ashoka's instructions. The second stage in this story of the coming of Buddhism to Ceylon, after the reconsecration of the king in the style of Ashoka and the delivery of the message of advice to him to become a Buddhist lay-disciple like Ashoka, was the introduction of the *Sangha* into the island. This, according to the chronicle, was the work of the great Buddhist leader in India, Moggaliputta, who sent an elder (*thera*) and four *bhikkus* to Ceylon to 'establish the discipline of the Conqueror',[6] that is, of the Buddha, in the island. The elder was Mahinda, Ashoka's son by his first wife, Devi. Mahinda had been a member of the *Sangha* for twelve years by the time he was sent to Ceylon, having been admitted to full membership of the Order at the age of twenty. On his arrival in Ceylon he made an occasion for meeting king Tissa when the latter was out hunting. Although Tissa had been reconsecrated according to Ashoka's instructions, he had not yet become a Buddhist lay-disciple, even formally. Having engaged the king in conversation, in order to find out what kind of mind he had, and having discovered the king to be a keen-witted man, Mahinda delivered to him one of the Buddha's discourses known as 'The Discourse on the Simile of the Elephant's Footprint'.[7] This covers a range of topics: it tells of the Buddha, 'a perfected one, a fully self-awakened one, endowed with right knowledge and conduct, a well-farer, knower of the [three] worlds, the matchless charioteer of men who are to be tamed, the Awakened One, the Bhagavan'.[8] It tells also of the *Dhamma* which he proclaims, and of the new standards of morality which are adopted by one who hears the *Dhamma* and is convinced of its truths; the sobriety and simplicity of life, the attitude of non-violence, the control of mind and senses which such a person develops, and how he loses all restlessness and worry, lives calmly, without doubts or perplexity. At the end of the discourse, its original hearer, a brahman, is recorded as saying,

> It is wonderful, good Gotama ... It is as if, good Gotama, one might set upright what had been upset, or might disclose what had been covered, or might point out the way to one who had gone astray, or might bring an oil-lamp into the darkness so that those with vision might see ... even so is *Dhamma* made clear in many a figure by the good Gotama.[9]

He then declares his resolve, in the usual three-fold formula, to resort to the Buddha, the *Dhamma* and the *Sangha* for as long as life lasts, asking the Buddha to accept him as a lay-disciple. The recital of the discourse by Mahinda is said to have had the same effect upon King Tissa, who at the end of it, together with his companions, similarly declared his intentions to resort to the Buddha, his *Dhamma*, and his *Sangha*.[10] The next day Mahinda was invited to expound the Buddha's teaching to the women of the royal household. Of the three discourses which he is said to have used on this occasion, one dealt with the various sad fates which had befallen those who dwelt in the world of ghosts as a result of their previous evil lives (*the Petavatthu*),[11] another by way of contrast described the happy state of those who dwelt in heavenly palaces because of their previous moral goodness (the *Vimanavatthu*),[12] and a third set out the four noble truths of Buddhist morality.[13] After they had listened to Mahinda, the women of the royal household became 'stream-enterers', that is to say, those who have embarked on the Buddhist life and have taken the initial step towards crossing to 'the further shore'. Many of the local townspeople, too, having heard of the arrival of Mahinda and his companions, and of the great impression they had made, came together in a crowd and asked for Mahinda to come out and address them. He did so, using on this occasion the *Deva-duta-suttanta*, or 'Discourse on the Heavenly Messengers', another homily cast in the form of popular legend, making use of the folk-beliefs in Yama, the god of death. His messengers, according to this *Sutta*, are old age, disease, and the fact of death, and they are meant to remind men of the transitoriness of human pleasure, and the wisdom of living a morally good life. As a result, many of these townspeople also, we are told, became 'stream-enterers'. During the following days even larger crowds assembled to be addressed by Mahinda, with correspondingly wider public adherence to the Buddhist morality and way of life.

As a suitable place for Mahinda and his companions to spend their nights, a place neither too noisy nor on the other hand too far removed from the city and difficult of access, the king presented them with a piece of parkland, the Mahamegha. It was here a little later that the *vihara* or 'residence' for the *bhikkhus* was built which was eventually to be known as the 'Great *Vihara*' of the city of Anuradhapura, and the headquarters of the Theravada school of Ceylon. An important feature of the proper establishment of such a residence for *bhikkhus* was the tracing out of its boundaries.[14] This was done in a ceremony performed by the king, who ploughed a great circular furrow round the area. Boundary marks were then set up along the circle which had been ploughed, and so the territorial 'parish' of the *bhikkhus*' residence was permanently delineated. When that had been done a dwelling-house and a refectory were built, and a place was reserved for the planting of a cutting from the bodhi-tree which was to be brought from India. A place within the park had been already allocated for the eventual building of a *stupa*.

PROVISION FOR A BUDDHIST POPULACE

The decision to build a *stupa* was partly in acknowledgement of the now wide adherence of the people of Anuradhapura to the Buddhist system, and partly in order, so it is said, to provide for the *bhikkhus* themselves an appropriate focus for their devotion. We are told that at the end of the rainy season Mahinda raised the matter with the king: 'We have had no sight of the Buddha for a long time, O Lord of men. We live as men without a master. We have no way of paying our respect to the Buddha.' The king was puzzled by this: 'I thought you told me that the Buddha had entered *nibbana*.' 'Yes,' they replied, 'but vision of the relics is vision of the Conqueror.'[15] (This is perhaps a crude translation, but it helps to suggest the double sense of vision which seems to be implied in the text.) The king replied that they knew already of his intentions to build a *stupa*, and added, 'I will build the *stupa*; you must find out about the relics.'

It is evident from the style of the Pali chronicles that already popular ideas of miracles and marvels had made themselves at home in the Buddhist tradition. As S. Paranavitana has put it:

Mahinda and his companions transport themselves by air from Vedisagiri to Mihintale, gods are at hand to make smooth the path of the religious teachers, and impress the multitude with the efficiency of their doctrines. Earthquakes which do no harm to anyone vouch for the veracity of the prophecies

... At sermons preached on important occasions, the *Devas* in the congregation outnumber the humans. Elephants, without anyone's bidding, indicate to the king the exact spot on which sacred shrines are to be built.[16]

It should be noted that the marvels which are related are not in any special sense *religious* phenomena, that is, connected with god or gods. If the *devas* are mentioned, so also are earthquakes and elephants, and feats of inter-continental air travel, so we must regard the appearance of the gods as simply part of a general background derived from the popular world-view of the time. Paravitana points out that 'in spite of this legendary overlay, the main event, i.e. that Buddhism was accepted by the people and the ruler of Ceylon' is attested by epigraphical evidence.[17]

The manner in which sacred relics were brought from India to Ceylon is similarly described in the chronicles in terms of superhuman marvels: an air-trip to the Hima-layas to visit Sakka, the Lord of the gods; a parasol that bowed down of its own volition in the presence of the relics, and an elephant which did the same; a relic-urn which moved through space of its own accord, and more quaking of the earth in connection with these events. What most concerns us, however, is the fact that very early in this complex process by which ancient Ceylon became a Buddhist state there was the building of a *stupa*, and that this was apparently regarded as a necessity. A similar necessity for the proper functioning of the system (that is, presumably, the system known to function in Asho-kan India) was the importation from India of a bodhi- or bo-tree. But the most important aspect of the estab-lishing of the Buddhist system (i.e., the *Buddha-sasana* or discipline) was the coming into existence of an in-digenously produced *Sangha*. A remark attributed to Mahinda[18] makes this clear. When Tissa asked him whether the *Buddha-sasana* was now well established in the island, Mahinda replied that it was, but that it had not yet become firmly rooted. 'When will it become firmly rooted?' asked the king. Mahinda's reply was: 'When a son born in Ceylon of Ceylonese parents becomes a *bhikkhu* in Ceylon, studies the *Vinaya* in Ceylon, and recites it in Ceylon, then the roots of the *Sasana* are deep set.' The first two of these requirements had already been met; a son born in Ceylon of Ceylonese parents had become a *bhikkhu*, Maha-Arittha by name, and had studied the *Vinaya* in Ceylon. Arrangements were then made for a recital or teaching session of *Vinaya* to take place in the presence of the king. This clearly portrays the intimate relation which was conceived to exist between the life of the *Sangha*, which was ruled by the Vinaya, and the life of the state, which was ruled over by the king. It emphasizes, too, the national, indeed, in a sense, even nationalist, character of the *Buddha-sasana*; its full realization involved the existence also of a Buddhist national state.

The *stupa* having been built by the king for the relics which had been brought from India, and the bodhi-tree, brought from India by Ashoka's daughter Sankhamitra, having been planted, the essential ingredients for the Buddhist state after the Ashokan pattern were all present: a king who was a Buddhist disciple; an indigenous *Sangha*; and provision made in the form of a *stupa* and a bo-tree for popular devotion to be expressed by the mass of the people, a large number of whom were now Buddhist adherents or lay-disciples.

The extent to which this outline of events is authentic historically, cannot be seriously doubted. It is certainly very like the pattern of the Ashokan Buddhist state, as we have seen it through the evidence of the inscriptions of Ashoka. If it be argued that this is a projection back into third century BC Ceylon of the Buddhist pattern of the chroniclers' own time, that is, the fifth and six centuries AD, then it is all the more noteworthy, that in sixth-century Buddhist Ceylon the pattern so closely adhered to what it had been in Ashoka's India eight centuries before. However, the Pali chronicles of the fifth century AD, which tell how Ceylon became a Buddhist state in the third century BC, tell also of the other missions of Ashoka at that time – into the Himalayan region for example. This was not a region in which the Sinhalese had any particular interest, yet the Sinhalese chroniclers recorded the tradition which had come to them. It was pointed out by T. W. Rhys Davids that the historicity of this mission to the Himalayas had been clearly confirmed by archaeological evidence found at Sanchi.[19] This suggests that what the chroniclers recorded was based on sound historical tradition, so far as the essentials are concerned, although, as we have seen, allowance has to be made for the extent to which the popular world-view of the time has affected the details of the story, by way of exaggerations and miraculous embellishment.

MODERN REJECTION OF THE IDEA OF THE EARLY BUDDHIST STATE

A modern Sinhalese Buddhist, Dr Walpola Rahula, finds himself somewhat embarrassed by the story of Buddhism having been 'established' in Ceylon in the way in which it is related in the chronicles. 'The idea of the "establishment" of Buddhism in a given geographical unit with its implications is,' he says, 'quite foreign to the teaching of the Buddha ... nowhere had he given injunctions or instructions regarding a ritual or a particular method of "establishing" the *Sasana* in a country. Buddhism is purely a personal religion.'[20] Apart from the fact that it is difficult to understand how a system of philosophy which denies the validity of the concept of an individual person can be called 'a personal religion', a more important issue is raised when, in continuation of this line of thought, Dr Rahula says: 'The notion of establishing the *Sasana* or Buddhism as an institution in a particular country or place was perhaps first conceived by Ashoka himself', and adds that 'Ashoka was the first missionary king to send out missions for the conversion of other countries.'[21] Since

Ashoka was also, according to Dr Rahula, an 'organizer and psychologist', he thought up a suitable ceremonial which could be used to demonstrate to the ordinary people that the new 'religion' was now established among them.²²

Dr Rahula is by implication making two claims: first, that Buddhism had by Ashoka's time already been reduced from being a comprehensive, humanistic theory of existence, with an accompanying social and political philosophy, to being a spiritual cult, a purely 'personal religion', with no societal dimension at all; second, that Ashoka radically changed the character of Buddhism, in that he was the first person to conceive the idea of the Buddhist state, an idea which, in Rahula's view, is 'quite foreign to the teaching of the Buddha', and that it was this radically-changed Buddhism which Ceylon received. A great Ceylon Buddhist of the fourth century did not think so; Buddhaghosa records that the Buddhism of the city of Anuradhapura was as that of India at the time of the Buddha.²³ Since the first part of this book was devoted to showing that the idea of a Buddhist society co-terminous with the political state *is* implied in the discourses of the Buddha, there is no need to make any further comment on either of Dr Rahula's contentions. The significance of his view of Buddhism as 'purely a personal religion' is that it indicates the extent to which some modern Buddhists, in their desire to expound Buddhism in terms the West will understand, have tended to assimilate Buddhism to the other 'isms' which are lumped together under the general title of 'religions' and of these it is particularly Protestantism (known in Ceylon continuously since the coming of the Dutch in the middle of the seventeenth century) which seems to provide Rahula's model of what a religion should be. For, among the variety of Western religion, it is Protestantism (as seen in its characteristic form in the USA) which has been proud of its individualism over against all collectivism, of its dislike of constitutional links between church and state, of its encouragement of free enterprise over against ideas of corporate social responsibility, and its insistence that in the end all that matters is the destiny of the individual's indestructible soul, that is, either eternal salvation or eternal damnation. This certainly 'is purely a personal religion', and it is in these terms that some Buddhists in Ceylon, exposed at fairly close quarters to Protestant influences, have sought to interpret Buddhism. Buddhist history, in Ceylon and elsewhere, cannot fail to be a source of confusion and embarrassment to those who wish to see Buddhism in such purely 'personal' terms.

SUBSEQUENT HISTORY OF THE BUDDHIST STATE IN CEYLON

By the end of Mahinda's life, some forty-eight years after his arrival in the island, the pattern of the Ashokan Buddhist state had been faithfully reproduced in all its essentials: Buddhist king, *Sangha* and people; this was the pattern of society implied in the discourses of the Buddha, realized in the reign of Ashoka, and still accepted as the classical norm when the Ceylon chronicles were compiled eight or nine centuries later.

This pattern persisted throughout much of the succeeding centuries, with interruptions during periods of invasion and foreign rule by South Indian kings. But whenever and wherever a Sinhalese king ruled in Ceylon there was usually some kind of approximation to the classical pattern of the Buddhist state. The tradition was maintained through the centuries with varying degrees of stress and strain until the many dynasties of the Sinhalese kings came to an end in modern times, with the annexation and political control of the whole island by the British in 1815. Throughout the entire period from the time of Tissa, when Ceylon became a Buddhist state, until 1815, it was accepted that in the state of Ceylon only a Buddhist could by right be ruler of the country. Dr Rahula cites epigraphic evidence from the tenth century AD to the effect that 'the king of Ceylon had not only to be a Buddhist but also a Bodhisattva'.[24] We may note the occurrence of this belief in Burma, too. Rahula quotes a Sinhalese work which is even more explicit on the subject of the inalienable right of the Buddha over the island of Ceylon: 'This Island of Lanka [25] belongs to the Buddha himself; it is like a treasury filled with the Three Gems [26] ... Even if a non-Buddhist ruled Ceylon by force awhile, it is a particular power of the Buddha that his line will not be established.' [27] This concept of territorial proprietorship, which as Rahula shows, continues down to the nineteenth century, is striking evidence of the political dimension which was an accepted feature of Buddhism in its classical form. There is a clear parallel here with the concept of *dar-ul-Islam*, the territory which belongs to Allah, in the tradition of Islam, which also, as we noted in chapter 2, was in its original form a civilization before it was reduced to a religion. In the Buddhist case there is the additional point that, certainly by the tenth century, it was explicitly held that the *Sangha* conferred kingship, 'selecting princes for the throne, and supporting their favourites, even to the extent of violating the succession'.[28]

To attempt to compress, or even to comment on, the long history of the Buddhist state in Ceylon over a period of more than two thousand years, in the space at our disposal here, would be ludicrous. What can be done, with some profit perhaps, is to select a few characteristic 'moments' in that history. Some will be moments of prosperity, peace and honour; others will be moments of adversity, distress and shame. Both kinds are well represented in Ceylon's history.

The first half of the first century BC[29] in Ceylon was occupied by the reigns of three kings: *Duttha-gamini* (101–77 BC), *Saddha-tissa* (77–59 BC), and *Lanja-tissa* (59–50 BC). Each of these reigns presents a different facet of Buddhist civilization in Ceylon.

RECIPROCITY BETWEEN KING AND SANGHA

Duttha-gamini's reign commenced at a time of crisis for the state. The north of the island was occupied by Tamil invaders from South India. The Sinhalese Buddhist dynasty had withdrawn from Anuradhapura to a town called Mahagama in the region known as Rohana, in the south of Ceylon. After forty-four years of Tamil occupation of the northern part of the island, the young prince Duttha-gamini succeeded to the throne of the Sinhalese kingdom. He was deeply committed to the ideal of a restored Buddhist polity throughout Ceylon.

Even before his father's death, Duttha-gamini had begun to make preparations to march against the Tamil king, Elara; he had raised a large force from among the Sinhalese in the southern part of the island, and at the head of this force he now set out for Anuradhapura. Reaching the bank of the Great Ganga river of Ceylon, which formed the frontier between the Tamil-occupied north and the rest of the island, he said: 'I will go to the land on the further side of the Ganga in order that the *sasana* (of the Buddha) may be made bright.'[30] As a token of this intention and because the sight of them would be auspicious and give his men security, he took also five hundred *bhikkhus* with him. The chronicler emphasizes that Dutthagamini's campaign, which quickly began to be very successful, was not prompted by motives of personal aggrandizement or power, but had as its aim the restoration of Buddhist polity to the whole island: 'Not for the pleasure of having dominion do I make this effort, but always with the intention of establishing firmly the *sasana* of the Buddha.'[31]

Having defeated the Tamil king, and achieved what was necessary for the whole island to be once again a Buddhist state, Duttha-gamini reflected on the cost in human lives which this had necessitated and was overcome with remorse: 'he, looking back upon his glorious victory, great though it was, knew no joy, remembering that thereby was wrought the destruction of millions of beings.' [32] His reign from then onwards was marked by the kind of activity which showed his devotion to the Buddhist tradition. He undertook the building of a new *stupa*, and with it a great new college (*vihara*) for the *Sangha* which took three years to complete; he had a palatial nine-storeyed meeting hall built, in which the *Sangha* could hold the twice-monthly *uposattha*-ceremony [33] and which incorporated also a library and places for study and the discussion of problems. The pillars which supported this vast building can still be seen at Anuradhapura. But the most meritorious of his works, in the view of the chronicler, was the construction of the Great *Stupa*.[34] Whereas the story of the building of the new college, the Maricavatti, is told by the chronicler in twenty-six verses, and that of the building of the great meeting hall in forty-eight verses, the story of the preparations for, and the building of, the Great *Stupa*, the obtaining of relics, the making of the relic chamber and the enshrining of the relics, takes altogether 340 verses. The same scale of valuation seems to be reflected in the book of the king's meritorious deeds, which, we are told, was read out when the king was on his deathbed,[35] for the record of the amounts expended on these three works is given as being in the proportioin 19: 30: 1,020. This great memorial shrine was, in the words of Malalasekere, 'the most stupendous and the most venerated of those at Anuradhapura'.[36] Not only was it the largest and most splendid *stupa* to have been built in Ceylon, but it is said to have been the largest anywhere in the Buddhist world at that time.[37] A great deal of prominence is given by the chronicler to the fact that this undertaking of Duttha-gamini was carried out without any use of forced labour (the normal method of getting public work done in the ancient world) but rather by the employment of workmen who were paid fair wages. Various kinds of welfare services which Duttha-gamini provided for the people are also mentioned, including eighteen centres at which medical treatment and medicines were made available.[38] It is significant that in

the Ceylon tradition Duttha-gamini is connected with the
Buddha, not only as his disciple but also as his kinsman.
According to the Great Chronicle tradition he was a direct
descendant of Gotama's paternal uncle, Amitodana.[39]
Moreover it is foretold that from the Tushita heaven into
which Duttha-gamini entered at his death, as the proper
reward for his piety, he will eventually be reborn on earth
in the days of the next Buddha, Metteyya. The two will, in
fact, be sons of the same mother and father: 'The great
king Duttha-gamini, he who is worthy of the name of king,
will be the first disciple of the sublime Metteyya; the
king's father will be his [Metteyya's] father, and the king's
mother his [Metteyya's] mother. The younger brother Sad-
dhatissa will be his second disciple . . .'[40]

It was Saddha-tissa, the younger brother mentioned
here, who succeeded Duttha-gamini at his death. He, too,
is remembered in the Buddhist tradition of Ceylon as a
king who 'accomplished many works of merit'.[41] His reign
of eighteen years was one of peace; he inherited the
stable situation which his elder brother had brought about,
and the most notable aspect of his reign from a public
point of view appears to have been the steady programme
of *vihara*-building which he carried out. The close and
cordial relationship which existed between the king and
the *Sangha* during his reign is illustrated by a story found
in a fourteenth century work.[42] In this compilation in
Sinhalese of episodes from Indian and Ceylon Buddhist
history we are told that during Saddha-tissa's reign the
famous elder, named Buddharakkhita, delivered a discourse which lasted through the whole night. The king,
having arrived late, unannounced and unexpected, and
not wishing to cause a disturbance, remained standing outside the hall. The Ceylonese style of public hall, with its
open sides, makes it easy to hear from such a position, and
there he remained until the discourse ended, at dawn.
When the speaker learnt that the king had been so long
outside he said, 'You are king, sire, and not accustomed to
such discomfort. How was it possible for you to remain

standing outside throughout the night?' The king replied that he would willingly stand listening to such a discourse not one night, but many nights in succession. The two of them thereupon embarked on a discussion of the *Dhamma*, and so impressed was the king that he offered to resign his throne in favour of the other. The elder returned the compliment, with the significant words: 'Do thou, O King, rule the country on behalf of the *Dhamma*.' [43]

Whatever the authenticity of this story, its importance for our present concern lies in the evidence which it provides of a continuing tradition in Ceylon, from at least the time of the chroniclers of the fifth century to this Sinhalese source in the fourteenth century, a tradition that the kings of Ceylon are the agents of the Buddhist *Dhamma*, and that the great kings are those who maintain close and sensitive relationships with the *Sangha*.

Another incident from Saddha-tissa's reign shows that the role of the king in relation to the *Sangha* was not only that of the acceptance of moral guidance and the putting into effect of the requirements of the *Dhamma*, but also of reminding the members of the *Sangha* of the standards of conduct required of them as guardians and exponents of the *Dhamma*. According to the great commentator Buddhaghosa, writing in the fifth century, the easy conditions which the *Sangha* enjoyed during Saddha-tissa's reign, as a result of both his and Duttha-gamini's liberality, and the prosperity of the times, appear to have brought about a slackening of discipline among the *bhikkhus* of Anuradhapura. By way of reprimand, Saddha-tissa discontinued his alms to them, and gave the alms to the *bhikkhus* of Cetiyapabbata only. Thereupon the lay people asked what was the reason for this. The function of the lay people in cases of disagreement between king and *Sangha* on more than one occasion in Ceylon Buddhist history appears to have been to lend their support to whichever side could show itself to be in the right. On this occasion, by way of reply, the king the next day resumed his almsgiving to the *bhikkhus* of Anuradhapura, and now that the people's attention had been drawn to the matter, he was able to justify his temporary suspension of alms 'by pointing out to the people the unsatisfactory manner in which the *bhikkhus* behaved in accepting the food',[44] that is, in a greedy and disorderly manner.[45]

Duttha-gamini's attitude towards the *Sangha* had been one of extreme respect and veneration; it was that of a king who had made strenuous efforts and ventured much on behalf of the Buddhist tradition, and who reverenced above all those who were the guardians of that tradition. Saddha-tissa also had shown a high respect for the *Sangha*, as we have seen, but this was for the *Sangha* at its best, personified in the wisdom and eloquence of Buddharak-kita. To the *Sangha* at considerably less than its best he was prepared to show his disapproval, to the extent of withdrawing his economic support of its unworthy members. Both these kings, in their attitudes to the *Sangha*, are representative of many others in the history of Ceylon since their time. There is, however, yet another type of relationship, and that is represented by Lanja-Tissa.

THE SANGHA, THE STATE AND THE PEOPLE

At the death of Saddha-tissa the chief ministers of state and the whole assembly of the *bhikkhus* of the Thuparama came together to discuss the question of the succession. For reasons which we are not told, they decided to consecrate Saddha-tissa's second son, Thulatthana, as king, rather than his first son, Lanja-tissa. It has been suggested that Thulatthana was known to be more likely to work in harmony with the *Sangha* in the maintenance of the Buddhist state, or, to put it in other words, that those responsible were 'choosing the better man'.[46] With the support of the *Sangha*, therefore, Thulatthana was consecrated king. When Lanja-tissa, who was in the south of Ceylon, heard of it he travelled to Anuradhapura and 'having seized'[47] (which probably means 'having killed') his brother Thulatthana, he took command of the state himself. For the next three years relations between Lanja-tissa and the *Sangha* were very strained. He showed them disrespect, we are told, and neglected them,[48] thinking to himself, 'They took no notice of seniority.'[49] The chronicler appears to consider that Lanja-tissa was in the wrong, however, since he goes on to tell us that after three years a reconciliation was effected, and Lanja-tissa made atonement, or, literally 'imposed a punishment on himself'[50] by devoting a large amount of money to build additional embellishments to the various shrines at Anuradhapura, spending 300,000 pieces of silver here, another 100,000 there, and so on, and distributing new sets of clothing to 60,000 *bhikkhus*. This 'atonement' suggests that he was regarded as the guilty party, and therefore, by implication, that the action of the chief ministers and the *Sangha* in naming and consecrating Thulatthana as king had been justified. This view of a fifth or sixth century Buddhist chronicler conflicts with those modern writers who, starting from the presupposition that *bhikkhus* are and always have been a-political, take the view that the members of the Sangha were in the wrong in their 'intervention in political matters',[51] as it is described by one; or their 'unfortunate intervention in politics in an attempt to place their favourite on the throne in violation of the law of succession', as an earlier modern writer had put it.[52] It is hardly justifiable to suggest, as another does,[53] that this 'interest in the affairs of state' on the part of the Buddhist *Sangha* was a new thing in the first century BC, unless, of course, the Buddha is not to be reckoned a Buddhist. The fifth century chronicler has the advantage of writing from within what was as yet an unimpaired Buddhist civilization, rather than from a Buddhist civilization mutilated by foreign political domination, and infected by alien notions that Buddhism is, like Protestantism, a 'religion', and that, therefore, it is improper for it to have a national, political and social dimension.

The chronicles from which most of our information

concerning the Buddhist history of Ceylon is derived were the work of *bhikkhus*. The compilers were *bhikkhus* and the sources which they used had also been produced by *bhikkhus*. That members of the Buddhist Order should in one generation after another devote so much of their time to producing what are, in effect, dynastic histories, is in itself a significant fact. The major characters throughout these chronicles are the kings: first Ashoka and then, in the present case, the kings of Ceylon, and in the case of other chronicles the kings of Burma [54] and of Thailand.[55] The royal activities in which the chroniclers are most interested are those undertaken on behalf of the Buddhist Order in particular, and also on behalf of the people generally. In Wilhelm Geiger's words, the chroniclers tell us 'of the *viharas* built by the king, of the repairs he had undertaken on the more ancient buildings, of his bounty to the needy, the poor and the sick, and above all to [the Sangha]'.[56] Those who maintain that political and economic affairs lie outside the range of interest of Buddhism have a difficult task in explaining the very great interest shown by generations of Buddhist chroniclers in affairs of state and the condition of the people.

Nowhere is this interest shown more clearly than in the continuation of the Great Chronicle, which although it is known as the 'Little' Chronicle (*Culavamsa*) in fact adds a further sixty-four chapters to the thirty-six contained in the Great Chronicle. These additional chapters continue the history of the Buddhist state in Ceylon from the end of King Mahasena's reign, in 362 AD, to the coming of the British and the end of the kingdom in Ceylon in 1815. This is the work of several chroniclers, each of whom extended the story to his own time, in the thirteenth, the eighteenth, and the nineteenth centuries respectively.

The condition of the people suffered badly, for example, from the civil war which lasted for the greater part of the seventh century. In sixty-five years there were fourteen changes of king. These dynastic struggles, although fought 'with mainly mercenary troops in a limited area round the capital',[57] nevertheless had a disastrous effect on the welfare of the country. Commenting on the struggles of the second quarter of the century the chronicler tells us that 'each [of the two kings] drove out the other in turn. But the whole people, suffering under the wars of these two kings, fell into great misery and lost money and field produce.'[58] Another equally offending aspect of these kings' activities was their contemptuous and vandalistic attitude towards the symbols of the Buddhist *sasana*. One of them seized everything of value that he could find in the three great *viharas* of the Buddhist Order in the capital, and 'broke in pieces the golden images and took the gold for himself and plundered all the golden wreaths and other offerings'. At another shrine 'he took away the golden crowning ornament on the temple and smashed the umbrella on the *cetiya* (*stupa*) which was studded with costly precious stones.'[59]

Another feature of the disturbed political situation was, as B. J. Perera points out, that kings thus engaged in more or less continuous local conflict could not give their attention to the proper administration of the country's affairs, and these suffered in consequence.[60] Moreover, needing all the support they could possibly get from the nobility or from dignitaries and high officials of the state, the feuding kings were not in any position to risk alienating them by taking too careful an interest in the administration. Thus, one of the proper functions of a good Buddhist king was neglected; the nobility increased their power, and epigraphic evidence bears eloquent testimony 'to the travails of the masses under the officialdom of these days'.[61] It is important to notice that the chroniclers are concerned not only with the *Sangha*, and the relationship of kings with the *Sangha*, but also with the general condition of the citizens of the state, and their treatment at the king's hands, both in matters relating to economic and general welfare, and in those things which concerned the maintenance and proper observance of the Buddhist tradition, the *sasana*.

THE REIGN OF PARAKKAMA BAHU I

Of the *Culavamsa* as a whole, approximately a third is
devoted to one king, Parakkama Bahu I, whose reign
covered the period 1153–86 AD. Just as in the first and
second parts of the *Mahavamsa* it is Devanam-piya Tissa
and Duttha-gamini who stand out as the central figures, to
be given epic treatment, in the continuation, the *Culavamsa*, it is undoubtedly Parakkama Bahu who receives
this treatment. 'There is no name in the annals of Sinhalese history,' writes Dr Malalasekere, 'which commands
the veneration of the people in such measure as that of this
prince of the "mighty arm", Parakkama Bahu, since he
united in his person the piety of Devanam-piya Tissa and
the chivalry of Duttha-gamini.' [62]

A good deal of change had occurred in the Buddhist
state of Ceylon, however, between their reigns and his.
There had been changes in the nature of Buddhism, both
within the *Sangha* itself, and in the popular practices
which had come to be associated with Buddhism among
the people as a whole, and there had been considerable
social change, mostly in the direction of a decline in the
general welfare, both of the nobility and of the poorer
people. At the outset of his reign as king of Ceylon, from
his new capital at Polonnaruva, Parakkama Bahu, we are
told, thought thus:

By those kings of old who turned aside from the trouble of
furthering the laity and the Order . . . has this people aforetime
been grievously harassed. May it henceforth be happy and may
the Order of the great Sage – long sullied by admixture with a
hundred false doctrines, rent assunder by the schism of the
three fraternities and flooded with numerous unscrupulous
bhikkhus whose sole task is the filling of their bellies – that
Order which though five thousand years have not yet passed is
in a state of decay, once more attain stability. Of those people
of noble birth who here and there have been ruined, I would
fain by placing them again in their rightful position, become
the protector in accordance with tradition. Those in search of

help I would fain support by letting like a cloud overspreading the four quarters of the earth a rich rain of gifts pour continually down upon them.[63]

His intention is seen to be three-fold: first, to reform and purify the Order, which had been affected by what today would be called revisionist doctrines, and purge its ranks of imposters and idlers; second, to restore to their proper status the dignitaries of the land; and third, to make provision for the sick and the needy. The chronicle then describes how all this was carried out, and is confirmed by epigraphical evidence.[64]

After describing the achievements of this great reign in detail for some six chapters, or 987 verses, the chronicler brings his account of the reign to a close with the words,

Thus Parakkama Bahu, the Ruler of men, by whom were performed divers and numerous kinds of meritorious works, who continually found the highest satisfaction in the teaching of the Master [the Buddha], who was endowed with extraordinary energy and discernment, carried on the government for thirty-three years.[65]

A great deal of attention is devoted by the chronicler to describing Parakkama Bahu's policy and practice because it was an outstanding example of the Buddhist ideal, although by no means the only example. Other kings of Ceylon, before and after him, approximated to this same ideal. Generous provision for the *Sangha*, and support for them in the study, preservation and public teaching of the Buddhist tradition was a primary duty of the kings of Ceylon. The building and equipping of shrines, in order to encourage the practices of meditation and the honouring of the Buddha, was another equally characteristic feature. Vigorous measures for improving the material condition of the people were also an important part of the Buddhist ruler's proper exercise of his power. The ensuring of an adequate food supply for a growing population required large irrigation works, and these were frequently undertaken by the Sinhalese kings. Dhatusena, for example, is remembered for the large reservoir which he had built, covering an area of ten square miles, whose waters were conveyed to the dry areas where they were needed by a canal fifty-four miles long. Parakkama Bahu was the author of a scheme to provide island-wide irrigation. 'In the realm that is subject to me,' he said,

there are, apart from many strips of country where the harvest flourishes mainly by rain water, but few fields which are dependent on rivers with permanent flow, or on great reservoirs. Also, by many mountains, by thick jungle, and by widespread swamps my kingdom is much straitened. Truly in such a country not even a little water that comes from the rain must flow into the ocean without being made useful to man.

According to the chronicles he made good the damage which time and neglect had done to the irrigation works constructed by earlier kings, and in addition carried out new construction projects which far exceeded the scope of anything which had been done previously.[66]

Another characteristic feature of Sinhalese Buddhist civilization was the attention which was given to establishing and maintaining centres for the treatment of the sick. 'This was the most highly advanced branch of the social services provided for the people by the state,' observes C. W. Nicholas.

The Chronicles often record additional endowments to the national medical service by several kings, and these statements are fully corroborated by the inscriptions. High dignitaries of state also founded or endowed hospitals. There were, in addition to general hospitals, homes for cripples, the blind and the incurable. Lying-in homes for women were established in several localities. Sick animals were also cared for.[67]

It is important to recognize the extent to which all this was associated with adherence to Buddhist values. The kings who were most active in promoting the welfare of their people were also most prominently concerned with the state of the *Sangha*, and with the encouragement of Buddhist morality throughout the kingdom through enhancement of Buddhist tradition, provision for teaching, and so on. The pattern of Sinhalese civilization agrees remarkably closely with that of Ashokan India, and both of them with the ideal structure of society which is adumbrated in the discourses of the Buddha.

The extent to which Buddhist tradition permeated the life of the people of Ceylon would have varied from place to place, and from one reign to another. In general it can be said that in Ceylon there was a gradual and steady growth throughout the centuries in the extent and the depth of permeation of popular religious cults and beliefs by Buddhist ideas and values, a process which is still at work today. The understanding of this process requires some analysis of the relations between Buddhism and popular religion, and to this subject we shall turn in the final chapter.

One further point which must be mentioned here, however, is the practice which had developed in Ceylon of donating land to monasteries. The land so donated provided the monastery with a regular source of food. The tenants of the land also provided services of various kinds for the monastery. This practice seems to have been established at least as early as the sixth century AD, for it is admitted in the Ceylon Chronicles that King Aggabodhi I (568–601) made grants of land and monastery-servants to one *Vihara*, and granted villages to others.[68] This, as Paranavitana points out 'was an innovation which went against the ideals of early Buddhism'.[69] The *Sangha* came to accept such grants as safeguards, ensuring a continuing economic basis for its life in hard times, such as they had in fact experienced under hostile kings, when the continued existence of the *Sangha*, and with it of the *Buddhasasana*, seemed to be threatened. 'The members of the *Sangha*, however, in order to satisfy their conscience, were expected to refuse when an offer of land grant was made, but to be silent when it was said that the grant was made to the *stupa* [the pagoda]'.[70]

By the time the capital city was shifted from Anuradhapura to Polonnaruva in the eleventh century AD, the 'biggest landowners were the monasteries, which owned far greater extents of fields, singly and in the aggregate, than any other private owners'.[71] The produce of the land belonged to the monasteries; some of the villagers who worked on the land received a share of this for their own use; others were tenants of cultivable land in return for the services they performed for the monastery.

There are numerous references to such grants of lands in the Ceylon chronicles; the practice of making grants is confirmed by the evidence of inscriptions, some dating from as early as the first century BC.[72] The practice was not confined to Ceylon, however; grants of land to Buddhist monasteries in India are well attested by inscriptional evidence. The reason given by the donor was almost always the enhancement of his own store of merit.[73] In Ceylon, since land belonging to monasteries was exempt from royal taxation, the permission of the king was required before a would-be donor was allowed to make the transaction. The form of petition which had to be submitted ran as follows: 'I am desirous of making this present to the *vihara* for my good, and I pray Your Majesty will permit me, as it is equally for your good.'[74] Acceptance of the gift by the *Sangha*, however, as we have seen, implied a tacit recognition of the economic vulnerability of the *Sangha* under the other, older arrangement whereby the *bhikkhus* depended on the generosity of lay people to supply their needs day by day. Under this arrangement, the king, as the leading layman, would usually be one of the most generous donors, and normally there was no real threat to the *Sangha*'s livelihood. But experience had shown that in troubled times, when the peace of the state was seriously disturbed, the very existence of the *Sangha* could be in danger. Seen from that point of view, the receiving of grants of land by the *Sangha* was wise and provident, but in times of prosperity the possession of such resources of wealth could become a source of corruption and a shifting away from the original perspective. In particular this seems to have happened in the case of some of the great monastic centres which developed in India, and can be seen as one contributory cause of the decline of the *Sangha* and, therefore, eventually of the virtual disappearance of Buddhist civilization from India. There were, however, other, more important reasons for the relatively short period that Buddhist civilization lasted in the land of its origin; the factors which brought it to an end had already been operating for many centuries. The rise of great and wealthy monastic schools (Nalanda, for example) only emphasized the retreat from the local 'parish' monasteries which was already far advanced in most parts of India, so successfully had the opponents of Buddhism done their work.

FORCES HOSTILE TO THE BUDDHIST STATE

Buddhist civilization was short-lived in India. The reason for this was that its two principal characteristics were opposed by two perenially powerful factors in the Indian situation. These two characteristics were Buddhism's humanistic stance, and its political–ethical implications. The first of these ran counter to the overwhelmingly theistic trend of the time, which found expression in a multiplicity of devotional cults, and succeeded in converting the *Buddha-sasana* into yet another of these. The second of Buddhism's major characteristics inevitably aroused the opposition of the priestly brahman class, who had their own theory of the state, one which honoured brahmans and made them indispensable, a role which Buddhist teaching certainly did not ascribe to them. Brahmanical opposition prevented any serious expansion and development of the Buddhist state in India after the death of Ashoka. The possibility which would appear to have been open to Buddhism in those circumstances was to return to what it had been before Ashoka, the blueprint of a civilization, an ideology waiting to be embodied once again in a social and political reality. But the nature of the Indian situation was such that even this dénouement was rendered impossible. Not only did Buddhism cease to be a civilization after Ashoka (apart from one or two temporary local or regional exceptions); it suffered also a transformation of its original humanistic character: it became a theistic religion.

We have already noted the rise in India, by the time of Ashoka, of a cult of Buddha as *bhagava* or lord, a development which was probably inevitable once Buddhism had been divested of political and public relevance. If any explanation for the remarkable intensity of the *bhakti* or devotional mood in ancient and medieval India is to be offered, the most plausible is that where men are totally cut off from participation in political processes, and from having any kind of responsibility, however small, for the course of mundane events, they are likely to find compensation in devoting themselves with intensified zeal to the affairs of a supramundane realm. This is a case which has been argued elsewhere by Guy Swanson, for example, in his book *The Birth of the Gods*. In Hindu India the mass of men were cut off from effective participation or the possibility of it; the difference between the Buddhist state and the brahmanical state is that, in the former, ordinary men of any level of society are able to enter the *Sangha* and thus become members of a body which has a recognized status and a real advisory and even admonitory role in relation to the political ruler. In a Buddhist state and society every man is a potential member of the *Sangha*. In a brahmanical state, however, such options are not open to the majority of ordinary men, only to the small élite of brahmans who act as ministers and advisers. No man has the option of becoming a brahman; only he is a brahman who is born to such a station. It is noteworthy that India has been of all countries of the world the most religious, if this is judged by the number and variety of deities which are worshipped, the bizarre extravagances which are associated with the devotion offered to them, and the widespread public acceptance of such ideas and practices. It is noteworthy also that India has in the past been renowned for her caste system – a system which irrevocably allotted a man his place in the social structure, at the head of which (in its traditional form) was a hereditary priesthood and an absolute monarch. The only word for 'government' in Hindu India was *Raj*, that is, king. Manuals of statecraft have been numerous in the course of Indian history, and they have been the work of brahmans. Visvamitra says that whatever act, on being done, is approved by the Aryans versed in the canon is law, and what they blame is held to be its opposite.[1] Politics in classical India, as represented by the great work of Kautilya (the brahman minister of state) and as practised by Indian kings and their hard-hearted advisers, writes U. N. Ghoshal, 'is based upon a creed of gross materialism, heartless cruelty and base superstition'.[2] It was partly for that reason, because of Indian experience of the antagonism between politics and ethics, that the early Buddhists sought to set forth a new relationship between the two, and worked for the establishment of a Buddhist state. But the political power of the brahman and the 'idiocy' (that is, the self-contained nature) of village life, which even now is still the life lived by 80 per cent of India's people, have supplemented and aided each other. It is difficult to resist the conclusion that the two together have not some close connection with the extreme and intense theistic devotion which also has characterized Indian life through the centuries.

THE RISE OF THEISTIC BUDDHISM OR MAHAYANA

We return to the point, therefore, that when its brahman enemies had brought to an end its one magnificent demonstration of how politics and ethics may be brought into harmony in the Buddhist state, it was virtually inevitable that in the Indian situation Buddhism should in large part be transmogrified into a theistic devotional cult. This change was expressed before very long in a material form, in the representation of the Buddha, the lord of the cult, in iconographical form, for the purposes of devotional ritual (see chapter 9, p. 205). The accompanying *ideological* consequence of the *bhakti* mood in India was the emergence of a conception of the Buddha as divine. It has been suggested that 'the raising of the Buddha to divine status in the Mahayana creed parallels the Roman deification of the Emperor in the same way that the aspiration to a creed promising salvation may be discerned in later Buddhism,

Roman literature of the Imperial period, and in Christianity.'[3] Certainly the material expression of this was, at first, in terms which were borrowed from Graeco-Roman culture. The earliest known *Buddha-rupas*, or Buddha 'images', as they are called in the West, which come from Gandhara, to the north-west of India, were adaptations of the concepts and techniques of Graeco-Roman sculptors, just as were the early representations of Christ in Christian art. 'It is not surprising,' writes B. Rowland, 'in the earliest Gandhara Buddhas to find Shakyamuni with the head of a Greek Apollo and arrayed in the *pallium* or toga, carved in deep-ridged folds suggesting the Roman statues of the period of Augustus.'[4] Later on the specifically Indian form of *Buddha-rupa* was produced, showing the Buddha seated, with crossed legs, in the characteristic *asana* or posture of the yogin. There were ancient antecedents in India for this kind of iconography; for yogic figures seated in this posture are found in the art of the Indus Valley civilization of the second millenium BC. In the still later stages of the development of the *Buddha-rupa* in India conventional devices were introduced in order to represent the supernatural quality and powers which had by then become essential features of the Mahayana conception of the Buddha. Together with such representations of the eternal, divine Buddha, there developed also an iconographical tradition of Bodhisattva-figures. In Mahayana doctrine the Bodhisattva was a being who had advanced, through many existences, to the penultimate stage where he was now on the threshold of Buddha-hood, and who had acquired great spiritual power, by means of which he was able to help other, lesser beings in their progress towards the ultimate goal. He, or more properly they, for a feature of the Bodhisattva idea in Mahayana Buddhist tradition is that there are many of them, were thus credited with 'saving' power, and were called on, in faith, by their pious devotees. Functionally they were indistinguishable from the many gods of Hindu India, and indeed some of them owed the characteristics attributed to them in the elaborate mythology which was woven around each of them, to Indian and Iranian folk-lore.

It will be seen that the emergence of the Bodhisattva-yana, or Mahayana school, was part of the general tendency present in all Buddhist schools to allow an open frontier so far as external relations with folk-culture were concerned. In the Theravadin tradition this open frontier was allowed in the interests of the *Sangha*'s expansion of its influence into cultural areas which were not yet permeated with Buddhist values. Such elements of folk culture which were thus brought within the realm of popular Buddhist practice were made subordinate to the Buddha and his *Dhamma*. The difference between the Theravada and the Mahayana schools was thus, to a large degree, in practice, a matter of different policies. More precisely, they differed on the question of how closely the *Sangha* should adhere to the original perspective, expressed in the *Vinaya* and the *Dhamma*, the Discipline and the Doctrine, which they had inherited. In the view of the matter which is being presented here it is suggested that the Theravadins were more effective in retaining the original perspective of a philosophy of human existence which had clear implications in the realm of government and social administration, while the Mahayana schools succeeded in transforming Buddhism into a mystical philosophy, another of the numerous varieties of Indian gnosticism, a system of belief in heavenly saviours and an ultimately unreal earth, of salvation by divine grace, through faith; in short, a theistic religion.

CONTRASTING FEATURES AND FORTUNES OF
MAHAYANA AND THERAVADA

Of the many factors which aided the growth of the Mahayana schools in India, two are outstanding and of particular relevance here. One was the greater influx into the Buddhist *Sangha* of men of brahmanical birth and up-

bringing, as a consequence of the royal approval of Buddhism in the Ashokan state. The other was that in the
aftermath of the Ashokan Buddhist state, and the resur-
gence of brahmanical state polity, it might well have
seemed that there was little prospect of a revived Buddhist
state of the Ashokan kind, and that the form of Buddhism
for the future was, therefore, the Mahayana.

In the event, it has been the Theravada form, committed to the concept of a Buddhist national and international structure, which has proved the more durable of
the two in South and South-East Asia. In the last resort
it was because the Theravadin *Sangha* retained its belief
in the value of a *socially-structured* Buddhism that it has
survived. The Mahayana schools, pre-occupied as they
were with metaphysical and mythological questions, were
largely indifferent to matters of social structure. Even the
social structure of the Buddhist community itself, which
was provided for in the *Vinaya*, was a matter of small
moment to those whose attention was fully engaged in
expounding the *voidness* of all concepts and constructs
whatsoever. The notion of '*bhikkhu-hood*', of becoming a
member of the institutional Order, is for the Mahayanist
not essential; it is at the most only an aid, advisable for
some, perhaps, but not necessary for all.[5] For those Mahayanists who do enter the Order, the *Vinaya* will be of some
interest, and indeed some Mahayanists have achieved
reputations as scholars of the *Vinaya*. But, in general, as
S. Dutt has observed 'the preservation by different sects of
the *Vinaya* rules in their respective canons does not mean
that the rules in their actual bearing on *Sangha* life or, in
other words, in the practical operative aspect, were taken
by all sects in the same way as by the Theravadin.'[6] It is
where the Theravada prevails today, in Ceylon, Burma,
Thailand, Laos and Cambodia, that the *Sangha* and the
Vinaya, as embodying its classical constitution, are regarded as basic and indispensable to the existence of Buddhism. It will be seen that the difference between the Theravada and the Mahayana is ultimately a difference about

Buddhism itself – whether, as in the tradition of the Theravada countries, it is to be regarded as a way of life and a culture, nourishing a civilization by means of which certain distinctive values are given political, social and economic expression in the life of the people; or whether it is to be regarded as a purely metaphysical or theosophical system.

The rivalry between these two points of view was not unknown in Ceylon, and it was with such schism that King Parakkama Bahu was concerned. But in Ceylon it was the Theravadin tradition which prevailed and which has endured. In India, however, the outcome was different. One of the areas where the Mahayana had met with most success was in the north and north-west of India. From the evidence provided by the Chinese pilgrim, Hsuan Tsang, it appears that even by the seventh century AD the scene in much of this area was one of desolation and ruin so far as Buddhism was concerned. In Gandhara over a thousand monasteries and most of the *stupas* were crumbling into ruins and there were few Buddhists left. Where *bhikkhus* were to be found, in Bolor for example, they were ignorant men, not observing the rules of the Order, and careless of their moral conduct.[7] In Kashmir, where both Hinayana and Mahayana existed side by side, the pilgrim found that conditions were better and that there were more than a hundred *viharas* in use, housing over 5,000 *bhikkhus*. The king favoured Buddhism, supported the *Sangha*, and received the pilgrim with great respect. Hsuan Tsang found a number of centres of thriving Buddhist learning and discipline in Kashmir and spent altogether two years there. Elsewhere, however, in the Punjab, the scene was largely one of desolate monasteries and few monks. In contrast, there were many temples to the gods of Hindu religion. What had happened here seems to have been repeated in most of the other areas of India where once Buddhism had existed in its classical form, that is, where the *Buddha*, the *Dhamma* and the *Sangha* had been recognized as its indispensable elements, providing its definitive form. When, in the development of Mahayana ideas and practices, one of these elements, the *Sangha*, was neglected or abandoned, Buddhism sooner or later ran into the shifting sands of Indian polytheism and was lost.

A question which may be raised at this point is why the Buddhist *Sangha* in India did not heed the warning which was provided by the fate of the *sasana* in areas which had once been strongly Buddhist, particularly the north-west and the south, but where, by the seventh century it was in decline or ruin. The disappearance of Buddhism from India did not happen in a day; it was so long-drawn-out a process that it might be thought that someone could have perceived the reasons for what was happening, and halted or reversed the process.

The Theravada school in India would appear to have been the obvious agency. It cannot be assumed that the Theravadins failed to see the danger. The very fact that the Theravadin tradition was maintained is evidence that there were those who were convinced that in the interests of the *Dhamma* this was the form of Buddhism to which loyalty should be given. And once or twice in the later centuries of Buddhist history in India – that is, between the seventh and twelfth centuries – the classical pattern, the Buddhist state, ruled by a king sympathetic to the aims and attitudes of Buddhism, did emerge. But in India the Theravadins were, as we have seen, at a particularly severe disadvantage. Since the form of Buddhism which they espoused presupposed a Buddhist ordering of society, it was inevitable that their programme and policy continued to be the special target for brahmanical attack. It has recently been argued by Lalmoni Joshi that just as brahman hostility undermined the Ashokan Buddhist state, so brahman hostility to Buddhism was more potent a cause of Buddhism's decline and final disappearance from India than the attacks of the Muslim Turks in the twelfth and thirteenth centuries. He argues that constant brahmanical hostility towards Buddhism succeeded in loosening Buddhism's hold on the Indian people even in areas where it had managed to retain some place, and that the anti-Buddhist propaganda in brahmanical literature was not a mere 'war of the pen' but was periodically accompanied by social boycott and royal edicts against those who violated the 'divinely ordained' scheme of *Caturvarnya* [the brahmanical four-class system] and forceful confiscation of landed property of Buddhist establishments by brahmanical kings.[8]

If this is so, we have at least two major reasons for the eventual final disappearance of Buddhism from India. One was the continuing hostility of the brahmans towards what they recognized had been and was a threat to their theory of the state and of society (a hostility which would be felt more keenly by the Theravadins, whose conception of Buddhism was in social-structural terms). The other was the self-weakening effect which was produced within Buddhism by the Mahayana school, which had more in common with brahmanical philosophy and was nourished by brahmanical learning. The essential social dimension of Buddhism was lost sight of in the excessively metaphysical preoccupation of the Mahayana school, and their contempt for what they held to be the unimaginativeness of the Theravadins who, in their view, were unnecessarily preoccupied with the regulations and the discipline of the *Sangha*, and with a form of practice in which the primary emphasis lay so unimaginatively on the simple pursuit of morality.

This is certainly the view of the matter which is suggested by the later history of Buddhism in Bengal. For some fifteen centuries altogether Bengal was a land in which the *Sasana* was alive and respected.[9] It was a largely Buddhist area when the Chinese pilgrim, Fa-hsien, visited it in the fifth century AD. Two centuries or so later, the Chinese pilgrim, Hsuan Tsang, visited various regions of Bengal and he too described the many temples and monasteries he found, although he seems to have been aware also of the beginnings of decay in some places. It appears that by this time the non-Buddhist shrines, the *devalayas*, were more numerous than were the Buddhist, and that the trend was in that direction. Even when, a century or so later, Buddhism was clearly in decline in other parts of India, there was a period of new development in Bengal under the Pala kings from the eighth century onwards. At least three great Buddhist centres of learning are known to have existed in Bengal during that period: Vikrama-sila, on the bank of the Ganges in central Bengal, Soma-pur, in the same area, and Jagaddala, in the Bogra district (now Bangladesh). From the description given by other Chinese pilgrims, and from archaeological discoveries, it appears that these were vast, elaborate complexes of magnificent buildings, each at the height of its prosperity providing places for well over a thousand monks, possibly many more. Some of the *bhikkhus* who at that time lived in the monasteries of Bengal adhered to the Mahayana, but there were many who were Theravadins.

However, certain aspects of the development of these great centres may also help to explain the subsequent disappearance of Buddhism from most of Bengal. One feature of the Buddhism which found its focus principally in these *mahavidyalayas* has been described in caustic terms by the Indian historian, D. D. Kosambi.

Clearly, this was nowhere near the Buddhism preached by the Founder in sixth-century BC Magadha. There still existed ascetic monks who travelled barefoot, slept in the open, begged their way on leavings of food, and preached to the villagers or forest savages in country idiom, but their status and numbers diminished steadily. The monk's prescribed garment of discarded rags pieced together had been replaced by elegant robes of fine cotton, excellent wool or imported silk dyed in the costliest saffron. One feels that the great Teacher ... would have been laughed out of the exquisite and magnificent establishments run in his name ...[10]

The tradition of learning at these centres was predominantly, though not exclusively, that of the Mahayana philosophers. Some of these Bengal centres of Buddhism

fostered the later development of Madhyamika and Yoga-
cara doctrine which moved in the direction of the Vajra-
yana or Tantra. In their excessive preoccupation with
metaphysical problems, the Mahayanists seem to have
lapsed into an attitude to matters of *Vinaya* discipline
which can only be described as somewhat more than
liberal. It is not surprising, therefore, that lay adherents,
the people of the villages, finding that the matters with
which the Mahayana philosophers were preoccupied were
far beyond their comprehension, turned their attention
more and more to ideas and practices which were at best
only marginal so far as the central doctrines of the Buddha
were concerned. They became absorbed in cults of female
deities, introduced in the first instance as female Bodhisattvas. These cults were directed towards the goal of
self-fulfilment and incorporated a variety of material derived from the folk-culture of Bengal. It was from these
that there then developed, as Sushil Kumar De observes,
'all the coarsening features of decadent Tantra, in both its
Hindu and Buddhist guises', and which 'with their mystic
exaltation of the female principle in the universe, and
their emphasis upon the religious value of sexual passion
and sexual use of women formed an undesirable legacy of
a great system'.[11] At a later stage these Buddhist folk-
deities were to be absorbed into the popular Vaishnavism
and Shaivism of Bengal under such names as Manasa, the
snake goddess, and Chandi the forest-goddess, who came
to be thought of as the spouse of the god Shiva. It was in
Vaishnavism that certain elements of Buddhism lived on
in Bengal, albeit considerably modified: for example, in
the democratic and anti-caste mood of Vaishnavism, its
strongly vegetarian emphasis, and its opposition to violence. Even the Buddha was afforded a place in Vaishnavism as *Buddha-dev*, one of the incarnations of Vishnu
and one of the many deities in the Hindu pantheon; pictures representing him so are frequently found adorning
the walls of Bengali houses today. But Vaishnavism in

Bengal can hardly be regarded as a successor to Buddhism in certain other of its aspects. J. C. Ghosh says of it that

... Vaishnavism was one of the main influences responsible for the intellectual black-out, and the emasculation of national life, in pre-British Bengal. This was due to its over-emotional nature, to the almost exclusive attention it paid to the life of love (*prem*) and devotion (*bhakti*) in preference to the life of thought (*jnana*) and action (*karma*). In its craving for union with a personal god it lived entirely absorbed in the emotion of love, and entirely preoccupied with how to intensify that emotion to the utmost. With its elaborately designed cult of love, and its frenzied mass singing (*kirttan*) and dancing, it induced those states of mystical ecstasy and trance (*bhav-dasa*) in which the intellect is blotted out and the powers of action are paralyzed.[12]

THE CRUCIAL ROLE OF THE SANGHA AND ITS DISCIPLINE

In addition to the hostility of the brahmans, two further aspects of the later history of Buddhism in Bengal now suggest themselves as possible reasons for its decline and disappearance: (1) what Kosambi calls the 'corrupting influence of wealth' in the great monasteries, which eventually dominated the scene so that the smaller local monasteries withered away; and (2) the excessively intellectual preoccupation of the Mahayana monks which resulted in the neglect of the basic elements of the *Buddha-sasana* at the level of the ordinary people and left the field entirely open to the invasion of popular Buddhism by luxuriant folk-cults.

It is important, however, to notice that it is not the attitude of tolerance towards popular cults and beliefs which, by itself, can be held responsible for the decline of Buddhism. The crucial factor in the survival or disappearance of a Buddhist culture embodying distinctively Buddhist values seems to have been the *Sangha*. It was argued in chapter 8 that the distinguishing characteristic of Buddhist civilization is the triangular relationship between *Sangha*, king and people. The optimum conditions for the maintenance of a flourishing Buddhist civilization are when all three are harmoniously related and functioning according to the classical pattern of the Ashokan state. However, there were times in Indian history when the cooperation of the king could not be counted on. In areas where Buddhism had formerly flourished, the *Sangha* might, with a change of dynasty, find itself deprived of royal support; the new dynasty might show a clear preference for some non-Buddhist ideology, such as Shaivism or Jainism. When this happened Buddhism did not thereupon disappear altogether from the region concerned. It might suffer an eclipse; it might, sometimes but by no means always, suffer persecution. But often it would be preserved in sufficient measure by a faithful *Sangha* to be able to revive again if and when conditions became more favourable.

Clearly, therefore, much depended on the faithfulness of the *Sangha*, that is, on their adherence to those norms and values which had been transmitted to them as their Buddhist heritage. In the development of the Mahayana there was a relaxing of hold upon these traditional norms and values; on the one hand there was an accommodation to brahmanical ideas, encouraged perhaps by what may have been the desire to placate or assuage brahmanical hostility towards the *Sangha*. In these circumstances adherence to traditional norms would suffer. The open frontier with popular cults and beliefs would no longer be controlled by a strong, tradition-oriented *Sangha*, and the consequence would be a further tilting of the balance against Buddhist values. If the withdrawal of royal support in what had been an area of Buddhist civilization occurred in such circumstances as these, the likelihood of the *Sangha*'s maintaining the Buddhist tradition until royal support was regained would be much slighter.

THE ECONOMIC BASIS OF THE SANGHA'S
EXISTENCE

However, there is a further aspect of the matter to be considered. Even in circumstances when the *Sangha* adhered to the traditional norms, it could scarcely survive as an institution if it were deprived of the support *both* of the king *and* of the people simultaneously. If in addition to deprivation of royal patronage, the *Sangha* should suffer for some reason loss of lay support it would then be almost impossible for it to maintain itself for long. If the *Sangha* was properly maintaining its traditions of morality of life and service of the people, if it was providing a source of teaching and exemplary conduct which the lay people would esteem, the only reason why the lay people would be likely to fail to support the *Sangha* would be that of economic stringency. That is to say, if the surplus of resources of food and materials which a society needs to have at its disposal for the feeding and clothing and housing of its *bhikkhus* were to be cut off, in some relatively permanent way, it would become virtually impossible to maintain the *Sangha* in that society any longer. This was very probably the case at the time of the devastating raids and territorial conquests made by the Turko-Afghan Muslims across north India in the twelfth and thirteenth centuries. These invasions seriously disrupted the agricultural economy. 'Muslim historians have recorded only the plunder of jewels, gold and silver, but they are almost silent about the forcible seizure of crops standing in the field or lying in the granary of the peasant', writes Bhakat Prasad Mazumdar.[13] Military campaigns were usually waged in the fine weather of the Indian cool season, after the harvest. It is obvious that expeditions in which sometimes as many as twenty thousand foot soldiers were engaged were not provided at the outset with food to carry with them for the entire campaign. It was, therefore, the custom whenever possible, in the waging of campaigns in India to time them to begin when the countryside was rich with harvest. At such a season the commander 'can obtain fodder [for his troops and horses] and at the same time inflict an injury on the other party, by destroying the crops standing in the fields.' [14] It was generally recognized that it was the cultivators who had to bear the brunt of the movement of armies, in the form of the loss of their food supplies. In the last quarter of the thirteenth century this is what was happening in East Bengal, which had been until then a strongly Buddhist area. The Muslim conqueror of the Tippera and Dacca districts, Tughral Khan, 'forcibly acquired a considerable wealth' in these parts in the year 1275 AD, a modern Pakistani historian records.[15] It can be assumed that the life of the countryside suffered accordingly, so that the economic surplus out of which the *bhikkhus* had been supported would exist no longer. It is significant that Tughral Khan immediately made a very handsome gift of money to a dervish for the building of a Khangah near Dacca; effective steps were taken to colonize the whole area with Muslims, while non-Muslims began to migrate out of the district.[16]

Thus an area in which, until then, the *Sangha* had continued to maintain the norms of Buddhism, now became incapable of providing the basic economic support which the continued existence of the *Sangha* required. The *bhikkhus* would be forced either to put off their robes and cease to be *bhikkhus*, or to migrate to the neighbouring territories of Burma and Tibet, while the monasteries of East Bengal fell into decay and were overgrown, to disappear, often without trace.

12 The Survival of Buddhist Civilization in Ceylon

ECONOMIC AND POLITICAL CAUSES OF THE CONTRACTION OF THE BUDDHIST STATE

In the classical three-fold structure of the Buddhist state, where king and *Sangha* and people each had their proper and necessary part to play, the crucial member of the trio was the *Sangha*. But the classical structure could be damaged when any one of the three ceased to be able to function in the normal manner. We have seen that in India the loss of a Buddhist laity able to support the *Sangha* could lead to the *Sangha*'s disappearance. We have now to consider how in Ceylon the loss of Buddhist kingship in the modern period has also had lasting effects of an adverse kind. The role of the king in the classical pattern of the Buddhist state is to protect the *Sangha* and promote the *Dhamma*, both by his support of the *bhikkhus* and by wise legislation designed to promote a society with a public ethos of the kind in which Buddhist morality can be pursued by the maximum number of the people. When there is no longer a Buddhist king these functions go by default; if alien cultural and ethical values are introduced there may be a falling away from Buddhist values on the part of the people, and eventually perhaps on the part of the *Sangha* also. This is what can be seen to have happened in Ceylon since the beginning of the sixteenth century. The story has been told often enough before, in a variety of ways.[1] What follows is a brief recapitulation of the main events in order to show how they illustrate the delicate nature and workings of Buddhist civilization.

The kind of misfortune which befell Buddhism in Bengal at the end of the thirteenth century: namely, a violent and determined invasion by the bearers of an alien culture, occurred in Ceylon some three centuries later. There were, however, a number of external attacks from south India after the death of King Parakkama Bahu I in 1186 which weakened the kingdom and aggravated the political and administrative decay which had set in by the close of the twelfth century. Added to this there were internal dissensions. The irrigation system established by Parakkama Bahu gradually fell into disrepair and the land in the dry zone of north central Ceylon, deprived of its water supply, became desolate. The former economic prosperity of the region, where the royal capitals had been, now gave way to crop failure, famine and disease. During the following centuries malaria seems to have made its appearance in Ceylon, to sap the vitality of the people still further.[2] There was a general shift of population away from the dry northern and south-eastern plain to the wet, western lowlands. The great monasteries and pagodas of northern Ceylon were deserted and fell into ruins and were almost forgotten until their rediscovery in the twentieth century.

A new centre of government was established at Dambadeniya, thirty miles inland from the west coast. The elders of the *Sangha* gathered there, and together with the king, they made an attempt to revive and purify the life of the *Sangha*, and establish a proper discipline once again after the dislocation and general decline of the preceding years. The vitality of the *Sangha* recovered, and by the middle of the fourteenth century its reputation in the Theravadin countries of South-East Asia was sufficiently high for the Thai king to invite the head of Ceylonese *Sangha* to come and reorganize the *Sangha* in Thailand. On a number of occasions during the fourteenth century members of the Burmese, Thai and Cambodian *Sanghas* visited Ceylon to study canonical texts and monastic discipline and organization, and then to return to their own countries to put into effect what they had learned.

By the end of the fifteenth century, however, a decline had once again begun in Ceylon. The country was divided politically, so that a deputation from Pegu, in Burma, which arrived in Ceylon in 1476, found it impossible for some time to reach the capital because of rebel forces which stood in the way. By 1477 the island was divided between three kingdoms, Jaffna in the north, Kandy in the central highlands, and Kotte in the western lowlands. The ruler of the last of these, the king of Kotte, claimed to be lord of the whole island, but his claim had little foundation in fact. Many of the coastal towns were in the hands of Muslim traders and merchants. The political division of the rest of the island, and the disintegrating effect of this on the Buddhist civilization of Ceylon at the end of the fifteenth century has been described by G. P. Malalasekere. Apart from the coastal towns the rest of the island was

governed by chieftains holding mimic courts at various centres. These petty tyrants, even more degenerate in their character than they were humiliated in station, no longer manifested the patriotism and the zeal for the public welfare which had so significantly characterized the former sovereigns of Ceylon. They had ceased to occupy their attention with the advancement of religion or with the development of institutions calculated to benefit the people.[3]

The island's food supply had been seriously affected by internal disturbances, and the shortage was such that food had now to be imported from south India. The divided and depressed state of the country was inevitably reflected in the condition of the *Sangha* which was, once again, at a low ebb. We noticed earlier how prominent is the concern of the chroniclers of Ceylon with the relationship between king and *Sangha*; they sensed the vital importance of this relationship, and it is clear that 'the decline of the one reflected the lapse of the other'.[4]

It was in this condition that Ceylon was confronted by the first of the invaders from Europe, the Portuguese, whose ships dropped anchor off the west coast in 1505. From then onwards Ceylon was not to be free of European domination for four-and-a-half centuries. In Ceylon, as in the other lands the Portuguese invaded, the sequence of events was conquest and conversion. Like modern urban gangsters, they moved in to give the king of Kotte their 'protection'. Subsequently, a young prince of Kotte, entrusted to Portuguese priests for education, was converted to Christianity. At his death he bequeathed the whole island to the Portuguese, an act of generosity which was both unnecessary and unrealistic. The part of the island which was his to bequeath was already well under their control, and as for the rest, his claim was fictitious. Extensive confiscation of Buddhist *Sangha* buildings and land greatly enriched the Christian religious orders in the island. The *bhikkhus*, displaced in the lowlands, moved up country to Kandy, and the *Sangha* virtually disappeared from the western coastal plain. Portuguese priests took over not only the property of the *Sangha* but also its place in the rural society of the lowlands. They presented a form of Christianity which was tolerant of local cults and beliefs, and the transition so far as the village people were concerned, from folk religion within a Buddhist framework to folk religion within a Catholic framework, was not too uncomfortable for those who did not resist. It is clear that the Portuguese, through their own sufferings during the early days of their settlement in the island, 'came closer to the people of the country than either the Dutch or the British'[5] who succeeded them. Many of their priests, moreover, were from the indigenous population of south India, and it was partly the zeal and devotion of these humble men which won adherents to Catholicism in Ceylon, and maintained the Catholic community during the time of persecution under the Dutch.

The kingdom of Kandy, in the central highlands, thus became the residuary upholder of Buddhism in Ceylon. There the traditional pattern of king, *Sangha* and people was preserved. During the middle decades of the eighteenth century a considerable revival of the *Sangha* was brought about, largely through the initiative of the Kandyan kings, Siri Vijaya (1739–47), and his successor, Kitti Siri (1747–82).

THE EIGHTEENTH-CENTURY REVIVAL OF BUDDHISM UNDER IMMIGRANT RULERS

It is interesting that both these kings were foreigners. The previous king, Narinda Singha, had married a princess from Madhura, in south India, and with her to Ceylon had come her brother, Siri Vijaya. At the death of Narinda there was some dispute over the succession, and one party at court favoured the claim of a son of Narinda's by a concubine. But this candidate withdrew voluntarily and Siri Vijaya, who was strongly favoured by others at court, succeeded as king. The case is interesting for the light it throws on the acceptance by the Kandyan chiefs only seventy-six years later of another foreign 'claimant' to the throne – the British governor, Robert Brownrigg, whom they expected to slip into place and maintain the traditions of a Buddhist state as other foreigners had done (see p. 261). King Siri Vijaya also took as his queen a princess from south India (from Madhura) and she too was accompanied to Ceylon by her brother, Kitti Siri, and their father. Again, therefore, at the death of Siri Vijaya, a south Indian prince became king of Kandy. Not only did he become king, but like his brother-in-law he became an enthusiastic upholder of the Buddhist state. During Siri Vijaya's reign young men began to come forward, as they had not done for some time, to take the robe as novices (*samaneras*) in the Buddhist *Sangha*. Arrangements were made by the king and his household for all such novices to be properly instructed in the tenets of Buddhism. Funds were made available for the production of Buddhist manuals of instruction. The king encouraged the holding of public festivals, and occasions for the public teaching of *Dhamma*. He had Buddha statues erected in many places, new *cetiyas* built, and old shrines restored. The one important measure which needed to be taken for the revival of a Buddhist state was the reconstitution of the *Sangha*. The higher ordination, or *upasampada*, that is, ordination as *bhikkhu*, was no longer possible in Ceylon, as there is a requisite number of *bhikkhus* to form a chapter and carry out such ordination and they could not be found. Aided by the Dutch, who provided him with a ship, Siri Vijaya sent envoys to Pegu (lower Burma) and Ayudhya (capital of the Thai kingdom) to request *bhikkhus* from those kingdoms to come to Ceylon to carry out the *upasampada*. But both expeditions suffered shipwreck; in the first case only one, and in the second a mere handful of survivors returned to Ceylon to tell what had happened.[6]

Success was achieved, however, during the reign of Kitti Siri. A man of great virtue, according to the Pali chronicle, and devoted to the *Buddha*, the *Dhamma* and the *Sangha*, he had already made a resolve to restore and protect the Sangha in Ceylon.[7] Accordingly he sent messengers, with gifts, and a letter in the Pali language, to the Thai capital, Ayudhya. There the envoys were received with honour, and the Thai king made arrangements at once for a chapter of *bhikkhus* to go to Ceylon. The whole party, 'with books on the doctrine and the monastic discipline [which were lacking in Ceylon] . . . a golden image of the Buddha, and a superb golden book, a magnificent royal letter, gifts of various kinds, and dignitaries of the King of Ayudhya [as envoys]' came safely to Ceylon.[8] In July 1756 a great ceremony of ordination was held in Kandy and many novices, some of whom had waited long for this occasion, were made *bhikkhus*. The newly ordained were instructed by the members of the *Sangha* who had come from Ayudhya, and the king himself drew up a code of conduct for their guidance, in accordance with the precepts of the *Vinaya*. A revival of Pali learning followed, and a renewal of literature activity. It was recognized that the concern of the *Sangha* with the ills which afflict mankind covered ills of mind and of body. So, in addition to giving themselves to the study of *Dhamma* and its practice for the purification of men's minds, the *bhikkhus* took up the study of medicine too; this was another result of the revival of learning.

THE IMPACT OF THE BRITISH INVASION OF CEYLON

By the end of the eighteenth century British naval interests in the coastal waters of India had led to the capture by Britain, from the Dutch, of the large harbour and port of Trincomalee, on the north-east coast of Ceylon. This happened in 1782, and thus encouraged, in 1796 the British seized the port of Colombo, also from the Dutch. Dutch power in the island thus came to an end, and the maritime provinces passed into the hands of Britain, to be declared a Crown Colony in 1802. The surviving kingdom of Kandy, in central Ceylon, was now surrounded by a new band of foreign adventurers.

The circumstances in which, in 1815, the Kandyan kingdom, at whose head was a young man of nineteen, became a British colony, entail a story of treachery which does no credit to the Sinhalese traitor, Pilame Talawe, who was the prime mover, or to Frederick North, the British governor who encouraged him in his murderous intentions. That was in 1798, two years after the British had seized Colombo from the Dutch (with the aid of Swiss mercenaries whom they bought over from Dutch service). North was confided in by the would-be assassin, and in his eagerness to make the most of the opportunity to set up a military protectorate at Kandy, comments Sir James Tennent, 'Mr North not only forbore to denounce the treason of the minister, but lent himself to intrigues inconsistent with the dignity and honour of his high office.'[9] It was, however, ten years after North had departed from Ceylon that the train of events he had set in motion finally brought about a situation in which North's successor, Robert Brownrigg, was able to order the British troops to march into Kandy to restore order and take the young king prisoner. On 2 March 1815 the king was solemnly deposed and his entire realm vested in the British crown. The Convention of Kandy, a form of agreement which the British drew up, set out the conditions under which the new regime would operate; it stated that a 'tyrannous' king had been deposed for having waged 'war' against Britain, and that 'for the time being' the control of the kingdom would be in the hands of the British governor. This agreement, which was signed on behalf of the king of England on the one side and the chieftains of Kandy on the other, included a clause (Article 5), which read as follows: 'The religion of Boodhoo [the Buddha] professed by the chiefs and inhabitants of these provinces is declared inviolable; and its rites, ministers and places of worship are to be maintained and protected.'

The Sinhalese version of this document, however, makes it clear that it was Sinhalese Buddhism, in its *popular* as well as its *monastic* aspect which was meant, since reference is made both to the 'religion of the Buddha and to the *Agama* [religion] of the *Devas* [local gods], and protection is promised to the *Viharas* [Buddhist temples] and the *Devalayas* [temples of local gods]'.[10]

This is important, because it indicates that it was not only the 'pure' Theravada which the British government undertook to protect, but the whole range of popular Sinhalese religion. One important, indeed essential, element of Buddhism they had, however, removed when they deposed the king of Kandy. For without a king the traditional structure of the Buddhist state was seriously distorted; it meant that there was no longer a Buddhist civilization in Ceylon. Buddhism had, in fact, been reduced to a religion, and that is what the British called it.

What had been taken away when the king was deposed was the guardianship of the Buddhist ethic in its public and social dimension. There was no longer a Buddhist who possessed political authority which he could use to promote the kind of society which would foster the values and practices of Buddhism. What is more, with the setting up of their rule over the whole of Ceylon, and the commercial enterprises which they soon introduced, the British very seriously affected the nature of Sinhalese society over the next century and a half, introducing alien values and attitudes, and doing so in such a way as to give high prestige to these alien values compared with the traditional values of Buddhist Ceylon.

The campaign on the part of Christian missionaries to have the connection between Buddhism and the British government severed had made use of three major arguments: that Buddhism was a system of idolatry; that 'interference' in the religion of the country by the British would be interpreted by the people of Ceylon as implying approval of that religion; and that the only thing which kept Buddhism alive was the support of the State.[11] Each of these three arguments was the expression of a half-truth. Sinhalese Buddhism, it is true, including as it does the cults of local and Indian gods and spirits, certainly appears, at the popular village level, as the kind of paganism which was most frequently described by nineteenth-century missionaries as 'idolatrous'. That the appearance which Sinhalese Buddhism thus presents is due to the tolerance of the beliefs of unsophisticated people by a highly sophisticated and rational system of analysis is a point which the cultured Western despisers of this particular 'idolatry' have missed. Again, it was not so much 'interference' as non-interference in the religion of their country which the Buddhists of Ceylon felt they had a right to expect from their alien overlords; the complaint now, as then, is not that the British failed to 'approve' of Sinhalese Buddhism, but that they positively disrupted it by severing an important connection, a connection which had traditionally existed between the religion of the people and the ruler of the people. However naive their religious system might be, it was the right to maintain it intact which was being disputed. In a similar fashion

Christians in a Western country might feel themselves alienated from a government which took positive measures to undermine their religious beliefs and practices on the grounds that their religion was superstitious or idolatrous. Finally, Spence-Hardy and his missionary colleagues, in their contention that it was only Government support which kept Buddhism in Ceylon alive were comforting themselves with what was at most only a half-truth. It is true that the Buddhist state requires for its full and proper functioning the cooperation of a ruler whose policy and legislation is in keeping with the *Dhamma*. But, as events have shown, it is untrue to say that the Buddhist culture and civilization will inevitably disappear as soon as the country is deprived of such a ruler. The crucial element in the classical Buddhist structure is the *Sangha*. In Ceylon the *Sangha* survived, albeit for a time much handicapped and weakened, and it is to this fact that the survival of Buddhism in its traditional form in Ceylon must be credited.

The fact remains that the promise which the British government had made in 1815, in Article 5 of the Convention of Kandy, was not kept. In England, William Wilberforce, an evangelical Member of Parliament, stated his objection to the clause more openly: it would, he feared, prevent missionary attempts to convert the Buddhists of Ceylon to Christianity; he objected, moreover, to the religion of the Buddha being described as 'inviolable'.[12] Nevertheless, as K. M. de Silva points out, 'the Kandyans believed that the relationship between Buddhism and the British Government defined in 1815 was to be permanent.'[13] For them, with their long tradition of Buddhism as something more than a religion – the tradition of a Buddhist state – it was perfectly natural that the authority in whom (so they had been led to believe) they had vested political power over what had always been a Buddhist state should maintain it as such. It was necessary, for the proper working of a Buddhist state, that there should be an authority corresponding to that of a king,

which would function as a Buddhist king would, to promote the welfare and maintain the institutions of a
Buddhist population. This was perceived by Tennent,
who wrote:

> ... it is not *protection* which they look to us for ... It is not
> our *management* they want ... But what they really want
> under the semblance of interference and appearance of control
> is really our identification with their religion and the prestige
> of the Government name as associated with their appointments
> and patronage.[14]

What the Kandyan chiefs were expecting would simply be
a repetition of what had happened before; the Nayakkar
dynasty, whose kings had ruled Kandy since 1739, had also
been of foreign, that is, of south Indian origin, as we have
noted earlier. But he who ruled a Buddhist state, whether
he was south Indian or English, would, the Kandyans supposed, rule it according to the hallowed tradition of Buddhist Ceylon.[15]

That they were naïve is understandable. The Kandyan
kingdom had been largely cut off from the affairs of the
wider world, and its people were disposed to think in terms
of their Buddhist tradition and its values. They did not
understand at first what it was that had come to them with
the arrival of British troops and a British governor in
Kandy. They could not be expected to understand the
complex commercial rivalries of the European nations, of
their navies and armies in South-Asia as well as in Western
Europe, and how this was now involving their simple and
remote kingdom in the hills. When, in 1817, they began to
get an inkling of how different the new situation really
was from anything which had been experienced before,
they made their protest, in a rebellion against those whom
they now recognized as alien overlords. The rebellion was
crushed, and with British power already considerably
stronger than in 1815, it became possible for the British
Government in Ceylon to make a new Proclamation, on 21
November 1818, which showed a considerably less defer-
ential attitude both to the chiefs and to Buddhism.

HOW BUDDHISM IN CEYLON BECAME
A 'RELIGION'

From 1818 onwards the speed of Westernization of Ceylon
was accelerated. Educational developments were directed
away from traditional learning within the context of Buddhist culture, and led either in the direction of secularism
or Christianity (evangelical, Catholic, or Church of England). The young Sinhalese found it necessary to avail
themselves of these new forms of education if they were to
be appointed to government posts and continue to have
any part at all in the running of their country. Monastic
education declined correspondingly in importance and in
quality.

To some extent, however, this was a stimulus to Buddhism. It could be seen that all depended now on the
Sangha. The role of the *bhikkhus* as the voice of Buddhism, critical of un-Buddhist acts on the part of alien
rulers, was now greatly enhanced. It was this reaction to
the enslavement of the traditional way of life to Western
values during the British colonial period which first drew
bhikkhus into direct political activity in Ceylon.[16] In spite
of the disabilities which the *Sangha* suffered, such as the
alienation of monastery lands and property, and the by-
passing of the monastic educational system, it managed to
survive the one hundred and thirty years of British rule
after the destruction of the kingdom of Kandy. During
the latter half of this period it benefited from the encouragement and help which had now begun to come from
Western sympathizers, notably the American Colonel H.
S. Olcott, and from Madame Blavatsky and Mrs Annie
Besant who came from England. Ludowyk has pointed to
an important modification in the Buddhist response to
Christian missionary activity: 'it had perforce to express
itself in forms decided for it by Christian activity ... the
battle joined had to be fought with weapons similar to
those used by the Christian missionary; hence such things
as Buddhist Sunday Schools and even Buddhist carols'.[17]

In this way Buddhism in Ceylon gradually became even more of a 'religion', as the modern West understands the term.

But this was largely in respect of the face which it turned to the West. So far as the wholly Sinhalese, village situation was concerned the frontier with local deities and cults remained open, and the *relative* importance of this within Sinhalese Buddhism as a whole may well have increased as the public status of the *Sangha* declined. The extent to which folk-beliefs and practices have been allowed to coexist in close association with Buddhism in Ceylon has for long puzzled the more superficial Western observers. The juxtaposition of Buddhist devotion and popular Sinhalese cults has given rise to Western judgements in terms of 'syncretism' or 'corruption'. This is illustrated in the procedure followed by the Sinhalese Buddhist when he visits a *vihara*. He does very much as his Buddhist forebears would have done in ancient Anuradhapura.[18] He goes first to the *stupa* (or *dagaba*), and circumambulates it, keeping it on his right. He pays his respect to the Buddha, whom the *stupa* represents, by offering flowers and also perhaps lights (in the form of a coconut oil lamp) and incense. After that it is usual to venerate the bodhi-tree. Finally, he visits the *Buddha-rupa*, usually kept in a shrine-room or temple, and venerates that in the same manner. But in the same compound, or temple-enclosure, there may be, in addition to the three items to which Buddhist ceremonial respect has been offered, another temple, devoted to specifically Sinhalese deities, local or national, or possibly to deities of Hindu India. After, but only after, respect has been offered at the Buddhist places, he visits the *devalaya*, in order to seek some particular immediate mundane boon: to pray for the birth of a child, or for a relative's recovery from illness, or for success in some business venture.

Another of the features of Sinhalese Buddhist culture which has often confused and perplexed the outside observer is its public pageantry, when, for example, the Tooth

Relic is taken out of the Temple at Kandy and carried in procession round the city for all the people to venerate. This, too, has given rise to questions from non-Buddhists about the justification for such practices, or objections that this is alien to what is found in the Pali canon, and is not Buddhism, or not 'pure' Buddhism. It is only recently that the inner cohesion of Sinhalese Buddhism has begun to be understood in the West, largely through the writings of social scientists. It will therefore be useful at this point to provide a brief survey of some of their work.

MODERN SINHALESE BUDDHISM FROM THE VIEWPOINT OF SOCIAL SCIENCE

Until just over a decade ago, Western accounts of Sinhalese Buddhist religion, whether descriptive or analytical, were hard to come by. Copleston [19] devoted less than a sixth of his *Buddhism, Primitive and Present in Magadha and Ceylon*, to contemporary Sinhalese Buddhism. Most of the book consists of descriptive writing of a largely impressionistic kind, and clearly indicates the viewpoint of the writer, that of a Christian missionary-bishop. T. W. Rhys Davids's article in the *Encyclopaedia of Religion and Ethics* on Ceylon Buddhism provides the kind of scholarly treatment of the history, doctrines, and monastic structure of Theravada Buddhism that one would expect from this great Pali scholar, but has disappointingly little about the popular practice of Buddhism which he, as a resident of Ceylon, might have given us. Sir Charles Eliot [20] devoted four pages to some aspects of the contemporary practice and structure of Sinhalese Buddhism and to the relationship between the life of the monasteries and that of the lay people. He speaks of three religions within Sinhalese Buddhism: 'local animism, Hinduism, and Buddhism are all inextricably mixed together'.[21] He notes that the practice of Buddhism in Ceylon entailed a 'pageantry' and an 'ornate ritualism' which 'is not authorized in any known canonical text'.[22] Copleston speaks of 'the two Buddhisms' in Ceylon. On the one hand there is the moribund tradition of the lay people and the villages; on the other there is that of the Pali texts and the monasteries and of the educated élite of Colombo, which in his day was alive with the spirit of revival. Between these two, he considered, there was an extreme divergence.[23] For while the Buddhism of the educated classes claimed to be compatible with modern scientific thought, it was tolerant of much superstition and polytheism.[24] Ceylon Buddhism was, he said, 'inconsistent, just where inconsistency does the most harm'.

This apparent dichotomy within Sinhalese Buddhism had, however, already been noted by the seventeenth-century Englishman, Robert Knox, who spent eighteen years in Ceylon. Among other examples of what Ludowyk has called Knox's 'power of observation and his ability to see the essentials'[25] was his now frequently quoted dictum that the Sinhalese have 'Budu for the soul, and the gods for this world'. By 'the gods' is meant the whole complex of rituals and beliefs associated with local and national deities. Knox perceived that there was an important difference in function and status between the two cults.

There is much in Sinhalese practice to support the notion of two religions, Buddhist and non-Buddhist, co-existing side by side, or even, to some extent, syncretistically. This can be seen, for example, in the practice of pilgrimage, and in the hospitality given to non-Buddhist cults within the precincts of Buddhist temples. While there are places of pilgrimage which are of a primarily Buddhist character, the sacred city of Anuradhapura, for example, there are others which are associated primarily with the guardian deities of Ceylon, such as Kataragama, a famous shrine in the jungle of the dry-zone of the extreme south-east of the island. Nur Yalman records that 'thousands of pilgrims from Ceylon and South India, Buddhists as well as Hindus (and even Muslims and Christians) flock to this deserted locality and bring it alive for a few weeks every year.'[26] There are other shrines which combine both

Buddhist and non-Buddhist elements, such as Sri Pada (Adam's Peak): this is revered from a Buddhist point of view on account of the foot-print of the Lord Buddha which is found on its summit, and it is held sacred, too, as the abode of the Sinhalese god, Saman. Leonard Woolf in his novel of Sinhalese life, *The Village in the Jungle*, gives an account of a pilgrimage of village people to the shrine of the Hindu god 'Kandeswami', in which he notes their acceptance of the fact that 'though the god is a Tamil god, and the temple a Hindu temple, the *kapuralas* (that is, the ministrants) are all Buddhists and Sinhalese'.[27]

We have noted that within the precincts of temples devoted to the Buddha there will often be found subsidiary shrines called *devalayas*, devoted to Hindu and Sinhalese gods. These, and other similar features of Sinhalese practice, have led Western observers in the past to regard the situation as one of the 'corruption' of Buddhism by 'animism', or else to speak of Buddhism in Ceylon (as in Burma and Thailand) as merely a thin veneer covering the 'real religion' of animism, or yet again to regard it as an example of thorough-going religious syncretism.

Some rather different accounts of the cultural structure of the Theravada countries of South Asia have become available recently in the writings of social scientists who have worked in that area in the past decade or so. The most notable names in connection with Ceylon are those of Ryan, Obeyesekere, Ames, Yalman and Evers.

In 1958 Bryce Ryan, a sociologist, provided a valuable descriptive account of the main features of the two elements in Sinhalese culture, Buddhist and non-Buddhist.[28] In chapter 6 of *Sinhalese Village*, 'From Buddhism to the wonderful world', he describes the features of Sinhalese belief and practice which are related more directly to the Buddha and his teaching; in 'The wonderful world: gods and demons', chapter 7, Ryan deals with the non-Buddhist features, viz., the cults of Hindu, local Sinhalese, and planetary deities, the placation of demons, and various magical practices. The important point to be kept in mind is that there is a large overlap in the clientele of the Buddhist shrine and that of the gods, an overlap which includes the majority of the lay people. 'Pure Buddhism', comments Ryan, 'is a philosopher's abstraction. Sinhalese Buddhism is pure; Buddhists are not. The Sinhalese are Buddhists, but in the same breath we may as rightly say that the Sinhalese are believers in numerous gods, sub-gods and demons, and that non-Buddhist supernaturalism in the form of planetary influences, wood-sprites, sorcery, and ghosts is ubiquitous.' [29]

In Ryan's view, a real distinction exists, not merely at the level of anthropological analysis, but in the consciousness of the villager himself, between Buddhist and non-Buddhist beliefs and practices. So far as the Buddhist aspect is concerned, both for monks and laymen, attention is focussed chiefly on the acquiring of merit. The attainment of *nirvana* is held to be far beyond the reach of ordinary man in this age; gaining merit is a more practicable immediate goal, and is at the same time consistent with acceptance of the idea of *nirvana* as the ultimate goal. Merit is acquired principally by various forms of worship and by the practice of almsgiving or generosity. Over against this, and distinct from it, Ryan sees the variety of belief in supernatural powers and the accompanying various practices of astrology, spirit-propitiation, exorcism, and so on. These 'powers', in his view, are not hierarchically graded, except that 'the Buddha stands above all others, and toward Him there is unique reverence and worshipfulness.' [30] Demons are regarded as agents of illness and other various human disorders. Belief in demon-caused disease, he notes, tends now to be confined to those illnesses of a more mysterious kind, not readily amenable to treatment by Western medicine. Astrology, he considers, is given the place of a natural science rather than a metaphysical belief-system.

However, Ryan indicates that the two spheres are not entirely distinct. The chanting of *pirith* by Buddhist monks as a 'generalized antibiotic' against evil influences, and pilgrimages to sacred shrines have both to be placed somewhere between these two spheres. 'If the *pirith* ceremony takes us one step into the borderland between philosophic Buddhism and practical supernaturalism, the pilgrimage to sacred shrines is at least midway between these theoretically distinct spheres.' [31] Elsewhere he speaks of *pirith* and pilgrimage as representing a merging of Buddhism and the cult of the gods. 'In the former the power of the Buddha is given supernatural quality, and in the latter the merger is a wedding of convenience between Lord Buddha and the gods.' [32]

Obeyesekere sees the relationship between them in terms of hierarchy. In the first place there is the hierarchy of supernatural powers, with presidential status ascribed to the Buddha. 'The positions of all other supernatural beings derive, directly or indirectly from, or are measured against, this initial presidential status of the Buddha.' [33] Below the Buddha are the guardian deities of Ceylon, and below these are gods of local authority or power, who are thought of as subservient to the national deities, and as their attendant ministers. Below these comes the host of demons who are able to punish people with disease, and below them the spirits of dead men, ghosts who are often spiteful and harmful. Corresponding to the hierarchical structure of the pantheon is the gradation of symbolic gestures used in connection with the various rituals. This is a marked feature of Sinhalese practice, and has been well summarized by Obeyesekere as follows:

The Buddha as head of the pantheon, is worshipped with the hands on the head or forehead. In rituals in Buddhist temples, vegetarian foods and fruit juices are placed on his altar, and he is honoured with incense and flowers. The gods are worshipped with the hands farther below or with the fists clenched and placed against the chest. Since gods are considered noble beings (and even potential Buddhas), they too are offered vegetarian foods, auspicious flowers, and incense. This respectful obeisance is not given the demons at all – they are offered neither auspicious flowers nor incense, but are typically invoked with certain flowers considered inauspicious and with resin, an inferior incense ... Hence the kind of offering symbolizes status in the pantheon.[34]

Obeyesekere presents this account of the pantheon in the context of his argument that Sinhalese Buddhism, the popular religion of Ceylon, is to be understood as a 'little tradition', subordinate to the 'great tradition', which is the Theravada Buddhism of South-East Asia as a whole.

Robert Redfield's concept of great and little traditions is here used by Obeyesekere and applied to the Ceylon situation because, in his view, it makes possible a more realistic analysis than is to be found in those accounts of South-East Asian Buddhism which employ the notion of different cultural 'layers' or 'strata', one on top of the other. It also avoids the necessity to deal with the folk religion of these countries in terms of 'animism' – 'a convenient label under which one could subsume beliefs or customs he did not fully comprehend, or was impatient with'.

The important point here is that Sinhalese Buddhism is to be viewed in its entirety as 'a single religious tradition', that is, an integrated system, and not a juxtaposition of radically different or competing elements, Buddhist and non-Buddhist; nor even a situation of peaceful coexistence of disparate elements. Just as there is a single pantheon of the Buddha, gods, demons and lesser supernatural beings, so also the whole range of Sinhalese Buddhist belief and practice displays a single, consistent structure, or constitutes, as Obeyesekere calls it, a 'moral community'. In his view, moreover, Sinhalese Buddhism is locally institutionalized in each village, so that the religion of the village can also be seen, 'for methodological purposes as a· unitary structure', that is, a smaller moral community. This Obeyesekere works out in detail, arguing that the local village ritual, differing slightly from one village to another, 'validates the social structure of the village, defines its limits, and demarcates the village as a moral community over which the (local) gods have protective jurisdiction and authority'.[35] The rituals and values which are common to the Sinhalese, the rituals associated with the national deities of the island, contribute the wider moral community of Sinhalese Buddhism; and, finally, the rituals and values associated with the Buddha constitute the 'great' moral community of Theravada Buddhism. The little tradition of Sinhalese Buddhism is thus linked quite consistently (*pace* Copleston) with the great tradition of South-East Asian Theravada Buddhism by a common set of meanings, derived from the great tradition: *karma*, merit, *dana* (giving, or generosity), *sila* (morality), '*arahant*-ship' and *nirvana*. 'The common salvation-idiom,' says Obeyesekere, 'is the ideological channel which facilitates movement from one tradition to the other', that is, from 'great' to 'little', or the reverse. But in the different countries of Buddhist South-East Asia the salvation-idiom is phrased in different languages, so to speak; that is, in terms of the different local peasant cultures. This, he says, agrees with Robert Slater's conclusions regarding Burmese Buddhism, in his book, *Paradox and Nirvana*,[36] that it is Buddhism and not animism 'that constitutes the governing ethos of the people'.

Whereas Obeyesekere lays great emphasis on the continuity of hierarchical structure from local village religion to pan-South-East Asian Buddhism, Ames and Evers are concerned to emphasize the degree of conceptual difference within the Sinhalese situation. Ames argues that although the Sinhalese may in practice fuse Buddhist, and what he calls 'magical-animist' practices, they never confuse them.[37] There is a clear distinction, he says, in the mind of the villager between the sacred ritual of Buddhism and the profane ritual of magical-animism. Ames sees the policy of Buddhist *bhikkhus* in allowing the practice of local cults alongside the cult of veneration of the Buddha, as mainly one of accommodation. He quotes the words of one of the *bhikkhus*:

People are going to propitiate the deities anyway, no matter what we say. Besides, Buddha never said they should not; he never said it was demerit. Therefore, if we keep shrines in our temple compounds, whatever their reason for coming, people will at least come – and learn to venerate Buddha while invoking the deities.[38]

This Ames regards as a case of dangling carrots before the horse, or, in this case, the peasant, and points out that Buddhism is not the only religious system to do this. He finds a parallel in the 'sacramentals' of Catholicism, as distinct from the sacraments. When local or national deity shrines are placed within the precinct of the Buddhist temple, this is in order 'to bring magic under the control of the monks, and the spirits under the suzerainty of the Buddha'. It is not, he emphasizes, syncretism. There is still a radical division between the concerns of a man when he is venerating the Buddha and when he is engaging in the rituals of magical animism. Veneration of the Buddha and the acquiring of merit thereby is concerned with the trans-temporal world; the spirit cults are concerned very much with this world and its immediate day-to-day needs. The dichotomy is not between the great tradition and little tradition, as separate unitary systems, though connected by a progression of values; at every level the dichotomy is between other-worldly (*lokuttara*) and this-worldly (*laukika*) values and aims.

Ames suggests that these two Pali terms, *lokuttara* and *laukika*, as they are used by the Sinhalese, have meanings very close to Durkheim's concepts of 'the sacred' and 'the profane'. His explanation of the existence of these two levels in Sinhalese Buddhist practice is that it is due to the nature of Buddhist doctrine. There is only one way to salvation, in the Buddhist view; it is very difficult and the goal is far distant. 'For the ordinary Buddhist, salvation is considered very difficult because it demands arduous meditation; it is very distant because the necessary practice takes thousands and thousands of rebirths.' [39] Ames, unlike some earlier Western observers of Buddhism, avoids falling into the error of saying simply that its practice entails a complete turning of one's back on this world and renouncing all interest in it and its affairs. 'Because of the evaluative supremacy of the world-negating *nirvanaya* ideal, relations with the world are always strained. But because of the concern with rebirth and comfort, relations with the world are also necessary and important.'[40]

On the basis of his analysis of Sinhalese practice in terms of sacred and profane concerns, Ames proceeds to identify four religious sub-systems which he claims have developed within Sinhalese Buddhism as a consequence of the remote nature of the Buddhist goal, i.e. *nirvana*. The first sub-system is that which is wholly concerned with the sacred, namely, the Buddhist religious belief-system, with its own special practices and institutions. The second and third sub-systems are the temple-estate, and the nation-state. These are, at best, only quasi-sacred. The fourth sub-system is that of the spirit cults, which the Sinhalese regard as entirely profane (*laukika*). This four-fold analysis Ames develops in detail in the course of a review and interpretation of the whole spectrum of Sinhalese religious and non-religious practices. Buddhist practice, whether it be meditation, or merit-making by means of worship, generosity of action, and so on, is directed solely towards an other-worldly end. No immediate mundane benefits are expected. Ames emphasizes particularly the non-reciprocal intention in Buddhist giving, whether to monks or to one's neighbours. One does not give in order to receive any reciprocal boon. In the magical cults, however, this is precisely what one does expect: to receive an immediate boon in return for offerings made. The spirit-cults, unlike Buddhist practice, cater for needs which are 'specific, concrete and mundane'.[41]

Just as Ames rejects the great tradition/little tradition dichotomy, so also he rejects the earlier notion that there are three 'religions' existing side by side (as Eliot suggested) namely, the religion of the Buddha, Hinduism and the deity-cults, and the cults of hobgoblins and spirits. In his view there is one system which has reference to the sacred; it embraces both monk and layman, without radical separation between them, in a pyramidal structure of different types of practitioners and graded activities and statuses, from the lowliest kind of merit-making at the bottom of the pyramid to the highest kind of meditation-practice at the top. This is Sinhalese religion. In contrast, there is another system of belief and practice, which has reference to the profane, that is, to the spirit-cults. This is Sinhalese magic. It will be seen that Ames's dichotomy owes something to the kind of distinction between religious and magic made by Malinowski, as Ames himself acknowledges.

The two systems interact, in ways which can be fairly clearly traced. Ames does this, representing the interaction in diagrammatic form.[42] Between these two systems, polarized in terms of the religion/magic distinction, come the two intermediate sub-systems of the temple-estate and the state. All owe their special characteristics to the nature of Buddhist religion. For example, the state, in the Sinhalese tradition of the pre-British period, was what it was because 'the King was dedicated to upholding the faith and protecting (Buddhist) religious institutions ... this was the political aspect of religion'. The spirit-cults, similarly, hold their position in the culture of Ceylon, not by their own right so much as by right of the need which Buddhist religion creates in day-to-day life, by virtue of the remoteness of its salvation-ideal. Ames points out that where the salvation-ideal is modified, in the direction of becoming less remote, the status of the spirit-cults is also modified as a consequence: that is, the need for this kind of cult depreciates. 'It is precisely the modern Buddhist enthusiast who believes that salvation is attainable within this or the next few lives who also claims that magic is superfluous.'[43]

Hans-Dieter Evers agrees with Ames's analysis in general, and from the point of view of his own studies of the Buddhist *Sangha* provides supporting evidence of the clear-cut theoretical distinction between the two realms, sacred and profane, Buddhist and non-Buddhist. The distinction is clearest, he finds, in the case of the respective roles of Buddhist and non-Buddhist cult-specialists – that is, the *bhikkhus* and the magicians or exorcists. It is with these that Evers is primarily concerned. At the level of the non-specialist lay people the two realms overlap. But it is significant, Evers points out, that among the lay people there are no sectarian divisions along Buddhist/non-Buddhist lines. The same constituency of laymen participates in both kinds of rituals. 'Doctrinal differences have, as a matter of fact, not led to social differentiation and the formation of sects.' [44] Since the same group of laymen may hold both sets of beliefs, this suggests that these are not different, competing sets of religious doctrines, but rather that one set is religious (having reference to the sacred), and the other is non-religious, mundane or secular (having reference to the profane). Evers sees Buddhism as constituting the religion of the Sinhalese, but he sees it as an 'incomplete religion', that is, it leaves certain kinds of mundane needs uncatered-for, which have to be met by secular agencies. There is, however, in this concept of an 'incomplete religion' some confusion of definitions. If Ames's Durkheimian analysis is adhered to, it will be seen that a religion is 'complete' when it meets men's needs with reference to the sacred. The meeting of mundane needs is not primarily or properly the business of religion, even though religion by the values it fosters, may have an effect on the way secular agencies meet secular needs.

Yalman's concern is almost wholly focused on the non-Buddhist rituals, within which he finds, as an important and interesting feature, a binary structure. That is to say, the basic purpose of the rituals appears to be to bring about a desired end which will be the reverse of some present, undesirable situation. There is thus a structure of opposed categories: sickness and health, enmity and friendship, and so on. He finds that this characterizes Buddhist belief and practice also, so that there is a parallelism of structure between the two systems, Buddhist and non-

Buddhist. Yalman's primary concern to some extent by-passes the important question of the total structure of Sinhalese culture, as Ames observes. However, in so far as Yalman appears to accept a general distinction between Buddhist and non-Buddhist rituals his analysis does not conflict with Ames's. Ryan's account also implies a distinction of a kind between 'Buddhist' and 'the wonderful world' of gods and demons; the latter, says Ryan, is 'no more than casually associated with the Lord Buddha and that which is of the gods'.[45]

Broadly, therefore, two kinds of analysis of the Sinhalese religious-cultural situation are possible. There is that of Obeyesekere, who sees a hierarchy of closely structured moral communities of belief and practice in which Buddhist and non-Buddhist elements in varying degrees form integrated systems, and which can be compared with one another in terms of 'little tradition' and 'great tradition'. On the other hand, there is that of Ames, who identifies two distinct realms of belief and practice, sacred and profane, each of which has its own complete, self-contained structure. Nevertheless, the two realms affect each other: the kind of emphasis which is being made at any given time within the Buddhistic monastic-lay system will have its effect upon the nature and the status of the secularly-oriented-ritual system.

These two views of Sinhalese religion and culture have some important implications for the interpretation of contemporary ideological and social change in Ceylon. If Obeyesekere's analysis is accepted, the consequences of the modernization and industrialization of Ceylon are likely to be that damage will be done to the structure of these holistic cultural systems or moral communities, in so far as they are increasingly infiltrated by alien ideas and, more important, techniques for dealing with everyday human cares and ills. The effect of modernization will be construed as being one of secularization, in the sense in which Bryan Wilson, for example, uses it, meaning thereby a loss in the social importance of religious beliefs and rituals.

If Ames's analysis is accepted, a rather different view of the same process becomes possible. The distinction between sacred and profane areas of concern enables us to see modernization as a process which may affect one of these more immediately and more drastically than the other; it is not the whole structure of Sinhalese Buddhism which is likely to be affected, but only that system which has secular needs as its field of interest. Illness, for instance, will, in the process of modernization, be regarded less and less as the work of demons, who need to be placated or exorcized; the appropriate remedy will be seen increasingly in terms of scientific medical knowledge.

However, complications are likely to arise in the course of modernization. For the astrological and spirit-cults are restorted to for reasons other than illness; they may be used, for example, by those who seek a change of luck, or to remedy a personal grievance, or to gain some personal advantage. This may explain why these cults show little sign of becoming obsolete in modern Ceylon. The author, when in Ceylon in 1970, was told by informants that the number of people resorting to the *devalaya* shrines in the Colombo area had shown no decrease, but rather the reverse. This is not difficult to understand; in conditions of rapid modernization like those in the Colombo area, awareness of personal stresses and strains may become more acute, as it appears to have done in Japan since the end of the Second World War.[46] Ceylon suffers also from an internal conflict of cultures, Buddhist and Western. The gap left by the removal from what had been a Buddhist state of one of its most vital functionaries, the Buddhist king, and the introduction of alien institutions and values may have been a prime cause of social and cultural tension of a complex order, a classic case of *anomie*, which is reflected in the increasing tendency of Sinhalese people to resort to the *devalayas* for the remedying of immediate and urgent personal disabilities and ills. More research of a comparative nature is needed on this question.[47]

THE UNACKNOWLEDGED IMPORTANCE OF
POLITICAL AND ECONOMIC FACTORS

What seems to emerge from this review of Buddhist civilization in India and Ceylon is that it was not openness to the local cults which weakened Buddhism; this was, if anything, a means of integrating Buddhist and non-Buddhist, Buddhist and not-yet-Buddhist practices, aims and ideals. What weakened Buddhism in both India and Ceylon was its sensitivity and vulnerability to *political* assault and change, and also to *economic* depression or change, whenever discontinuance of an agricultural surplus left the *Sangha* unprovided for and unable to survive.

The difference between the economy of the wet-rice-growing river plains and that of the hills is an important factor in the geographical distribution of Buddhist culture and civilization within any major region, whether in India, Ceylon, or South-East Asia. The difference between the two types of economy and their associated cultures has been admirably dealt with by Edmund Leach, although too few students of Buddhism pay attention to the kind of distinctions to which Leach has drawn attention in connection with Burma.[48] Certainly, the large part played by the economic factor does not appear to be recognized, or at least admitted, by many modern *bhikkhus*. The author found this to be the case in discussion of population growth and control in Ceylon and Thailand.[49] That, however, is one of the issues whose discussion cannot adequately be attempted within the scope of the present book. A brief look at some of these issues may, however, be allowed in the concluding pages.

Epilogue: Beyond the Present Horizons

We have now seen in general outline the characteristic development of a Buddhist civilization in certain parts of India, followed by its decline and virtual disappearance. We have observed the same kind of development, in its essential features, in Ceylon, but here the decline was later and was arrested in time to preserve Buddhist civilization in principle, although its classical structure in Ceylon has since been damaged by European invasion and conquest.

BEYOND INDIA AND CEYLON

No attempt has been made, since it would be impossible within the space available, to deal with the development of Buddhist civilization in those countries outside India where the Mahayana has been the predominant form in which Buddhism spread: that is, in China, Japan, Korea, Tibet and Vietnam. Moreover, in the characteristic form of Buddhist civilization with which we have been concerned here, the *Sangha* is one of the principal and indispensable elements. Since the Mahayana accords less importance to the *Sangha*, the structure of the Buddhist civilization which would have to be traced in the Mahayana countries would be of a somewhat different kind. Moreover, Buddhist civilization as we have characterized it places a high value on the adherence to Buddhism of the political ruler, in order to make possible the kind of political and economic structure which will facilitate the pursuit of Buddhist morality by the maximum number of the citizens of the state, since in this more humanistic form of Buddhism primary importance attaches to human moral effort. Where the adherence of the ruler could not be secured, it was rather more as a theistic religion of supernatural salvation that Buddhism made its way. The outstanding example of this is to be found in China throughout much of the history of Buddhism in that land, although it is to the later rather than the earlier period that this properly applies.

However, it is worth noting that in certain of the countries where the Mahayana form has prevailed, notably Japan and Tibet, the introduction of Buddhism was jointly the concern of the political ruler, who wished his country to adopt Buddhist culture and civilization, and of the *Sangha*, who had already entered the country or were brought in to cooperate with the ruler in setting up a Buddhist state. It is clear that in these cases, therefore, the essential characteristics of Buddhist civilization were recognized, and duly realized.

In Japan, for example, Buddhism was introduced at a time when 'a central authority was being established and the classes and tribes of the numerous islands were being welded into a nation', and when 'communication with the Korean peninsula provided a continual stimulus to change and movement'.[1] The first Buddhists to enter the country, from Korea, were artisans and scholars who came as the bearers of the various arts of civilization.[2] In AD 538 a delegation was sent to Japan by the Prince of Kudara, a principality in the south of Korea, and this was accompanied by Buddhist *bhikkhus*, with Buddhist literature and articles for ceremonial use. The ruling class in Japan was divided over the new ideology: some favoured it and some did not. The division reflected a struggle for political supremacy among conflicting interests. The triumph of those who favoured Buddhism came with the accession of Prince Shotoka to the regency of the country in 593. His reign, says Anasaki, was 'the most epoch-making period in Japanese history, and it was marked by the striking advance of Buddhist influence and continental

civilization. He became the founder of Japanese civilization ...'[3] The public proclamation of Buddhism as the
state religion of Japan was accompanied by the founding
of a Buddhist institution, or group of institutions – a
temple, where provision was made both for ceremonies for
study of Buddhist philosophy and sciences by the
bhikkhus, and for their residence; an asylum for orphans
and old people; a hospital; and a dispensary.[4]

The political ruler acting as Buddhist head of state,
concerned to establish a Buddhist style of public life, with
appropriate institutions for the public welfare, in conjunction with the *Sangha* and on behalf of the people – this
agrees closely with the pattern of Buddhist civilization
established in India by Ashoka eight centuries earlier.

Similarly, it was a Tibetan king, Sron-btsan-sgam-po,
who, about a century later, sought to introduce Buddhism
into his country. A knowledge of its characteristics as a
religious culture and civilization had come to him through
his marriage alliances with Nepal and China. Success was
eventually achieved when a Buddhist teacher from north-
western India, who understood the need for the 'open
frontier' between Buddhist philosophy and popular ideas
in the making of a Buddhist state, was invited to assist in
the task. At a later period of Tibetan history, in the
eleventh century, when Buddhism needed to be restored,
it was a member of the Tibetan royal family who urged
the great Atisha to leave Bengal and go and live in Tibet
for the sake of the rebuilding of Buddhist civilization in
that country.[5]

The even more important case of Buddhist civilization,
which there is not the space to deal with adequately here,
is that of South-East Asia. Particularly significant are the
Theravada Buddhist countries of mainland South-East
Asia: Burma, Thailand, Laos and Cambodia. The fact
that a recognizable civilization of the kind with which we
have been concerned survives in these countries today is
due in large part to two factors. First, there was the work
of the *Sangha* in gaining the adherence of the early rulers

of the Burmese and Thai kingdoms to Theravada Buddhism. Second, there was the influence of the continuing tradition of Sinhalese Buddhism, which at various times in the history of Ceylon's relations with these South-East Asian countries had a stimulating effect on their development as Buddhist states. Such was the case in the late eleventh century when the Burmese kingdom of Pagan came to the help of the kingdom of Ceylon in resisting invasion by the Cholas of South India, with the result that Pagan benefited by the contact her *bhikkhus* had with the Pali Tipitaka tradition in Ceylon. Again, as a result of Parakkama Bahu's reform of Buddhism in Ceylon in the following century, *bhikkhus* from the Mon kingdoms of what is now south Burma and central Thailand, from the Burmese kingdom of Pagan, and from the Malay kingdom of Ligor (the modern Nakorn Si Thamarat in South Thailand) all greatly benefited, in learning and in understanding of the methods of Buddhist analysis and mind training, as well as in the experience of monastic and social organization which they gained as a result of the visits to Ceylon which so many of them made during the twelfth and thirteenth centuries.

South-East Asian kings played an important part in the growth and flowering of Buddhist civilization in the countries of the mainland during these centuries, especially Anawrahta, king of Pagan in the eleventh century, and Rama Kamhaeng, king of the newly established Thai kingdom of Sukhothai in the thirteenth century. As a result of the policies pursued by kings and *Sangha* during these formative centuries, the Burmese and Thai, and eventually also the Laos and Cambodian people of the river-valley states, became supporters of the *Sangha* and willing participants in the benefits which Buddhist civilization brought them. Not all of the peoples of the mainland countries were brought within the aegis of Theravada Buddhism, however; the hill people remained largely untouched, with certain special exceptions, such as the people of the Shan States of eastern Burma and north-west

Thailand. But in the main it was the valley people who became Buddhists, and whose ricefields provided the surplus which maintained and still maintains the *Sangha* in those areas, enabling it to function in what is still, in Thailand especially, its classic and traditional role within a Buddhist civilization. The part played by wise and far-seeing kings such as Mongkut and Chulalongkorn in nineteenth-century Thailand in preserving Buddhist civilization and guiding its development in the conditions of the modern world, or the part played by a rash and unwise king such as Thibaw, the last Buddhist king of Burma, who precipitated his country's final conquest by the British in 1885, and thus brought about a disruption of the Buddhist state, are part of a larger story which must be told elsewhere.[6]

BEYOND 'RELIGION'

Buddhism, like any other living tradition, has developed and changed in the course of its history. As we survey the ground which has been covered here, it is possible to distinguish several major 'types' of Buddhism. There is the Buddhism of the pre-Ashokan period, of which the fullest, though not the only evidence, comes to us through the Pali canon. The emphasis in this early period is predominantly humanistic; the *Buddha-sasana* is a system of mind training, for the restructuring of human consciousness, and thus, ultimately of human society. At this stage Buddhism may be characterized broadly as a humanistic ethic seeking full embodiment in a political and social community, an ideology seeking to become a civilization.

The next stage is Ashokan Buddhism. At this stage Buddhism has realized its potential as a civilization; the cooperation of the *Sangha*, the political ruler and the people has been secured, and a Buddhist state has, in principle, come into existence. This does not mean that all the people have accepted Buddhist values and are acting upon them, or that they all understand the Buddhist doctrines of man, the world and human destiny. But the conditions have been established in which a gradual and steady approximation to these values becomes possible for the whole people. What is more, Buddhist values are given recognition in the structure and the laws of the state. The national state is not, however, the ultimate goal; the vision is of a reconstituted humanity which goes beyond the national to the international community. The Buddhist ruler does what is in his power to commend Buddhist civilization to fellow-rulers, as Ashoka did to his friend and contemporary, King Devanam-piya Tissa of Ceylon. In such efforts to extend Buddhist civilization the members of the *Sangha* cooperate with the ruler or, in many cases, prepare the way for such royal enterprise by their own efforts in making known the *Dhamma*, as the *Sangha* did in north India before the time of Ashoka, and as the Mon *bhikkhus* of South-East Asia did, before the accession of King Anawrahta in Burma, and King Rama Kamhaeng in Thailand. There is no question, however, of either the national Buddhist state, or some international community of Buddhist states which might eventually come into existence, being the ultimate goal in view. The *Dhamma*, as it comes to us in the Pali texts of Ashokan Buddhism, adumbrates a reconstituted humanity, in the social and political sense, but the vision is of more than that. It is recognized that the social structure has important consequences for men's understanding of the human situation and affects their attempts to cope with it and to improve the human condition. This is recognized in Pali Buddhism to an extent which has not always been properly appreciated by Western writers about Buddhism. But a reconstituted social structure is not the ultimate goal, or the final answer. Alvin Gouldner has criticized his fellow-sociologist, Talcott Parsons, for making the social system the answer to man's mortality, which he says, Parsons regards as the 'tragic essence' of the human condition. 'Over and against man's animal mortality, Parsons designs a "social system" that, with its battery of defences and equilibrating devices, need never run down. What Parsons has done is to assign to the self-maintaining social system an immortality transcending and compensatory for man's perishability.' What this theoretical effort of Parsons assumes, adds Gouldner, is the immortality of the social system and, particularly, the American social system.[7] The same kind of objection might conceivably be raised against a theory of Buddhist civilization in which the Buddhist state was held to be the ultimate goal, the reality which comprehended, without remainder of any sort, the whole of the Buddha's teaching. This would be a mistake, for there is clearly recognizable, too, in Pali Buddhism the sense of *the sacred*, as that which transcends all historical and empirical entities. 'There is, O *bhikkhus*, that which is not-born, not-become, not-made, and not-conditioned. If this not-born, not-become, not-made, and not-conditioned were not, then there would be apparent no release from that which is born, become, made and conditioned.'[8] Another name in Pali Buddhism for this absolute which transcends the empirical world is *nibbana*.

It is clear that it is this transcendent reality which is 'the sacred' in Pali Buddhism. Whatever is venerated for its 'sacred' character is in Buddhism that which has a very close or special relationship to *nibbana* – the *Dhamma* which proclaims it, the *bhikkhus* who are the bearers of the *Dhamma* and may in some cases be close to *nibbana*, and the *stupa* which symbolically represents it.

In speaking of Buddhist 'values', therefore, we are speaking of values which are derived from the affirmation of this transcendent sacred reality; Buddhist norms of action are norms which lead men towards *nibbana*. To affirm the sacredness of *nibbana* as the source of Buddhist values does not, however, contradict the characterization of Pali Buddhism as humanistic. It is partly in order to distinguish Pali Buddhism from the Mahayana and from Hinduism that we have characterized it in this way, that is, have emphasized its contradistinction from belief systems which are theistic. And it is to distinguish the Buddha's attitude, as it is portrayed in the Pali canon, from the brahmans and theists of his day, that he may be characterized as 'secular', that is, in contradiction to these 'religious' figures.

But there is a positive reason, too, for describing as humanistic a system of belief and values which centre upon the affirmation of the reality of *nibbana*. For this reality, according to the Pali Buddhist view, is discoverable by man without divine aid; it was so 'discovered' by, or, more properly, it was a man who was 'awakened' (*buddha*) to this reality and who then proclaimed it to others, that they also might become 'awakened' to it. This is not to say that 'awakenment' or enlightenment is immediately available to any and every man. The necessary prerequisite is moral purification, purification of body and consciousness. For humanity in general this is the primary requirement which will inevitably absorb most of its effort and concern. But the implication is that humanity has it within its own power to achieve this; the doctrine is in that sense humanistic. It is humanistic also in that it sees human nature as the highest of the various levels of existence, in the sense that it is only from existence at the level of human nature that *nibbana* is reached. Even the *devas* or celestial beings must come to birth in the human realm in order to be within range, as it were, of *nibbana*. It is no contradiction, therefore, to say that Pali Buddhism has its concept of the transcendent 'sacred', and at the same time that it is a humanistic belief-system. Belief in the sacred does not necessarily imply theistic belief, nor are humanism and a sense of the sacred incompatible.

In the actual situations which Buddhist civilization entailed in India and Ceylon there was often a mixing, or at least juxtaposing, of values. The values held by the member of the *Sangha* who was far advanced in the Buddhist way would have been notably different from those of the villager in Ashoka's India, the villager who had barely as yet come under the influence of the *Dhamma*. Hence it was that with the establishing of

Buddhism as a civilization there also went a dilution of the quality of the values held throughout the Buddhist state, compared with their much higher quality when the Buddhist community contained scarcely any 'laymen', but only *upasakas*, or followers. Now, in Ashokan Buddhism, the *putthujana* or 'ordinary man' was a constituent member of the Buddhist civilization; for him *Dhamma* had to be commended; he had to be encouraged and exhorted to live according to this *Dhamma* which had become the guiding principle of the state.

It was this aspect of Buddhist civilization in Ashokan India, the inclusion of large numbers of 'the masses' within the Buddhist state, in conjunction with the tolerant attitude of the *Sangha* towards the view of life and of the world from which the ordinary man started, which in time produced an important modification. This was the 'popularization' of Buddhist beliefs, in terms of spirits and celestial beings, and it was popularized Buddhism which formed one of the principal components of the third stage of Buddhist development, the post-Ashokan theistic Buddhism which is called Mahayana, or Bodhisattvayana. As we have seen, it is the role of the *Sangha* which is crucial in this kind of situation. The *Sangha*, as the bearer *par excellence* of *Buddhist* values, can successfully deal with such popularized Buddhism, so long as it is allowed to retain its proper status in the Buddhist system as the respected embodiment of wisdom and exemplar of morality. Where the *Sangha*'s status is diminished, or its existence is a matter of indifference, effective permeation of popular culture by Buddhist values ceases to be possible. In India this is what happened eventually, but not before Buddhist civilization in its Ashokan form, in which the *Sangha*'s crucial role was recognized, had been planted in Ceylon. There the proper role of the *Sangha* was retained and safeguarded. This book has attempted to look as carefully as possible within the space available at the difference in the factors present in India and Ceylon, and to suggest some answers to the question why it was that in

India, where Buddhism began, the *Sangha*'s place was undermined, and with it the whole of Buddhist civilization, while in Ceylon the *Sangha*'s essential place was preserved, and Buddhist civilization with it. The factors which have been identified as important are three; they are: *political* – seen in the attitude of rulers, hostile or friendly towards the *Sangha*; *social* – that is, the existence or absence of social classes, such as the brahmans, who are antagonistic to the *Sangha*; and *economic* – that is, the continuing ability of the economy of a country to support the *Sangha*.

Although we have not dealt with South-East Asia, the principles are the same there, too. The *Sangha* survived because it retained the support of political rulers, at least until the British conquest of Burma disrupted Buddhist civilization in that country; and without such disruption until the present day in Thailand. It survived because it was not opposed by any seriously powerful social class or group acting as a rival for the allegiance of the people, and offering a rival ideology of the state, as happened in India. It survived, too, because in the Theravada regions of South-East Asia, that is, the rice-growing river-valleys and plains, agriculture can produce enough and to spare for the present population of the region; there has, therefore, until now, always been a surplus out of which the *Sangha* can be supported.

We have seen from the history of Indian Buddhism that the economic basis of the *Sangha*'s life can be of two kinds. There is the situation in which it is supported by large-scale munificence on the part of royal patrons or very wealthy merchants. And there is the other, older system, that of local support by village people, contributing out of their agricultural surplus to the feeding of the *bhikkhus* and to the upkeep of the monasteries. In the latter case the organization, as in modern Burma, is very simple, like that of the primitive *Sangha*. Mendelson describes it as 'made up, in the main, of small discrete units ultimately responsible to themselves alone: monks living alone or in small groups with perhaps a small entourage of novices and schoolchildren, supported by the village on whose outskirts their monastery was built'.[9] When the economic basis of the *Sangha*'s life is of this kind it is less exposed to the risks of a change of dynasty or the death of wealthy patrons; its basis is wider and, normally, more secure.

On the other hand, when the *Sangha* is a large landowner there is, we have seen, the danger to its life in the alienation from the needs and concerns of the ordinary people which can easily take place, as well as the attraction which the *Sangha* then holds for unworthy entrants. Nor is the land-owning *Sangha* entirely secure from the possibility of economic shortage, for this can come about whether the *Sangha* owns the land or not, by failure of crops, or destruction of crops by invading troops, or merely by defection on the part of the laymen on whom the *Sangha* depends for the cultivation of its land. On balance, the largest guarantee of security and well being for the *Sangha* appears to be found in the system of the 'many small discrete units', supported in each case by the local people.

BEYOND BUDDHISM

Whether or not the increase in population in the Theravada countries is now running at such a rate that, before long, it will exceed the optimum size which allows an agricultural surplus to exist, sufficiently great to support both the non-agriculturally productive sectors of the national economy *and* the *Sangha* as well, is an open question. It is conceivable that the economies of Burma and Thailand could be so adversely affected by the present rate of population increase that a situation could be reached in which it would be difficult to maintain the *Sangha* at its present size and, therefore, its present level of effectiveness. What we have outlined here of the history of Buddhist civilization in India and Ceylon suggests that such an eventuality could seriously threaten the continued existence of Buddhist civilization in South-East Asia.[10]

The Sinhalese Buddhist writer, Dr Walpola Rahula, takes the view that Buddhism *lost* something when it was adopted by Ashoka as a 'state religion'. The framework of reference which this book has attempted to set forth requires a different way of describing that development, and its consequences. Rahula holds that what was formerly a 'religion' gradually developed into 'an ecclesiastical organization with its numerous duties, religious, political and social'. Once this has happened to a religion, he continues, it has to change with the times, or perish.[11] In the view of the matter which has been presented here, one has to say, in contrast to Rahula's interpretation of the matter, that when an ideology for the restructuring of human nature and society becomes a religious cult, it gradually loses some of its original spirit of rationality and political relevance, and its professional representatives or bearers degenerate into a merely religious organization; that it is impossible for a psycho-social philosophy, once it becomes a religious cult, to maintain its effectiveness. The time then comes when it has to change, and reform, or perish; it has to purge itself of what were once popular, cultic, polytheistic religious ideas and practices. These may still retain their hold among rural people, but their days are numbered in a modernizing world. (Other forms of superstition may flourish in urban societies, but not these.)

The Buddhist *Sangha* seems now, however, to have accepted the role of being the professional bearers of a religious cult, one of the several religious alternatives open to men to choose from. Rahula's views are by no means unrepresentative. In the case of Theravada Buddhism, a great deal of the early Ashokan perspective, in which Buddhism was seen as a civilization, has certainly been preserved in one sense, through the preservation by the Theravadins of the Pali texts and their teaching. But Theravada Buddhism as it actually exists today, in Ceylon and South-East Asia, is by no means identical with the Buddhism of the Ashokan period. Much has been acquired along the way since then in the form of devotional practices, institutional organization, and commentaries on the doctrine. In some Asian countries Buddhism retains a good deal of its original concern with the public dimension of life as distinct from the private world of soul-salvation, its character as an ideology capable of integrating a religiously and even culturally pluralistic society. It is in Western countries, on the whole, that there is the strongest insistence on regarding it as a religion competing with other religions; this is a view of it which is shared by some of its adherents, and the adherents of other faiths with which, in Western countries, it coexists.

Some of those citizens of Western countries who have come to call themselves 'Buddhists' affirm that what they have embraced is a religion, on the grounds that man has an innate need for religion and that nothing else but a religion can meet this need. This is a need which they feel, and which they believe has for them been met in Buddhism. There must, they say, be devotional practice, worship, mythology, faith; without these man cannot live, or cannot live at his full stature. 'Buddhism is still a religion, not a philosophy or a system of ethics, by neither of which alone can men live ... We may wish to prune religion of all myth but it should not be overlooked that myths represent man's attempt to express the ineffable and his attitude towards it. A spiritual vacuum must be avoided.'[12]

Certainly Buddhism has *become* a religion, and began to move in that direction within five hundred years from the time of the Buddha's death. But the intention here has been to demonstrate that, in origin, it was the ethos and the philosophy of a civilization. The Buddha was an 'analyst', not a propounder of dogmatic truth, and early Buddhism was characterized essentially by its rationalism (see chapter 7). The human 'need' to which the Buddha addressed himself was not that of man's need for religion, but man's need to overcome his condition of self-centredness, and to identify with a greater, completely comprehensive reality. If man has any innate spiritual 'need', it would appear to be this, rather than religion. Religion provides *one* of the possible ways in which men identify with some all-embracing reality, but there are others. The assertion that religion is a basic human need can be countered by the fact that large numbers of men today live without resort to religion. Whether such men live adequately, or according to the deepest needs of their nature, is controversial. An equally tenable view is that men who live by religion are, partially at least, opting out of this world in favour of another, and therefore are not living fully in this world. Identification with that reality in relation to which the individual self is forgotten, the most comprehensive reality of which man is aware, which 'sanctions' man's existence,[13] can for some men lead to humanistic rather than religious activities. The man without a religion is not a man without values; the values by which he lives are differently derived. Acceptance or rejection of a particular religious position is governed to a large extent by the values which a man embraces, whether they are values he has always held (that is, inherited, or traditionally-received values), or whether he has recently come to hold them. Some people, holding certain sets of values, will take the view that they (and the rest of mankind) have an innate need for devotional practices, for mythology, for belief in a 'world' other than this one; this may itself be the value judgement from which they start. Others, with different sets of values, may not hold this view. Buddhism, especially in Westernized urban situations, has come to be very largely a system of belief and practice which appeals to certain of those who hold the former view, but does not appeal to those who do not feel any need for religion, and do not consider that this is a universal human need. For them, Buddhism is largely irrelevant, as irrelevant as any other religion, although they may acknowledge that it fills a need, and is true, for those who adhere to it.

The fact that Buddhism has, especially as it is understood in the West, arrived at the position where it has this specialized 'religious' character, is an illustration of the perennial religion-making tendency which appears to operate as actively in modern as in ancient societies. It is a continually recurring tendency, but this fact is not necessarily an indication of a universal human *need*, any more than the perennial recurrence of cholera epidemics in the hot season in India is an indication of men's *need* to have cholera. To point out that this religion-making tendency exists, and that it can and does transform into a religious cult, with its attendant mythology, a movement which started out as something quite different, is a proper part of the task of the historian of religion.

FROM THE ANCIENT INDIAN REPUBLICS TO THE MODERN REPUBLIC OF INDIA

Buddhism began as a theory of human existence with implications for human social structure, a philosophy not dependent in any way on theistic belief or theistic sanctions, nor having any divine revelation as its starting-point, and yet tolerant of the theistic beliefs current in the contemporary society, and capable of providing a way of transition from irrational to rational attitudes. In these respects at least, one can observe certain similarities between it and the secular constitution of the modern Republic of India. The fact is not without significance that the founders of the Republic adopted, as its emblem, a famous piece of sculpture known as the Sarnath Lion Capital of the emperor Ashoka, together with the other symbol of the Buddhist state, the Wheel of *Dharma* (*Dharmacakra*). It must be emphasized, however, that the Buddhist affinities, such as they are, of the modern Republic of India, are with the Ashokan state, not with Buddhism as it has now come to be practised, as one 'religion' among others.

The Buddha, it will be recalled, is represented in the Pali texts as favouring a republican form of government. But in the political circumstances of the Buddha's time monarchy seemed to be the only viable system, and the compromise which early Buddhism effected was one by which a republican community (the new *Sangha*), the prototype of a restructured human society, functioned as an advisory body to the monarch. In this way, in Ashokan India, the individualistic brahmanical conception of monarchy was modified in the direction of a *limited* degree of republicanism. So far as the religious beliefs and cults of the day were concerned the Ashokan state adopted the role of the tolerant patron of them all.

The Republic of India, unlike Britain, for example, and some of the other states in modern Asia, does not officially favour any one particular religion. Nor is its head of state required, either by tradition or by the Constitution, to be an adherent of a certain religion. On the other hand, it promises 'to secure to all its citizens ... liberty of thought, expression, belief, faith and worship'.[14] The political structure is one of elected representative government, the basis of the franchise being one man (or woman), one vote. This in itself is a remarkable testimony to the trust which the makers of the constitution placed in the people of India, since 85 per cent of them are non-literate. The trust appears to have been justified, as a political scientist outside India observed even as early as 1960.[15] The Constitution also sets out explicitly that, as a sovereign democratic republic, India intends to secure for all her citizens social and economic justice and equality of status and opportunity. It is perhaps significant that Jawaharlal Nehru, whose part in the shaping of the Constitution was very considerable, was himself strongly influenced by Buddhist ideas, and that the chairman of the body set up to prepare a 'Draft Constitution' (published in 1948) was Dr Ambedkar, who himself later became a Buddhist, together with a large number of the community of the Mahars, to which he belonged. The caste structure, one of the salient features of traditional, post-Buddhist Hinduism is not merely not recognized in India's Constitution; it is by implication rejected. Jawaharlal Nehru as Prime Minister of India until 1964 vigorously pursued this line of policy; as W. H. Morris-Jones has put it, so frequently did he inveigh against communal and caste divisions that the composers of newspaper headlines were 'hard pressed to make the theme arresting'.[16] The final point in this brief comparison is that the Constitution of India guarantees the rights of the individual, but carefully balances this with an equal emphasis on the unity of the nation, and the security of the state itself. In making this double emphasis the Indian Constitution guards against 'the tendency to engender an atomistic view towards society' which in the USA, for example, has resulted from emphasis on individual rights over against the common welfare.[17]

Criticism of the doctrine of caste, tolerant neutrality where all other religious beliefs and practices are concerned (so long as they are consistent with public safety and well-being), concern for social and economic justice, the promotion of rational attitudes and policies wherever possible and an avoidance of measures which would encourage atomistic individualism – these features of modern India's Constitution do not in themselves constitute Buddhism, but to some observers they may suggest that the same kind of problems which were engaging serious attention in the Buddha's day have in modern times been recognized afresh, and are being dealt with in a similar spirit. There is no question, of course, of 'Buddhism' and the ideology of the Republic of India being equated. In the case of the former the *Dhamma* is set out at great length and in great detail; the ideology of the latter has no such explicit exposition. In one sense there was no need in the latter case to set out the ideology, for this had been done already by one of India's greatest sons, the Buddha. It may well be that unconscious echoes of the *Dhamma* are to be heard in the Constitution of the Republic. As in the case of the Ashokan stage, what was envisaged in the way of social reconstruction did not immediately become a reality. The Constitution has to be implemented. But this is the direction in which India has chosen to move and in which she has already begun to advance. Between the republics of ancient India and the Ashokan Buddhist state there is a recognizable historical link, in the *Sangha*. Between the Ashokan state and the modern Republic of India there is again a recognizable affinity; even though the intervening period in this case is much longer, and the genealogy is more complex, what is aimed at in the Constitution of the twentieth-century Republic shares this same family likeness. The important point of difference between the Ashokan state and the modern Indian Republic is that in the former, the *Sangha* was present as an essential element in the socio-political situation. In the latter it is not present, except in an extremely minor role, in certain parts of India, where it has in modern times begun to be reintroduced.

Notes

NOTES ON CHAPTER 1

1 The Pali word *bhikkhu* is often translated into English as 'monk', but this word, with its European connotations of a life apart from other men, is misleading.
2 *Census of India, 1931*, Vol. XI, Rangoon, 1933.
3 *Rayngankansasanapracampi 2508* (Annual Report of Religious Affairs for 1965), Ministry of Education, Bangkok, p. 397.
4 E. B. Tylor, *Primitive Culture*, 4th ed., 1903, Vol. I, p. 424.
5 E. Durkheim, *The Elementary Forms of the Religious Life*, Chapter 1, Section 2.
6 Melford E. Spiro, in *Anthropological Approaches to the Study of Religion*, ed. by Michael Banton, 1966, p. 88 f.
7 *D.* II, p. 156.
8 *Udana*, VIII, 3.

NOTES ON CHAPTER 2

1 E. Nottingham, 1967.
2 E. Nottingham, p. 38.
3 *Voice of Buddhism*, Vol. 8, No. 3, Kuala Lumpur, September 1971, pp. 50–57.
4 For some expansion of this point, see Trevor Ling, 'Buddhist Values and the Burmese Economy', in *Patterns of Buddhism*, ed. by Ninian Smart, 1973. See also pp. 223–4 and 266–7 in this book.
5 *The Middle Way* (Journal of the Buddhist Society of London) in 1971 listed some thirty such groups, but the list is by no means exhaustive.
6 The new suburb of Malaysia's capital, Kuala Lumpur.
7 In the journal of the Buddhist *Missionary Society of Kuala Lumpur, Voice of Buddhism* (September 1971, p. 50) we

read that 'in the years that followed the formation of the Buddhist Missionary Society in 1962, Buddhism [in Malaysia] underwent a major transformation. From a stagnant religion it has become a living force in this country.'

8 It should be noted that, in the view of some Indian historians, there was no Aryan entry *into* India; the movement was in the other direction: in this view, that is, a language and a culture moved *out* of India and spread into other parts of Asia and Europe.

9 See T. O. Ling, *A History of Religion East and West,* sections 1.3 and 1.5.

10 A. B. Keith, 1928, p. 443.

11 *The Laws of Manu,* trans. by G. Buhler, *SBE,* Vol. XXV, Oxford 1886.

12 *Muhammedanism,* London, 1911, p. 75.

13 *Jesus and the Zealots,* 1967, p. 26.

14 *Jesus and the Zealots,* p. 24.

15 *Jesus and the Zealots,* p. 25.

16 S. G. F. Brandon, *History, Time and Deity,* 1965, pp. 189 ff.

17 L. Wirth, 1964, p. 3 f.

18 D. E. Smith, 1963, p. 6 f.

NOTES ON CHAPTER 3

1 The traditional date for the birth of Gotama is, according to the Buddhists of Ceylon and South-East Asia, 623 BC, and for the death, 543 BC. Thus, the 2,500th anniversary of the decease was celebrated in 1956/7. According to modern scholarship, however, the dates should be sixty years later, that is, 563 and 483 BC respectively.

2 D. D. Kosambi, 1956, 137.

3 B. C. Law, 1932, xx.

4 It is important to distinguish between the 'Middle Country' of ancient India, which was called *Madhyadesa,* and the modern state of *Madhya-Pradesh*; the two are geographically different areas.

5 M. Shafi, 1960, p. 8.

6 *IGI,* Vol. I, p. 293.

7 *IGI,* Vol. I, p. 293.

8 This picture of India in the Buddha's time as a land of abundant food is one which some readers may find surprising, since it is commonly believed in the West that

India has an 'age-old problem of poverty and hunger', to quote one recent example of this sort of ignorance. The widespread hunger of the Indian peasants, who invaded the city of Calcutta in the Bengal famine of 1943, is a relatively modern phenomenon. In 1943 the reason lay partly in distribution problems but the long-term reason was the low productivity of Indian agriculture by the end of the British period. Under British rule a landlord system developed which led to insecurity of tenure by tenant-cultivators, in the division and redivision of plots of land, to the point where farming became uneconomical. Cultivators fell into the hands of excessively usurious money lenders. In these circumstances they had little opportunity of increasing the productivity of the land. Moreover, the rate of population increase might have been less serious in its effects had India been able to develop industrially as the Western countries themselves had done and as Japan, free from foreign rule, was able to do. India's industrial development was limited to a few enterprises which were compatible with British economic interests – railways, coal mining to supply the fuel, a small iron industry mainly for the same purpose, jute and cotton milling, the development of which was limited by the interests of Dundee and Lancashire rivals, some sugar refining, glassware and matches. The Industrial Revolution which was needed to relieve India's growing population of its equally fast-growing poverty was not allowed to begin until independent India embarked on the first of her five-year plans in 1951. See P. S. Lokanathan 'The Indian Economic System', in *Economic Systems of the Commonwealth* ed. by Calvin B. Hoover (1962), for a short summary.

For a severe criticism of British economic policy in India by one who was an avowed admirer of British political and legal institutions see Romesh Dutt, *Economic History of India*, 2 vols., (2nd ed. 1906). For a longer account of the more recent situation, see Nasir Ahmoud Khan, *Problems of Growth of an Underdeveloped Economy – India* (1961).

In the India of old there was food in plenty; a significant pointer is the widespread traditional use of fasting as a moral discipline; this is more likely to arise in a situation where people are well fed and need such a discipline than in one where they are already undernourished.

9 *Diod*.II.36; quoted in A. Bose, 1961, p. 122.
10 J. W. McCrindle, 1877, p. 55.
11 D. D. Kosambi, 1956, p. 128.
12 e.g. *Jat.* 547, 499, 518, etc.
13 R. R. Gates, 1948, p. 339.
14 D. D. Kosambi, 1956, p. 106 f.
15 M. M. Singh, 1967, p. 201.
16 J. Beaujeu-Garnier, 1966, p. 55.
17 J. Beaujeu-Garnier, 1966, p. 126.
18 M. M. Singh, 1967, p. 247 f.
19 M. M. Singh, p. 240.
20 A. Bose, 1961, p. 226.
21 *Arthasastra*, II, 1, 48.
22 A. Bose, 1961, p. 226.
23 *sarvamatthi*: This rather imaginative etymology is derived from the Pali form of the name of the city, *Savatthi*.
24 A. Cunningham, 1871, pp. 407–14.
25 *IGI*, Vol. VIII, p. 112.
26 E. B. Cowell (ed.), *Jataka Tales*, Vol. II, 1895, p. 223.
27 See pp. 157 ff.
28 Such as, for example, the ruins of Kaushambi (modern Kosam) 25m. SW of Allahabad.
29 A. Bose, 1961, p. 204.
30 Bose, p. 204.
31 *DDPN*, Vol. II, p. 276.
32 M. S. Pandey, 1963, p. 144.
33 See p. 121.
34 *DDPN*, Vol. I, p. 765 f.

NOTES ON CHAPTER 4

1 U. N. Ghoshal, 1966, p. 189.
2 Ghoshal, p. 186.
3 Ghoshal, p. 188.
4 Ghoshal, pp. 192 f.
5 For a comprehensive account of both the theory and the practice of government in the period under review see Ghoshal, 1959 and 1966.
6 See Rhys Davids, *Dial.*, Pt. III, 1966, pp. 87 ff.
7 Ghoshal, 1959, p. 65.
8 Ghoshal, 1966, p. 532.
9 Manu is the father of the human race in Indian mythology;

he is regarded also as the first and greatest king and prime lawgiver. P. V. Kane, in his *History of Dharmasastra* (Poona, 4 vols., 1930–46) Vol. I, pp. xxv f, comes to the conclusion that the *Code of Manu* belongs to the period from the second century BC to second century C.E. in its present form, with possibly an earlier original.

10 *The Law Book of Manu, SBE*, Vol. XXV, p. 217.

11 Pratap Chandra Ray, the *Mahabharata*, Calcutta, 1883–96.

12 A manual of statecraft and political philosophy composed by a brahman minister of state, probably of the early Mauryan empire. See p. 186.

13 A. II. 74–6, trans. as *Gradual Sayings*, Vol. II, pp. 84 f.

14 See D. Mackenzie Brown 1968, p. 39; and *The Law of Manu, SBE*, Vol. XXV, pp. 40–41.

15 *The Law of Manu, SBE*, Vol. VII, p. 44.

16 See Ghoshal, 1959, pp. 92 f and 131 f.

17 *Arthasastra*, I, 4 and 5.

18 *Mahabharata* XII, 56, 39–40.

19 U. N. Ghoshal, 1966, p. 119.

20 J. C. Brown and A. K. Dey, 1955, p. 178.

21 Brown and Dey, p. 178 f.

22 There are, of course, six possibilities, which may be set out as follows. If A represents monarchy, B urbanism and C individualism, the six possible causal sequences are:

1 A...B...C
2 A...C...B
3 B...C...A
4 B...A...C
5 C...B...A
6 C...A...B

The three which have been mentioned in the text (6, 1 and 3) seem the strongest.

23 Durkheim, 1969, Bk. II, chapter 2.

24 Durkheim, Bk. II, p. 262.

25 Durkheim, Bk. II, p. 403.

26 Durkheim, Bk. II, p. 403.

27 Wirth, 1964, p. 70.

28 Wirth, p. 71 f.

29 E. Fromm, 1942, p. 23.

30 Fromm, p. 23.

31 C. Drekmeier, 1962, p. 55.

32 It should be emphasized that 'urbanism' in this case means the single-city urbanism of the monarchies of ancient India.

NOTES ON CHAPTER 5

1 As represented, e.g., in the Gupta period (fourth to sixth centuries AD) and throughout medieval Indian history down to the end of the Vijayanagar kingdom in S. India in the early sixteenth century.

2 S. N. Dasgupta, 1922, p. 42.

3 There has been considerable discussion as to whether the Upanishads are the work of brahmans, or of the *kshatriyas*, i.e., the nobleman class, some at least of whom were critical of the brahmanical sacrificial system, and proposed these ideas, found as the *Upanishads*, as an alternative. On the whole it seems that the *Upanishads* fairly early gained acceptance by the brahmans and that they may be regarded as broadly within the category of brahmanical literature.

4 Dasgupta, 1922, p. 22.

5 Dasgupta, 1922, p. 22.

6 *Dial.*, Pt I, p. 163.

7 *Dial.*, Pt I, p. 180.

8 *Dial.*, Pt I, p. 164.

9 *Dial.*, Pt I, p. 182.

10 *Brahma Jala Sutta*, 21. See *Dial.*, Pt I, pp. 16 ff.

11 *Vin. Texts, SBE*, Vol. XX, p. 152.

12 *Sutta Nipata*, 927.

13 That is, the RgVeda, SamaVeda, and YajurVeda *samhitas*.

14 M. Bloomfield, writing at the end of the nineteenth century records, however, that influential scholars of Southern India at that time still denied the genuineness of the Atharva as a Vedic text. (See *SBE*, Vol. XLII, pp. xxviii ff.)

15 *HCIP*, Vol. II, p. 464.

16 *HCIP*, Vol. III, pp. 370 f.

17 See Bhattacharya, 1969.

18 *Dial.*, Pt I. p. 31.

19 *Middle Length Sayings*, Vol. I, p. 211.

20 *Middle Length Sayings*, Vol. I, p. 212.

21 *Theragatha* and *Therigatha*.

22 *Vin.* II, 115.

23 T. O. Ling, *Buddhism and the Mythology of Evil*, 1962, p. 80.

24 A. K. Warder, 1956, p. 47.
25 Warder, p. 47.
26 S. Dutt, 1962, p. 47.
27 Dutt, p. 47.
28 Warder, 1956, p. 47.
29 L. S. S. O'Malley, 1910, p. 3.
30 Warder, 1956, p. 48.
31 T. W. Rhys Davids, *Dial.*, Pt I, 1956, pp. 69 f.
32 Warder, 1970, p. 40.
33 B. Barua, 1921, p. 305.
34 *DPPN*, Vol. II, p. 398.
35 *Dial.*, Pt I, pp. 65–95.
36 *Dial.*, Pt I, p. 70.
37 On the Jains, see: H. von Glasenapp, *Der Jainismus*, 1925;
   S. T. Stevenson, *The Heart of Jainism*, 1915.
38 *Dial.*, Pt I, p. 171.
39 *Dial.*, Pt I, p. 73 f.
40 *Dial.*, Pt I, p. 75; see also pp. 37–41.

NOTES ON CHAPTER 6

1 *Buddhism: its Essence and Development*, 3rd edn., 1957,
   p. 34.
2 See H. H. Wilson, 1856, pp. 248 ff.; E. Senart, 1875; H.
   Kern, 1882–4.
3 T. R. V. Murti, 1955, p. 287.
4 A. Bareau, 1966, p. 17.
5 T. W. Rhys Davids, 1959, p. 20.
6 D.I.92. See *Dial.*, Pt I, p. 114.
7 *Dial.*, Pt I, p. 113.
8 *Vin.*II.183; *D.*I.90; *Jat.*, I.88.
9 E. B. Cowell, *Jataka Tales*, 1901. Vol. V–VI, p. 92.
10 D.III.117. See *Dial.*, Pt III, p. 111.
11 E. B. Cowell, *Jataka Tales* (No. 522), Vol. V–VI, 1905, pp.
   64 ff.
12 See N. Wagle, 1966, p. 28.
13 See R. K. Mookerjee, 1969, p. 374.
14 *HCIP*, Vol. II, p. 366.
15 See *M.*I.163–5. *Middle Length Sayings*, Vol. I, pp. 207–9.
16 D. Chattopadhyaya, 1969, pp. 95 f.
17 *ABORI*, 1968, p. 444.
18 *M.*I.163.

19 E. J. Thomas, 1949, p. 51.
20 *M.I.*168. *Middle Length Sayings*, Vol. I, p. 212.
21 For the story of Yasa, and subsequent events, see *Vin.*, Vol. I, pp. 15–20.
22 *DPPN.*, Vol. I, p. 794–8.
23 *DPPN.*, Vol. I, p. 798.
24 See *Samantapasadika* I.9.
25 *Dial.*, Pt II, p. 79.
26 *Dial.*, Pt II, p. 92.
27 *Dial.*, Pt II, p. 103.
28 *Dial.*, Pt II, p. 125.
29 *Dial.*, Pt II, p. 161.
30 *Dial.*, Pt II, p. 199 ff.
31 *MahaSudassana-Jataka* (No. 95). See E. B. Cowell, Vol. I, 1895, pp. 230 ff.
32 *D.I.*4.
33 *Dial.*, Pt I, p. 4 n. 3.

NOTES ON CHAPTER 7

1 *Ariya-pariyesana Sutta*. *M.I.*160 ff. See *Middle Length Sayings*, Vol. I, pp. 203 ff.
2 *M.I.*167. See *Middle Length Sayings*, Vol. I, p. 210 f.
3 *M.I.*27 f. See *Middle Length Sayings*, Vol. I, pp. 27–9.
4 See *Dial.*, Pt II, pp. 4 ff.
5 *Dial.*, Pt II, p. 23 ff.
6 In Indian thought the mind is included as the sixth sense. Like other senses, it is regarded as having its characteristic organ – the brain.
7 D. L. Snellgrove, *Buddhist Himalaya*, 1957, p. 15.
8 Nyanatiloka, 1956, p. 138.
9 Nyanatiloka, p. 140.
10 Buddhaghosa, *Visuddhimagga*, VII.3.
11 Buddhaghosa, *Visuddhimagga*, XXL.3.
12 For fuller details of the relationship of the three-fold to the eight-fold way see the author's article in S. G. F. Brandon, *A Dictionary of Comparative Religion*, p. 257 f.
13 G. S. P. Misra, 'Logical and Scientific Method in Early Buddhist Texts', *JRAS*, 1967–8, p. 54.
14 'Vibhajjavado ... aham ... naham ... ekamsavado': *M.II.*469.
15 Max Weber, 1963, p. 125.

16 *Middle Length Sayings*, Vol. I, p. 251.

17 Karl Marx, 'Theses on Feuerbach', in *K. Marx and F. Engels on Religion*, Foreign Languages Publishing House, Moscow, n.d., p. 72.

18 Narada Thera, 1964, p. 408.

19 See, for example, K. N. Jayatilleke, 1963, and G. S. P. Misra.

20 Misra, p. 64. See chapter 7, note 13.

21 *BSOAS*, Vol. 18, 1956, p. 46.

22 B. Malinowski, *Magic, Science and Religion and other essays*. Doubleday Anchor Books, 1954, p. 17.

23 There were (1) the school whose tradition is embodied in the Pali canon of Ceylon – the *Sthaviravadins*, forerunners of the *Theravadins*; (2) the school which developed in northern India, known as the *Sarvastivadins*, whose literature is in mixed *Buddhist-Sanskrit*; and (3) one of the schools of the Mahayana, known as the *Yogacarins*, which also developed in India.

24 The *Abhidhamma* is the essence of Buddhist teaching; it is the *Dhamma*, in the sense of the discourses of the Buddha, reduced to the bare bones. The 'bones' consist of abstracts, numerical analyses, lists of properties, conditions, etc., involved in mental processes, their relations, and inter-relations, and the new formations, in terms of restructured states of consciousness, which may result. These bones are sometimes very dry bones indeed, and the seven books which make up the *Abidhamma-Pitaka* (the third section or collection in the three-fold *Tipitaka* of the canon) make very tedious reading. The non-Buddhist reader may wonder if such dry bones could ever have lived. What has to be remembered is the context of *Sangha* life and moral striving in which such subjects were studied, and still are studied, in the Buddhist countries of South-East Asia. See the articles '*Abhidhamma*' and '*Abhidhamma Pitaka (Theravada)*' in *A Dictionary of Buddhism* by Trevor Ling. Scribners, 1972, for further details and bibliographical notes.

NOTES ON CHAPTER 8

1 R. Tagore, 1931, p. 70.

2 Still more misleading is the usage adopted, even in modern Buddhist countries (following European, often Portuguese, usage), of calling *bhikkhus* 'priests'.

3 See *Oxford English Dictionary* under 'Monk'.

4 Dutt, 1962, p. 36.

5 Khaggavisana Sutta, Sections 35–75.

6 For further information on the technical aspects of meditation see Buddhaghosa, *Visuddhimagga*; for a condensed account see E. Conze, *Buddhist Meditation*, 1956.

7 *A*, I.253.

8 K. N. Jayatilleke, 1967, p. 498.

9 Vinayan Texts, Vol I, p. 305.

10 Jayatilleke, 1967, p. 490.

11 Dutt, 1962, p. 56.

12 Dutt, 1962, p. 54.

13 The religious–philosophical treatises which slightly preceded the *Upanishads* were known as *Aranyakas*, or 'Forest Writings'. The name for the third of the four *ashramas* or stages of life in the brahmanical scheme was that of the *vanaprastha* or 'forest-dweller' – that is one who dwelt in the forest as a hermit.

14 For a fuller account of this stage of Buddhist development, see Dutt, 1962, pp. 45–65.

15 *D*.II.100. *Dial.*, Pt II, p. 107.

16 *D*.II.100. *Dial.*, Pt II, p. 108.

17 Dutt, 1962, p. 86.

18 Sharma, 1968, p. 241.

19 For the view that the *Sangha* was organized simply in imitation of the tribal *sanghas*, see Jayaswal, *Hindu Polity* (3rd edn., 1955) p. 86, and for the view that it was a deliberate attempt to perpetuate an obsolescent institution, see D. P. Chattopadyaya, *Lokoyata*, 1959.

20 Jayatilleke, 1967, p. 518.

21 G.De, *Democracy in Early Buddhist Sangha*, Calcutta, 1955, p.xv.

22 *D*.II. 76 f.

23 One of the two major classifications of the traditional canonical literature of Buddhism, the other being the collection of the Buddha's discourses known as the *Sutta-Pitaka*. A third collection of material, the *Abhidhamma-Pitaka* was added later. See Note 24 to chapter 7. The *Vinaya* ('Discipline') contained the *Patimokkha*, or list of offences to be avoided, various other regulations concerned with the life of the Order, and some narrative sections dealing with the early history of the order. (For an English transl. see

SBE, Vols. 13, 17 and 20.)

24 *Mahavagga*, X.

25 *Cullavagga*, XII.2, 8.

26 in Pali, *Sangha-bheda*.

27 Dutt, 1962, p. 84.

28 Criteria of Buddhist orthodoxy and unorthodoxy are to be found, e.g., in *Vin*.II.10.

29 *D*.II.74 ff. See also chapter 6, pp. 101 ff., above.

30 Sharma, 1968, p. 241.

31 See, e.g., *Middle Length Sayings*, Vol. I, p. 293 ('uninstructed ordinary man'); *Gradual Sayings*, Vol. I, p. 25 ('uneducated manyfolk'); Vol. IV, p. 108 ('common average folk'), etc.

32 *Sutta Nipata*, 859.

33 *M*.I.239.

34 *S*.IV.201.

35 *S*.IV.196.

36 *A*.IV.157.

37 *A*.I.27.

38 *Sn*.706.

39 *Sn*.816.

40 *S*.IV.206.

41 *Sn*.351.

42 *A*.I.147; *S*.II.94 f.

43 *A*.III.54.

44 *A*.I.267; II.129.

45 *A*.IV.206.

46 *A*.II.163.

47 *M*.I.1, 7.

48 *A*.IV.68.

49 *A*.IV.157. In addition to the references in the Pali canon given in this paragraph, see also, for similar references: *M*.III.64; 227; *S*.I.148; *S*.II.151; III.46, 108, 162.

50 Sharma, 1968, p. 242. See also L. Whibley, *Greek Oligarchies, their Character and Organisation*, London 1896, p. 187. Whibley's further point about the Greek oligarchies, that the multitude were to be 'excluded from citizen rights', does not apply to the Buddhist attitude to the common people.

51 *Sigala-vada Sutta*: *D*.III. 180–193. See *Dial.*, Pt III, pp. 173–184.

52 i.e., Buddhaghosa.

53 T. W. Rhys Davids, *Buddhism*, London, 1890, p. 148.

54 See, e.g., the accounts given by J. G. Scott in *The Burman: His Life and Notions*, 3rd edn., 1909; H. Fielding Hall, *The Soul of A People*, 4th edn, 1902; Manning Nash, *The Golden Road to Modernity*, 1965.

55 By this word in the *Sigalovada Sutta* was meant heaven, the *devaloka*, as an *immediate* goal. The longterm goal remained, of course, beyond rebirth in heaven, *nibbana*.

56 E. Durkheim, *Elementary Forms of the Religious Life*, Collier Books, New York, 1961, pp. 355 f. (The emphasis is mine. – T.L.)

57 *A.I.*211 f. See *Gradual Sayings*, Vol. I, pp. 190–92.

58 See, e.g., the collection of discourses to Pasenadi contained in the *Kosala Samyutta* (*S.I.*68 ff). See *The Book of the Kindred Sayings* Vol. I, pp. 93–127.

59 *DPPN*, II, 285 f.

60 Whose work, *A History of Indian Political Ideas*, has been adjudged 'the most scholarly and comprehensive work on the subject ever to have been written'. (A. L. Basham in *BSOAS*, London University, Vol. 25 (1962), p. 178.)

61 Ghoshal, 1959, p. 69.

62 E.g., *Jat.* 194, 334, 407, 501, 521, 527, 533, 534, 540, 544.

63 *Jat.*V.378.

64 Jayatilleke, 1967, p. 530.

65 See, e.g., *Jat.*V.222 ff.

66 E. B. Cowell, 1905, p. 115.

67 *Gradual Sayings*, Vol. II, p. 85.

68 *Jat.*334.

69 *Dial.*, Pt I, p. 175 f.

70 *Dial.*, Pt II, pp. 199–217.

71 *Cakkavatti-Sihanada Su.*

72 *Dial.*, Pt III, p. 65.

73 *Dial.*, Pt III, p. 66.

74 *Dial.*, Pt III, p. 67.

75 *Dial.*, Pt III, p. 69 f.

76 Ghoshal, 1962, p. 73.

77 See *Gradual Sayings*, Vol. III, p. 114 f.

78 *A.I.*76 f. See *Gradual Sayings*, Vol. I, p. 71.

79 Ghoshal, 1962, p. 79.

80 *balacakram hi nisraya dharmacakram pravartate*. Jayatilleke, 1967, p. 530.

NOTES ON CHAPTER 9

1 *K. Marx and F. Engels On Religion*, Foreign Languages Publishing House, Moscow, n.d., p. 42.

2 In the Marxist case this is contained largely in K. Marx: *Economic and Philosophic Manuscripts of 1844*, transl. by M. Milligan, Moscow, 1959.

3 See R. K. Mookerji, 'Chandragupta and the Maurya Empire', in *History and Culture of the Indian People*, Vol. II, chapter 4; and B. G. Gokhale, *Asoka Maurya*, New York, 1966, chapter 1.

4 *HCIP*, Vol. II, pp. 31 ff.

5 See P. H. L. Eggermont, *The Chronology of the Reign of Ashoka Moriya*, Leiden, 1956.

6 See B. G. Gokhale, *Asoka Maurya*, 1966, Chapter 2.

7 Gokhale, 1966.

8 Gokhale, 1966, p. 107.

9 *Mahavamsa*, V.66.

10 *Appamada-vagga*, found in the *Sutta-Nipata*.

11 *Mahavamsa*, V.34–72, English transl. by W. Geiger, 1912 (1960), pp. 28–32.

12 See L. S. Perera, 'The Pali Chronicles of Ceylon' in *Historians of India, Pakistan and Ceylon*, ed. by C. H. Philips, 1961.

13 See J. Bloch, *Les Inscriptions d'Asoka*, Paris, 1950, and E. Lamotte, *Histoire du Bouddhisme Indien*, Louvain, 1959, Addenda, pp. 789 ff. For an English transl. see R. Thapar, *Asoka and the Decline of the Mauryas*, Oxford, 1961, Appendix V, pp. 250–66; or Gokhale, 1966, Appendix, pp. 151–70.

14 The question of what is meant by the gods mingling with men will be dealt with later – see p. 200.

15 R. Thapar, *Asoka and the Decline of the Mauryas*, 1961, p. 259. I have amended the punctuation after 'if they are earnest' in order to express the meaning of the original more clearly. See Bloch, 1950, pp. 147–8.

16 Identified as the modern town of Kanakagiri.

17 The three are: The Bairat Stone Inscription, the Barabar Hill Cave Inscription, and the Kandahar Inscription. See J. Bloch, 1950, pp. 154, 156, and E. Lamotte, 1959, p. 793 for the text of these.

18 This title occurs 59 times in the 29 inscriptions. In one of them, the Seventh Pillar Edict, it is repeated 10 times.

19 See R. K. Mookerji in *HCIP*, Vol. II, p. 73.

20 The title *Piyadassi*, which may be translated loosely as 'the Splendid', is frequently used as a name for Ashoka in the inscriptions.

21 The Thirteenth Major Rock Edict, transl. by Thapar, 1961, p. 256 f. See Bloch, 1959, pp. 125–8, for text.

22 Just as the *Chakravartin* is conventionally referred to as 'father' so Ashoka declared 'all men are my children' (Second Kalinga Rock Edict, Thapar, p. 258).

23 Thapar, p. 266; Bloch, p. 172.

24 Thapar, p. 261; Bloch, p. 154 f.

25 Thapar, p. 261; Bloch, p. 157. For the story of the modern discovery of this pillar, in the forests of the Nepal border, see S. Dutt, *The Buddha and Five After Centuries*, 1957, chapter 2.

26 Eleventh Major Rock Edict: Thapar, p. 254 f; Bloch, p. 120.

27 Third Major Rock Edict: Thapar, p. 251; Bloch, pp. 96–7.

28 Fourth Major Rock Edict: Thapar, p. 251; Bloch, pp. 98–9.

29 Thapar, p. 266; Bloch, p. 172.

30 Thapar, p. 262; Bloch, p. 162.

31 Thapar, p. 266; Bloch, p. 171.

32 For convenience, an analysis of the expositions of *Dhamma* in the Ashokan inscriptions is given below; set out synoptically this enables the evidence, on which the summary given in the text of chapter 9 is based, to be seen at a glance:

| Major Rock Edicts | | | Pillar Edicts | |
Third	Fourth	Eleventh	Seventh	Second
(1) obedience to parents	obedience to parents	obedience to parents	obedience to parents	
(2) good behaviour to friends and relatives	deference to relatives	generosity to friends and relatives	[see (14) below]	[see (14) below]

| | Major Rock Edicts | | | Pillar Edicts | |
	Third	Fourth	Eleventh	Seventh	Second
(3)	generosity (*dana*) to brahmans and shramanas	deference to brahmans and shramanas	generosity (*dana*) to brahmans and shramanas	regard for brahmans and shramanas	
(4)		obedience to elders		deference to elders	
(5)				obedience to teachers	
(6)			good behaviour to servants, etc.	regard for servants, etc.	
(7)				regard for the poor and wretched	
(8)	not to kill living beings (*anarambho*)	abstention from killing (*anarambho*)	abstention from killing (*anarambho*)	abstention from killing (*anarambho*)	
(9)		non-injury to living beings (*avihimsa*)		non-injury to-living beings (*avihimsa*)	
(10)	to spend little				
(11)	to have minimum possessions				
(12)					few faults and many good deeds
(13)				mercy	mercy
(14)				charity (*dana*)	charity (*dana*)
(15)				truthfulness	truthfulness

| | *Major Rock Edicts* | | | *Pillar Edicts* | |
	Third	Fourth	Eleventh	Seventh	Second
(16)				purity	purity
(17)				gentleness	
(18)				virtue	

33 First Major Rock Inscription: Thapar, p. 250; Bloch, pp. 92–3.

34 Kandahar Bilingual Rock Inscription: Thapar, p. 260.

35 Fifth Pillar Edict: Thapar, p. 264; Bloch, pp. 165–6.

36 Fourth Major Rock Edict: Thapar, p. 251; Bloch, pp. 98–9.

37 Eighth Major Rock Edict: Thapar, p. 253; Bloch, pp. 112–13.

38 Second Major Rock Edict: Thapar, p. 251; Bloch, pp. 93–5.

39 A *kos* is approx. 2 miles, and 8 kos = 1 *yojana*, or the normal distance for a day's march for soldiers in those days in India.

40 Thapar, p. 265.

41 *Dhamma mahamatra*.

42 Fifth Major Rock Edict: Thapar, p. 252; Bloch, pp. 102–4.

43 Thapar, p. 250; Bloch, pp. 90–91.

44 Ninth Major Rock Edict: Thapar, pp. 253 f; Bloch, pp. 113–15.

45 Minor Rock Edict 'from Suvarnagiri': Thapar, p. 259; Bloch, p. 146.

46 Barabar Cave Inscriptions I and II, and Seventh Pillar Edict: Thapar, pp. 260 and 265; Bloch, pp. 156 and 170 f.

47 As Ghoshal (1966), for instance, does.

48 D.II.118.

49 See T. W. Rhys Davids, *Dial.*, Pt I, pp. 272–3, and his *Buddhism*, 1890 (1962), pp. 174–7.

50 D.II.141. See *Dial.*, Pt II, p. 154.

51 D.II.141. See *Dial.*, Pt II, p. 154.

52 Dutt, *The Buddha and Five After Centuries*, 1957, p. 169.

53 Dutt, p. 167. See also B. Rowland, *The Art and Architecture of India*, 3rd edn, 1967, n. 1 to chapter 6, p. 279.

54 The Pali Chronicles credit him with building numerous *cetiyas*, or *stupas*. See *Mv*.V.175. See also Dutt, p. 171; and Rowland, p. 48.

55 For modern examples of this, see Ling, *A History of Religion East and West*, 1968, pp. 371 ff.
56 Philip S. Rawson, *Tantra*, Arts Council of Great Britain, 1971, p. 33.
57 Thapar, 1961, p. 255.
58 Dutt, 1957, p. 217.
59 Kathavathu, 176–7.
60 Kathavathu, pp. 178–9.
61 Kathavathu, p. 202.
62 See, e.g., *Milinda's Questions*, Vol. I, transl. by I. B. Horner, 1963, IV.6, in which 'the natural weakness of the Lord's physical frame' is repeatedly mentioned.
63 For a summary of the debate, particularly between Hariprasad Sastri and H. C. Raychaudhuri, see Thapar, pp. 198–205.
64 *Manu*, IX.225.
65 *Manu*, V.89.

NOTES ON CHAPTER 10

1 This is Buddhaghosa's commentary on the *Vinaya-Pitaka*. See G. P. Malalasekere, 1928, pp. 94 f.
2 Malalasekere, 1928, pp. 45 f.
3 *Mahavamsa*, XI.19, transl. by Geiger, 1912, p. 78.
4 *Mahavamsa*, XI.28–32, transl. by Geiger, pp. 79 f.
5 *Mahavamsa*, XI.33–36, transl. by Geiger, p. 80.
6 Pali: *jinasasanam patitthapetha*. Geiger's translation as 'found the religion of the Conqueror', reflects modern conceptions and is possibly misleading. The word *sasana* means strictly 'a discipline', or 'teaching'.
7 Strictly, 'the lesser discourse on ... etc.' (*Culahattipadupama–Suttanta*). In its context as a discourse of the Buddha it is found in the *Majjhima-Nikaya*, I.175. See *Middle Length Sayings*, Vol. I, transl. by I. B. Horner, London, 1954, pp. 220–30.
8 M.I.179.
9 M.I.184. *Middle Length Sayings*, Vol. I, p. 230.
10 *Mahavamsa*, XIV.23, transl. by Geiger, 1912, p. 93.
11 This is a separate book, found in the *Khuddaka-nikaya*.
12 Also a separate book of the *Khuddaka-nikaya*.
13 The *Sacca-samyutta*, found in the *Samyutta-nikaya*. For the four noble truths, see above, chapter 7, p. 111.

14 According to Buddhist custom already established in India.
15 *dhatusu ditthesu ditthohoti jino*: *Mv.*XVII.3.
16 C. W. Nicholas and S. Paranavitana, 1961, p. 49.
17 Nicholas and Paranavitana, 1961, pp. 49 f.
18 *Samantapasadika.*
19 *Buddhist India*, 1959, pp. 299 ff.
20 Rahula, 1966, p. 54.
21 Rahula, 1966, p. 55.
22 Rahula, 1966, p. 55.
23 *Visuddhi Magga*, I.91.
24 Rahula, 1966, p. 62.
25 The correct name of the island. The name 'Ceylon' is a European corruption.
26 That is, the Buddha, the *Dhamma* and the *Sangha*.
27 *Pujavaliya*, Colombo, 1926, p. 656. See Rahula, 1966, p. 63.
28 See Rahula, 1966, p. 69 f.
29 The dating followed here is that of Wilhelm Geiger, based on the evidence of the chronicles, and set out in detail in his translation of the *Culavamsa*, Vol. II, pp. ix–xi. On the other hand, according to the chronology followed by Nicholas and Paranavitana, 1961, these three regions cover the period 161–109 BC (p. 341).
30 *paragangam gamissami jotetum sasanam aham Mv.*XXV.2. Alternatively, the words might mean, that the *sasana* (of the Buddha) might be made clear.
31 *rajjasukhaya vayamo nayam mama, sadapi ca sambuddh-asasanasseva thapanaya ayam mama. Mv.*XXV.17.
32 *Mahavamsa*, transl. by Geiger, p. 177.
33 The ceremony at which the Vinaya regulations which govern the life of the *Sangha* are recited, and any infringements are confessed and dealt with.
34 *The Mahā Thūpa* – known also as the Ruvanveli Dagoba – 'the Relic Chamber of the Golden Sands'.
35 *Mv.*XXXII.1–47.
36 Malalasekere, 1928, p. 35 f.
37 Nicholas and Paranavitana, 1961, p. 67.
38 *Mv.*XXXII.38.
39 See E. W. Adikaram, 1946, p. 65, n. 3.
40 *Mv.*XXXII.81–2.
41 *Mv.*XXXIII.13.
42 *Saddharmalankaraya*, Colombo edition, n.d., p. 123.
43 Malalasekere, 1928, p. 40.

44 Adikaram, 1946, p. 71.
45 See Buddhaghosa's commentary on the *Vibhanga, Sammo-havinodani*, 473.
46 Adikaram, 1946, p. 73.
47 *gahetva*: Mv.XXXIII.19.
48 Or 'caused them to decline': *parichapayi*. Mv.XXXIII.20.
49 *na janimsu yathavuddham*.
50 *dandakammattham*. Mv.XXXIII.21.
51 Adikaram, 1946, p. 73.
52 Malalasekere, 1928, p. 40.
53 Rahula, 1966, p. 81.
54 The *Sasanavamsa*, composed in Burma in 1861 by a *bhik-khu* named Pannasami.
55 The *Jinakalamali-pakaranam* composed in Thailand, in the early sixteenth century by Ratanapanna, a Thera of Thailand.
56 *The Culavamsa*, Part I, transl. by Wilhelm Geiger and C. M. Rickmers, Colombo, 1953, p.v.
57 B. J. Perera 'Some political trends in the late Anuradha-pura and Polonnaruwa period', in *Ceylon Historical Journal*, Vol. X, 1960, p. 60.
58 *Culavamsa*, 44.130. English transl., Pt I, p. 86.
59 *Culavamsa*, 44.133.
60 Perera, 1960.
61 Perera, 1960, p. 63.
62 Malalasekere, 1928, p. 175.
63 *Culavamsa*, LXXIII.2–8.
64 See Nicholas and Paranavitana, 1961, p. 215.
65 *Culavamsa*, LXXIX.86.
66 For details of Parakkama Bahu's irrigation works see Nicholas and Paranavitana, 1961, pp. 256–9, and for those of earlier kings, pp. 159–62.
67 Nicholas and Paranavitana, 1961, p. 170.
68 Mv.XLII.16–24.
69 Nicholas and Paranavitana, 1961, p. 111.
70 Nicholas and Paranavitana, p. 111.
71 Nicholas and Paranavitana, p. 169.
72 Nicholas and Paranavitana, p. 111.
73 B. M. Morrison, 1970, p. 115.
74 R. Pieris, 1956, p. 73.

NOTES ON CHAPTER 11

1 Ghoshal, in *HCIP*, Vol. III, 1970 (3rd edition), p. 343.
2 Ghoshal, 1970, p. 343.
3 Rowland, *The Art and Architecture of India*, 3rd edn., 1967, p. 281.
4 Rowland, 1967, p. 78.
5 See Dutt, *Buddhist Monks and Monasteries of India*, 1962, p. 169.
6 Dutt, 1962, p. 174.
7 Hsuan Tsang, Vol. I, p. 240.
8 Lalmani Joshi, 1967, p. xvii.
9 For the evidence that Buddhism had reached Bengal in the Ashokan period see the author's 'Buddhism in Bengal' in the S. G. F. Brandon Memorial Volume, 1973.
10 Kosambi, 1965, p. 178.
11 Sushil Kumar De, 1961, p. 26.
12 J. C. Ghosh, 1948, p. 24.
13 Bhakat Prasad Mazumdar, 1960, p. 170.
14 Mazumdar, 1960, p. 171.
15 *Dacca District Gazetteer*, 1969, p. 49.
16 *Dacca District Gazetteer*, 1969, p. 49.

NOTES ON CHAPTER 12

1 See, e.g., Ludowyk, 1966; Malalasekere,1928, G. C. Pieris, 1963; P. E. Pieris, 1920.
2 See Nicholas and Paranavitana, 1961, chapter 18.
3 Malalasekere, 1928, p. 259. On this period see also J. E. Tennent, 1859, Vol. II, chapter 1; and P. E. Pieris, 1920, *passim*.
4 Ludowyk, 1966, p. 9.
5 Ludowyk, p. 12.
6 *Mv*.XCVIII.
7 *Mv*.XCIX.7–11.
8 *Mv*.C.73–6.
9 Tennent, 1859, Vol. II, p. 76.
10 de Silva, 1965, p. 64, n. 2.
11 R. S. Hardy, 1893, pp. 12 f, p. 44.
12 P. E. Pieris, 1950, pp. 596 ff.
13 de Silva, 1965, p. 65.
14 Quoted by de Silva, 1965, p. 65.

15 On the Sinhalese view regarding the inalienable right of the Buddha over the island, see above, chapter 10.

16 de Wijesekere, 'Theravada Buddhist Tradition Under Modern Culture' in *Proceedings of the 11th Congress of the International Association for the History of Religion*, 1968.

17 Ludowyk, 1966, p. 116.

18 See Rahula, 1966, p. 284.

19 Copleston, 1908.

20 C. Eliot, 1921, Vol. III, pp. 41–4.

21 Eliot, Vol. III, p. 42.

22 Eliot, Vol. III, p. 48 f.

23 Copleston, 1908, pp. 275 f.

24 Copleston, p. 282.

25 Ludowyk, 1962, p. 171.

26 N. Yalman, 1966, p. 210.

27 L. Woolf, 1913, p. 106.

28 B. Ryan, 1958.

29 Ryan, p. 90.

30 Ryan, p. 106.

31 Ryan, p. 101.

32 Ryan, p. 105.

33 Obeyesekere, 1963, p. 143.

34 Obeyesekere, 1966, p. 10.

35 Obeyesekere, 1966, p. 16.

36 R. L. Slater, *Paradox and Nirvana*, Chicago, 1951.

37 M. Ames (i), 1964, p. 78; (ii) 1964, p. 35.

38 Ames (ii), p. 37.

39 Ames (ii), p. 25.

40 Ames (ii), p. 27.

41 Ames (i), p. 80.

42 Ames (ii), p. 40.

43 Ames (ii), pp. 47 f.

44 H.–D. Evers, 1965, p. 98.

45 Ryan, 1958, p. 90.

46 On Japanese religious movements since the Second World War, see Clark B. Offner and Henry Van Straelen, *Modern Japanese Religions*, 1963; D. C. Holtom, *Modern Japan and Shinto Nationalism: A Study of Present-Day Trends in Japanese Religions*, Revised edn., 1963; Harry Thomson, *The New Religions of Japan*, 1963; H. N. MacFarland, *The Rush Hour of the Gods*, 1967; *The Sociology of Japanese Religion*, ed. by Kiomi Morioka and William H. Newell,

1968; H. Byron Earhart, *Japanese Religion: Unity and Diversity*, 1969.

47 Another feature of Sinhalese culture which is of importance to social anthropologists, but which has not been dealt with here, is the relationship between Buddhism in Ceylon and the caste system. On this, see E. R. Leach, 1960, for further references. The degree to which the Buddhist community in Ceylon recognizes caste distinctions appears to be a case of a feature of 'pan-Indian civilization' (Leach, 1960, p. 5) proving stronger than the resistance to it which is implied in Buddhist theory.

48 See Leach, 1954, especially chapter 2.

49 See Ling, 'Buddhist Factors in Population Growth and Control', *Population Studies*, Vol. XXIII, No. 1, March 1969, pp. 53–60.

NOTES ON EPILOGUE

1 M. Anesaki, 1930, p. 51.

2 Anesaki, p. 52.

3 Anesaki, p. 57.

4 Anesaki, pp. 57 f and see also Ling, *History of Religion East and West*, 1968, pp. 239 f.

5 See Ling, p. 248.

6 The subject of Buddhist civilization in South-East Asia is a large and important one, and deserves treatment in a separate work.

7 Gouldner, 1970, pp. 433 f.

8 *Udana*, VIII.3.

9 Mendelson, 1964, pp. 86 f.

10 See note 49 to chapter 12.

11 Rahula, 1966, pp. 76 f.

12 Review by Murial Clark in *The Middle Way*, London, Vol. XLVII, No. 1, May 1972, p. 49.

13 See chapter 1, p. 18.

14 Preamble to the Constitution. See D. D. Basu, 1962, p. 25.

15 R. N. Spann, 1963, p. 23.

16 W. H. Morris-Jones, 1971, p. 55.

17 D. D. Basu, 1962, p. 43.

Abbreviations

A.	Anguttara Nikaya (Pali text)
ABORI	Annals of the Bhandarka Oriental Research Institute
Arthas-astra	*Kautilya's Arthasastra*, transl. by R. Shamasastry, 8th edn., 1967
BSOAS	*Bulletin of the School of Oriental and African Studies*
D.	*Digha Nikaya* (Pali text)
Dial.	*Dialogues of the Buddha*, Pt I, Pt II and Pt III (see bibliography under Davids, T. W. Rhys)
Diod.	*Bibliotheca Historica of Diodorus Siculus*, in J. W. M'Crindle, *The Invasion of India by Alexander the Great*, 1893, pp. 269–301
DPPN	*Dictionary of Pali Proper Names*, 2 vols, by G. P. Malalasekere
Gradual Sayings	*The Book of the Gradual Sayings*, Vol. I, Vol. II and Vol. V by F. L. Woodward, 1932, 1933 and 1936; Vol. III and Vol. IV transl. by E. M. Hare, 1934 and 1935
HCIP	Bharatiya Vidya Bhavan's *History and Culture of the Indian People*, Vols. 1–10
IGI	*Imperial Gazetteer of India*, 9 vols., ed. by W. W. Hunter, 1881
Jat.	*Jatakas* (Pali text)
JRAS	*Journal of the Royal Asiatic Society*
M.	*Majjhima Nikaya* (Pali text)
Mv.	*Mahavamsa* (Pali text)
S.	*Samyutta Nikaya* (Pali text)
Skt.	Sanskrit
Sn.	*Sutta Nipata* (Pali text)
SBE	*Sacred Book of the East*
Vin.	*Vinaya Pitaka* (Pali text)

List of Works Cited in the Notes

ADHYA, G. L. *Early Indian Economics*, 1966

ADIKARAM, E. W. *Early History of Buddhism in Ceylon*, 1946

AMES, M.
  (i) 'Buddha and the Dancing Goblins: A Theory of Magic and Religion' in *American Anthropologist*, Vol. 66. Part I, 1964
  (ii) 'Sinhalese Magical Animism and Theravada Buddhism' in *Religion in South Asia*, ed. by E. B. Harper, 1964

ANESAKI, M. *History of Japanese Religion*, 1930, reprinted 1963

BAREAU, A. *Les Religions de l'Inde*, 1966

BARUA, B. *A History of pre-Buddhistic Indian Philosophy*, 1921

BASU, D. D. *Introduction to the Constitution of India*, 2nd edn., 1962

BEAUJEU–GARNIER, J. *Geography of Population*, transl. by S. H. Beaver, 1966

BHATTACHARYA, T. *The Cult of Brahma*, 2nd edn., 1969

BLOCH, J. *Les Inscriptions d'Asoka*, 1950

BOSE, Atindranath. *Social and Rural Economy of Northern India*, 1961

BROWN, D. Mackenzie. *The White Umbrella: Indian Political Thought from Manu to Ghandi*, 1968

BROWN, J. C. and DEY, A. K. *India's Mineral Wealth*, 3rd edn., 1955

CHATTOPADHYAYA, D. *Indian Atheism*, 1969

COPLESTON, R. S. *Buddhism Primitive and Present in Magadha and in Ceylon*, 2nd edn., 1908

COWELL, E. B. (ed.) *Jataka Tales*, Vols. I–II, 1895; Vols. III–IV, 1901; Vols. V–VI, 1905.

CUNNINGHAM, A. *Geography of Ancient India*, 1871

DASGUPTA, S. N. *History of Indian Philosophy*, Vol. I, 1922

DAVIDS, T. W. Rhys. *Buddhist India*, 8th edn., 1959

Dialogues of the Buddha, Pt I, 1899; Pt II, 1910; Pt III, 1921. repr. 1956, 1965 and 1966

DE, K. *Vaisnava Faith and Movement*, 1961

DE SILVA, K. M. *Social Policy and Missionary Organisation in Ceylon, 1840–55*, 1965

DE WIJESEKERE, O. H. 'Theravada Buddhist Tradition under Modern Culture', in *Proceedings of the 11th International Congress of the International Association for the History of Religions*, Vol. I, 1968

DREKMEIER, C. *Kingship and Community in Early India*, 1962

DURKHEIM, E. *The Division of Labour in Society*, English transl. by George Simpson, 7th impression, 1969

DUTT, S. *Buddhist Monks and Monasteries of India*, 1962

ELIOT, C. *Hinduism and Buddhism*, 3 vols., 1921

EVERS, Hans-Deiter. 'Magic and Religion in Sinhalese Society' in *American Anthropologist*, Vol. 67 (i)

FROMM, E. *The Fear of Freedom*, 1942

GANGULI, B. N. (ed.) *Readings in Indian Economic History*, 1964

GATES, R. R. *Human Ancestry from a genetical point of view*, 1948

GEIGER, W. *Mahavamsa, or the Great Chronicle of Ceylon translated into English*, 1912, reprinted 1964
    Culavamsa, being the more recent part of the Mahavamsa, Pt I and Pt II, 1928, reprinted 1953

GHOSH, J. C. *Bengali Literature*, 1948

GHOSHAL, U. N. *A History of Indian Political Ideas*, 1959
    A History of Indian Public Life, Vol. II: The Maurya and pre-Maurya period, 1966

GOKHALE, B. G. *Ashoka Maurya*, 1966

GOULDNER, A. W. *The Coming Crisis in Western Sociology*, 1970

HARDY, R. S. *The British Government and the Idolatry of Ceylon*, 1839

HSUAN TSANG *Buddhist Records of the Western World*, 4 vols., transl. from the Chinese by Samuel Beal, reprinted 1957

JAYATILLEKE, K. N. *The Principles of International Law in Buddhist Doctrine*, 1967 (private circulation only)
    Early Buddhist Theory of Knowledge, 1963

JOSHI, L. *Studies in the Buddhistic Culture of India*, 1967

KEITH, A. B. *A History of Sanskrit Literature*, 1928

KERN, H. *Der Buddhismus und seine Geschichte in India*, 1882–4

KOSAMBI, D. D.
  (i) *An Introduction to the Study of Indian History*
  (ii) *The Culture and Civilisation of Ancient India*, 1965

LAMOTTE, E. *Histoire du Bouddhisme Indien: des origines à l'ère Saka*, 1958

LAW, B. C. *Indological Studies*, Vol. III, 1954

LEACH, E. R. *Political Systems of Highland Burma*, 1954
  Aspects of Caste in South India, Ceylon and North-West Pakistan, 1960

LING, T. *History of Religion East and West*, 1968

LUDOWYK, E. G. *The Story of Ceylon*, 1962
  The Modern History of Ceylon, 1966

MAHAVAMSA (Pali text) edited by Wilhelm Geiger, 1908, reprinted 1958

MAJUMDAR, B. P. *Socio-Economic History of Northern India*, 1960

MALALASEKERE, G. P. *Dictionary of Pali Proper Names*, 2 vols., 1937, reprinted 1960
  The Pali Literature of Ceylon, 1928, reprinted 1958

M'CRINDLE, J. W. *Ancient India as described by Megasthenes and Arrian*, 1877

MENDELSON, E. M. 'Buddhism and the Burmese Establishment' in *Archives de Sociologie des Religions*, Vol. 17, 1964

MOOKHERJEE, R. K. *Ancient Indian Education, Brahmanical and Buddhist*, 4th edn, 1969

MORRIS-JONES, W. H. *The Government and Politics of India*, 3rd (revised) edn, 1971

MORRISON, B. M. *Political Centers and Cultural Regions in Early Bengal*, 1970

MURTI, T. R. V. *The Central Philosophy of Buddhism*, 1955

NARADA, Thera *The Buddha and his Teaching*, 1964

NICHOLAS, C. W. and PARANAVITANA, S. *A Concise History of Ceylon*, 1961

NOTTINGHAM, E. 'Buddhist Ethics and Economic Development' in *World Buddhism Vesak Annual*, 1967

NYANATILOKA, *Buddhist Dictionary*, 1956

OBEYESEKERE, G.
  (i) 'The Great Tradition and the Little in the Perspective of Sinhalese Buddhism', in *Journal of Asian Studies*, Vol. 22 (2), 1963

(ii) 'The Buddhist Pantheon in Ceylon and its Extensions', in *Anthropological Studies in Theravada Buddhism*, ed. by Manning Nash, 1966

O'MALLEY, L. S. S. *Bengal District Gazetteers: Birbhum*, 1910

PANDEY, M. S. *The Historical Geography and Topography of Bihar*, 1963

PIERIS, G. C. *Ceylon Today and Yesterday*, 2nd edn, 1963

PIERIS, P. E. *Ceylon and the Portuguese, 1505–1658*, 1920
Sinhale and the Patriots, 1950

PIERIS, R. *Sinhalese Social Organisation: The Kandyan Period*, 1956

RAHULA, W. *History of Buddhism in Ceylon: the Anuradhapura Period*, 2nd edn, 1966

RYAN, B. *Sinhalese Village*, 1958

SENART, E. *Essai sur la legende du Buddha*, 1875

SHAFI, M. *Land Utilization in Eastern Uttar Pradesh*, 1960

SHARMA, J. P. *Republics in Ancient India, c. 1500 BC to 500 BC*, 1968

SINGH, M. M. *Life in North-Eastern India in Pre-Mauryan Times*, 1967

SMITH, D. E. *India as a Secular State*, 1963

SPANN, R. N. (ed.), *Constitutionalism in Asia*, 1963

SWANSON, G. *The Birth of the Gods*, 1960

TAGORE, Sir R. *The Religion of Man*, 1931

TENNENT, Sir J. E. *Ceylon*, 2 vols., 1859

THAPAR, R. *Asoka and the Decline of the Mauryas*, 1961

THOMAS, E. J. *The Life of the Buddha*, 3rd edn, 1949

WAGLE, N. *Society at the Time of the Buddha*, 1966

WARDER, A. K. *Indian Buddhism*, 1956

WEBER, M. *The Religion of India*, 1958
The Sociology of Religion, 1963

WILSON, H. H. 'Buddha and Buddhism', *JRAS*, Vol. XVI, 1856

WIRTH, L. *On Cities and Social Life*, Chicago, 1964

WOOLF, L. *The Village in the Jungle*, 1913, reprinted 1961

YALMAN, N. 'Dual Organization in Central Ceylon' in *Anthropological Studies in Theravada Buddhism*, ed. by Manning Nash, 1966

Acknowledgements

I should like to express my indebtedness to the following friends for their helpful discussion and criticism of various parts of this work: to Professor R. C. Pandeya, and members of the staff and research scholars of the Buddhist Studies Department, University of Delhi, for allowing me the opportunity of conducting a seminar on the subject-matter of chapter eight; to Professor D. L. Jayasuriya, head of the Department of Sociology in the University of Colombo, for the opportunity of rehearsing some of the theme of this book at an earlier stage of its development at a seminar of the Urban Studies Unit; to Dr Debiprasad Chattopadhyaya and his wife, Dr Alaka Chattopadhyaya, for the gracious hospitality they extended to me, in their home in Calcutta, and, together with Dr Devavrata Bose, for the stimulating comments they made and the suggestions they offered. I am grateful also to the editorial board of *Religion* (Oriel Press, Newcastle) for permission to reproduce, in slightly revised form, a contribution published originally in that journal, to the editor of *Vesak Sirisara* (Colombo), and to the editor of *The Aryan Path* (Bombay).

T.O.L.

Index

MORE ABOUT PENGUINS
AND PELICANS

Penguinews, which appears every month, contains details of all the new books issued by Penguins as they are published. From time to time it is supplemented by *Penguins in Print*, which is our complete list of almost 5,000 titles.

A specimen copy of *Penguinews* will be sent to you free on request. Please write to Dept E P, Penguin Books Ltd, Harmondsworth, Middlesex, for you copy.

In the U.S.A.: For a complete list of books available from Penguin in the United States write to Dept CS, Penguin Books Inc., 7110 Ambassador Road, Baltimore, Maryland 21207.

In Canada: For a complete list of books available from Penguin in Canada write to Penguin Books Canada Ltd, 41 Steelcase Road West, Markham, Ontario.

SOME BOOKS ON RELIGION AND MYTHOLOGY
PUBLISHED BY PENGUIN BOOKS